To my dad:

Dad, I wrote a book about bikes. I know how proud you would be.

And to my friend Greg Flusche:

Next time wear your helmet.

And to three-time World Driving Champion Ayrton Senna (the man I loved to hate):

Olé Senna. Obrigado, adeus, bravo!

Table of Contents

AMERICA BY MOUNTAIN BIKE *MAP LEGEND*

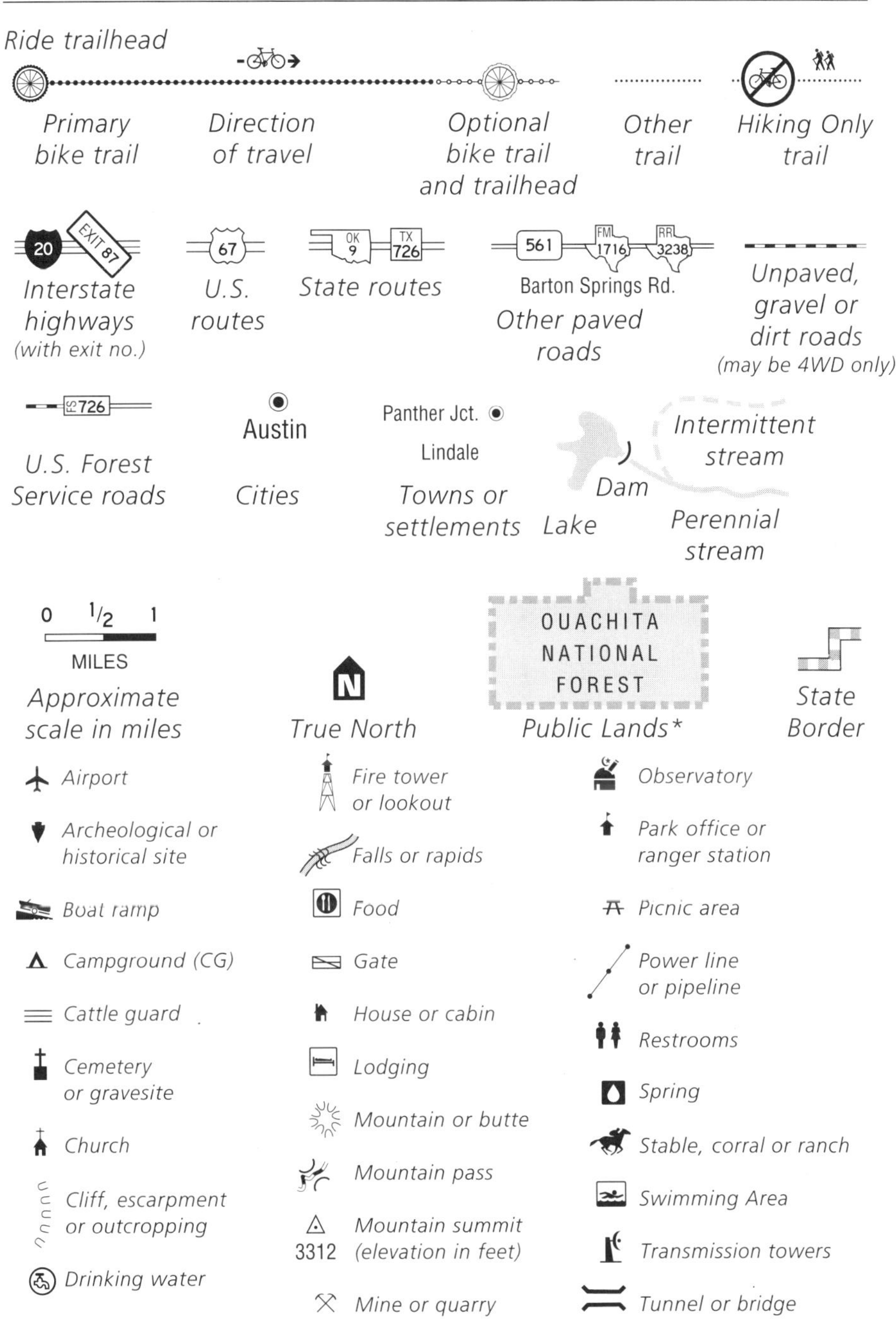

*Remember, private property exists in and around our National Forests.

List of Maps

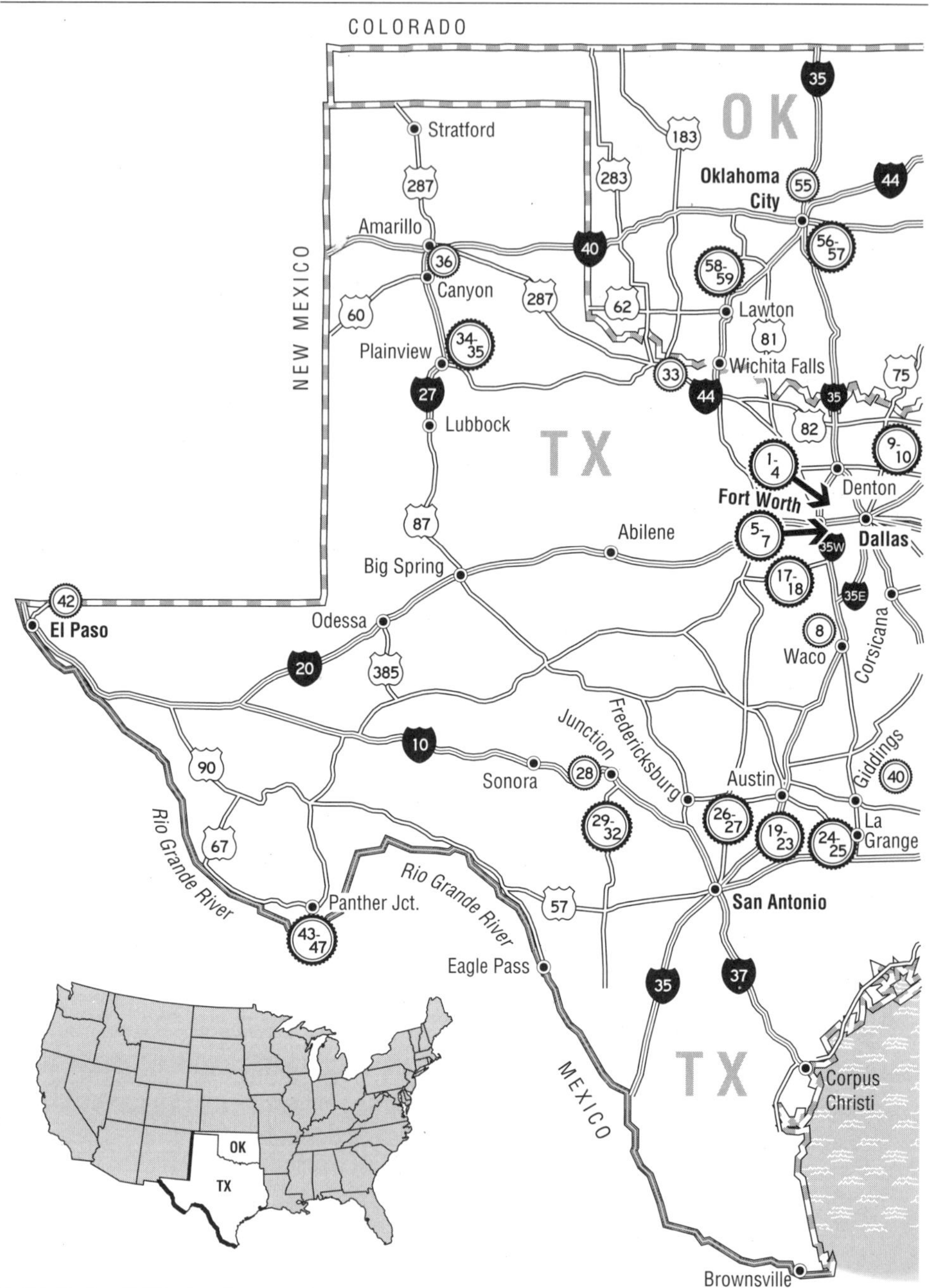
COLORADO
NEW MEXICO
OK
TX
Stratford
Amarillo
Canyon
Plainview
Lubbock
Oklahoma City
Lawton
Wichita Falls
Denton
Fort Worth
Dallas
Abilene
Big Spring
Odessa
El Paso
Waco
Corsicana
Junction
Fredericksburg
Sonora
Austin
Giddings
La Grange
San Antonio
Panther Jct.
Rio Grande River
Eagle Pass
MEXICO
Corpus Christi
Brownsville

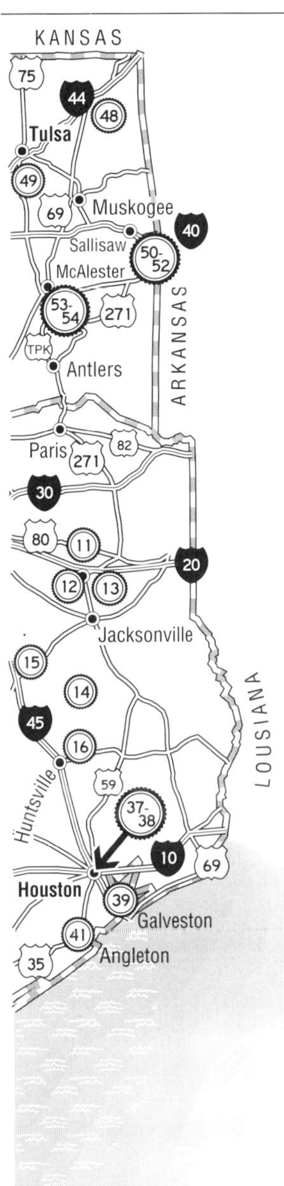

TEXAS

North Texas/Dallas Fort Worth

1 L. B. Houston Nature Trail
2 Northshore Trail
3 Knob Hill Park Trail
4 Horseshoe Trail
5 Boulder Park Trail
6 Windmill Hill Preserve Trail
7 DORBA Trail
8 Cameron Park Trail
9 Sister Grove Park Trail
10 Bonham State Park Trail

East Texas

11 Tyler State Park Trail
12 East Texas Rails-to-Trails
13 Martin Creek Lake State Park Trail
14 Double Lake Trail
15 Big Brown Creek Primitive Area Trail
16 Huntsville State Park Trail

Central Texas and the Texas Hill Country

17 Cedar Brake Trail
18 Fossil Rim Ride
19 Town Lake Hike and Bike Trail
20 Barton Creek Greenbelt Trail
21 Emma Long Park Trail
22 Forest Ridge Preserve Trails
23 Old Homestead Trail
24 Bluff Creek Ranch Trail
25 Rocky Hill Ranch Trails
26 Hill Country Rifle Range Trail
27 Wolf Mountain Trail
28 Walter Buck Wildlife Management Area Trails
29 Hill Country Wilderness Trail
30 Hermit's Trace Ride
31 Spring Falls / Bandera Creek Ride
32 Comanche Bluff / Chiquita Falls Ride

The Texas Panhandle

33 Copper Breaks State Park Trail
34 Quitaque Canyon / Los Lingos Rails-to-Trails
35 Caprock Canyons State Park Trail
36 Capitol Peak Trail

The Gulf Coast

37 Ho Chi Minh Trail
38 Barker Dam Ride
39 Jack Brooks Park Trail
40 Lake Somerville Trailway
41 Brazos Bend State Park Trail

Far West Texas

42 Trans Mountain Trails

The Big Bend Country

43 Hot Springs Ride
44 Old Maverick Road
45 Glenn Spring Road
46 Glenn Spring Loop
47 Old Ore Road

OKLAHOMA

48 Whispering Pines Trail
49 Turkey Mountain Park Trails
50 Old Military Road
51 Boardstand Trail
52 Horsethief Springs Trail
53 Little Bugaboo Creek / Whiskey Flats Ride
54 Hog Camp Ride
55 Arcadia Lake Trail
56 Stanley Draper Lake Trails
57 Clear Bay Trail
58 Twelve Miles of Hell
59 Medicine Bluffs Ride

Acknowledgments

I gush about my club, the Dallas Off-Road Bicycle Association (DORBA), but the members really do deserve recognition. This group revolutionized mountain biking in Dallas in the late 1980s by coalescing many like-minded and proactive individuals in the general Dallas area into a nationally respected and accomplished trail-building machine. Before I ever knew what DORBA was, they were meeting with city park boards and county commissioners to gain access to what has become an excellent range of legal riding opportunities for mountain bikers of all skill levels.

Because I don't want to leave anybody out and hurt their feelings, I am not even going to try and remember the names of all the special souls I should thank for helping me put this manuscript together. (I know you all thought you were doing most of the work most of the time anyway.) Instead I am going to offer a hearty "thank you" to all those who have ever dragged his or her butt out of a comfortable bed early on a cold Saturday morning and grabbed some hiking boots and a pair of loppers to be at the trail at 8 or 9 A.M. to do their duty. If you have the right attitude about trail work, it is all just conditioning anyway. Consider it cross-training.

Thank you for making the sacrifices that keep the trails in place even though helmetless gonzo savages ride like mudhole surfers and don't realize YOU are where the trails come from. We were all young once.

At some point I really need to thank my roommate Kennis for putting up with me while I was writing this book. She bankrolled my travels, corrected my grammar, and tried more than once to keep a current itinerary of my wanderings while I was researching this manuscript. Thanks to her I actually finished (almost on schedule) and ended up with something to be proud of. Thank you for your patience and support. The check is in the mail. Don't forget to empty the dishwasher before you go to bed. Are those cockatiel fajitas ready to go on the grill?

I should also thank the staff of the Texas Parks and Wildlife Department. Without them I would drive into unknown camps late at night with no idea where my spot was. There are no finer state employees, except my mom. Oh yeah—"Hi, Pat."

I also have to thank my editor, Dennis Coello, who found me, out of hundreds of Texas or Oklahoma mountain bikers, and offered me the opportunity to fascinate you all with my drivel. Dennis has become a good friend and comrade, and he is a patient and thoughtful boss.

Keep up the good work, all of you. See you on the trail. Bring your bike and we'll ride later.

P.S.—God bless every soldier and every peace officer who ever died to protect my freedom. Thank you.

Foreword

Welcome to *America by Mountain Bike,* a 20-plus-book series designed to provide all-terrain bikers with the information they need to find and ride the very best trails everywhere in the mainland United States. Whether you're new to the sport and don't know where to pedal or an experienced mountain biker who wants to learn the classic trails in another region, this series is for you. Drop a few bucks for the book, spend an hour with the detailed maps and route descriptions, and you're prepared for the finest in off-road cycling.

My role as editor of this series was simple: First, find a mountain biker who knows the area and loves to ride. Second, ask that person to spend a year researching the most popular and very best rides around. And third, have that rider describe each trail in terms of difficulty, scenery, condition, elevation change, and all other categories of information that are important to trail riders. "Pretend you've just completed a ride and met up with fellow mountain bikers at the trailhead," I told each author. "Imagine their questions, be clear in your answers."

As I said, the *editorial* process—that of sending out riders and reading the submitted chapters—is a snap. But the work involved in finding, riding, and writing about each trail is enormous. In some instances our authors' tasks are made easier by the information contributed by local bike shops or cycling clubs, or even by the writers of local "where-to" guides. Credit for these contributions is provided, when appropriate, in each chapter, and our sincere thanks goes to all who have helped.

But the overwhelming majority of trails are discovered and pedaled by our authors themselves, then compared with dozens of other routes to determine if they qualify as "classic"—that area's best in scenery and cycling fun. If you've ever had the experience of pioneering a route from outdated topographic maps, or entering a bike shop to request information from local riders who would much prefer to keep their favorite trails secret, or know how it is to double- and triple-check data to be positive your trail info is correct, then you have an idea of how each of our authors has labored to bring about these books. You and I, and all the mountain bikers of America, are the richer for their efforts.

You'll get more out of this book if you take a moment to read the Introduction explaining how to read the trail listings. The "Topographic Maps" section will help you understand how useful topos will be on a ride, and will also tell you where to get them. And though this is a "where-to," not a "how-to" guide, those of you who have not traveled the backcountry might find "Hitting the Trail" of particular value.

In addition to the material above, newcomers to mountain biking might want to spend a minute with the glossary, page 306, so that terms like *hard-pack, single-track,* and *water bars* won't throw you when you come across them in the text.

Finally, the tips in the Afterword on mountain biking etiquette and the land-use controversy might help us all enjoy the trails a little more.

All the best.

Dennis Coello
St. Louis

Preface

Our story takes us back to those thrilling days of yesteryear, when Campy was King and Japanese was Junk . . .

In 1984 an old touring buddy, Mark Treadwell, bought the first mountain bike I had ever seen up close, a chrome Ross. I thought, "Hey, this mountain bike deal looks neat, but it is just another California fad." You could not have convinced me it was as much fun as I now know. Riding a mountain bike is like being ten years old again, out in The Woods, wandering the trails with your friends. At least that is what my early years were like, in a suburb of Oklahoma City in the 1960s. We never thought about who might have built those trails, and to this day I have no idea where they came from, but boy they were fun to ride. Whoopty-doos and bermed turns and creek crossings, about the same as what I like to ride now. I had a gold Schwinn Stingray with a slick back tire, a sissy bar, a banana seat, and butterfly handlebars. Just like a few thousand other young American males of my day.

The Woods were not exactly my parent's favorite place-for-me-to-be-found, but they were on the way to school and several other locales I frequented, and all my friends hung out there and rode their bikes. Just about any time I had a free afternoon I could be found there, happily fishing or looking for snakes, or just wading along the creek. Oh, to be young again, eh?

So then I grew up and forgot off-road cycling. My dad moved us to a fair-sized town in the panhandle of Texas, not far from what the locals called The Cap Rock. This area of Texas is very similar to the Grand Canyon, only on a much smaller scale. I spent a lot of time exploring the canyons and really developed a hunger for the outdoors. Thus began my love affair with trails. I had motorcycles, and I did a fair amount of off-roading with them. Are you beginning to see a pattern forming here?

Then, in about 1974, I fell back in love with the bicycle and bought the fanciest one I could find. A few years later, while going to college in Austin, I wandered into the co-op bike shop looking for a set of toe clips for my bike. I knew just enough about cycling to know that serious bikies used trap pedals. While I was there, I saw this thing hanging from the ceiling. It was like some fine piece of precision-tooled machinery, all jewel-like finishes and impossibly skinny tires. Cupid and his arrows found me, and I knew: Someday, I would own a bike comparable to what I had discovered that day in Austin.

Later I moved to Dallas. It took about three more years before that custom bike came home with me. This happened just a couple of years before I saw the Ross I mentioned earlier. About the same time a company named Specialized was marketing a bike called the StumpJumper. The rest is history.

I bought my first mountain bike in 1990, long after numerous friends tried to convince me it was a blast to ride one. (These people were from California, so I was a little leery and kept talking about fads.) I did not know of any places to ride, so I just used my mountain bike to bash curbs and try daring stuff in a culvert near my house. Then a friend in Hot Springs, Arkansas, got a mountain bike and started bragging about all the trails in his area, and said I should grab my bike and come up sometime.

I went to visit my friend and his family, and coincidentally, we were to go to a mountain bike festival in the nearby Ouachita National Forest that weekend. I got to the festival not really sure what to expect. Sitting in the parking lot of the campground, waiting for the first ride of the festival to begin, I noticed that this girl waiting next to me was wearing a shirt that said Dallas Off-Road Bicycle Association. I tossed her a "Hey, I'm from Dallas, who are you?" She explained that her husband was the president of the club and introduced me to him and several other DORBA members who had driven up for the festival. "Oh yeah, we come up every year for this," they repeated almost in unison.

I got my first taste of real mountain biking there, in Arkansas, and guess what happened? Cupid and the arrows again, big time! As soon as I got back to Dallas, I joined the club and started finding out about trails in my area. There were some pretty good ones. Nothing like the Ouachita Mountains in Arkansas, but fairly serious for around here. I started hanging out with the DORBA crowd and going to meetings and workdays and rides. It was not long before I determined that I had found my true calling. The purpose of all those years I had spent sweating over my Campagnolo stuff had been to give me the endurance I would need to develop the strength I would need to be the mountain biker I wanted to be.

Well, here we are in 1995. Shimano is king, mountain bikes are the hottest thing around, and on a regular basis I climb on a soapbox and try to convince my fellow mountain bikers that they need to help maintain the trails. It is inconceivable that some fool thought this was only a fad.

Cowabunga, dudes and dudettes, *señors y señoritas*. Let's get this reading stuff out of the way so we can ride. I hope you get as much enjoyment from exploring the pages of this book as I did creating them for you.

Charles Buddy Cypert
Dallas, Texas
Internet: chuck.cypert@lunatic.com
TEXAN BY CHOICE, NOT BY CHANCE

P.S.—While researching trails in Oklahoma, I decided to stop by and check on the place I describe above as "The Woods." What did I find but several ten-year-olds gleefully jumping ramps and being adolescent males! Only the equipment has changed in 25 years; the kids still love big air. Thank you, Lord.

Good Advice

Do right and risk the consequences!
—Sam Houston, frontier statesman

This is the part of my book where I am your mom. Some people say mountain biking is a controlled crash. This is a dangerous sport, and the opportunities to get hurt or stranded or otherwise inconvenienced are way many. Use good judgment in attempting technical challenges. If in doubt, get off and walk. Remember the TGIF rule: "too gutsy—inverted fast!" I have seen many skilled riders leave skin on the trees and rocks along various trails, and I am sure this is something we all expect to happen occasionally. It pays to minimize the opportunities for injuries. Bleeding just a little is a good way to get the m-dolphins flowing, but a serious injury will keep you off the bike while you heal. This is just about always during great cycling weather, it seems (voice of experience).

Wear a helmet, eye protection, gloves, and even sleeves sometimes if the situation warrants it. The "wear a helmet" thing may get old after a while, but I promise you that if I try to go very far without one, I *will* crash into something with my head. It never fails. Don't leave home without your brain bucket. I never pass the end of the driveway without mine.

If the trails are muddy, stay off them. Every ounce of dirt you carry away to wash down the drain at the car wash or at home is an ounce of trail. This soil will never be replaced, so don't waste it. It is the raw material that mountain bike trails are made from.

If you are allergic to poisonous plants, you must either take the proper precautions or find another sport. The same goes if you are scared of snakes. If you ride a mountain bike on mountain bike trails long enough, you *will* meet a few snakes. Leave them alone, go on, and everybody will be happy. Both of these cautions are intended to keep you out of trouble on and off the bike. Try to develop the good habit of being observant. That way, when you stop by the trail to take a break, you'll automatically do a scan of the ground nearby to verify that there are no dangers, instead of stepping off the bike and into a pile of water moccasins.

We got yer chiggers. If you don't know what they are, let me introduce you. They are little tiny insects that crawl into your skin and live, the whole time causing an irritation in the spot they enter that itches like 50 mosquitoes and lasts for a month. Which brings us to mosquitoes. We have 'em and they are very persistent. Carry good repellent and use plenty. When you find a slow-developing mosquito bite that lasts and lasts, it is already too late—the chiggers have you. When I get them bad, I may have 50 or 60 bites. I have heard of and tried many home remedies. None cure the bites; they only kill the bugs. I have painted the bumps with fingernail polish (clear is obviously preferable) and I have taken a sponge bath of ammonia. Not a fun date, I can tell you. Especially when you get a drop in the old nether regions. Yoweee baby! If you find something better, please let me hear from you.

Learn to handle your machine in a competent manner before you attempt to ride the trails I call hard or dangerous. Getting in over your head in the technical stuff and then getting hurt *es no macho, es muy stupido.* It does our sport no good at all to have beginners get maimed on expert trails. It makes all of us look bad, and slows traffic.

Carry plenty of water, more than you expect to use. You can always pour it out when you return to your car if you did not drink it. Better safe than sorry. Don't be such a gram-counter that you leave that extra bottle at the car to save yourself a quarter pound of weight on the bike and then cramp and have to walk home. To quote Mark Twain, "Sometimes too much to drink is barely enough." That might possibly be out of context, but the gist of his statement still holds true in our case. In the summer keep a bottle of sunscreen handy, even if you like those weird cycling tan lines. Skin cancer is a major killer.

Learning first aid would in no way be a waste of time, and carrying at least a rudimentary first-aid kit into the boonies would show what a well-prepared and competent cyclist you are. And impress the girls and guys in your group.

Try to make a habit of doing a reconnaissance run around trails you have never been on before blasting full-speed-ahead into the trees. It might save you some skin or prevent a broken bone or two. Hey, it only makes good sense to be prepared and to appear to be a wise rider, even if you are really a gonzo maniac. Your friends will be impressed.

Be polite to other trail users. Equestrians and pedestrians use many of the trails in this book. Mountain bikers have sort of a questionable reputation in some people's eyes. You have seen the coverage of races on TV and pictures on the covers of magazines. It makes us all look like technoracerhead weenies who blast around at full speed all the time. That meshes too easily with the impression a hiker gets if you go screaming by him on the trail, unannounced, spraying mud or a cloud of dust in his face. If you behave this way, we will gradually start to have access to less and less land and fewer and fewer cool trails. Don't be the jerk that gets mountain bikers kicked off some trail somewhere. Please.

Carry your patch kit and pump, and maybe some tools, even if you don't know how to use them. Necessity is a mother. The places I am going to take you will provide many opportunities to catch a flat tire or snap a derailleur. If you have the stuff and you see a stranded comrade, stop and offer assistance. Someday you may be the one standing by the trail whining about

Many riders just like this will grow up to become mountain bikers. If they grow up. Get a helmet, dude.

your broken gears or flat tire. What goes around comes around. Be a Boy Scout; be prepared.

I have to put in a disclaimer about some of the maps you will find in this book. In many cases, accurate maps of the trails in a given area simply do not exist. Without aerial photographs (extremely expensive) or without having ridden the trails while using a global positioning system (still prohibitively expensive; I went for a new tent instead), it is impossible to give you an exact map of all the trails in some locations. Therefore I have put a note on the ones that are approximated, indicating that they are sometimes at best a general description of the area of the desired trails.

I have done my best to keep you on track by trying to give you what I feel you need to know to stay out of trouble. Some trail directions include advice about landmarks or habits to use when approaching forks in the particular trail. Some trails have many such forks. Some of my maps are much more an indication of area borders of myriad trails than a deadly accurate depiction of what is there. Give me a break, I did the best I could with what I had to work from, and I spent plenty of time backtracking to stay located my own damn self. If you get lost, then I did not do my job well. Feel free to send me e-mail chewing my butt if you are unhappy. All I can do is ignore you or put you in my mail reader's twit filter.

I am pretty good at this, so if I lose you from time to time, try to be patient. Go back to the last spot where you knew for sure where you were and work your way from there in an outward spiral looking for blazes or bike-signs. If the place is that badly established, I probably didn't put it in the book. I found some trails that were exceedingly well marked, and some that disappeared within a few miles of the trailhead. I think I did okay. If you are a klutz, be careful. Take somebody who has some Indian in them or something. Or, if you aren't a girl, take a girl with you; at least she will stop and ask directions.

Okay, all the griping is over. Get out there and ride and have fun.

Introduction

A BRIEF GUIDE TO THIS GUIDE

At the risk of sounding redundant I am going to give an explanation of what the various headings in a chapter mean (to me):

Ride number: Pretty obvious. If you don't think so, you need to find another sport.
Trail name: What the signs at the park call it, or what most of the local riders call it.
Note: The information in the next six headings is included in the introductory paragraphs to each ride.
Length: How many miles make one lap (loop trail) or round-trip (out-and-back trail). As accurate as my bike computer (close enough for mountain bike work).
Configuration: Whether the trail is a) some form of "loop" that will bring you back to where you started and not touch the same piece of dirt twice, b) an "out-and-back," where you ride all of the same dirt twice, c) a "point-to-point" that is so long or difficult that you may want to be dropped at one end and picked up at the other by some sort of support crew (basically the same as an out-and-back without the -and-back), or d) some bizarre combination of all or some of the above.
Difficulty: Ha ha ha ha ha. Grain of salt, dear hearts. Remember that I race. If I say "hard trail," and you have only been riding a year, well, maybe you should wait another year or so. Definitely DO NOT TRY TO KEEP UP WITH YOUR FRIENDS IF THEY ARE BETTER THAN YOU. If you have to go, then take your time and do the ride at your own pace. Get off the machine and walk ALL the deadfalls and EVERYTHING scary. Or run the risk of serious injury or terrible humiliation and sore body parts. If I say it is an easy trail, then I believe it to be something the average parents could ride with their children (ALL WEARING HELMETS, OF COURSE). Within this guide is every shade in between those two extremes.
Condition: It is black gumbo or it is sandy or rocky or gravel or whatever particular surface is the challenge-of-the-day for this ride. Single-track is one-lane; it may be wide, as in three or four feet, or maybe narrow, as in less than your handlebars. Double-track is two-lane and was probably a road long

ago. Jeep roads are wide enough for a four-wheel vehicle but very rugged. Dirt or gravel roads are generally active public roads and will be carrying automobile traffic.

Scenery: People who live in Texas or Oklahoma know how to love it here and see the beauty in the countryside. If you are from Colorado Springs, you will probably laugh your pedals off when you hear me say something is very scenic. Lighten up a little, okay? If I think the views are special or the trees are memorable or I saw a cool bird, then maybe I just have better eyes than you. Maybe I am just biased. I like it here.

Highlights: Anything neat about the area or the trail. I am a history nut, so expect tons of cowboy and Indian stuff. If there are any other notable points or interesting bits around, I have attempted to report them. If I bore you, then one of us needs to get a life. I ain't saying which one of us.

General location: What corner or slice of which state we are dealing with. I sort of divided Oklahoma up into eastern, central, and western. Texas is a little more complicated; North Texas, East Texas, Central Texas or the Hill Country (mostly interchangeable), the Panhandle, West Texas, the Gulf Coast, and the Big Bend Country.

Elevation change: In feet above sea level. 50′ is fifty feet. I like to tell you where the highest and the lowest spots are. If the situation is really that cut-and-dried, then my job is as easy as reading the topographical maps. If it is constant up and down, I will tell you so in the introductory part about "Difficulty." If you have an altimeter on your bike, then you really need to lighten up.

Season: Hmmmmm. The weather in the winter can bring anything from 0s to 70s, so the seasons here are often a day-to-day deal. If a trail grows over in the summer, and I was unlucky enough to detect that at the time (some real horror stories here, folks), then I will tell you. If the mud is bad for long periods during the wet season, I have tried to tell you that too. If the hunters take over during deer season, then too bad. They are a trail-use group, too. And my brother, Steve, is one of them.

Services: I have tried to find you a convenience store near the trailheads, and I have tried to find you a phone near the same location. And water, and a bathroom. I failed sometimes through no fault of my own. Some locations are just too remote. I have also noted that for you. If you need anything else, then take the proper precautions and plan ahead.

Hazards: Some trails have stickers, some have steep and sudden land formations, some have wild animals or snakes or terrible insects. Some are just far from anywhere to get help. If there are horses or motorcycles or pedestrians or other interruptions to our progress, I will tell you. If there are bullets or artillery shells flying nearby, I will tell you that, too. And I am not kidding.

Rescue index: This is an index of whether or not you are likely to get rescued if you get hurt, or what extreme effort might have to be executed to get you out of where you missed the turn. I have tried to give you the nickel tour on what will be required to get help. It may be no more than reiterating the obvious—i.e., get to the pavement and flag down a car to get you to the nearest pay phone to call 911. Practice safe wrecks. Pack in a pal. Remember the buddy system. Misery loves company. Don't ride into *terra incognita* alone. *Capice?*

Land status: Many of the best trails are on private property, but plenty are on public lands of some sort. State and national parks have contributed much to the available trail miles within the scope of my efforts. In a few spots, groups of concerned citizens have formed coalitions to purchase and protect areas where the nature and wildlife were threatened. Or maybe they purchased an old railroad bed and turned it into a trail.

Maps: I have drawn maps where it was humanly possible for me to do so. If the area is fairly simple, it really helps. If there are maps of the area before I get there, that helps too. I just get topos and plot it out from what I already know. If it is a hopeless maze of single-track that forms a web across some elbow in a river somewhere, then I drew you a map of the boundaries or landmarks that I used to keep my bearings. If the ranger has better maps than me, I have told you that, too. In all cases I have wrapped this section up with the names of the United States Geological Survey (USGS) 7.5 minute series, 1:24,000 scale, topographic quadrangles (commonly called quads). These show terrain contours and much information useful for navigating in the wild. Plus, they are just about the perfect scale for mountain biking. They are sort of large but can be easily folded to show just what you want to see and the surroundings.

Finding the trail: Where to start. How to stay on. How to tell your support crew where to look for you if you don't come back.

Sources of additional information: I have given you the address of the park or the land manager thereof if we are on public land. If the ride is private, I have tried to convince the owner that we are okay, so take it easy. Drop them a note of thanks if you really enjoyed the trip. Typically this is where I stuck the name of the nearest bike shop I could locate or make friends with. Sometimes I mention interested parties that are involved with the particular trail, like maybe a bike club or two.

Notes on the trail: Where I stuck all the other junk. Like cool places to camp or neat stuff to do nearby, or other myriad details. Anything that did not seem to fit elsewhere.

Let's go. I'm ready to roll some rubber on some rocks.

Chuck Cypert

ABBREVIATIONS

The following road-designation abbreviations are used in the *America by Mountain Bike* series:

CR	County Road
FM	Farm to Market
FR	Farm Route
FS	Forest Service road
I-	Interstate
IR	Indian Route
US	United States highway

State highways are designated with the appropriate two-letter state abbreviation, followed by the road number. *Example:* TX 6 = Texas State Highway 6.

Postal Service two-letter state codes:

AL	Alabama
AK	Alaska
AZ	Arizona
AR	Arkansas
CA	California
CO	Colorado
CT	Connecticut
DE	Delaware
DC	District of Columbia
FL	Florida
GA	Georgia
HI	Hawaii
ID	Idaho
IL	Illinois
IN	Indiana
IA	Iowa
KS	Kansas
KY	Kentucky
LA	Louisiana
ME	Maine
MD	Maryland
MA	Massachusetts
MI	Michigan
MN	Minnesota
MS	Mississippi
MO	Missouri
MT	Montana
NE	Nebraska
NV	Nevada
NH	New Hampshire
NJ	New Jersey
NM	New Mexico
NY	New York
NC	North Carolina
ND	North Dakota
OH	Ohio
OK	Oklahoma
OR	Oregon
PA	Pennsylvania
RI	Rhode Island
SC	South Carolina
SD	South Dakota
TN	Tennessee
TX	Texas
UT	Utah
VT	Vermont
VA	Virginia
WA	Washington
WV	West Virginia
WI	Wisconsin
WY	Wyoming

TOPOGRAPHIC MAPS

The maps in this book, when used in conjunction with the route directions present in each chapter, will in most instances be sufficient to get you to the trail and keep you on it. However, you will find superior detail and valuable information in the 7.5 minute series United States Geological Survey (USGS) topographic maps. Recognizing how indispensable these are to bikers and hikers alike, many bike shops and sporting goods stores now carry topos of the local area.

But if you're brand new to mountain biking you might be wondering "What's a topographic map?" In short, these differ from standard "flat" maps in that they indicate not only linear distance, but elevation as well. One glance at a "topo" will show you the difference, for "contour lines" are spread across the map like dozens of intricate spider webs. Each contour line represents a particular elevation, and at the base of each topo a particular "contour interval" designation is given. Yes, it sounds confusing if you're new to the lingo, but it truly is a simple and wonderfully helpful system. Keep reading.

Let's assume that the 7.5 minute series topo before us says "Contour Interval 40 feet," that the short trail we'll be pedaling is two inches in length on the map, and that it crosses five contour lines from its beginning to end. What do we know? Well, because the linear scale of this series is 2,000 feet to the inch (roughly 2 ¾ inches representing 1 mile), we know our trail is approximately ⅘ of a mile long (2 inches × 2,000 feet). But we also know we'll be climbing or descending 200 vertical feet (5 contour lines × 40 feet each) over that distance. And the elevation designations written on occasional contour lines will tell us if we're heading up or down.

The authors of this series warn their readers of upcoming terrain, but only a detailed topo gives you the information you need to pinpoint your position exactly on a map, steer yourself toward optional trails and roads nearby, plus let you know at a glance if you'll be pedaling hard to take them. It's a lot of information for a very low cost. In fact, the only drawback with topos is their size—several feet square. I've tried rolling them into tubes, folding them carefully, even cutting them into blocks and photocopying the pieces. Any of these systems is a pain, but no matter how you pack the maps you'll be happy they're along. And you'll be even happier if you pack a compass as well.

In addition to local bike shops and sporting goods stores, you'll find topos at major universities and some public libraries, where you might try photocopying the ones you need to avoid the cost of buying them. But if you want your own and can't find them locally, write to:

USGS Map Sales
Box 25286
Denver, CO 80225

Ask for an index while you're at it, plus a price list and a copy of the booklet Topographic Maps. In minutes you'll be reading them like a pro.

A second excellent series of maps available to mountain bikers is that put out by the United States Forest Service. If your trail runs through an area designated as a national forest, look in the phone book (white pages) under the United States Government listings, find the Department of Agriculture heading, and then run you finger down that section until you find the Forest Service. Give them a call, and they'll provide the address of the regional Forest Service office from which you can obtain the appropriate map.

TRAIL ETIQUETTE

Pick up almost any mountain bike magazine these days and you'll find articles and letters to the editor about trail conflict. For example, you'll find hikers' tales of being blindsided by speeding mountain bikers, complaints from mountain bikers about being blamed for trail damage that was really caused by horse or cattle traffic, and cries from bikers about those "kamikaze" riders who through their antics threaten to close even more trails to all of us.

The authors of this series have been very careful to guide you to only those trails that are open to mountain biking (or at least were open at the time of their research), and without exception have warned of the damage done to our sport through injudicious riding. My personal views on this matter appear in the Afterword, but all of us can benefit from glancing over the following International Mountain Bicycling Association (IMBA) Rules of the Trail before saddling up.

1. *Ride on open trails only.* Respect trail and road closures (ask, if not sure), avoid possible trespass on private land, obtain permits and authorization as may be required. Federal and State wilderness areas are closed to cycling.

2. *Leave no trace.* Be sensitive to the dirt beneath you. Even on open trails, you should not ride under conditions where you will leave evidence of your passing, such as on certain soils shortly after rain. Observe the different types of soils and trail construction; practice low-impact cycling. This also means staying on the trail and not creating any new ones. Be sure to pack out at least as much as you pack in.

3. *Control your bicycle!* Inattention for even a second can cause disaster. Excessive speed can maim and threaten people; there is no excuse for it!

4. *Always yield the trail.* Make known your approach well in advance. A friendly greeting (or a bell) is considerate and works well; startling someone may cause loss of trail access. Show your respect when passing others by slowing to a walk or even stopping. Anticipate that other trail users may be around corners or in blind spots.
5. *Never spook animals.* All animals are startled by an unannounced approach, a sudden movement, or a loud noise. This can be dangerous for you, for others, and for the animals. Give animals extra room and time to adjust to you. In passing, use special care and follow the directions of horseback riders (ask, if uncertain). Running cattle and disturbing wild animals is a serious offense. Leave gates as you found them, or as marked.
6. *Plan ahead.* Know your equipment, your ability, and the area in which you are riding—and prepare accordingly. Be self-sufficient at all times. Wear a helmet, keep your machine in good condition, and carry necessary supplies for changes in weather or other conditions. A well-executed trip is a satisfaction to you and not a burden or offense to others.

For more information, contact IMBA, P.O. Box 412043, Los Angeles, CA 90041, (818) 792-8830.

HITTING THE TRAIL

Once again, because this is a "where-to," not a "how-to" guide, the following will be brief. If you're a veteran trail rider these suggestions might serve to remind you of something you've forgotten to pack. If you're a newcomer, they might convince you to think twice before hitting the backcountry unprepared.

Water: I've heard the questions dozens of times. "How much is enough? One bottle? Two? Three?! But think of all that extra weight!" Well, one simple physiological fact should convince you to err on the side of excess when it comes to deciding how much water to pack: a human working hard in 90-degree temperature needs approximately ten quarts of fluids every day. Ten quarts. That's two and a half gallons—*12* large water bottles, or *16* small ones. And, with water weighing in at approximately 8 pounds per gallon, a one-day supply comes to a whopping 20 pounds.

In other words, pack along two or three bottles even for short rides. And make sure you can purify the water found along the trail on longer routes. When writing of those routes where this could be of critical importance, each author has provided information on where water can be found near the trail—if it can be found at all. But drink it untreated and you run the risk of disease. (See *Giardia* in the Glossary.)

One sure way to kill both the bacteria and viruses in water is to bring it to a "furious boil." Right. That's just how you want to spend your time on a bike ride. Besides, who wants to carry a stove, or denude the countryside stoking bonfires to boil water?

Luckily, there is a better way. Many riders pack along the effective, inexpensive, and only slightly distasteful tetraglycine hydroperiodide tablets (sold under the names Potable Aqua, Globaline, and Coughlan's, among others). Some invest in portable, lightweight purifiers that filter out the crud. Yes, purifying water with tablets or filters is a bother. But catch a case of Giardia sometime and you'll understand why it's worth the trouble.

Tools: Ever since my first cross-country tour in 1965 I've been kidded about the number of tools I pack on the trail. And so I will exit entirely from this discussion by providing a list compiled by two mechanic (and mountain biker) friends of mine. After all, since they make their livings fixing bikes, and get their kicks by riding them, who could be a better source?

These two suggest the following as an absolute minimum:

tire levers
spare tube and patch kit
air pump
allen wrenches (3, 4, 5, and 6 mm)
six-inch crescent (adjustable-end) wrench
small flat-blade screwdriver
chain rivet tool
spoke wrench

But, while they're on the trail, their personal tool pouches contain these additional items:

channel locks (small)
air gauge
tire valve cap (the metal kind, with a valve-stem remover)
baling wire (ten or so inches, for temporary repairs)
duct tape (small roll for temporary repairs or tire boot)
boot material (small piece of old tire or a large tube patch)
spare chain link
rear derailleur pulley
spare nuts and bolts
paper towel and tube of waterless hand cleaner

First-Aid Kit: My personal kit contains the following, sealed inside double Ziploc bags:

sunscreen
aspirin
butterfly-closure bandages
Band-Aids
gauze compress pads (a half-dozen 4" × 4")
gauze (one roll)
ace bandages or Spenco joint wraps
Benadryl (an antihistamine, in case of allergic reactions)
water purification tablets
Moleskin/Spenco "Second Skin"
hydrogen peroxide, iodine, or Mercurochrome (some kind of antiseptic)
snakebite kit

Final Considerations: The authors of this series have done a good job in suggesting that specific items be packed for certain trails—raingear in particular seasons, a hat and gloves for mountain passes, or shades for desert jaunts. Heed their warnings, and think ahead. Good luck.

Dennis Coello

TEXAS

> If I owned Hell and Texas I'd rent out Texas and live in Hell.
> —General Philip H. Sheridan

Texas, the Lone Star State. A few words about Texas and Texans are in order at this point. I moved to Texas from Oklahoma in 1969, but I am still a "damn Yankee" to my friends who were born here because I am originally from north of the Red River. Don't worry; it is just a joke. Texans love to see themselves as a cut above the average American, and they like to tease folks from other states for not being Texans. As soon as you open your mouth and some geographically specific accent pops out, it happens: they know, and they will proceed to identify you as "a foreigner." The best way to respond is to ignore it. Just play along. Someday you will get a Texan where you live, and you can turn the tables on him. Otherwise, you will not meet friendlier and more honest folks anywhere. The older residents love to tell stories from their youth and regale you with historical information, because the state's past is very colorful.

Though I cannot claim Texas as a birthright, there is something special about how I can answer when someone asks me where I am from: Dallas. That one word says it all. People don't ask if you mean Dallas, Texas, because they know there is only one Big D. Dallas and Texas and Texans have become famous worldwide, though some of that fame may be infamy. To live here is to fall in love with the heritage, if you can ignore the blistering summer heat.

The name Texas comes from *tejas,* some old Spanish word for "friendly." The name was applied to a tribe of Indians the original Spanish explorers met early in their travels through this part of North America. The Spaniards were impressed with the Indians' friendliness and openness. So, we all know what happened to those Indians, eh? Maybe this friendly stuff ain't all it's cracked up to be? But the original meaning still applies to the residents of today, which you too will find if you just relax around them and ignore the "everything is bigger in Texas" idiom.

Texas became the U.S.A's 28th state on December 29, 1845. For ten years before that, it was the Republic of Texas. This probably explains the native habit of seeing yourself as slightly larger than life. Texans declared (March 2, 1836) and then won their independence from Mexico with the assistance of many early frontiersmen, such as Tennessee native Davy Crockett and Louisiana gentleman Jim Bowie. Both caught bullets at a church down in San Antonio (March 6, 1836). Everyone has heard of the Alamo, and most people know about the massacre that occurred there, but only people raised here are aware of all the other battles that were fought and how much Texan and American blood was spilled winning Texas's independence from Mexico. These are a very proud people, and they have extremely long memories.

Until the late 1800s Texas was mostly wide-open land. Earlier than that, parts of the state were mainly populated by Indians or outlaws, so many areas figure prominently in some serious gunfights. After the War for Southern Independence (a.k.a. War between the States, War for States' Rights, or Civil War), farmers used barbed wire to fence in huge areas, and this spelled the end of free rangeland. This also brought the end of being able to wander from place to place uninhibited.

Trail riding is undergoing something of a revival in Texas. Many equestrian clubs have annual trail rides, complete with chuckwagons and period costumes. After all, this is a state with a rich heritage of people wandering around at will out in the boonies. At one point in our history it was possible, and fairly common, for people to ride from one end of the state to the other—something like 800 miles—and never see a fence. Those were the days of cattle drives and buffalo, cowboys and Indians, and the Texas Rangers and the outlaws. I like to see myself as a modern-day cowboy in some ways; my horse just prefers Gatorade to oats.

Though the equestrian set would probably disagree with me, in a lot of ways I think mountain biking has enhanced trail awareness and access to trail areas by getting a lot of mainstream people outdoors and into the woods. These people have rediscovered the joys of nature and the Texas our forefathers knew and loved. We just prefer the easy storage of a mountain bike to the high maintenance of a horse.

Words of caution, again. Watch for poison ivy and snakes. Just about any area where the trails run under a canopy of hardwoods will have poison ivy, poison oak, or poison sumac. I have never been terribly allergic to this stuff, so I am not good at identifying it. If you are one of those folks whose skin reacts to these plants, learn what they look like. They are *very* common on shaded trails.

Snakes are also fairly common. I have seen the poisonous ones while mountain biking in Texas, so I promise you they are out there. Rattlesnakes, copperheads, and especially cottonmouth water moccasins can be a definite threat to you when you are on trails in Texas. The last two are the most dangerous simply because they are so aggressive. Either one will go out of its way to chase you and try to bite you, while rattlers typically will try to go the other way. If you see a snake, and you are not a herpetologist, leave it alone. Snakes eat their weight in rodents and are very valuable members of the animal kingdom. Just let them be and you will not have any trouble. If you make a stop on the trail, look where you are stepping before getting off the bike. One time a friend of mine almost stepped right in the middle of a pile of water moccasins because he was not looking where he was going. It would not have been pretty, I promise you, so be alert. Of course we would have taken him to a hospital—just as soon as we had stopped laughing at the numskull for ignoring everybody. (We were yelling at him not to move, but he just kept backing up.)

The weather is also a worthy opponent of the Texas mountain biker. Storms can blow in with a suddenness that will surprise you. In an hour or two a fluffy cloud on the horizon can turn into a monster hailstorm, and there may be nowhere to hide. Always keep an eye tuned to the sky. Like Texans are fond of saying, "if you don't like the weather, wait a few minutes; it will change." And though it never gets real cold in many parts of the state, the Panhandle gets some pretty severe winter weather just about every year. To quote another Texas axiom, "There is nothing between Amarillo and the Canadian border but a barbed-wire fence, and the top two strands are down." The heat in summer months can be very severe, so carry plenty of water with you to the trailhead and have at least two bottles on your bike. Dehydration brings on cramps and can cause a trip that started as big fun to end with a miserable death-march back to where you parked.

Also, much of the land where the trails were built is fairly delicate. Stay on the trail. Do not ride if the trail is muddy enough that the stuff sticks to your tires. Be careful and keep locked-brake skidding to a minimum. The main enemy of Texas mountain bikers is EROSION. The more an area gets abused by people locking their brakes and skidding, or by being ridden on when very wet, the more of it washes away in the next rain. Several trails in other parts of the country have been closed because of negligent users. Let's keep Texas land managers from having to close our trails. Carry your trash out with you, especially flattened inner tubes, and ride responsibly. Think about the future. This attitude is what has helped us gain access to the land we build the trails on. This attitude is also what mountain biking and true mountain bikers are all about.

North Texas and the Dallas–Fort Worth Metroplex

Home sweet home. This is the part of my state I am most familiar with and best able to tell you about. To the continuing surprise of a lot of area mountain bikers, there are some great trails around here. All of the mountain bike trails in this part of Texas were built and are maintained by volunteers, mostly from the Dallas Off-Road Bicycle Association. There are no mountains or real "wilderness" areas, but several locations could be considered remote. Especially if you have just locked your keys in the car (both sets, of course). Please keep this in mind when going out for a trail ride, as most trails have no facilities for acquiring drinking water or mechanical assistance. A cellular phone might be a good addition to your equipment in case an emergency should arise, along with a good selection of tools, a pump, and a patch kit. And a spare car key (taped somewhere on the bike).

Many of the trails in this area are on land held by the U.S. Army Corps of Engineers as flood control right-of-way, since many are near area reservoirs maintained by the Corps. Park rangers are very supportive of the rights of trail users, but bear in mind that most of the trails are multi-use facilities and that you will be sharing the trail with hikers and runners, as well as local nature groups and the occasional equestrian club. Few of the biking trails in this area also allow equestrian usage, though it is not unheard of to meet horse traffic from time to time. Follow the IMBA rules concerning yielding to other traffic. In other words, everybody else has the right-of-way over bikes.

Carry a patch kit and spare tube and pump, because if you do not have flat-proof tubes you WILL eventually need these items. North Texas is home to mesquite, honey locust, and bois d'arc trees. It is not uncommon to see a hundred three-inch thorns attached to a tree limb within inches of the trail. I am not making this up; just about everything in the outdoors here sticks you or bites you. Some of these trails are on reclaimed land that was once used for dumping trash (illegally, of course), and nails can be a problem. When I started trail riding, I had eight patches in my rear tube alone in the first week.

Also, keep in mind that this is a big city and it has a lot of mountain biking enthusiasts. Being careful around blind turns is a must on the out-and-back trails. It is a good idea to have a handlebar bell on your bike and to use it often when approaching blind corners. If you meet another rider on a difficult hill, the one going up has the right-of-way. Other considerations are listed on a trail-by-trail basis where they apply.

DORBA member Tony Linthicum demonstrates that not all off-road rides are in remote locations.

Dallas has 911 service, so in an emergency go to a phone and dial 911. Some of the outlying rural areas may not be hooked up on this yet, and you might just have to dial 0 and tell the operator what your problem is. Follow the posted instructions if you are using a pay phone. Another interesting note that might prove helpful is that DORBA has a voice-mail hotline with mailboxes for trail conditions at each of the facilities we maintain. Call and follow the instructions to get the latest trail-poop.

I have listed trail workdays for the trails in my area, as most of the local ones are maintained by my club and have a regular maintenance schedule. Don't be bashful—come out sometime and join a work party. They normally run about three hours, and lots of us bring our bikes for a ride afterward. You can meet the people who are directly involved with creation and maintenance of the facility and have some fun too. We trim trees, build bridges, and try to educate trail users with the code of the hills. Trail work is not nearly as daunting as it may seem. Everybody who comes out does it from a love of the land and our sport. There are ladies, there are kids, there are even nonriders at these events, so don't not come because you are not SuperRider. Most of the SuperRiders are too busy tearing up the trails to lower themselves to pick up trash or move dirt. Trail work is really therapeutic for those of us who live fast-paced city lives, and you might pick up some information about other cool places to ride or just meet some really nice people.

Please, do not laugh when a cyclist from around here calls something "technical." For some people this stuff is the only trail exposure they have ever had. So if you are a state champ from somewhere, keep it in perspective. The same goes for the word "hill." I always laugh when some Colorado biker comes down here and asks why it is so flat. Hey, we do the best we can with what we have. And we have fun. If you just want to gripe about how easy our trails are, you are not going to make a lot of friends among local cyclists. And don't complain about doing laps on a closed loop if you are accustomed to 25-mile-long trails. If North Texas is too easy for you, stay tuned. We are just getting started. Wait until we head to West Texas, because you haven't seen the wide-open spaces yet.

Each ride description has a section labeled "Season." We have two types of seasons in Texas and Oklahoma—the wet ones and the dry ones. The winters are usually not so bad that they keep you off the trails for very long. You will read that my advice concerning season is more directed at what kind of shape the trail is in when it is wet. Sometimes the conditions are just too bad. Do not slam through mud puddles; slow down or even get off the bike and walk around if you find a bad one. Please. Every ounce of dirt you carry out adds to erosion. Tread lightly and preserve the trails. One other caution I note where it applies is that hunting season should keep you off certain trails. Otherwise our trails may typically be enjoyed year-round. If in doubt, call one of the numbers listed in the "Sources of additional information" sections.

RIDE 1 *L. B. HOUSTON NATURE TRAIL A.K.A. CALIFORNIA CROSSING*

This is an excellent easy trail in the midst of one of America's largest cities. With a length of just over four miles and cutoffs that will allow riders to avoid parts of the trail, this is a ride anyone can enjoy. You could push a wheelchair around with ease, but many places are definitely too tight for a tandem or trailer. (Since first writing this, though, I have been nearly decapitated by the stoker on a tandem because I leaned out from behind a tree one night to yell "boo" and scare what I thought was a single but was really the captain. I

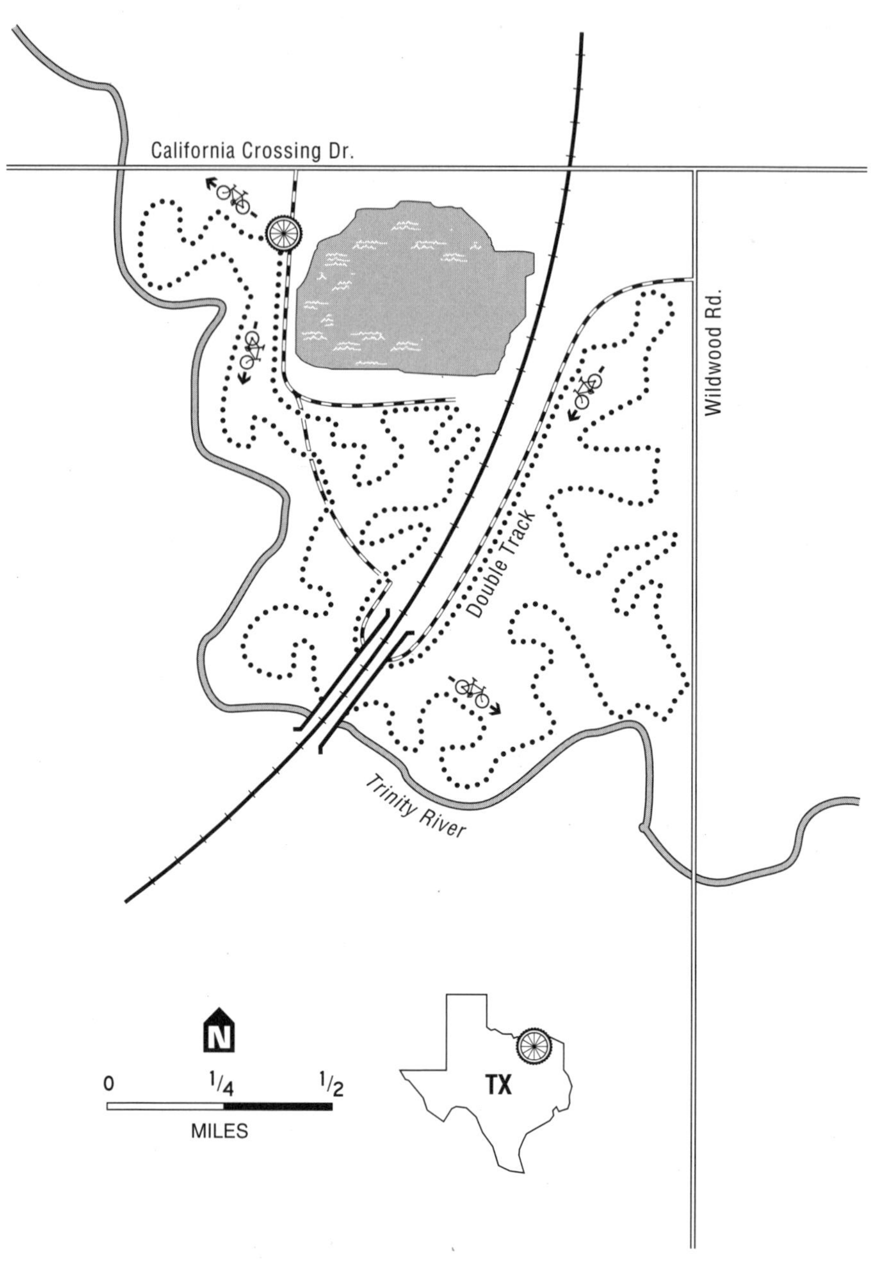

Note: *This trail has many more twists and turns than indicated.*

should revise that to say "most tandems"). No climbing or technical skills are required, but nevertheless, this is a very fun trail. My favorite one, in fact, since it is a ten-minute drive from where I live.

The configuration is a winding loop in rich riparian hardwoods that for the most part follows the Elm Fork of the Trinity River but never crosses it. The trail lies in the floodplain, and the surface is river silt and decomposing leaves, what the locals call black gumbo mud. When slightly wet, this stuff is as sticky as any surface you could ever ride. Sometimes you may find yourself wishing you had not, as it can be so gummy it sticks to your tires, bike, feet, and anything else that touches it. It holds water for a long time when completely saturated. Plus, the single-track is almost entirely shaded, so even a little rain makes the surface stay tacky for days. It is normally rideable within a few days of rainfall, but when deep tire tracks or puddles of water can be observed from the parking lot, don't try it. You will probably be okay in the trees, but the open sections will find you carrying a bike that weighs more than you ever dreamed.

Some beautiful bends in the river are accessible from the trail, and if you are a nature watcher, you'll appreciate the many opportunities for spotting local fauna. Lots of big, old trees, an adjacent pond or small lake that many people fish on, and mucho poison ivy. Texas Stadium, home of the four-time World Champion Dallas Cowboys, is visible on the other side of the river from one spot. Welcome to L. B. Houston. It can offer some interesting riding for beginners or those wishing to hone their bike handling skills.

Another interesting fact about this park is that within a stone's throw of the trailhead is a shallow spot in the river where wagon trains used to cross on their way to California, hence the nickname California Crossing. People say you can still see the depression from the old wagon road, and a historical marker indicates the spot. The marker is on the opposite side of California Crossing Drive from the trail at L. B. Houston Park, in what is known officially as California Crossing Park.

The name L. B. Houston belonged to the man who restructured and reorganized the Dallas Parks and Recreation Department in the 1930s. Apparently old Mr. Houston was quite a character, and the folks I have spoken with who knew him said he was a very straightforward and down-to-earth sort who would jump down into a ditch and introduce himself to the workers, *muy pronto,* when he was head of the department. A very memorable old coot about sums it up, as best I can tell. I'll bet he would have understood mountain bikers if he were alive today.

General location: The trail is located in the northwestern sector of Dallas, between Dallas and Las Colinas, just south of West Northwest Highway.
Elevation change: Not worth mentioning. A couple of small creek crossings, not more than ditches really. The whole park lies between elevations 410′ and 420′ above sea level.

L.B. Houston Trail is an excellent place to learn basic mountain bike skills. It is also a good place to hunt mosquitoes.

Season: During the dry months this trail is always well groomed and in excellent shape, though some corners may break up slightly and become crumbly. Within a few days of a light rain, this trail can offer some excellent grip and make for exciting riding.

Services: This trail is located right in the midst of the city. Nearby (less than one-half mile) is West Northwest Highway, a major thoroughfare with all manner of convenience stores and eating places. The only dedicated mountain bike shop in Dallas, Mountain Bike Innovations, is about a mile away.

Hazards: Traffic on this trail is expected to circulate in a counterclockwise direction. Almost all local riders know this, and it is marked, but be alert for knuckleheads going the wrong way. Very near the trailhead, immediately after a sharp left-hand turn, the river runs against the right side of the trail. This could be called a dangerous spot. There's a steep drop from the bluff into the river if you get too wide. Once you have ridden by this drop-off, you will be able to fix its location in your mind, and it will not sneak up on you again. Otherwise, it may surprise you the first time by. Stay to the left against the trees and you will be fine. The only other dangers come from the trees that line the trail and the heavy concentration of poison ivy in the park. The trees will lean out and grab your handlebars, and the ivy is everywhere. If you are allergic, take precautions.

Also, parallel to part of the trail is an elevated railroad track. Take care when making the turns under the trestle, because some old pilings are broken off nearly flush with the ground. Be wary, too, of the trains passing overhead on the trestle: one of our members and his daughter were nearly beaned by a bag of garbage tossed from a train.

Rescue index: The entire trail is within walking distance of a major paved road, West Northwest Highway. Looking around every time you pop out of the trees will show you several spots where you can bail out and go directly back to the trailhead parking lot without having to make a complete loop of the trail. Cutting a lap off the back side of the trail may require riding some old double-track that is overgrown with weeds. Pay phones are located at the convenience store on Newkirk and West Northwest Highway, and a bike shop (Mountain Bike Innovations) is caddy-cornered from there. Don't ask me where that expression comes from—it is Texan for the diagonal or opposite corner.

Land status: This is a city park and belongs to the Dallas Parks and Recreation Department.

Maps: They are not readily available, though Mountain Bike Innovations has a good one and Steve will probably let you copy it if you want. The 7.5 minute quad for this trail is Irving.

Finding the trail: Go west on West Northwest Highway from the point where West Northwest Highway passes under Interstate 35E. Keep going past the intersection of Loop #12 and West Northwest Highway, to the light at Newkirk Road, and turn left. At the stop sign, make an immediate right onto California Crossing Drive. Go west about a mile, passing over the railroad crossing. Just past the small lake you will see a parking lot on the left (south) side of the street. A monument in the parking lot identifies this as L. B. Houston Nature Trail. From the parking lot, go through the gate and proceed to the right into the trees and onto the trail, circulating counterclockwise. The main track is not crossed by any others, and if you just stay on it you will not get lost.

Sources of additional information:

Dallas Off-Road Bicycle Association
18484 Preston Road
#102-106
Dallas, TX 75252
(214) 579-5540

Mountain Bike Innovations
2053 West Northwest Highway #90
Dallas, TX 75220
(214) 432-0095

Notes on the trail: Since its resurrection in 1991, the original nature trail has grown to approximately 4 miles in length, consisting mostly of tight single-track, with some double-track connecting sections of the trail, especially along the railroad and near the start/finish area. There are no rest room or drinking fountain facilities, but there is ample parking in the parking lot or along California Crossing. Because it is a heavily wooded area in the middle of a big city, the park is home to a lot of wildlife. Armadillos and rabbits are common, along with many species of birds, and several riders have reported seeing a bobcat running on the trail. If you ride this trail in the spring, summer, or fall, I recommend that you carry some insect repellent in case you have to make a stop, as the mosquitoes in this area are very numerous. Numerous? Heck, they're overpowering, and if you stop you are doomed. This is one of the few trails that DORBA rides where we do not spend a lot of time by the trail practicing our conversational skills.

RIDE 2 *NORTHSHORE TRAIL A.K.A. LAKE GRAPEVINE*

Here you have the most popular North Texas mountain bike trail. At present it stretches nearly ten miles, from Rockledge Park (by the Grapevine Lake dam) to just west of Twin Coves Park, on the north side of Grapevine Lake. About a mile of it is abandoned roadway, but the rest is fine North Texas single-track.

The Northshore Trail is an out-and-back trail that follows the shoreline of Grapevine Lake, sometimes right on the beaches. It combines a few miles of old motorcycle and horse tracks with specifically constructed single-track mountain bike and hiking trails. These lands have avoided being developed into homesites because they lie on United States Army Corps of Engineers (USACE) property that forms the flood control easement for the reservoir.

This place covers the gamut of difficulty ratings: The western end has some difficult technical sections, with some short climbs and many tight, challenging switchbacks and rocky sections. This end is also mostly in the woods. The eastern end opens up somewhat, to longer downhills and some very fast flat beaches. Going from end to end and back is going to wear you out unless you are a very fit rider, and even then. Along the way are many creek crossings, but we DORBA members have bridged them or otherwise made them passable. Be prepared to yield to pedestrian and other bicycle traffic, which will likely be considerable: according to the Corps estimates, from 750 to 1,000 visitors come here in a busy weekend.

Soil conditions vary from location to location, but generally there is an abundance of sand and rocks. The sand may be powder or small gravel, and the rocks will typically be sandstone outcroppings or pieces of the same. Some areas on the farthest western reaches have more clay in the soil. This soil is darker and capable of holding water when wet. Usually, however, the sandy sections are dry enough to ride within a day or so of a fair amount of rain. You will see many spots where work has been done repeatedly to try and preserve a particular hill by trying to save the trees on it. Retaining walls and water breaks are therefore common, as are small bridges. If you ride this trail and conditions are wet enough that your bike and body are collecting mud, the rangers can and will cite you for a violation of the "trail closed to bikes when muddy" rule. And with good reason. A Texas mountain biker's worst enemy is not necessarily land developers, it is EROSION. While you are tooling along, notice that in many areas the trail is dug into the ground to a disturbing depth. While it is true that much of this damage was done by the early motorcycle riders, even more is the result of runoff rainwater carrying the soil away. Every time you skid your tires while braking, you contribute. Ditto every time you fly through a mud hole. With the volume of use this facility gets, every little bit hurts. Abuse it, and we all lose it. Members of the Sierra Club hide here and wait to photograph mountain bikers acting like asses, so don't.

The area north of the lake is called Cross Timbers for the dense tangle of woods. When you are not hidden in the trees, you will be offered some gorgeous views of the lake. Sunsets and sunrises can be spectacular from some of the high bluffs on the eastern end. Visible on the far side of Grapevine Lake are marinas and parts of the city of Grapevine. Except for the fact that the trail is plainly established and marked, it would be easy to forget how close you are to the metropolis, until the next big jet overhead. You are only a few miles from one of the largest airports in the world, and directly off the end of its main runways.

There is lots of parking, and there are many access points and swimming, day camping, fishing, and water skiing opportunities. These are all popular attractions to people visiting Grapevine Lake, and from what I have been able to glean, this is THE sailboat lake for the Metroplex area. Several towns are located nearby, so you can come here to get "away from it all but not too far." Plus, with the heavy level of use, you are never far away from assistance. During the summer months, you may even meet one of the Trail Patrol crews. These volunteers ride the trail and offer assistance to those in need, hopefully promoting goodwill between trail users.

General location: It is called the Northshore for the simple fact that it covers much of the north side of Grapevine Lake, starting at the dam and stretching west for several miles. All the way to US 377 someday, we hope.
Elevation change: The highest point in the park is just over 600′ above sea level, and the normal pool elevation of Grapevine Lake is 535′, though I think the lake is usually slightly higher than that.

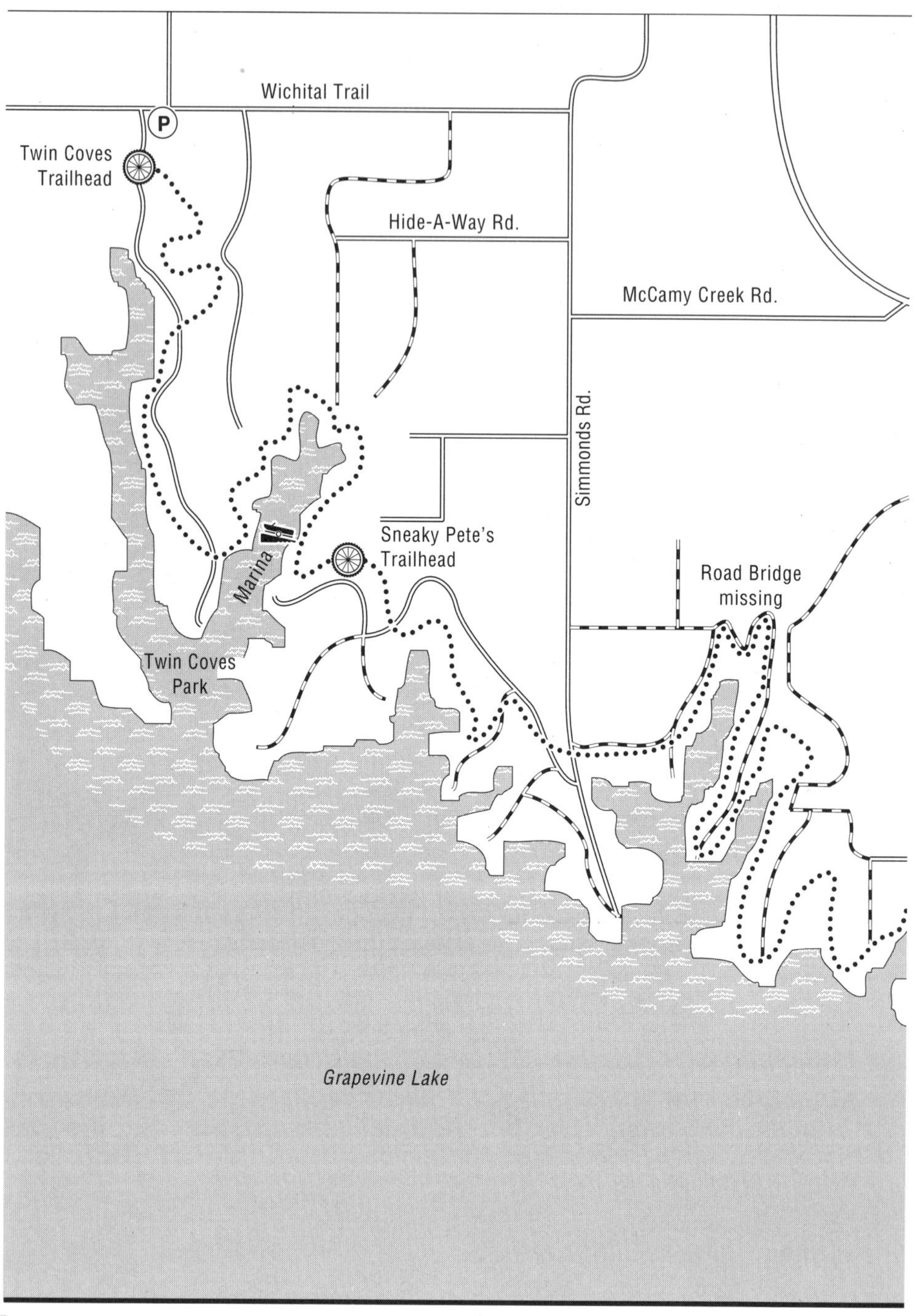
Wichital Trail
P
Twin Coves
Trailhead
Hide-A-Way Rd.
McCamy Creek Rd.
Simmonds Rd.
Sneaky Pete's
Trailhead
Marina
Road Bridge
missing
Twin Coves
Park
Grapevine Lake

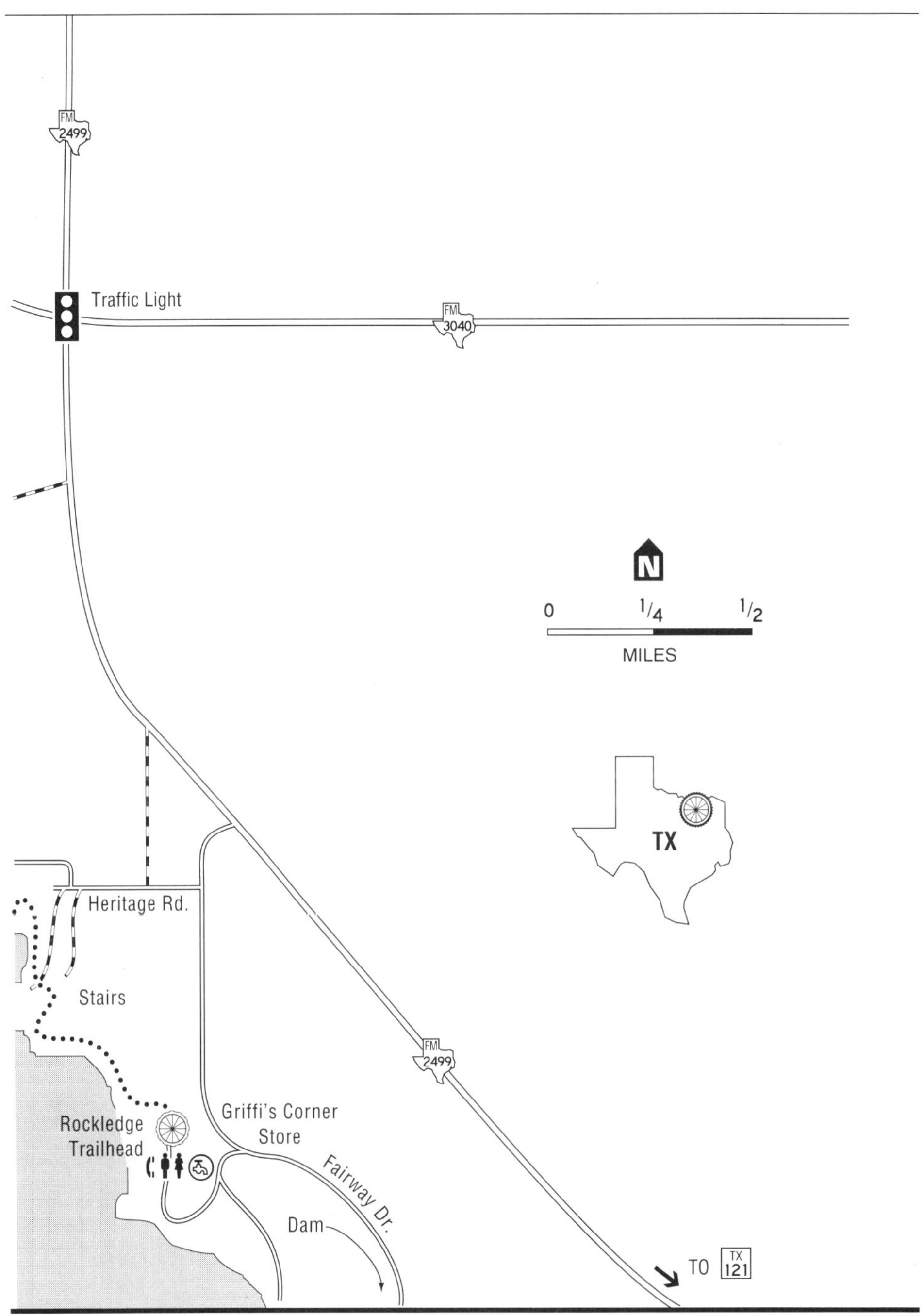

FM 2499
Traffic Light
FM 3040
N
0
1/4
1/2
MILES
TX
Heritage Rd.
Stairs
Rockledge Trailhead
Griffi's Corner Store
Fairway Dr.
Dam
TO TX 121

Season: Thank you, Texas, for another good year-round trail. The sandy sections drain really well and are usually dry enough to ride within a day of rain, but some of the areas under the trees may stay sticky for days after getting wet. Rule of thumb: If it sticks to your tires and gets slung onto your bike and collects there, it is too wet to ride. I have seen huge sections of the trail underwater as a result of flooding in the area, but that is an exceptional occurrence. The Corps has control over this land and can elect to close the trail to cyclists if they deem it too muddy for riding. Or for good if we destroy it. Please obey their wishes.

Services: For help or munchies, the city of Grapevine, to the south, is your best bet. And the town of Flower Mound is north just a few miles on FM 2499. Both offer a selection of eateries and convenience stores. Bluebonnet Bicycles is in Lewisville, maybe 10 miles away, and Mountain Bike Innovations in Dallas is only about a 20-minute drive.

Hazards: Almost too numerous to mention. There are several places where the trail follows a bluff along the lake, and a fall from one of these bluffs would be dangerous. Part of the trail follows an abandoned paved roadway that has a washed-out bridge near the eastern end. At this point the trail drops down through the creek bed on the south side of the huge hole in the pavement. *This is definitely a point to be wary of, because missing the turn where the trail dips into the creek would mean certain injury when you dive off the end of the road and onto your Oakleys.* Several places have gates to pass through in spots where the trail crosses a road. Go ahead, do a wheelie over them. Right, that's what people always say, but I have only seen one or two people try. At the road crossings, people in cars come flying down through there way too fast, so be extremely careful crossing the roads. Always STOP-LOOK-LISTEN before blasting across even a gravel road. Many fast sections combine with places where the trail surface is very loose, so taking a tumble is always in the back of my mind here. Especially when I am already bleeding and the m-dolphins are speaking to me. This trail has many fast drops into blind turns, so do a reconnaissance ride before going full tilt into any of them. There could be an unexpected bridge or gully or opposing traffic just around the bend. Watch out for: joggers (a cross-country running club uses this trail extensively, and some of its members are also members in good standing of my club); hikers (the Boy Scouts use and help maintain this trail, and Sierra Club groups are a common sight); and people walking unleashed dogs (a violation of park rules but common nevertheless). Less than a mile from the Rockledge Park trailhead is a stairway that you MUST portage. To attempt to ride it would be to die. I must stress the "watch for idiots on bikes" rule because I personally know several people who have been hurt in collisions here.

Rescue index: This place is so spread out that breaking down several miles from where you parked is always a possibility. Several sections of the trail pass within a stone's throw of residential neighborhoods or cross park roads and fishing trails. The chances of locating assistance in an emergency are good.

Rules can be fun. The Northshore Trail at Grapevine Lake has some worthy ones. Help keep the trails open by using them.

Flagging down a fellow biker or a passing car is your best bet, though I personally would not be above knocking on someone's door and asking for help if I needed medical attention for an injured person. I helped load an injured rider into a helicopter ambulance in some guy's front yard out here one day, so take heed. Most of the mountain bikers around here are friendly enough that if they see you stranded they will often ask if you need help. Some will even offer to give you a lift to your car from where they are parked if you can make it that far. Bailing out and picking a paved road to use as an escape route to your parking spot is more than feasible. Just remember that east/west Wichita Trail and north/south Simmonds Road intersect, and you should be able to navigate back to where you are parked on generally good cycling roads.

Land status: The trail is located on flood control right-of-way held by the U.S. Army Corps of Engineers as operators of the Grapevine Lake flood control reservoir. The trail is contained within and policed by the City of Flower Mound.

Maps: Fairly good maps are available at the Corps headquarters and Visitor Center located on FM 2499 just north of the intersection with TX 121. The quads for this trail are Grapevine and Lewisville West.

Finding the trail: There are several popular trailheads with ample parking. DORBA people usually start their rides from the Sneaky Pete's trailhead, but just about everybody else starts from Rockledge Park.

Rockledge Park trailhead: Located at the north end of Grapevine Lake dam, this is a day-use campground with covered picnic tables and fire grates. Go north on Long Prairie Road from TX 121, past the Army Corps of Engineers headquarters and over the dam and spillway. Turn left at the signs for Rockledge Park, across the road from the Griffi's Corner store. This park opens at 9 A.M. and closes at 10 P.M. The gate is locked when the park closes. There are rest rooms and a pay phone at the trailhead.

Sneaky Pete's/Murrell Park trailhead: Located near the Murrell Park marina and Sneaky Pete's restaurant, this spot lies roughly in the center of the trail. Leave Dallas on Interstate 635 West toward Grapevine and D/FW Airport. Go west until you see where the road splits; the left fork goes to TX 121 South and the airport and the right heads for Bethel Road/TX 121 North. Take the fork to the right and get on TX 121. You will only be on TX 121 long enough to change lanes all the way to the left to catch FM 2499 toward Flower Mound. Go north on FM 2499 to the traffic light at FM 3040 and turn left, going west. (The road signs here say Flower Mound Road.) Go to the first street, McKamy Creek Road, and turn left. Go to the end of McKamy Creek Road, and at a three-way stop sign, turn left onto Simmonds Road. Follow the signs for Sneaky Pete's and Murrell Park. You go for a mile or so on flat ground, then the road suddenly drops over a small hill. This is the entrance to Murrell Park and only one of three very dangerous places where the trail crosses the pavement (unexpectedly for the cars). Be very careful; go slow. Go to the stop sign and turn right. You will pass some rest rooms near the boat ramp, the trail (again), and a water fountain (it tastes terrible, so bring your own). Follow the paved road as it curves around. Shortly after a sharp left turn, you will cross the trail again and immediately turn right, following more signs for the restaurant and marina. About a quarter of a mile past the turn, before the marina, there is a parking area on the right, by the sign kiosk and park bench. It is unusual not to see several mountain bikers hanging around the parking lot, so you will likely recognize the place. Park here and go through the gate and onto the trail. Going right (south) on the trail takes you to the easy part, and going left (north) takes you to the more difficult and technical sections.

Twin Coves Park trailhead: Follow the directions for the Sneaky Pete's trailhead as far as the end of McKamy Creek Road and the three-way stop sign. Turn right on Simmonds Road at the three-way stop and follow it to the intersection with Wichita Trail. Turn left on Wichita Trail and follow the signs for Twin Coves Park. Follow the park road down to the picnic area just before the entrance to Twin Coves Park. There are places to park and a few picnic tables near the trailhead. As at the Sneaky Pete's trailhead, the trail runs two different directions from the trailhead here—toward and away from the sign kiosk. If you proceed westerly, the trail winds around in the hills near the trailhead and has some very nice off-camber switchbacks and technical sections that are definitely worth exploring. There is presently only about a mile of trail to the west, but someday . . . Otherwise, the most technically demanding sections are the other way, east, toward the main body of the trail and the other trailheads.

Sources of additional information:

Dallas Off-Road Bicycle Association
18484 Preston Road
#102-106
Dallas, TX 75252
(214) 579-5540

Mountain Bike Innovations
2053 West Northwest Highway #90
Dallas, TX 75220
(214) 432-0095

U.S. Army Corps of Engineers
Fort Worth District
Grapevine Lake
M(817) 481-4541 for the Corps office
M(817) 481-3576 for trail conditions

Notes on the trail: This trail has been recognized as a National Recreational Trail, and my club has won national awards for our involvement with and work on it. The trail was pioneered in 1987 by Tom "Switchback" Deans and a former ranger, Jerre Killingbeck, with the help of members of DORBA, which at that time was just starting to stretch its legs. A hearty thank-you is due all of these unsung heroes; where would we be without you? We've come a long way, baby, and we are not through yet. There are still a couple of miles of trail to be squeezed out of the available land, and with the help of the City of Flower Mound, someday the trail from the dam will connect to the Knob Hill Trail via a bike path parallel or near Wichita Trail Road.

As an aside, if you wish to ride the whole enchilada, it is wise to start at the Sneaky Pete's trailhead. You can ride the hard side to Twin Coves and back, stop and refill your water bottles, and then ride the easy side over to the dam and back. That way if you break down you are only a maximum of 5 miles or so from your car.

Workdays are the second Saturday of each month. When the days are short, our club has a regular Wednesday night ride from the Sneaky Pete's trailhead, so call the hotline and bring a headlight if you are interested. Equestrian traffic is strictly forbidden on this trail, but they still wander onto our land all the time.

RIDE 3 *KNOB HILL PARK TRAIL, A.K.A. WEST END TRAIL*

If you want to get away from it all, including other cyclists, have a ride out on the wild West End, as the Knob Hill trail is informally known. This is an excellent place to pack a picnic lunch (which for me consists of an extra bottle of water and a couple of pecan pralines) and a pair of binoculars, and just waste an afternoon. The total length from the US 377 trailhead to the far east end at present is over six miles. Starting from the Dome House trailhead will allow you to skip the hard parts if you want. Jumping off from the US 377 trailhead will let you tackle techno-stuff first, then cruise the flats.

The trail is an out-and-back running roughly diagonally between two perpendicular roads, US 377 and FM 1171. It roughly follows Denton Creek. You wind through some dense woods, then open up into huge fields of native grasses, and finally you find yourself riding along Grapevine Lake. By the lake the soil is very sandy, and it may even be powder in some places, because the more eastern reaches are horse country. The middle sections are sandy enough to drain and typically can be ridden a few days after a rain. Elsewhere, the soil contains more clay and is not very rideable when wet, particularly in the technical sections.

Over half the trail is almost perfectly flat, and as mentioned above, if you start near the Dome House trailhead you can ride the easy stuff over to where the part under the canopy is, turn around, and return to your car and barely break a sweat. The hard stuff is not mind-boggling, but one or two spots could be dangerous because they are fairly steep, and there is even a spot I am scared to try. The rest is rideable by most off-roaders. I would venture to say that this is a good one for the kids to try. But then, I have no kids, so I may not be one to judge.

Parts of this trail can be a bog for months during the wet season. I have ridden it, but I won't again. Regardless, I appeal to you to ride here when conditions allow, because this trail does not get enough use, and it is a really neat place. This is a primitive trail, much more so than the main Northshore Trail, and crossing creeks may mean getting your feet wet. During the hotter seasons, for an early morning ride—say about dawn—this place is wonderful. There are long stretches where you can putt along and daydream away your daily troubles.

In the fall this area is beautiful; all the hardwoods along the creek and perimeters of the open fields are ablaze with colors. On the other hand, in high summer this trail can be surrounded by ragweed that towers eight feet into the air, cutting off any breeze that might wander by, and most of the views as well. If the weather is hot, plan to ride here at night or early in the day before the mercury goes out of sight.

RIDE 3 *KNOB HILL PARK TRAIL*

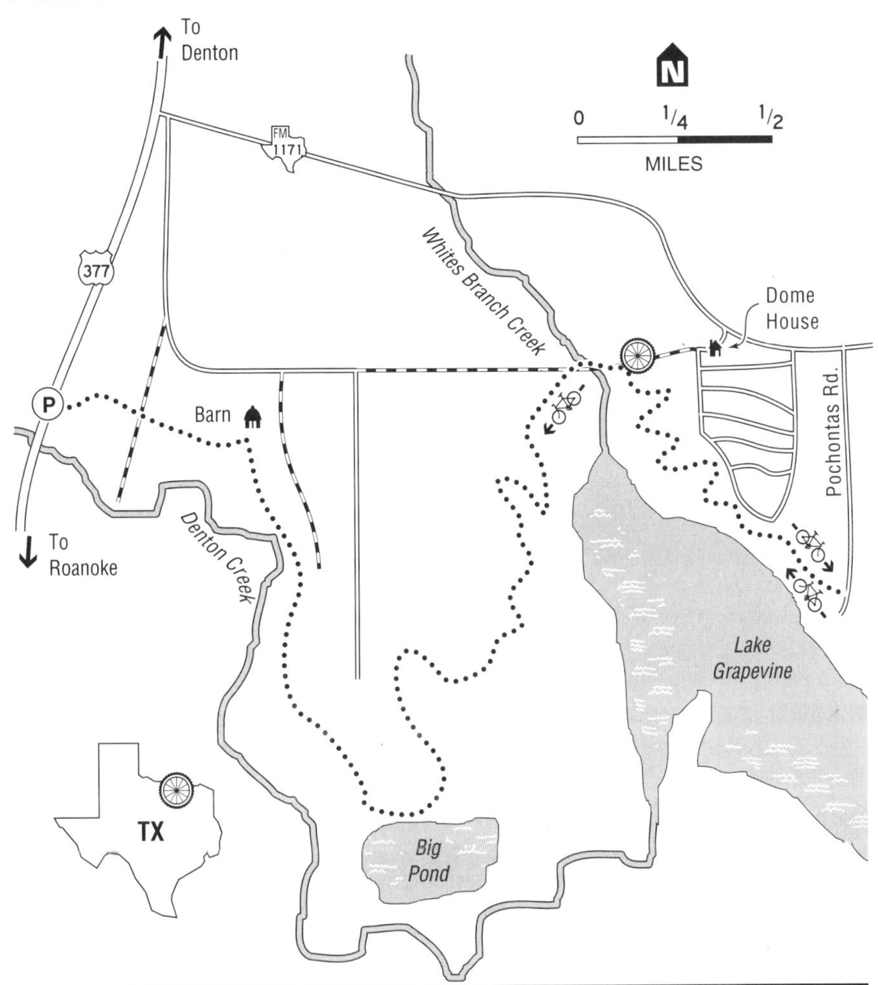

You will get an excellent cross section of North Texas terrain when you ride here. There will be some short, sharp hills, then some flat long fields of bluestem grass and various native flora, and you will even pass near enough to the lake to have some fair views of the water. There are a couple of benches scattered around, but for some reason the Corps hardly ever puts them in the shade. One is on sort of a lookout point, though. If you like to collect nuts, there are many pecan and walnut trees in the park. During season you might want to carry a bag to throw some in. If I ever spot that bald eagle I am always watching for, I think it will be somewhere along this trail. I love this place. If it just weren't so far out from town, I would practically live here.

General location: Half an hour northwest of Dallas, on the far west end of Grapevine Lake. More specifically, between Roanoke and Argyle, west of Flower Mound.
Elevation change: Overall, from the highest point to the water's edge, you only give up about 50′, so elevation-wise this trail is very comparable to the Northshore Trail.
Season: Knob Hill can be ridden year-round unless it is extremely wet. An evening ride here in the fall is a must for those fond of natural settings. In the summer, mosquito repellent is recommended if you plan to ride in the evening.
Services: None. Get water and supplies before going to the trailhead. Stop in Lewisville or Roanoke, depending on your direction of approach. Both have burger joints and convenience stores. The nearest bike shops are in Denton and Lewisville.
Hazards: Caution is a watchword here. There are several fast turns that tend to be covered with marbles or tree roots or a combination thereof, so take care when riding through fallen leaves or in the wet. The Knob Hill Trail is far enough from the city that hardly anyone rides here, so if you get hurt or break your bike, you are in for a long walk to the trailhead. In spite of the isolation, there are several blind turns to be wary of, and a bell is a worthy bike accessory to use on this trail.

There is equestrian access to the eastern parts of this facility, and bikers should observe IMBA rules. Watch for the two short, very steep creek crossings near the barbed-wire fence. They are tough enough that they should be attempted only by the most experienced riders; all others will probably want to walk.

As with many other trails in the area, cactus and thorny trees and bushes are the order of the day. Take a patch kit and pump. A first-aid kit with tweezers is a good addition to your gear for visiting this area. Snakes can be found almost anywhere here in the warmer months. Be careful and keep your eyes open, and if you see one, just keep going.
Rescue index: Hike to a road, stick out your thumb, and hope somebody will give you a ride back to where you are parked. Remember, the east/west road is FM 1171 and the north/south one is US 377. The best idea would be to stay on the trail and follow it to where you parked.
Land status: The U.S. Army Corps of Engineers take care of this property as flood-control right-of-way for Grapevine Lake. The trail is maintained by volunteers from the Dallas Off-Road Bicycle Association.
Maps: Nonexistent. Rumor has it that the original topographics were lost while the lake was being filled because someone left them at what unexpectedly became a submerged location. I did the best I could drawing one from memory. The quad, if you can find it, is Argyle.
Finding the trail: This gets sort of complicated, but I'll give it a try.

Knob Hill Trail is mostly for drier weather. DORBA member Ed Horn is the one with the big smile.

From Denton go south on US 377 to the intersection with FM 1171. Turn left (east) and go 1.7 miles to Old Cross Timbers Road. Turn right (south) by the Dome House, and about 50 yards west you will see the gate and parking area. Or keep going south past the intersection of FM 1171 and US 377 about one-half mile. The western trailhead is a small parking area and gate on the east side of US 377 just north of the bridge over Denton Creek.

From Dallas go west on TX 114 past Grapevine to Roanoke and the intersection with US 377. Go north on US 377 for 3.5 miles, and you'll see the western trailhead on the north end of the bridge. Or go another one-half mile north to FM 1171 and turn right to the Dome House trailhead.

From Lewisville, go west on FM 1171 to Old Cross Timbers Road, about 1.5 miles east of the intersection with US 377. Turn left and go past the Dome House to the parking area. It is one-tenth of a mile south of FM 1171.

Sources of additional information:

Dallas Off-Road Bicycle Association
18484 Preston Road
#102-106
Dallas, TX 75252
(214) 579-5540

Mountain Bike Innovations
2053 West Northwest Highway #90
Dallas, TX 75220
(214) 432-0095

U.S. Army Corps of Engineers
Fort Worth District
Grapevine Lake
M(817) 481-4541

Notes on the trail: Someday this trail may connect to the main stem of the Northshore Trail on the north side of Grapevine Lake, as it is actually considered by the Corps to be a part of the Northshore Trail. Since this trail was pioneered in 1992, whether mountain bikes or horses rule here has been a topic of some debate. The equestrian groups want to ride here, and with good reason. It is very suitable to four-legged traffic, and more positive contact between bikers and riders can only improve our relationship. A lot of "them" don't like "us," and vice versa. Don't be a jerk; if you see people on horseback, be friendly. Stop and let them pass, smile and wave, and everybody will be happy. We need more friends among "them," because the state is only so big, and we need to be able to share. They were here first, after all. Soapbox mode off: Enjoy—it's a neat trail. This is another place DORBA sometimes has night rides, so call the hotline. Night riding here is really fun during a full moon. Workdays for this trail, like the rest of the Northshore Trail, are on the second Saturday of each month.

RIDE 4 *HORSESHOE TRAIL A.K.A. SOUTH SHORE*

This trail is a point-to-point that turns into a loop of just over four miles when you hit the pavement for your return. This is recommended so that traffic circulates only in a roughly clockwise direction. Sorry, we did the best we could, but the residential area would not budge and let us build along their property. The Horseshoe Trail used to be called the South Shore Trail, but when the city of Grapevine took over from the feds, they had a ceremony, and now it's the Horseshoe Trail but no horses are allowed. You figure it out.

RIDE 4 *HORSESHOE TRAIL*

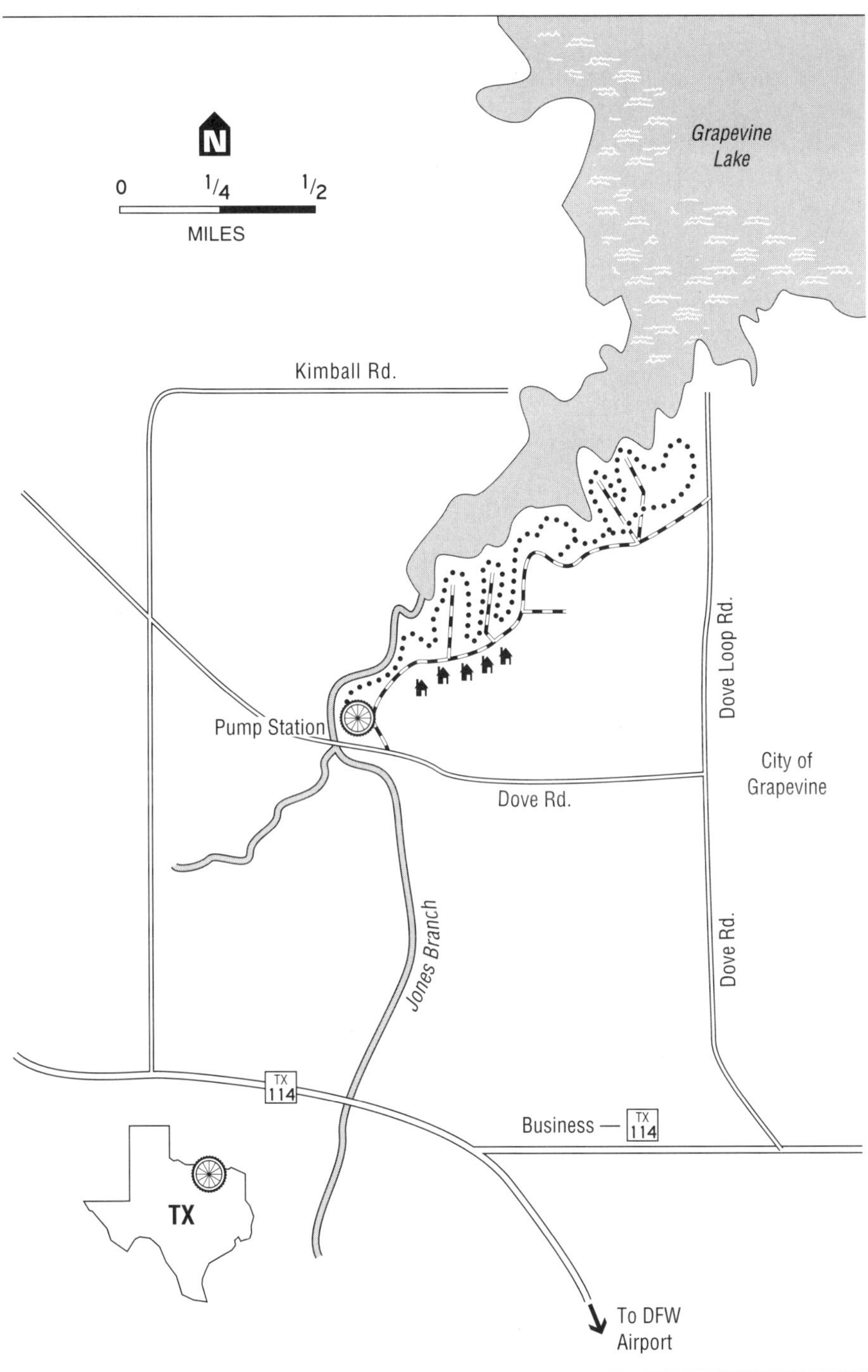

The loop winds around through the live oak and pin oak and post oak trees, occasionally offering views of Grapevine Lake or the adjacent housing developments. Not exactly world-class views, but a real good trail nevertheless. Your eyes need to be fixed on the trail anyway—there are some challenges in this park. Many of the turns are off-camber and have very short braking zones, and several of the short uphills are steep enough and have short enough entry areas to require quick and accurate gear changes.

The hard-packed sandstone and its light salting of loose sand combine to create a trail that is fast, slippery, and tight. If you break concentration for even a moment, you will go down or hit something. But go out here late some afternoon and cut a few laps, and your heart rate will get up there. Some of the newer sections are farther from the water and bring softer surfaces and faster turns. The trees are just as solidly attached to the ground, though.

A perfect example of the part of North Texas known as the Cross Timbers, the Horseshoe will not disappoint. This tight tangle of small trees, almost like large shrubs, is home to many a bird and squirrel. Again, riding farther from the water gets you into larger and older trees.

Ease of access and nearby facilities are the highlights of riding here. This is a City of Grapevine park and is located within the city limits in the Corp's old Oak Grove Park land. It was closed and decrepit for a long time, but the friends of DORBA are everywhere, even on the park board here.

General location: Grapevine, just a few miles north of Dallas/Fort Worth Regional Airport. On Jones Branch creek.

Elevation change: Maybe 40´, short and sweet.

Season: Year-round. Usually rideable within days of a rain, because the sandy soil drains very well.

Services: The trail is right in town, so there are numerous convenience stores located a short distance from the trailhead. The nearest bike shop is Mountain Bike Innovations back in Dallas, maybe 20 minutes away on TX 114.

Hazards: The slippery trail surface caused by the sandy conditions combines with the tight, tree-lined route to create an exciting series of twisty-turnies. You'll find ample opportunities to scrape a forearm or bang shoulders and hips on the trees. Since this place is only about 50 feet from some houses, look for pedestrians, especially little kids on BMX bikes. Late at night they like to cut down small trees about 3 or 4 feet up the trunk, leaving nice punji spears for the rest of us. And if you hear them shooting their pellet rifles, make lots of noise as you approach.

Rescue index: Ample. Once you get to the pavement, the parking area is no more than a mile away. Always go south, and any of the old roads you find will take you back to your car.

Land status: A City of Grapevine Parks Department facility. This was once a day use campground, but is now closed to automobile traffic.

Maps: Not readily available. The quad for this trail is Grapevine.

The Horseshoe Trail at Grapevine Lake is another trail providing large fun for small outputs of technical expertise.

Finding the trail: Follow TX 114 west past Grapevine to the traffic light at Kimball Road. Turn right on Kimball Road and go north to the four-way stop at Dove Road. Turn right on Dove Road and go east about a mile, to the park entrance parking area by the pumping station on the north side of Dove Road. Go through the gate and past the sign kiosk (noticing the date of the next workday, of course). The trail cuts off the road to the left, about 50 yards from the gate.

Sources of additional information:

Dallas Off-Road Bicycle Association
18484 Preston Road
#102-106
Dallas, TX 75252
(214) 579-5540

Mountain Bike Innovations
2053 West Northwest Highway #90
Dallas, TX 75220
(214) 432-0095

City of Grapevine Parks Department
(817) 481-0351

Notes on the trail: Expect lots of joggers and recreational cyclists on the roadway, since this park is adjacent to a large residential area. Another DORBA pal of mine is directly responsible for this trail; he serves both as DORBA trail steward and as a member of the City of Grapevine Parks Department. Workdays are on the first Sunday of each month.

RIDE 5 *BOULDER PARK TRAIL*

Here is a favorite trail of many Dallas mountain bikers. This trail is almost entirely single-track, almost completely varied in elevation, and sufficiently challenging that you will want to come back again and again to try and ace that one spot. The length is three to five miles per lap, depending on how much backtracking you do because you've gotten lost in the bewildering maze of interlacing trails. When properly flagged for a race, it is a winding loop with lots of convolutions. That is how Dallasites get so many running miles from so few square ones. Normally I have trouble making two circuits exactly the same because there are offshoots of the trail around every bend. Fear not, you can only get so lost that you spend ten minutes on the road getting back to your car and the trailhead.

The difficulty level for me is from medium to semi-tough, depending on the layout. I have heard expert-level riders say it is too easy, but we all know how they are. Some of the climbs I do not clean each time due to their technical difficulty, but all of it can be cleaned by the right rider. You will discover several fast downhills that you must respect if you want to live to see another trail, and you will find many good places to fall and land on your head, or arm, or ribs. Be careful until you find the line around all the turns.

The opportunities to get loose are many, because if you hit some of these turns too fast you will lose traction on the marbles and be in a slide before you realize. There are numerous limestone outcroppings and soft spots that provide challenging turns and climbs. If a race has been held here recently—and this is a popular location for races—you should take care in the faster turns, because they will have plenty of marbles. Did I mention the water crossings? They are steep and always slick, and there is one section along the creek bed, on loose rocks, that is slippery even when it is bone dry. Across some of the climbs you will find roots that will waste the power in your legs and leave you teetering, scrambling to unclip your feet and straddle that top tube.

This is not a trail for scenery unless you like beautiful trees, which I do. No great vistas, but lots of good examples of the motto of local flora—"See me or I will bite you." Otherwise, not really much to brag about unless you like to hear airplanes flying overhead. Red Bird Airport is right on the other side of Red Bird Lane from the trail, and you are under the planes' final approach for landing or initial climb out, depending on the fickle Texas weather.

Long ago this trail was a training area for the local National Guard unit, and people have told me of finding old shell casings and places where it was obvious that tanks or guns had been dug in. Try to ride it with someone who knows it so you can get all the local history. Lots of parts of this trail have colorful names, such as Dead Dog Turn, Hercules Club Turn, and Red Ball Loop, just to name a few. Some are pretty obvious, and some refer to various points of interest along the trail. A lot of riding has been done here over the years. Motorcycles and four-wheel-drives ruled for a long time, but at present the Dallas Parks and Recreation Department sees fit for this to be nonmotorized traffic only. Amen. The mountain bikers go crazy here.

General location: The trail is very near Redbird Mall and the I-20/US 67 mix-master, in the south-southwestern sector of Dallas.
Elevation change: Lots (for Dallas). The highest point in the park is around 700´ above sea level, and the lowest is near 600´.
Season: Boulder Park is a good year-round facility. Under normal conditions it has usually dried enough to be ridden within a day or two of a medium rain. Some of the climbs may stay slippery for several days, and you could find puddles along the creek at the same time.
Services: Practically within sight of the trailhead are Redbird Mall and Camp Wisdom Boulevard, both of which have numerous eating places and convenience stores.
Hazards: Plenty. The water crossings can be extremely slippery, and you rush up to them with very little warning as you drop out of the trees, rear wheel searching for braking traction. Many places on the trails have limestone outcroppings, which make for lots of marbles and can turn a fast downhill sweeper into a contest of high-speed controlled drift. Creek banks that drop 15 feet to the water are not uncommon, and getting lost or turned around is a real possibility here. Not to worry—you are in the middle of several million people, so you are not going to starve or anything like that. Just keep trying other trails until you hit someplace you recognize. Also, the normal poison ivy and crazy biker warning is in effect at this facility. Be especially wary when the leaves are down or the dark parts of the trail are wet. That piece of trail may look just fine, but it could be hiding old Mister Bustyerass. Also, stay out of the church parking lots and off their property.
Rescue index: If you are hurt, you can wait—someone will very likely come along, since this is a heavily used trail. If you get lost, go to the top of the hill. Then keep going until you hit a road or find the large church on Boulder Drive. A four-lane road is either Red Bird Lane (east/west) or Boulder Drive (north/south), and a big highway is US 67 and its access road (northeast/southwest).
Land status: The land is held by the Dallas Parks and Recreation Department.
Maps: Maps are generally not readily available. The 7.5 minute quads for this trail are Duncanville and Oak Cliff.

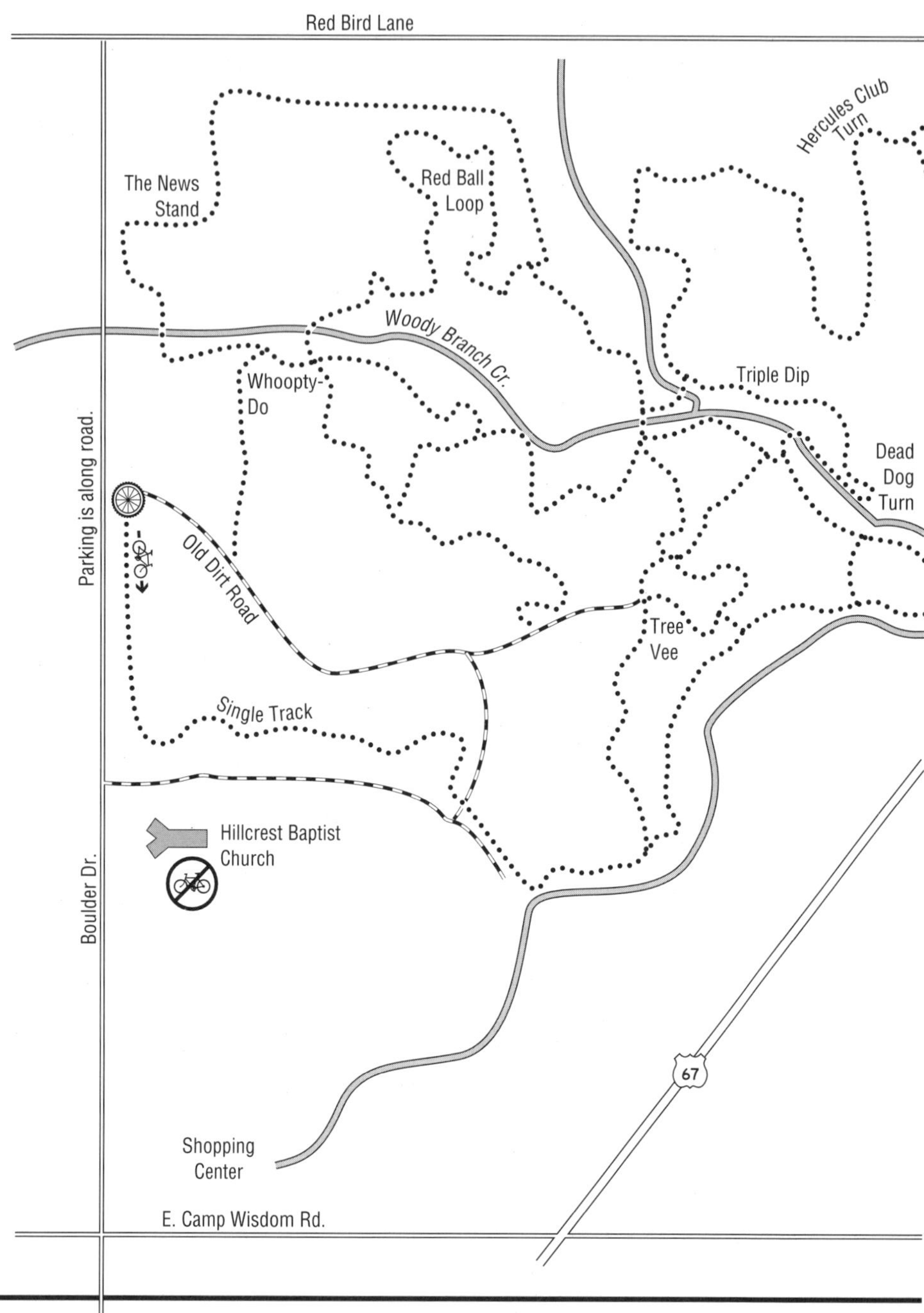
Red Bird Lane
Hercules Club Turn
The News Stand
Red Ball Loop
Woody Branch Cr.
Whoopty-Do
Triple Dip
Dead Dog Turn
Parking is along road.
Old Dirt Road
Tree Vee
Single Track
Hillcrest Baptist Church
Boulder Dr.
67
Shopping Center
E. Camp Wisdom Rd.

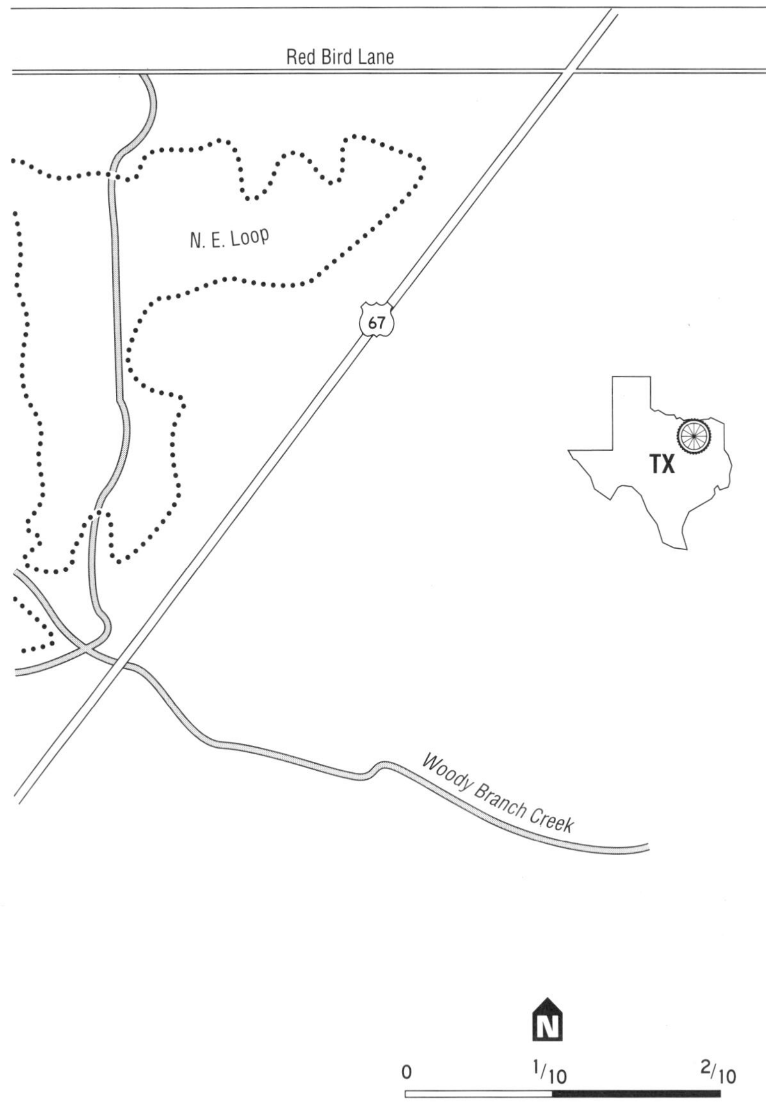

Note: *Map courtesy of DORBA's Steve Mayo.*

DORBA member Joe Warner often leads rides and workdays at Boulder Park. Hey Joe (sorry, I had to use that), thanks for everything you have done for DORBA and our sport.

Finding the trail: Go south from downtown Dallas on I-35E until you reach the split where US 67 bears to the right toward Cleburne. Follow US 67 south to Camp Wisdom Road, then right (west) to the first light, Boulder Drive. Turn right and follow Boulder Drive over the hill past the churches and park along the street. At present Boulder Drive is under construction, but parking is allowed along it. Go right—back toward Camp Wisdom, through the trees—and follow the trail. If you go straight into the trees, you will be going contrary to the accepted direction, which is counterclockwise.

Sources of additional information:

Dallas Off-Road Bicycle Association
18484 Preston Road
#102-106
Dallas, TX 75252
(214) 579-5540

Richardson Bike Mart
84 Dal-Rich Village
Richardson, TX 75080
(214) 231-3993

Notes on the trail: This trail has hosted the Dallas leg of the Texas State Championship Mountain Bike Series and is considered by some to be the best trail in Dallas. It is fairly smooth, very fast, and easily accessible from anywhere in town. There are many restaurants where you can unwind afterward in the mall directly south (across Camp Wisdom on Boulder Drive). A full lap is nearly five miles, and there is never a shortage of folks on the trail during good weather. Considering the amount of traffic this place gets, it is usually in pretty good shape. Workdays are on the third Sunday of each month, 9 A.M.

RIDE 6 *WINDMILL HILL PRESERVE TRAIL*

At present we have a single-track loop of about three miles for you to ride. We are waiting for the city to finish paving Wintergreen Road through the park before we get too exuberant. That way they don't build over the top of what we are working on. This is a nice quiet place for the most part; it backs up to a couple of residential neighborhoods. That usually guarantees joggers and kids on BMX bikes, and Windmill Hill is sure not to disappoint.

At one place the trail crosses over a bridge that spans Stewart Branch creek. This bridge commemorates the life of one Stevie Ray Vaughn, local musician. Perhaps you have heard of him? The exact connection between the famous blues guitarist and this park is nebulous. In his will he donated a part of his estate to the park system, and Windmill Hill got this bridge and the monument near the entrance. Stevie Ray loved his local parks, and local music fans revered him.

These lands were abused by the four-wheel-drive and motorcycle set until the city of DeSoto finally closed them off. A friend of DORBA on the park board wants to eventually plow all the old dirt roads under and start fresh by building top-quality single-track in their place. Does that sound like a plan to you? One weird thing about this place is that it actually lies partially in two different cities: DeSoto and Duncanville.

You can work up a sweat here from exertion, but it's not a real hard trail. The single-track winds around in the trees and manages a few meager technical challenges. Technical exercises take the form of root hopping in the middle of climbs and some loose conditions. Mostly, though, it is very rideable—nothing impossible—and it's short, so bailouts are no problem. The local kids love to BMX here. They do jumps and crazy tricks in an eroded bowl along one section of trail called "The Panhandle."

You never climb high enough here to get any good views over the trees, so scenery is mostly confined to the beautiful large trees that escaped being bulldozed when the city planned roads through here long ago. Windmill Hill is right in the backyard of a friend of mine, and its location right in the

RIDE 6 *WINDMILL HILL PRESERVE TRAIL*

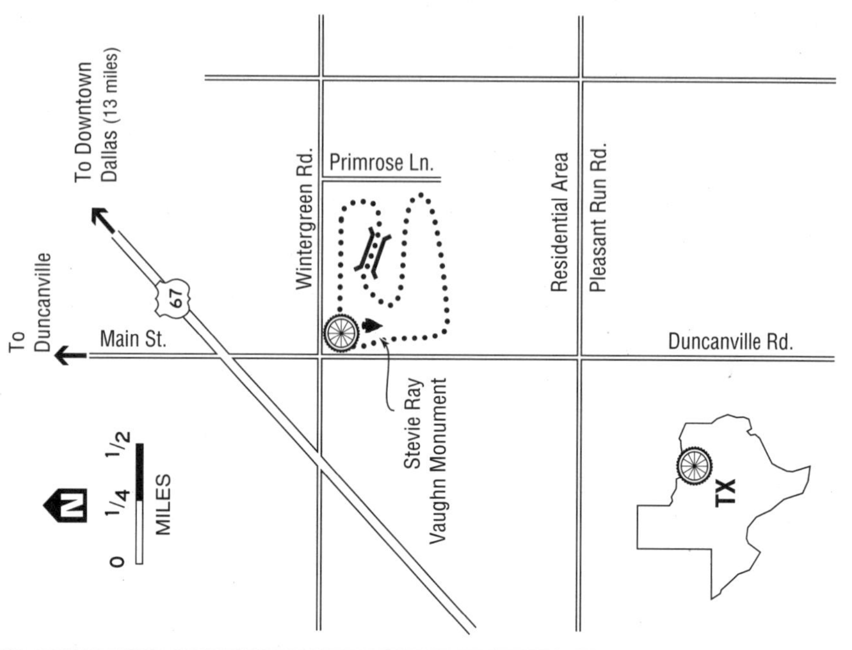

city makes it another of the trails with easy access from most parts of Dallas. Perhaps it's a good place for you to go check out some new equipment without committing yourself to a long ride far from your car.

General location: Duncanville/DeSoto. Southwest of downtown Dallas about 10 miles or so.
Elevation change: The variation is from a low of around 580′ above sea level up to around 650′.
Season: Year-round. Durable when a little bit wet. If you are getting muddy, it is too wet to ride. Have I mentioned that before?
Services: There is nothing at the trailhead. You are in DeSoto, though, so there are many convenience stores and eateries nearby.
Hazards: Marbles, poison ivy, and other traffic. Where small trees have been cut out of the trail, there are a few stubs that might catch a wheel and send you flying, especially when the leaves are down and hiding all that sort of stuff. The trees are firmly attached to the ground here, so try not to move any. Watch for low-hanging limbs; I always hit my head when I stand up to climb. Be careful.

A rider cleaning one of the few tricky sections of the Windmill Hill Preserve.

Rescue index: Good. Any direction you head will take you to a paved road within a short distance, but going east or west from the heart of the park would be most expedient.

Land status: City of DeSoto public park. No motorized vehicles are allowed.

Maps: Not readily available. The quad for this trail is Oak Cliff.

Finding the trail: From downtown Dallas go south on Interstate 35, toward Waco. After a few miles the highway will split, and US 67 will fork to the right toward Cleburne. Follow this road. In a few more miles you will pass I-20. Keep going until you see the exit for Duncanville Road/Main Street. Exit and go left (south) on Duncanville Road, and in about a mile you will see the entrance for the park and the parking area. Hit the trail on the east side of the parking area and wander around. The property is bounded on all sides by residences and paved roads, so you cannot get lost without major stupidity. And it is pretty small, so you can't get real lost anyway.

Sources of additional information:

Dallas Off-Road Bicycle Association
18484 Preston Road
#102-106
Dallas, TX 75252
(214) 579-5540

Mountain Bike Innovations
2053 West Northwest Highway #90
Dallas, TX 75220
(214) 432-0095

City of DeSoto Parks and Recreation Department
(214) 230-9650

Notes on the trail: At present the park has been sealed off from the motorized traffic, and the trail steward plans to heal some of the damage before we turn this into any more miles of trails. I would say that by 1996 this park should rank as a small but fine place to enjoy a few miles of fine North Texas single-track.

When you ride here, take a moment to think about the blues. This is an excellent opportunity to pay your last respects to one of North Texas's greatest musicians (apologies to Fort Worth's Van Cliburn) and one of America's true blues guitar legends. I for one will never forget a certain television "don't litter" campaign that featured a shot of Stevie, head bowed low over that old Strat, face hidden by the wide brim of the black hat he often wore. He ripped off a quick riff and raised his dark eyes to look straight at the camera and said, "Don't mess with Texas." Good advice any day of the week.

RIDE 7 *DORBA TRAIL A.K.A. CEDAR HILL STATE PARK*

The premier North Texas trail is at Joe Pool Lake and is named for my club, the Dallas Off-Road Bicycle Association. The present loop is just over seven miles in length, with a shortcut that offers you an optional shorter route of about three miles. There is enough land in the park that DORBA and Texas Parks and Wildlife Department (TPWD) plan to gradually double the trail miles. Situated near the White-rock Escarpment, this trail offers you the most dramatic elevation change of any terrain in the whole of Dallas County. One minute you can be loafing along by the lake, and the next you may be winding up the side of a hill where you climb to the highest point on the trail.

The DORBA Trail is a winding loop that crisscrosses 1,400 acres of prime mountain biking landscape. There is still a lot of development going on within this park, so by the time you read this there could be even more trail. When it is completed, we should be able to offer you variable loops of up to 12 miles of fairly intense riding. The present long loop is sufficient to hold you near enough to your maximum heart rate that two or three laps is about all most people can stand.

This is definitely one of the tougher of the Dallas area trails—at least, that is the general consensus of local mountain bikers. There are several short and steep climbs, and various abrupt creek crossings that require quick shifting and competent bike handling. In addition, there is plenty of tight single-track to keep you on your toes. Every plant along this trail has thorns, so this is a very good place to visit if you want to get flat tires, and lots of them. I would venture to say flat-proof tubes are the way to go.

Some of the downhills are that combination of fast and rough that your Carpal Tunnel Syndrome lives for. Several sections are fast S-turns that can be loose and covered with marbles during dry weather. These often swing into tight off-camber turns where you will find opportunities to experiment with bike handling skills you did not know you possessed. Under the trees the soil is darker and stays wet longer, while out in the open the ground can be hard as rock and sometimes offers you LARGE wheel-swallowing cracks during summer or extended dry spells.

Cedar Hill State Park and the DORBA Trail are located in the prettiest part of Dallas County, bar none—the White-rock Escarpment. From the hills you will find some great views of Joe Pool Reservoir and the bluffs along the escarpment. During the brief Texas fall, the hills are tinted with beautiful colors as the trees prepare to shed their leaves for the winter. If you could choose a place to build your dream home in Dallas County, it would probably be no more than a few miles from here.

This is a brand new state park, and its potential for providing recreational fun has barely been tapped. DORBA members sometimes have weekend camping trips here and bring their ski boats as well as their mountain bikes. The park has good swimming beaches and general camping facilities, as well as several day use areas that are great picnic sites, all only a short ride from the trail. There is also a set of hiking trails not connected to the DORBA Trail. Great bird-watching opportunities abound around Joe Pool Reservoir, especially along the dam (which is NOT located within the park's boundaries). You can circumnavigate the entire lake by bicycle on 20 to 25 miles of fairly good roads. Plus the road across the dam is closed to automobile traffic and makes for a nice quiet ride of about 8 miles round-trip. The DORBA Trail is another common location for local mountain bike races and will probably someday be used for a 24-hour race if I can get the sponsorship and interest generated. And if the ranger says okay.

General location: Cedar Hill State Park is on the eastern shores of Joe Pool Reservoir, in the southwest corner of Dallas, near the towns of Cedar Hill and Duncanville.

Elevation change: Another one with lots of elevation changes—for Dallas, anyway. The highest point in the park approaches 650´ above sea level (though the trail presently reaches only about 600´), while the normal pool elevation of the lake is 520´. Trust me when I say that you are up and down that mere 80´ over and over.

Season: Year-round, except in very rainy weather. The ranger wisely closes the trails when they are muddy. Visit this area when the trees are in color; you will learn a whole new respect for Texas scenery.

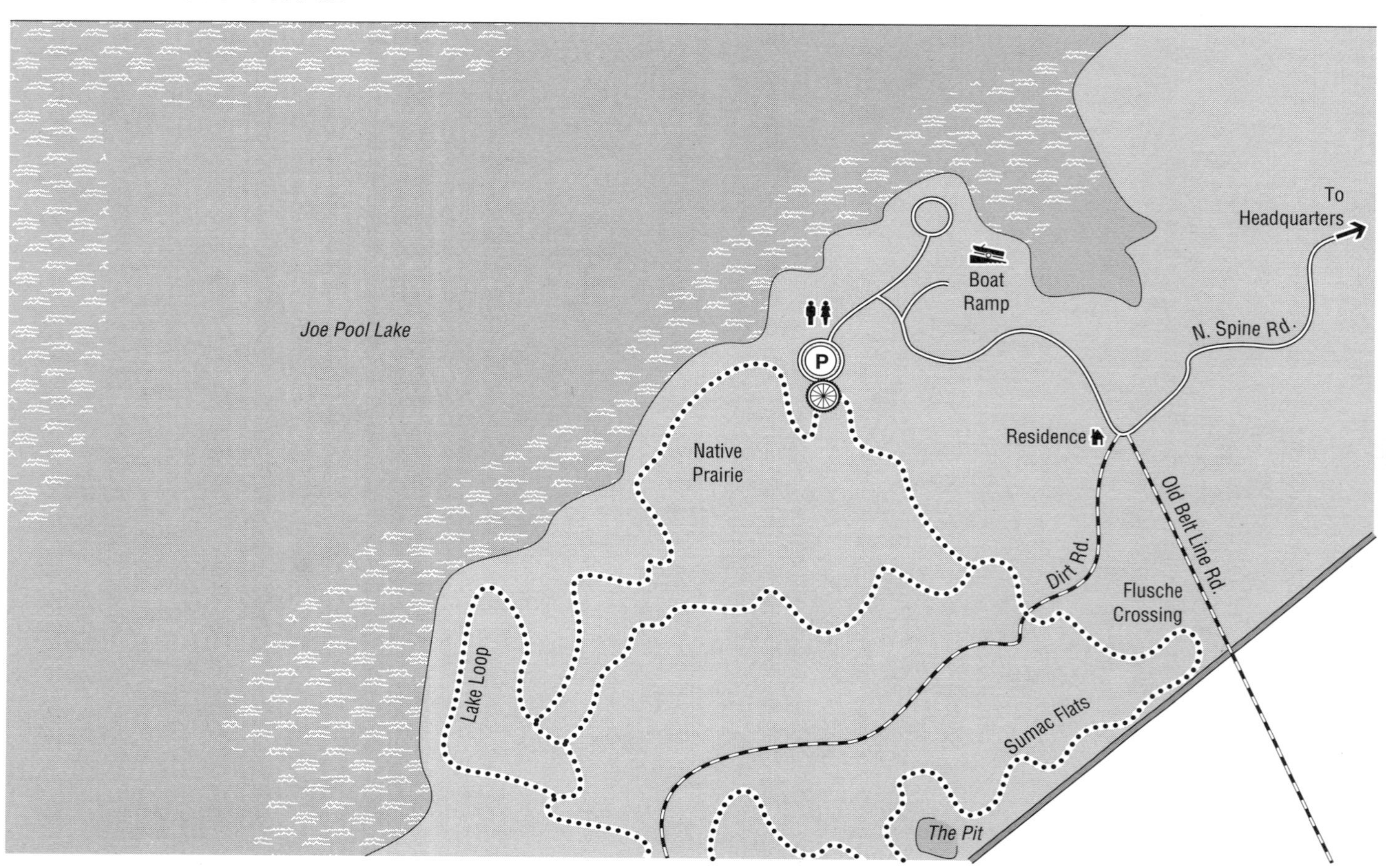
Joe Pool Lake
Boat Ramp
To Headquarters
N. Spine Rd.
Residence
Native Prairie
Old Belt Line Rd.
Dirt Rd.
Flusche Crossing
Lake Loop
Sumac Flats
The Pit

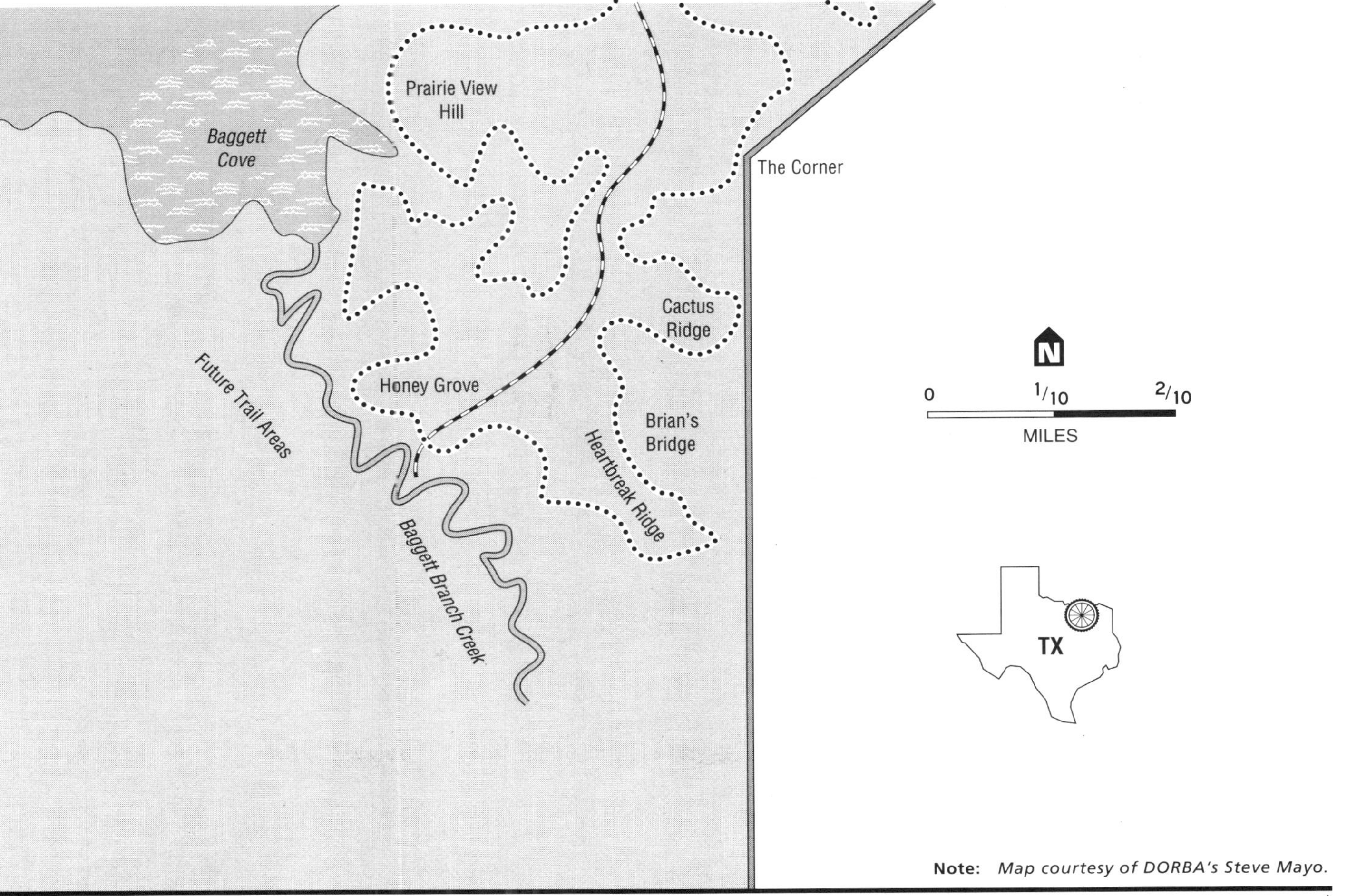

Baggett Cove
Prairie View Hill
The Corner
Cactus Ridge
Honey Grove
Brian's Bridge
Heartbreak Ridge
Future Trail Areas
Baggett Branch Creek
N
0
1/10
2/10
MILES
TX
Note: *Map courtesy of DORBA's Steve Mayo.*

The DORBA Trail at Joe Pool Lake, jewel of Dallas county rides. People with black stretchy shorts outnumber people with rifle racks.

Services: A soft drink machine and pay phone are located at the ranger station, and the marina has a small store that is open year-round. There are rest rooms and a water fountain near the trailhead. Cedar Hill is a short drive south on Farm to Market 1382, and there you will find all manner of eating places and convenience stores.

Hazards: I have left some skin around this trail in various places. The trees lean in, grabbing for your sleeves and handlebars, and I have seen large patches of poison ivy within inches of the trail. The surface can be very fast when dry, and during an extremely dry summer some areas can develop large cracks that threaten to swallow a wheel. These cracks are caused by shrinkage of the surface of the soil, a plight common to many Dallas-area trails.

Prickly pear cactus, honey locust, mesquite, and bois d'arc trees offer a wide selection of tire-piercing thorns that must be seen to be believed. You had better bring your patch kit and pump, along with a spare tube. In many places the trail cuts an S-turn right between two or three large patches of cactus, so watch for these. Also, several small bridges are located at the bottom of quick drops. You must have quick eyes and adjust your line to land on them squarely or risk a nasty spill. One or two of the descents will see you pushing 25 to 30 miles per hour if you go all out, so hold on tight. Mister Bustyerass definitely lives around every turn here.

Rescue index: As this trail gets plenty of traffic, I expect you will be able to snag a passerby if you are in need. Otherwise, it is a long walk through difficult terrain if you try to go cross-country and shortcut the trail; if you stick to the trail you will be much more likely to find help than hiking through the trees. The City of Cedar Hill is planning a road through the park. In the future this could make returning to the trailhead a much easier matter. And it will spoil the nice quiet atmosphere. Let us hope cooler heads prevail.

Land status: The land belongs to the State of Texas, and this facility is managed by the Texas Parks and Wildlife Department. Stop at the headquarters and tell them you love it.

Maps: Check with the ranger station at the gate, or call the Dallas Off-Road Bicycle Association trail steward. The quads for this trail are Cedar Hill and Britton.

Finding the trail: Go north from Interstate 20 on FM 1382, or go south from US 67 on FM 1382 to the main entrance for the state park. Ask the gate attendant for directions to the trailhead, but ask specifically for the DORBA mountain bike trail, because they have another series of short trails for hiking (worthy if you want to see a nice overlook). Traffic typically circulates clockwise, so when you reach the trailhead you will turn left onto the single-track just past the sign kiosk.

Sources of additional information:

Cedar Hill State Park
Box 941
Cedar Hill, TX 75104
(214) 291-3900

Texas Parks and Wildlife Department
4200 Smith School Road
Austin, TX 78744-3291
(800) 792-1112 for information only

TPWD Reservation Center
P.O. Box 17488
Austin, TX 78760-7488
(512) 389-8900 for reservations only

Dallas Off-Road Bicycle Association
18484 Preston Road
#102-106
Dallas, TX 75252
(214) 579-5540

Bicycle Tech
179 South Watson #410
Arlington, TX 76010
(817) 633-4799

Notes on the trail: There is a $3–5 charge for entering the state park to get access to the trail. You may purchase a Conservation Passport for $25 at the main entrance, and it will allow you access, as often as you like, to this and other state parks that charge a usage fee.

Until recently the head ranger was Jerry Hopkins, a good friend of DORBA. Jerry came to our meeting once and asked us if we would be interested in building trails on his land. It did not take long for DORBA to decide we needed to get that in writing, because it was just too good to pass up. We signed a letter of intent with him and began building trails. You should have seen the smile on his face when we held our first race. I think Cedar Hill State Park holds a couple of records for selling Conservation Passports, and that is certainly a direct result of having one of the best mountain bike trails in the area. To our pals at Cedar Hill State Park, and to all the members of DORBA who helped make it happen, thank you. This place is our open letter to the rest of the country showing how hard-core mountain bike nuts can work within the system and score big! To all those land managers in other areas who think mountain bikes don't belong, get real. Workdays are on the fourth Saturday of each month; feel free to come join the fun. The main park gate is closed and locked at 10 P.M., so call ahead for the combination if you plan to arrive late to camp.

RIDE 8 *CAMERON PARK TRAIL*

A lot of my friends call this the best trail in Texas. I'm not sure I would disagree with them, because this place has it all. When clearly flagged for a race, the laps vary from five to seven miles of fast single-track and long technical climbs. Unfortunately, it is seldom clearly flagged unless there has been a race. Since the area is laced with trails, to the point of almost being a maze, you should stick to the ones that have clearly been in recent use. Otherwise you can wander in circles for hours. Since it is so confusing, the best advice I can give is that you are riding around some hills and bluffs between the river and surrounding residential areas, so you can only go slightly astray.

This place reminds me much of Boulder Park, only on a slightly larger scale. It just *looks* like Boulder. You have the same dense woods, but the climbs are longer. There are some very fast descents that turn into slaloms and have you careening from one side of a gully to another over and over while avoiding tree roots and holes in the ground, all at your maximum heart rate and forward velocity. Some good-hard-fun riding.

Hey, it's technical; it's steep, it's long, and it's tight. There are some real tough off-camber turns where you must navigate between or around some trees while in a full skid with the back wheel. Mister Bustyerass is everywhere in Cameron Park. You can get hurt if you let your concentration slip for a second or two. This trail should be ridden with respect; take it for granted and you will get bitten.

Most of this trail is under the canopy, so the typical dark loamy soil is abundant, as are the loose stretches of broken limestone. The trail will always be slippery and a little soft in spots, but as long as it is dry, it begs to be ridden fast. Beat your brains out on the roots and rocky climbs, and wake that Carpal Tunnel Syndrome up on the blistering downhills. Either way, you will walk away from here with a respect for expert-class riders. I have watched them pass in sections where I am doing all I can just to stay upright and in some semblance of control.

The sections along the rivers are gorgeous. The Brazos is the most beautiful of the North Texas rivers. And the trees—man, the trees in this park are stunning during their color change. Driving into Waco from the north, you begin to question the sanity of whoever told you there was an awesome bike trail anywhere near this town. Once you drive into Cameron Park, though, you will be amazed that someplace that looks so flat from a distance can have so much elevation and such beautiful scenery.

This is another popular spot for Texas State Championship Series races, so popular that some years they host two. There is a really neat campground only two or three miles away by jogging trail, a place called Fort Fisher. It is right behind the Texas Rangers Hall of Fame and just off Interstate 35. The park even has a real Lover's Leap, according to the maps. The best trail in Texas? Could be.

General location: Along the southern shores of the Brazos River in western Waco. About 1.5 hours south of Dallas on I-35.

Elevation change: You soar from 370′ above sea level by the river to over 500′ at the highest points on the trail.

Season: Unrideable when freshly muddied. Period. It gets way too sloppy and slick to be usable. The rest of the time, hammer until your brains are fried, year-round. Be sure and tackle this place just after the leaves have fallen (yeah, right).

Services: Waco has two good bike shops. Plus, this is a city of nearly 100,000, so it can supply any other needs you might have. There are convenience

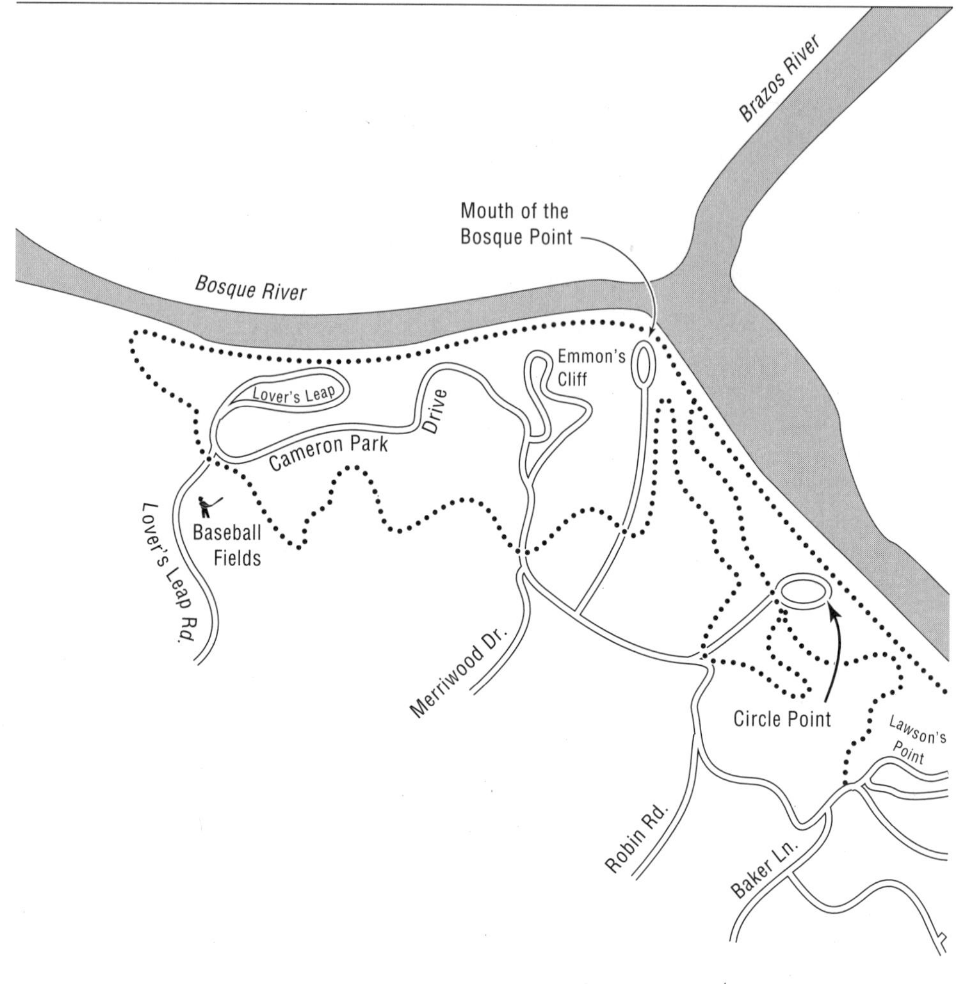

Note: *There are many more twists and turns than this map indicates.*

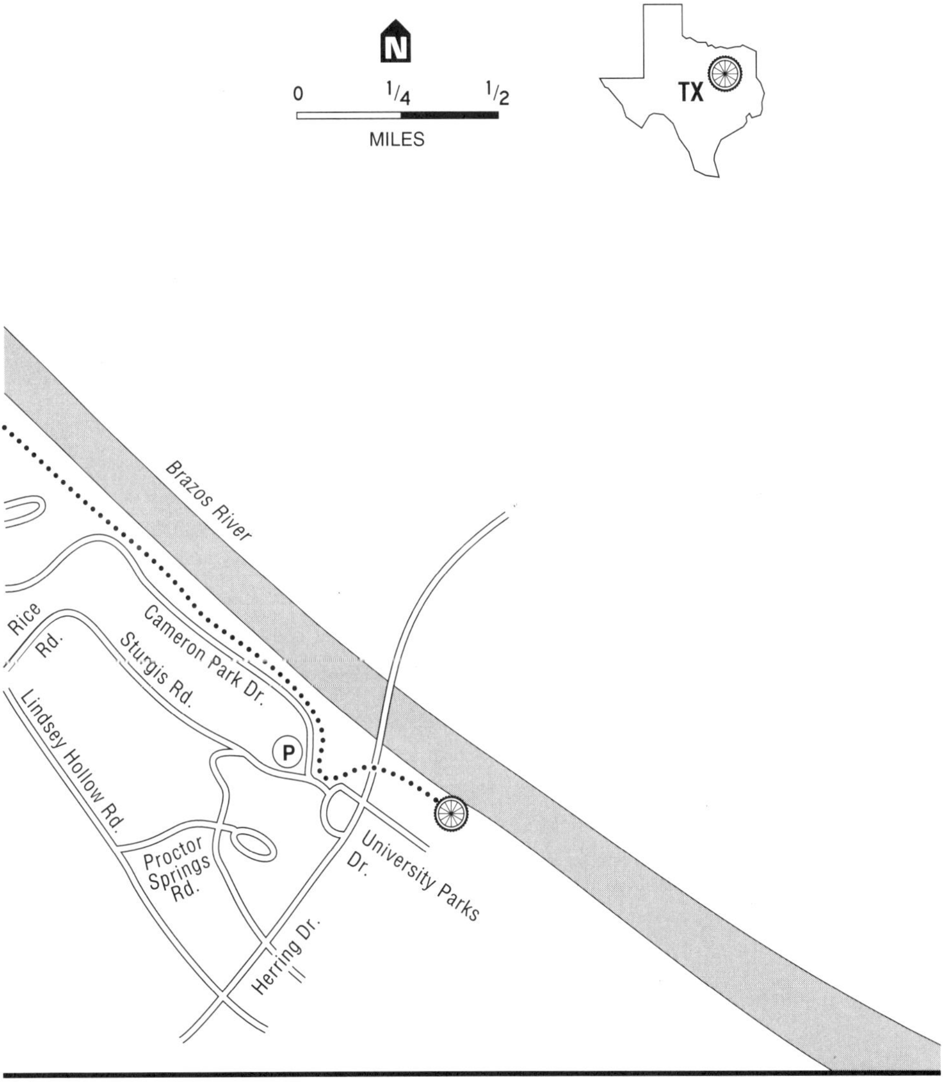

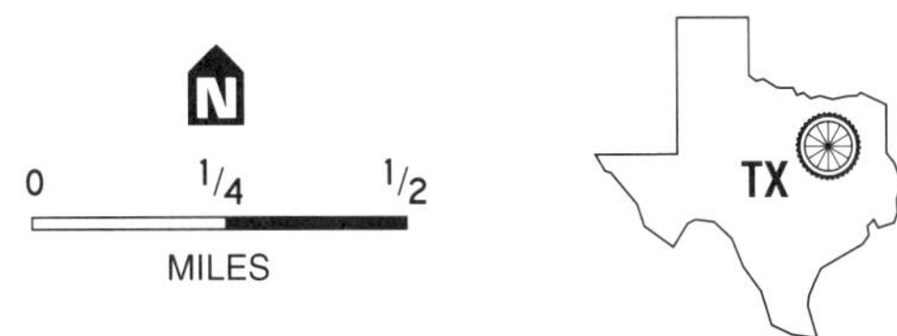
N
0
1/4
1/2
MILES
TX
Brazos River
Cameron Park Dr.
Rice Rd.
Sturgis Rd.
Lindsey Hollow Rd.
P
Proctor Springs Rd.
University Parks Dr.
Herring Dr.

stores on University Parks Drive where it passes under I-35, about 3 miles east of the park.

Hazards: Most hazards around here are tricky places on the trail, like fast off-camber turns or high-speed descents that require you to be watching far enough ahead to avoid obstacles in the trail. Also, Cameron Park has such an abundance of trails that it is quite easy to get turned around and wander in circles. The park is large enough to keep you busy for an hour or two trying to backtrack to a spot you recognize, but there's no real danger of getting lost. You will simply have to circulate, enjoying the technical challenges, until you come to a paved street or finally end up down by the river. If you hit a street, just keep heading in a northerly direction and you will eventually either find the entrance to the park again or hit the river. If you get to the river, turn right on the first trail you see and you will be headed back toward the entrance and parking areas.

Rescue index: The residential areas that surround the trails could probably be counted on for assistance in an emergency. Also, the popularity of this park insures that you will not lack for company if misery strikes. Like I mentioned above, if you need to find your way off the trail, go downhill to the river and head to the right; that will return you to the trailhead. The park's location in the middle of the city means that an ambulance is always just a few minutes away once you locate a phone.

Land status: The land here is a City of Waco public park.

Maps: Good luck. Let me know if you find a better map than the one in this book. The quad for this trail is Waco West.

Finding the trail: Go west on University Parks Drive from I-35 in Waco, approximately 3 miles. You will see signs indicating that you are in Cameron Park. Park anywhere along the road through the park. Follow Cameron Park Drive/University Parks Drive up to the top of the hill, where it ends at Baker Lane, and go across into the woods. If you turn right here onto Baker Lane, it runs down to Lawson's Point, where there is additional parking.

From here I have to tell you to refer to the map. You will be following the single-track through the woods. It branches and forks many times, so getting lost in the trees here is a very easy project. Keep the following boundaries in mind and you will be okay. The Bosque and Brazos Rivers bound you to the north and east, and the residential areas bound you to the south and west. You are riding in a narrow strip of cover along the area where the two rivers converge.

When you have had enough, head north to the river. Hang a right and you will eventually return to where you parked, if it was in sight of the water.

Sources of additional information:

Bicycles Outback
4705 Waco Drive
Waco, TX
(817) 772-BIKE

The city of Waco just appears flat from the highway. A few miles west are all the steep technical climbs you can stand.

Waco Chamber of Commerce
(800) WACO-FUN

Fort Fisher Campground
I-35 and University Parks Drive
(817) 750-5989

Notes on the trail: As I mentioned above, there are nice camping facilities at nearby Fort Fisher, and staying there will give you a good opportunity to visit the Texas Rangers Hall of Fame. When you are ready to ride, head over to the river and jump on the jogging path. Go left (west) all the way to the bridge at Washington Street, then get on University Parks Drive and continue west to the entrance of Cameron/Indian Springs Park. Ride hard and enjoy being free. Repeat as many times as necessary.

RIDE 9 *SISTER GROVE PARK TRAIL*

Shortly before I wrote this trail description, my club was granted access to the other half of the property in this park, and the present five miles should be increased—soon. This trail is way out from the big city and is another that sees too little use. To stand along the trail and listen to the wind rustle the bluestem grass is to regress a hundred years. I have many fond memories of rides DORBA has held here since the trail's birth in 1992. Come on out to Sister Grove Park and ride the single-track; the only thing you will hear is the sound of the wind, or maybe an occasional gunshot. Duck hunters infest the lake during season but are not supposed to get on our land.

The trail is a winding loop that takes you from the parking lot trailhead around through the trees and down near a small pond several times, then forces you to use the best of your technical skills to ascend briefly, and finally returns you to the trailhead, ready for another try at those fast sweepers.

This trail seems to be all uphill. It has some climbing and some extremely tight single-track. The ascents are direct, though laced with debris, and therefore require you to nail the line if you want to excel and be relaxed. The sections under the canopy have some excellent twisty-turnies where you will again need to be on the line to keep out of the trees. This is a fast trail, and it seems much harder than it should be if you're just examining the terrain on a map.

Trail conditions are on the rough side in the exposed sections. Some of the very fast downhills will make you see double because of how bumpy they are. The areas under the canopy are smooth, though you will encounter an occasional deadfall. The fast sweepers are almost surely slick with marbles, and they generally have a nice cedar tree or ten inside the apex.

The trail includes a breathtakingly nice example of a North Texas prairie. The dense hardwoods along the creeks and around the small pond are a haven to wildlife. The prairie sections are covered with Texas bluestem grass, and you will notice more of the familiar "stuff that bites you." The sections we are currently developing are near the pool of the lake and should provide some more variation in the trail, giving you access to the wetlands areas.

This is a popular spot for local astronomy clubs to set up their telescopes during interesting celestial events. This is also another excellent trail for birding, because it is in the middle of nowhere. There is a small pond (you cross its earth dam during part of your ride) that is heavily populated with frogs, and during warm summer evenings they will all get started singing at the same time and you can hear them all over the property. It carries a city boy away to come hang out here for a few hours. Enjoy.

General location: An hour northeast of Dallas, near the northern end of Lake Lavon.

Elevation change: You trade a few feet riding here. The highest point in the park is 560´ above sea level, and the pool elevation of Lake Lavon is normally around 490´.

Season: Often rideable shortly after a rain, it may be wet, but the ground is not real soft, so it will normally carry you without too much splatter. Some of the areas under the trees will be sticky for days, but DORBA has gotten the

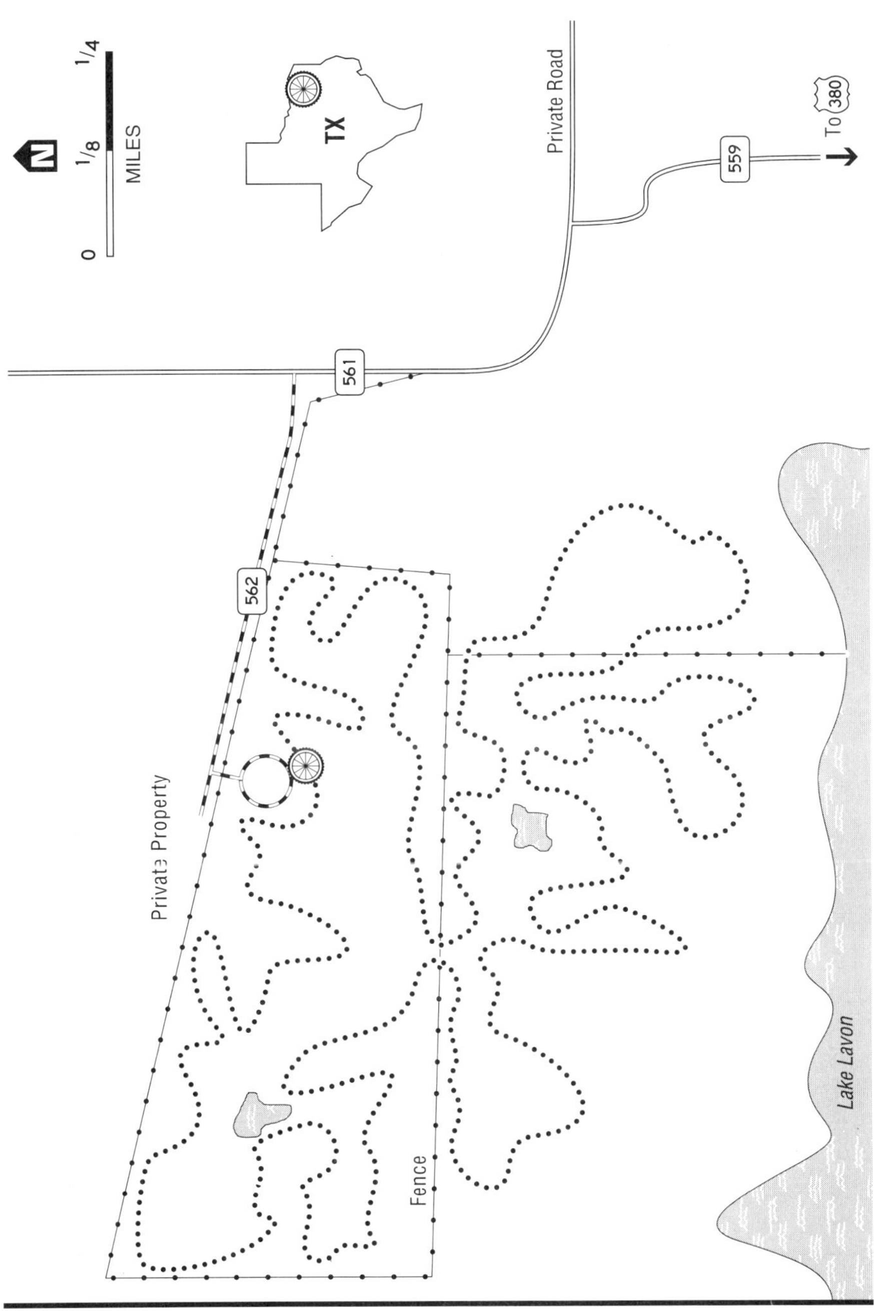
0
1/8
1/4
MILES
TX
Private Road
559
To 380
561
562
Private Property
Fence
Lake Lavon

worst ones navigable. As I mentioned above, duck hunting is allowed from the lake during the winter.

Services: Nonexistent. Princeton is the last town you go through coming from the west, and it has various burger joints, but the nearest bike shop I know of is in Plano.

Hazards: Most riders I know circulate clockwise, but traffic may be seen going in either direction. This trail is pretty far from any big towns, and the locals use it as access to Lake Lavon for hunting and fishing purposes, so it is not unusual to see kids on four-wheelers riding around in the park. This is illegal, but it happens nevertheless, and they have cut a few interesting trails of their own. Many of the fast turns are very loose, and the trail is generally very rough and bumpy when dry. This is another trail where giant cracks in the ground may appear in the summer. During the duck hunting season this area is open to hunters, but land-based blinds are prohibited. Nevertheless, on an early winter morning you will probably hear gunshots in the distance. Just wear bright clothing, hehehe.

Rescue index: You are in the outback here, and on most days you probably won't see many other bikers. If necessary, a hike across the prairie will allow you to shortcut some sections of the trail and proceed directly to the parking lot, which is located on one of the highest spots in the park. Keep going uphill until you get to the top, then look east to try and spot the Porta-potty at the park entrance. There are also trees in the center of the circular drive through the parking lot, and if they survive and grow any taller they should be easy to see from any clear spot in the park. There is a house at the end of County Road 562, but I have never met those folks. There are also houses along the other roads leading into the park. In an emergency, I will beat on a door until someone calls the police or an ambulance for me.

Land status: Sister Grove Park belongs to the Collin County Open Spaces Commission (CCOSC) and citizens of Collin County.

Maps: Contact CCOSC, DORBA, or Mountain Bike Innovations. The quad for this trail is Culleoka.

Finding the trail: From the town of McKinney, 30 miles north of Dallas on US 75 (Central Expressway), go east on US 380 toward Princeton and Lake Lavon. Just past Princeton you will go down a hill and find yourself on a long bridge across the middle of Lake Lavon. In the middle of this bridge is where CR 559 meets US 380 from the north. Turn left and go north on CR 559 to CR 561, then turn left. Follow CR 561 to the next road, CR 562, and turn left. Go about one-quarter mile and turn left at the sign for Sister Grove Park. This is the entrance to the park and leads to the circular parking lot. If you miss the turn, you will find yourself in Bubba's front yard, and his dogs will let you know you are not at the trailhead. Make a hasty retreat, because some of the residents of this house are the people who lost four-wheeler privileges when the park came under management by CCOSC. I don't think the kids around here are very fond of us now.

DORBA members Jeanne Patterson (second from left) and Cathi Layfield (center) accept awards for a job well done. They were instrumental in helping convert a forgotten piece of Collin County called Sister Grove Park into another great place to ride mountain bikes. Thanks ladies, we owe you big.

Sources of additional information:

Dallas Off-Road Bicycle Association
18484 Preston Road
#102-106
Dallas, TX 75252
(214) 556-0640

Mountain Bike Innovations
2053 West Northwest Highway #90
Dallas, TX 75220
(214) 432-0095

Collin County Open Spaces Commission
M(214) 424-1460 ext. 4618

The Heard Museum
One Nature Place
McKinney, TX 75069-9244
M (214)562-5566

Riders crossing a prairie of bluestem grass at Sister Grove Park.

Notes on the trail: The DORBA members who built this trail insist that it is occasionally used by "local dogsledders" as a practice course. Can you imagine there being dogsledders in Texas? Oh well, I have never seen them, but I have seen plenty of trails that were not built by us. This park is essentially in the middle of nowhere, so pack in what you will need.

The CCOSC occasionally has "prescribed burns" here, which basically consist of a controlled grass fire. Check with them or the Heard Museum in McKinney, because these burns are truly interesting to participate in. Also, the Heard Museum is an interesting place to visit if you find yourself in McKinney with time on your hands. The museum exhibits some personal belongings from one Bessie Heard, a longtime resident of McKinney and Collin County. This old gal went all over the world collecting things. She loved riding horses and going on safari in Africa. Some of the stuff she amassed is pretty neat, and admission is free. Check it out. The Heard

Museum is also the local raptor rehabilitation center. Whenever someone runs over an eagle or red-tailed hawk or vulture, if they have the presence of mind to notice, they can call the Heard Museum, and the raptor center there will take the injured bird and nurse it back to health as best they can. They usually have a pretty interesting collection of wounded fliers that are kept in captivity until they either are ready to go back to the wild or die of old age. A worthy use of leisure time, tending these birds. A last note on Sister Grove is that workdays are scheduled for the fourth Sunday each month.

RIDE 10 *BONHAM STATE PARK TRAIL*

Let's go ride an easy seven-mile loop in an out-of-the-way state park, someplace way off the beaten path. Bonham State Park is, strangely enough, right outside of the town of Bonham, Texas, and was wrought from land donated by this small North Texas town in 1934. It was built by the Civilian Conservation Corps and is typical of state parks the CCC built. It features a small lake, a bathhouse and swimming beach, cabins, and a mess hall that would provide good camping for a fairly large group.

The trail consists of a series of short trail segments that may be ridden consecutively to make one loop that runs about halfway around the lake. The trail surface is mostly hard-packed dirt with some stretches of gravelly limestone. In just a few spots, it is necessary to ride the paved park road for a short way to get from one segment to another. All pieces of the loop are well marked and in fact have some of the best trail signs of any state park I've seen.

The park is less densely forested than many but offers some prairie grasslands that burst with wildflowers in the spring. Many of these areas are visible from the mountain bike trail, and this trail makes a relaxing ride in all but the hottest weather. It is all fairly flat single-track and has only a few semi-technical stretches and mild hills. The trail is gentle enough to be ridden by cyclists of all skill levels.

General location: Bonham State Park is located a few miles southeast of the town of Bonham. This is northeast of Dallas about 1.5 hours by car.
Elevation change: The lowest point along the trail is around 610′ of elevation, and the highest probably reaches up to nearly 660′, but the changes are so gradual you will hardly notice.
Season: The trails here should be easily navigable in all but wet weather. Spring will probably bring the most enjoyment, because of the wildflowers that bloom then along stretches of the trails.
Services: The headquarters area offers just about anything you will need. There are showers and rest rooms, a pay phone, and a concession store nearby at the

swimming beach. The store is seasonally operated, so if you are in doubt you should call or acquire any supplies you need before heading over to the park. Bonham is very nearby.

Hazards: There are many low tree branches to watch for, and some sections of the trail have a loose surface of broken limestone that could cause problems if your speed is not controlled. Several plants native to this area possess thorns, and the cedar trees along the trail are sure to snag an arm or jersey if you get too close to them. Since you have to ride along the park road for a short stretch and cross a couple of active roads, you should take care to be observant of automobile traffic when you reach these places.

Rescue index: You should be able to get helped out of here if you need a rescue, but you will have to get back to the pavement, since there is normally not a lot of traffic on the trails. Looking at the map, you will see that you never wander real far from the pavement.

Land status: Here we have another fine Texas state park. It should always be so.

Maps: The fine folks at the headquarters have very nice maps for your perusal, free of charge. The quad for this trail is Bonham.

Finding the trail: To get to the state park, go south on TX 78 from Bonham about 2 miles to Farm to Market 271 and then 2 more miles to the turn for Park Road 24. This will carry you right by the fee station and trailhead and then on to the headquarters building.

Park at the headquarters area and unload your bike. Backtrack along the paved park road toward the entrance hut, a distance of about a mile. The first section of the loop, the M-1 segment, begins right across the road from the park entrance hut. Follow this trail as it winds among the trees and then reaches the pavement again. There you must turn right and follow the road for about one-quarter mile, until you see a sign indicating the M-2 cutoff, heading to the right. Follow M-2 as it winds around and around, crossing the bridge over the creek. Shortly afterward you will cross a private gravel road. Be careful here and watch for automobile traffic. Shortly after passing the cabins at the group camp area, you will begin the M-3 section. Follow this all the way around until it passes very near the lake's dam and, shortly thereafter, carries you back to the headquarters area. As you navigate the "M" sections, you will pass several "A" sections. These are typically shortcuts that will allow you to skip sections of the loop. Consult the map for exact definitions of each.

Sources of additional information:

Park Superintendent
Bonham State Park
Route 1, Box 337
Bonham, TX 75418
(903) 583-5022

RIDE 10 *BONHAM STATE PARK TRAIL*

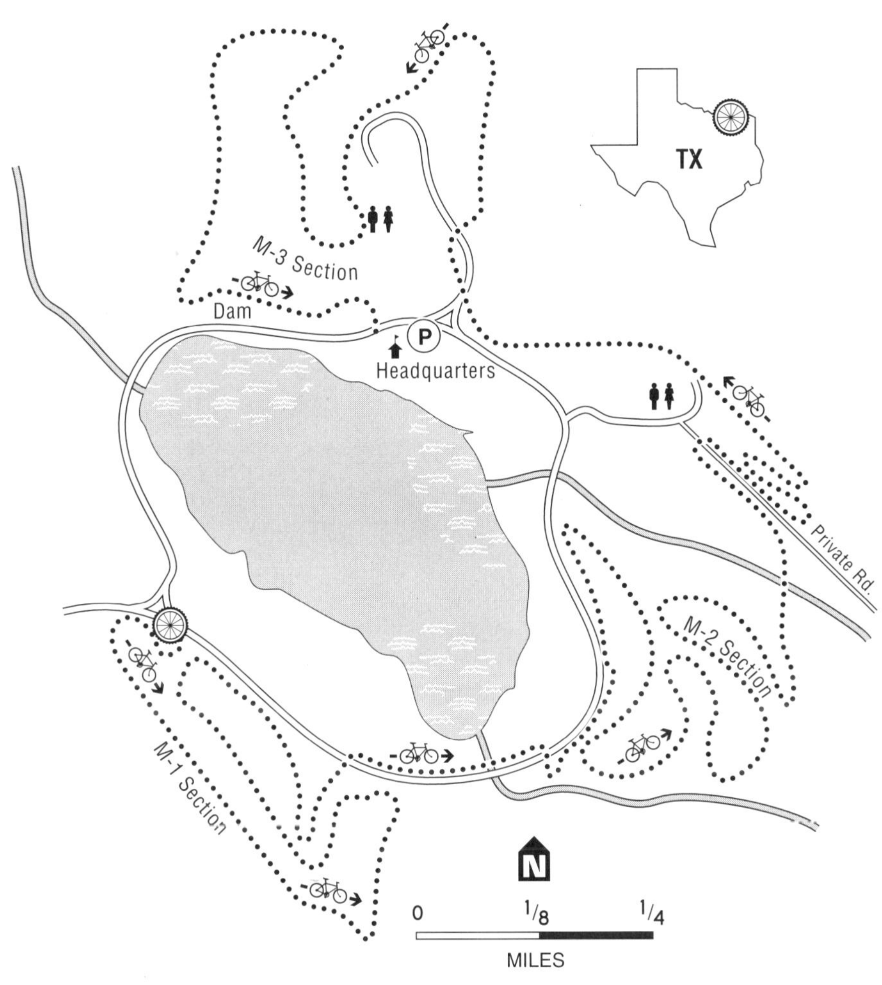

Texas Parks and Wildlife Department
4200 Smith School Road
Austin, TX 78744-3291
(800) 792-1112 for information only

TPWD Reservation Center
P.O. Box 17488
Austin, TX 78760-7488
(512) 389-8900 for reservations only

The summer sun can be blinding on the exposed sections of the Bonham State Park mountain bike trail. That is your author with the squint.

Notes on the trail: I have received some less-than-enthusiastic vibes from one of the employees at this park, both when I have called on the phone and again when I have visited. I think this person has very little regard for our hobby, but I have not been able to determine exactly why. Be on your best behavior so that her disdain remains unfounded. This attitude is highly unusual in state parks. Don't fret; you will be unhassled while you ride here.

East Texas

Now we move away from the Metroplex, into the piney woods and hills of East Texas. This is oil and timber country, with a few cattle thrown in for good measure. If you like hills, you are going to be happy part of the time. One interesting thing to note is that Tyler is the rose capital of the state; the many nurseries there produce some of Texas's prettiest cultivated flowers.

There are untold miles of dirt roads in this part of Texas, and any one can offer scenic views and relaxing rides. The state will sell you excellent maps of county roads, and from these you may be able to plan yourself some nice nonsingle-track trips if you like. See the "Clubs and Other Pertinent Groups" section near the back of this book for the addresses of good map sources.

RIDE 11 *TYLER STATE PARK TRAIL*

The first time I ever went to this park, I drove in late one night during a rainstorm. I had scheduled a camping trip and ride for my club and I was supposed to be ride leader, though I had never been here before. All week people were calling me and asking about the ride, but I had to keep telling them, "I have never been there. No, I don't know exactly where the trailhead is, but I am going with some friends who have been there several times. They say it's great, and you can ride there when it is wet." It was February at the time, a wet and evil time of the year in Texas. (I was born in February, by the way.)

This is a good trail; it has hard spots and plenty of technical challenges. At the time of this writing it is a closed loop of just over eight miles. This varies as new sections are added and old ones are closed off. Traffic generally circulates in a clockwise direction, mostly because that is the direction we always go when races are held here. It is tough riding, especially in the heat and humidity. Some of my pals have puked from riding it too hard during races. (You know who you are.)

The mountain bike trails at Tyler State Park are considered by many to be the finest single-track in the state. There are plenty of steep ascents and descents. There are tree roots and lots of debris in the form of deadfalls and loose rocks. Mostly, though, the trail is hard-packed dirt and sand that at times becomes small gravel. The surface here is nothing short of great, holding together and staying very rideable even during a rain. Some people say it gets better when wet. Yippeee!

RIDE 11 *TYLER STATE PARK TRAIL*

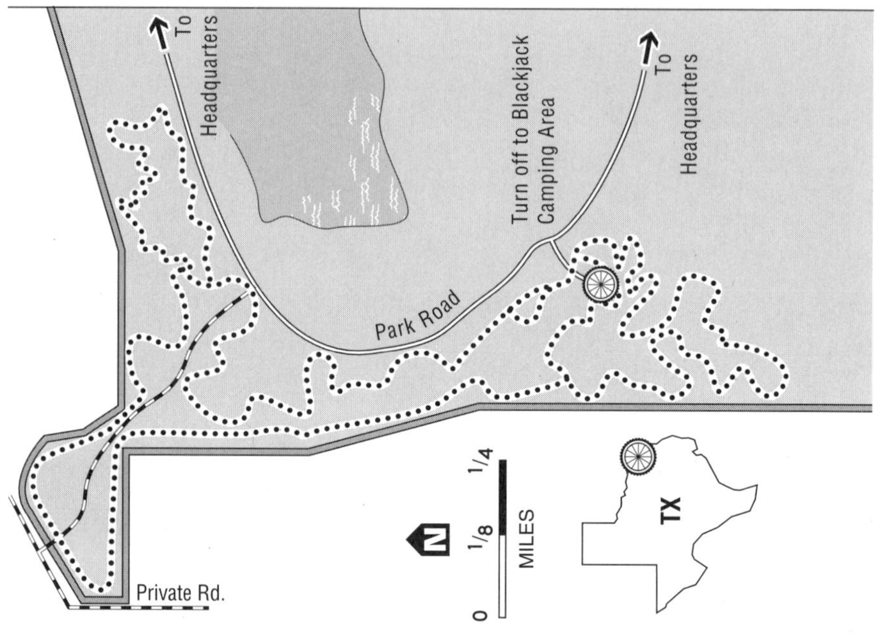

The trail is a main loop ("A") with a bailout ("B") that will provide shorter laps if you wish to stay near the trailhead. Both run through and up and down several small valleys in the piney woods area of East Texas, near a small lake. I have been told that the ranger has talked about letting the Tyler Bicycle Club build single-track all the way around the lake. That could mean one huge loop that would eventually rival anything in other states—take my word for it. The terrain around here is ideally suited to mountain bike trails. A construction project of this scale could return huge dividends to area cyclists who contribute—dividends in the form of glorious off-road cycling events. An impossible dream? I've met the guy who masterminded this place, and I think he is the man to make it happen.

With the dense population of pine trees, you will have only occasional glimpses of what is beyond the next hill. The camping areas around the lake offer some nice views, but that's not really why we are here, is it? If you take the opportunity to examine the landscape off to either side of the single-track, you will discover some of the prettiest lands in this part of the state. The forest is rich with wildlife, like armadillos, raccoons, and birds galore.

General location: Tyler State Park is a few miles north of Tyler, roughly 1.5 hours east of Dallas.

Elevation change: Looking over the topographical maps of the area, you will see that the lowest spot in the park is near 380′ of elevation and the highest reaches up to nearly 580′. While you're on this trail, you will trade 100′ or better on a regular basis.

Season: This place is really amazing; it can be ridden in the worst weather. If you ride during the summer, you should expect it to be a sauna, with temperatures reaching 100 degrees and humidity sufficient to make you think you are swimming.

Services: This is an excellent place from a support and resupply standpoint. The park has a concession building, but this is not a year-round service. There is a store right at the entrance that you can count on to be open any time of year and on Sunday. Pay phones are located at the park concession stand, the headquarters at the entrance, and the store across the road from the entrance. Tyler is only maybe a 10-minute drive, and anything you want is there, including bike shops. I would strongly recommend that you have dinner at least once at the Bodacious Bar-B-Q, located at the intersection of Farm to Market 14 and Interstate 20. Being quite the connoisseur of barbecue, I can only speak highly of their food.

Hazards: The usual cautions about screaming down those hills at full tilt are heavily emphasized, because there are roots and rocks and loose soil everywhere. When the leaves are down, be doubly careful. There are several small bridges over creeks, and many of them arrive with surprising suddenness. Some are signed as you approach from the blind side, but who reads those silly warning signs? If you see caution signs here, pay attention. The Tyler Bicycle Club does not put one up unless they mean it. You cross only one active road from the trail. This is paved, and it's the entrance to the Blackjack area. The trail briefly touches a dirt roadbed, but it is inactive.

Rescue index: Very good. Traffic levels are high enough that people are usually around, especially in nice weather. Lots of people camp here, so the road that rings the lake can be counted on to provide either assistance in an emergency or at least a smooth ride back to the parking area. There will be a few hills between your parking spot and anywhere you hit the road, however. In a couple of places the trail passes very near a paved county road that also has considerable traffic and could be expected to bring help or a nontrail way home. My last caution would be that here riders may circulate either direction and you should thus be watchful for approaching riders.

Land status: Another fine Texas state park. Thank you Texas Parks and Wildlife Department and old Pat Neff.

Maps: You can lay your hands on good maps at the headquarters near the entrance. They do not show elevation, but all the trail sections that have names are listed, and some are pretty funny. The quad for this trail is Tyler North.

Finding the trail: Tyler State Park is about 2 miles north of I-20 on FM 14. The normal trailhead is near the pavilion for the Blackjack camping area. From the parking area, go back the way you came in; you will see barricades

DORBA member Tina McCord also shares her loyalties with another bike club, the Wounded Ducks (the headdress is fluorescent duck feathers). Tyler State Park offers riders of all skill levels a chance to strut their stuff.

on either side before you get all the way back to the park road. These indicate where the trail crosses the drive and goes either direction. The next time you cross a paved road, you are back here. You might want to make sure you have your shorts on securely before hitting the trail.

Sources of additional information:

Tyler State Park
789 Park Road #16
Tyler, TX 75706-9141
(903) 597-5338

Texas Parks and Wildlife Department
4200 Smith School Road
Austin, TX 78744-3291
(800) 792-1112 for information only

TPWD Reservation Center
P.O. Box 17488
Austin, TX 78760-7488
(512) 389-8900 for reservations only

Tyler Bicycle Club
(903) 534-8890

Richardson Bike Mart
84 Dal-Rich Village
Richardson, TX 75080
(214) 231-3993

Bike-n-Sail
14204 Highway #110 South
Whitehouse, TX 75791-9801
(903) 561-4810

Notes on the trail: Tyler State Park opened in 1932, but you will never know it from the facilities. It is well maintained and clean, a testament to the hard-working staff of the Texas Parks and Wildlife Department. Tyler is also the first state park to have an official "Bikes Only" trail. Pedestrian traffic is not allowed, but I have seen runners here, and I am not about to yell at them. I will be even more supportive of them if they gain a reputation for helping maintain this trail.

RIDE 12 *EAST TEXAS RAILS–TO–TRAILS*

I joined the East Texas Rails-to-Trails Conservancy a couple of years ago and then forgot about it. Once when I was in Tyler for the weekend, I went to the bike shop and asked about it. The guy told me it was boring and flat. I thought, "Too bad, that project had a lot of potential." Well, I decided to ride it anyway, just to see. I mean, 20 miles of mountain biking trail is hard for a guy writing a book on the same to ignore. When the day was done, I had sort of a different analysis than the bike shop guys. I think a lot of that has to do with being from out of town. Plus, my eyes have a thing for the virgin trail.

The trail is a converted railroad bed that runs roughly 20 miles from just south of Tyler to a high spot called Love's Lookout, a place with a view. Most of the surface is small gravel—what an engineer calls aggregate. In some places it is even slightly grown up with grass. The rest is murderous deep gravel and crushed rock. This is a hard ride in spite of the gentle grade you find on old railroads. Keeping enough steam to get the bike through the real bad pockets is going to make your rear end sore the next day.

Since you are following a railbed, this trail is either an out-and-back or a point-to-point, depending on the availability of sag support. The time I rode it, I took the pavement back to Tyler. It had taken me much longer to get to the southern end than I had expected. (I stop a lot to shoot pictures and look

RIDE 12 *EAST TEXAS RAILS-TO-TRAILS*

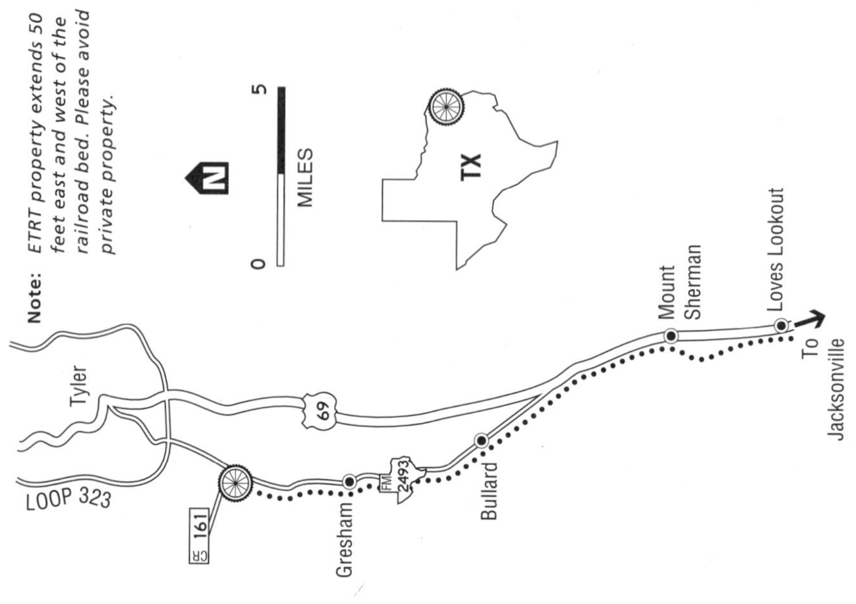

at hawks.) Unless you are a real glutton for punishment, I imagine you will also ride back on the roads if you lack a sag. Most of the time the wind is from the south, so I hope you will be able to enjoy having a nice Texas tailwind to kick you back to Tyler on the hardtop.

You can see the roads almost the whole way, and there are plenty of places to fill a bottle or grab a soft drink when you go through the small towns along the way. Once you reach Love's Lookout, you will be greeted with the longest view anywhere in this part of the state. It is surprising to find a spot with such a nice panorama after being closed in by the trees along the trail most of the time. In spite of these same trees, it will be plain that you are riding through people's front and back yards. There are houses and all sorts of buildings just off the trail, though this thins down to a few farms as you get farther away from Tyler.

Just south of Bullard is a historical marker that tells you the story of the Burning Bush religious colony that used to be near here. Look for it on the left just out of town, or watch through the trees for the signs along the road. Keeping an eye peeled to the highway will keep you in tune with where you are and also help you find the end of the trail, which is within sight of Jacksonville. I rode right on past it and up to some guy's fence because it wasn't marked.

With the gravel and all, this is a tough ride, but if training is your game you should give it a try sometime. It will hold you in the worst rain, maybe better than in the dry, and the ease of making a bailout and hitting fairly easy pavement home is enough to make up for the steady grind.

General location: The trail starts just on the southern end of Tyler. This is East Texas, home of East Texans.

Elevation change: This is interesting, because the mild grade of the trail is very deceptive. You start at an elevation of 460′, and until you hit Bullard you only gain and lose about 80′. Then you drop a little and the real grind begins. From Bullard to Mount Selman you go from right at 480′ to just over 700′ in maybe 5 miles. I thought it was my legs until I got a look at the topos. From Mount Selman to Love's Lookout you drop about 100′ gradually enough to think you have hit your second wind, then you gain it all back in maybe a mile. The grade seems longer and much worse than it really is at this point, because of lactic acid. Love's Lookout, near the southern trailhead, is over 710′.

Season: Boy, I wish I lived in Tyler, because on those rare days when it snows, this place would be a superb treat for hearty cyclists and equestrians. Ride here anytime, for sure. In the heat it would be great, because you can hit the Dairy Queen or Chevron stations along the way and get a cold drink.

Services: Every few miles you will find ample shopping, even on Sunday. From Mount Selman on there is nothing until you hit Love's Lookout (*if* the concession stand is open) or ride on south into Jacksonville. You will find stores there.

Hazards: When I rode it, all the washouts except one were bridged—with some very nice bridges, I might add. I did, however, run up to one spot where Mister Bustyerass was waiting. Even with the sun in my eyes, I saw him at the last moment and managed to bring my steed to a halt mere feet away from a deep washout in the trail. I could see where the missing railroad ties had probably held this old creek crossing together until they were pulled. Keep your eyes open, as always, for one of the snakes that love to lie across the trail during the spring. And watch out at the barricades, where roads cross. You should inspect every one of the dozen-plus roads, paved or not, for automobile traffic before crossing. These roads are all actively driven by Bubba and his pals in old pickup trucks with bad brakes. The trail also crosses many driveways that are not barricaded, so be careful of each place where a double-track crosses your path, and look before you leap.

Rescue index: The best chance of rescue for any trail I have ridden to date. The whole thing is never more than a mile from busy roads and is usually much closer. You could throw a rock (and there are plenty of them lying about) and hit a house or person or car most of the way, so a potential bailout or injury evacuation would be easily accomplished from almost anywhere along the trail. (You better be ready to run when you hit that person

Pilots have a term for it: Clear air/visibility unlimited. The East Texas Rails-to-Trails converted railroad bed offers many views just like this.

with the rocks, because they will probably return fire. Gearing is critical in these situations.)

Land status: East Texas Rails-to-Trails owns the title to about 75% of the land along the rail corridor; the other 25% is leased. ETRT will keep this open as a multi-use trail until the government decides it is in the best interest of the nation to take it back over and make it into a railroad again. In other words, this will probably never happen, and most likely there will always be a trail.

Maps: The ETRT or local bike shops can provide you with maps that are reliably marked with points of interest and parking or access to the trail. The quads for this trail are Tyler South, Bullard, and Mount Selman.

Finding the trail: From the intersection of Loop 323 South (on the south side of Tyler) and Farm to Market 2493, go south about 3 miles to County Road 164, then turn right (west) and go about one-quarter mile to where the trail crosses CR 164. It is plainly marked with barricades. Park and ride south until you have had enough or find a fence across the trail.

Sources of additional information:

East Texas Rails-to-Trails, Inc.
P.O. Box 7293
Tyler, TX 75711
(903) 595-5714

Tyler Bicycle Club
(903) 534-8890

Bike-n-Sail
14204 Highway #110 South
Whitehouse, TX 75791-9801
(903) 561-4810

Notes on the trail: The ETRT is a group of hard-working folks that got the authority and money to convert the unused railroad corridor into a multi-use trail. ETRT plans to pave portions of the trail but promises me there will always be a primitive-surface trail for us dirt-heads. Just remember that you might meet any nonmotorized form of transportation. Respect the rights of equestrian users and give them plenty of warning about your approach. Smile at the hikers and joggers, if you see any. I am sure other users enjoy this trail, but the time I rode it I only saw horse and bike tracks, and not another soul was there. I saw some great birds, though. And kids and dogs. Jointly and separately.

RIDE 13 *MARTIN CREEK LAKE STATE PARK TRAIL*

This is an easy six-mile set of single-tracks that zigzags around in a heavily wooded area along the shore of Martin Creek Lake. It is a noisy place because of the power plant on the south side of the lake, but the natural setting is quite peaceful. The lake was built for the power plant by Texas Utilities. Later, in 1976, they deeded the land to the state parks system.

The trail follows the lakeshore for a couple of miles, then parts of it diverge and enter another wooded area farther from the water. There are no real difficult technical obstacles, but I know people who could get hurt getting out of bed, so be careful, please. Parts are real flat, but the sections along the lake have a little bit of relief—nothing major. The trail is pretty sandy and is usually available for fun a day or so after some precipitation.

It is kind of hard to follow the exact route marked on the map, even though there are a few arrows in the form of wooden signs. There are so many other pieces of single-track crossing the trail that it gets sort of confusing. You may be content to stay along the lake and not try to find the piece that swings around and back up toward the entrance. Or maybe you are part Indian and want to explore. Have at it; there is another section of trail well worth investigating, just waiting for your eyes.

For you fishermen, the warm waters provide an excellent atmosphere and habitat for building monster bass, and the trail passes near enough to some

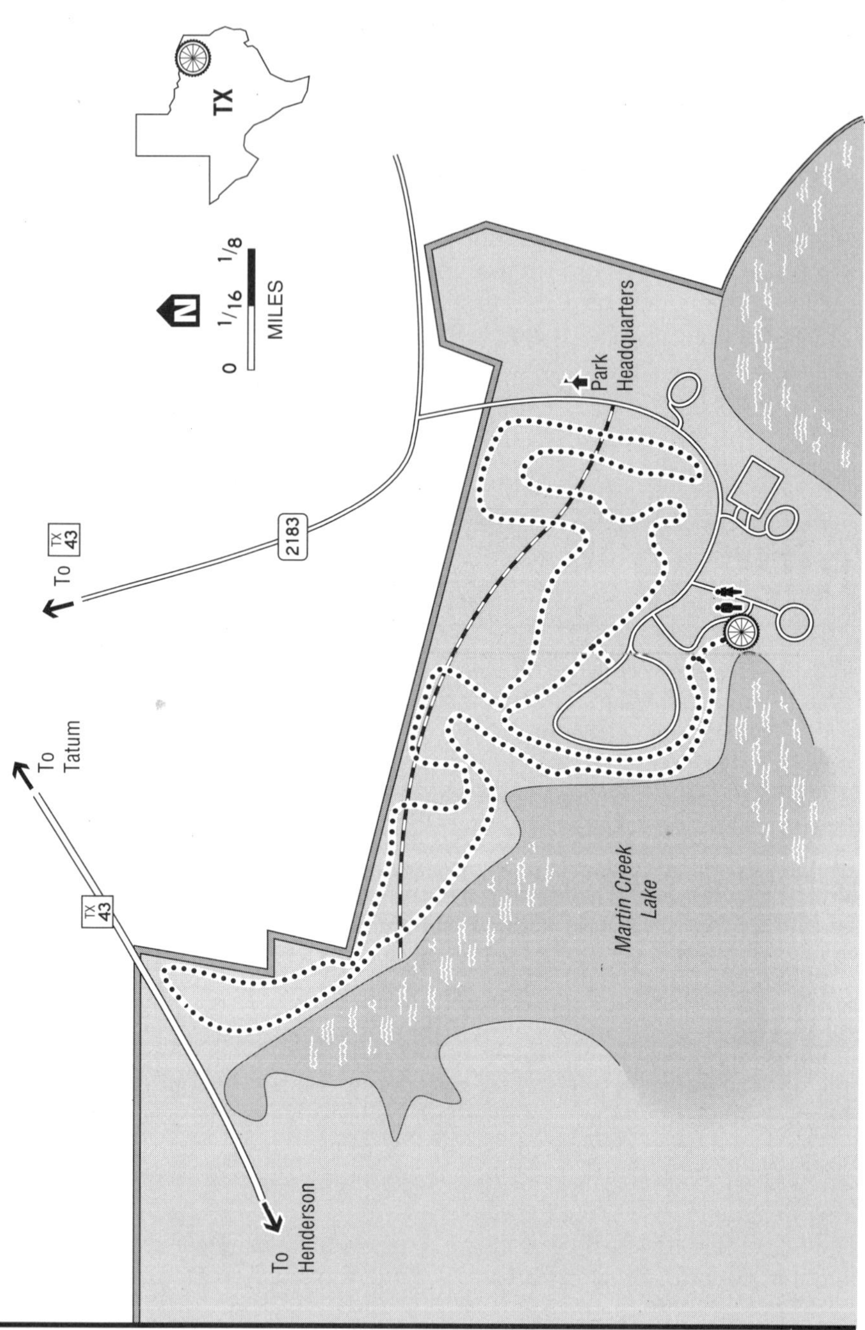
TX
N
0 1/16 1/8
MILES
To TX 43
2183
Park Headquarters
To Tatum
TX 43
Martin Creek Lake
To Henderson

open sections of shoreline that you might consider packing in your rod and reel. Buy a fishing license, though; don't tempt the game wardens.

For you history nuts, take notice that the main park road follows the path of Trammel's Trace. This was once a road used by early Indian travelers and settlers in wagon trains. Cool, huh? But don't drag your metal detector along and start looking for artifacts, because archeological items in this area are protected by law.

Hey, it is not Kamikaze Mountain or anything, but some folks are just happy to have somewhere to ride where the authorities won't yell at them. Warp eight is probably not appropriate for the trails at Martin Creek Lake State Park, but this place definitely has a few "warp fun" laps in it.

General location: Far into East Texas, about 20 miles southeast of Longview, you will find Martin Creek Lake State Park.
Elevation change: The normal lake elevation is 306′ above sea level, and the highest point in the park approaches 400′, but most of the trail is between the lake and 350′.
Season: This trail is pretty much a year-round facility except when the monsoons hit. Which can be anytime. Call ahead if you have any doubt. Try to see this place in the fall, when the trees are changing colors; it is really gorgeous.
Services: The headquarters has a pay phone and soda machine. Water and rest rooms are located at the trailhead. The nearest town is Tatum, maybe 6 or 7 miles northeast.
Hazards: Watch for hikers, because this trail gets a lot more of them than us. If you see a snake or an alligator, let it be and we will all go home happy and safe at the end of the ride. Otherwise, the typical hazards are the normal complement of low tree limbs and wooden bridges.
Rescue index: Since the terrain here is not extremely rugged, and you never wander far from civilization, it should present no major problem to hike out to the pavement if you need help or if you break down.
Land status: Another safe haven for nature in the form of a Texas state park.
Maps: The ranger will give you one of the best, free of charge. The quad for this area is Tatum.
Finding the trail: The state park is 3 miles southwest of Tatum on TX 43 and then south on County Road 2183.

Park across from the rest room building in the Broken Bowl screened shelter area. The trailhead is marked with a sign. Start riding and keep heading in a generally westerly direction, following the yellow flagging tapes that mark the trail. The trail winds around the trees and gradually leads over near TX 43 before turning back toward the trailhead and traveling right along the lake.

Before crossing the bridges over the creek on your outbound leg, you will see a place where some single-track branches to the right and goes northward, away from the lake. This connects to the single-track section behind the rest

A mountain biker could bring a rod and reel to Martin Creek Lake State Park and not be seen for hours. The lake is about 50 feet from this spot.

rooms near the trailhead, across the road from the sections near the lake. I for one had no luck finding the other sections this way; the trail appeared to be grown over or lost among the trees. What I did was, once I had returned to the trailhead from the loop along the lake, I rode down the paved road in front of the rest rooms. This will carry you past the trailhead for the hiking trail. You can follow the hiking trail north into the trees for just a short distance until you see where another piece of single-track crosses it. This is the rest of the bike trail. Hang a right and ride another loop, this one on flatter and more densely foliated territory. This part makes up nearly half the total trail miles and is a lot of fun. You will wind around in a big loop and return to the short hiking trail. Hang a right and hit the pavement back to your car.

Sources of additional information:

Martin Creek Lake State Park
Route 2, P.O. Box 20
Tatum, TX 75691
(903) 836-4336

Texas Parks and Wildlife Department
4200 Smith School Road
Austin, TX 78744-3291
(800) 792-1112 for information only

TPWD Reservation Center
P.O. Box 17488
Austin, TX 78760-7488
(512) 389-8900 for reservations only

Notes on the trail: This is another place where the staff will enthusiastically welcome your arrival to ride their trails. The facilities are clean and the people are nice. Hang a hammock between a couple of the trees and listen to the game on the radio. We will ride a couple of laps later. Don't drink too many beers.

RIDE 14 *DOUBLE LAKE TRAIL*

This place was a pleasant surprise. I had been in the vicinity researching the motorcycle areas in the Sam Houston National Forest and was lamenting the deep powdery conditions predominant in those areas. I drove over to Double Lake to camp, and it rained that night. I am not bashful about using seam sealant on any of my tents, so I stayed dry, but I was very concerned about what condition the trail might be in the next morning when I rose to cut a lap. *No problema*—the trail was fine. The sandy soil makes this trail usable in most conditions, even shortly after a mild rainfall.

This eight-mile single-track trail is arranged in sort of a squashed loop or upside-down U-shape. It crosses the paved park roads in three places, and you must be careful of automobile traffic in each of these locations. It is not extremely difficult or technical, but the speeds that are possible on the smooth surface of most sections will make a few of the corners interesting. Some of them will be loose and powdery where they occur suddenly and other riders have executed abrupt braking maneuvers. Exposed tree roots and maybe a deadfall or two will test your skills, but none of the climbing is dramatic.

This is good single-track, fairly easy and fun, fast and dependable in just about any weather. The area is very scenic, and the canopy of pine trees and hardwoods will keep you from needing any sunscreen. A swimming beach and concession stand are available near the tent camping areas, but please stay off of the park's nature trails, because they are for pedestrian traffic only. Also, be careful at the road crossings.

General location: Double Lake is near the town of Coldspring. The Sam Houston National Forest is home to the Double Lake Recreation Area.

Elevation change: The lake lies between 280′ and 290′ above sea level. The highest point along the trail is around 330′. You wind up and down a lot, but no severe climbing is required.

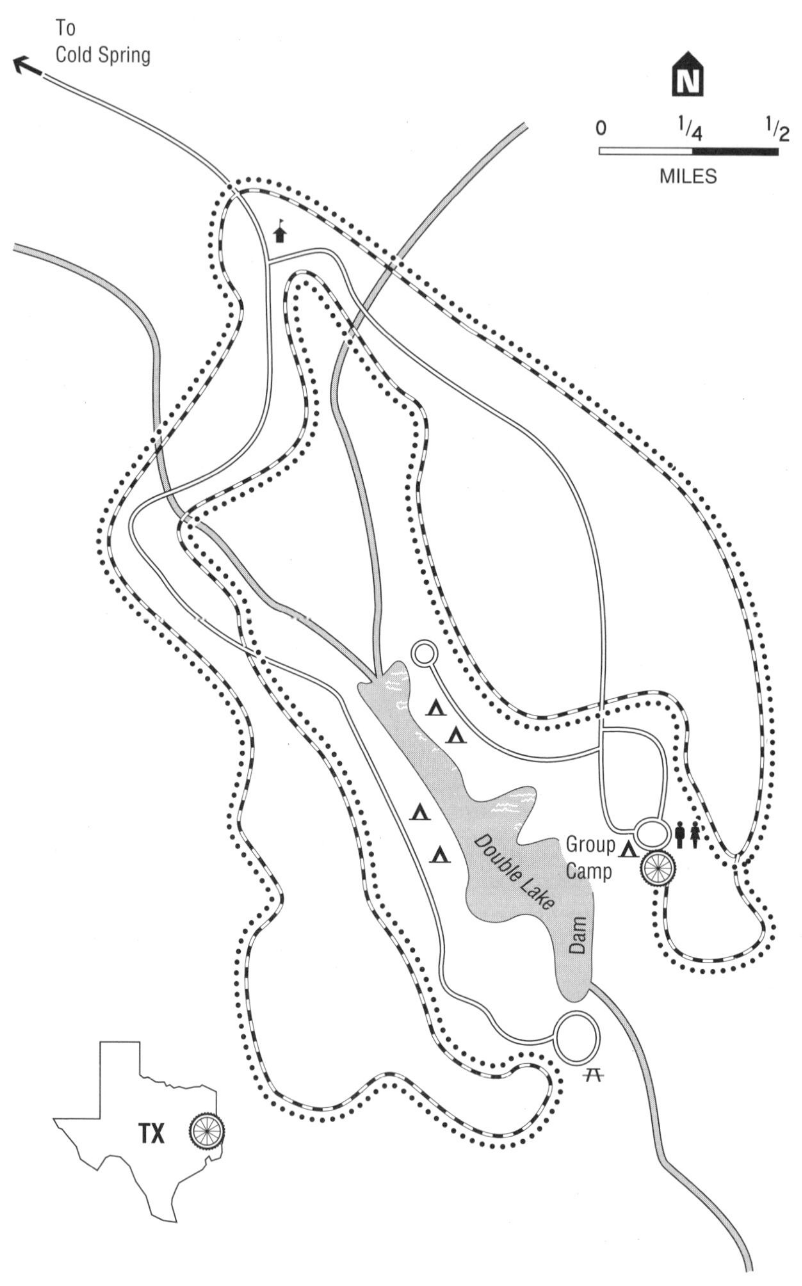
To
Cold Spring
0
1/4
1/2
MILES
Group
Camp
Double Lake
Dam
TX

A fine but little-known piece of single-track called the Double Lake Trail. HAMBRA helped the National Forest Service give us this eight-mile trail.

Season: This is a year-round facility, even rideable shortly after light to medium rainfall. Still, it always pays to phone ahead and check on the trail's status if you have a long drive ahead of you to get there.

Services: The concession stand has burgers and such, soft drinks and candy bars, etc. I have included their phone number in the information section; call to check whether they are open if you will need stuff after you get there. The camping areas have rest rooms with showers, and water is available at most of the campsites. There is a pay phone at the concession building. The nearest bike shop is far away, like probably Houston.

Hazards: I would strongly recommend watching for other riders and hikers using this trail. Other dangers include deadfalls across the trail, low branches, tree roots, and soft corners where the trail is loose from bikes locking their brakes. I strongly suspect that the mosquitoes in this area can be frightening, and snakes are always a possibility. You will cross the paved park roads in three places, and each of these is an accident waiting to happen if you don't look carefully before crossing any of them. Please don't get killed on any trail I have told you to ride. It would ruin my day and yours. This trail has a couple of short bridges, and you need to land squarely upon their faces to survive.

Rescue index: You have a very good chance to be saved if you need help here, because you never stray far from the pavement, and this is a popular park with cyclists, hikers, fishermen, and campers.

Land status: The Double Lake Recreation Area is national forest property, maintained and managed by the National Forestry Service.
Maps: Ask at the entrance if the booth is manned; the park staff has some excellent maps of the trail. Otherwise, ask at the concession building; they have maps of the Sam Houston National Forest, but may or may not have trail maps. The quad for this trail is Coldspring.
Finding the trail: From the town of Coldspring, go west on TX 150 a mile or two until you see Farm to Market 2025 fork to the south. About one-quarter mile south of this intersection, the road into the Double Lake Recreation Area heads to the east. Enter the park, and when you come to the fork in that road, take the left branch and follow it until it ends at the group camp area. Park near the rest room buildings. The trailhead is just behind them and is marked by a sign. Follow the trail from there and hang a left at the first fork so that you rotate roughly clockwise and have all the trail markings facing you. Have a blast. After you come back around and see the signs for the spur back to the parking area, you may follow them or do another lap. The road makes for good bailouts if necessary, so have fun.

Sources of additional information:

District Ranger
Sam Houston National Forest
308 North Belcher
Cleveland, TX 77327
(713) 592-6461

Terri Jenkins
Outdoor Recreation Planner
San Jacinto Ranger District
(713) 592-6462

Houston Area Mountain Bike Riders Association
(713) 856-9732

Double Lake Concession & Boat Rental
Highway 2025
Coldspring, TX
(409) 653-2795

Notes on the trail: This trail is maintained by one of our friends—the Houston Area Mountain Bike Riders Association (HAMBRA). They do a lot and are a driving force for educating area riders and keeping local trails open and rideable. Thank you very much; y'all have some fine trails.

The Sam Houston National Forest is named for a man from Virginia and Tennessee. Old Sam was quite the character, and if you ever develop an interest in frontier history, you will cross paths with him again and again.

The man was integral to Texas statehood, the first president of the Republic of Texas, and an all-around excellent human being.

RIDE 15 *BIG BROWN CREEK PRIMITIVE AREA TRAIL*

This is an easy out-and-back trail that will take you three miles into the woods around Fairfield Lake and then return you to the parking area with barely a sweat. (Total distance: 6 miles.) Take the kids on their single-speed BMX bikes or Grandma on her three-speed Sears and Roebuck cruiser, and everybody will have a great time. The trail is sandy, but thanks to the absence of equestrian traffic, it is typically very firm and rideable. Most of the year the trail is nearly covered with pine needles, and in autumn it may all but disappear in places due to fallen leaves.

Near the start you will pass a bench on the edge of a very scenic small pond. If you haul your fishing rod in, you can stop and try your luck with the panfish that populate these waters. In about two miles you will pass a rest room with drinking water and some primitive campsites. This is the Big Brown Creek primitive camping area, hence the trail's name. Then, near the end of the trail, you can see a mud hole that is the wallow for several feral pigs that live in this heavily wooded area. If this spot sounds interesting, ask the ranger to show you on the map where to find it.

The trail winds through the piney woods until you reach a clear-cut that marks the route of the pipeline that bisects Fairfield Lake. The ranger plans to install a boat dock and some primitive campsites near this clearing to offer boaters a place to pause, set up a volleyball net, and burn a few hot dogs.

The Big Brown Creek primitive camping area offers hikers a quiet place to spend the night, and bikers may find it ideal as a place for a nice picnic lunch and a few casual hours of relaxation in the woods. If you plan to visit in the early hours or during the evening, you should carry plenty of insect repellent, because the mosquitoes here are amazing.

If you glance about as you ride the trail, you will see many birdhouses along the way that were constructed and installed by local nature groups and youngsters. This area abounds with wildlife: Deer, raccoon, skunk, armadillo, and all other forms of familiar Texas critters await your knobby perusal. Don't step in the hog wallow.

General location: About 2 hours south of Dallas, and approximately the same distance north of Houston.

Elevation change: F–L–A–T! Not tabletop, but close. The lake is listed as having a normal pool elevation of 320′ above sea level, and the highest point (the parking area) is around 340′.

RIDE 15 *BIG BROWN CREEK PRIMITIVE AREA TRAIL*

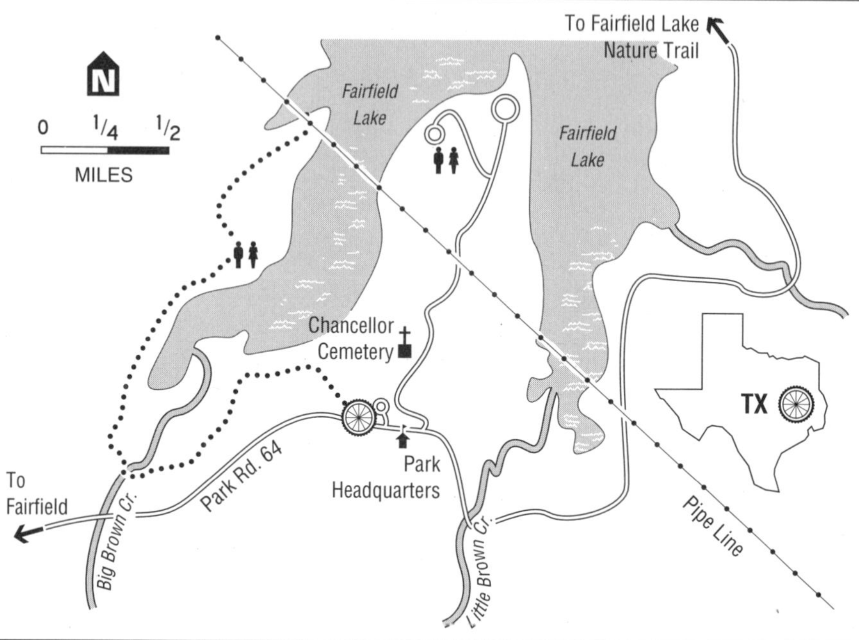

Season: I think the soil here probably drains real well, since it is so sandy, but a hard rain would turn the trail into pudding. Ask about trail conditions at the headquarters.

Services: A pay phone is located near the rest rooms at the Cooks Ferry campground. The nearest stores are in Fairfield, and the nearest bike shop is far away—in Dallas or Houston, to the best of my knowledge.

Hazards: The normal cautions about pedestrian traffic certainly apply here, because this *was* a hiking trail until a year or so ago, when the ranger decided to get a bike. Soon after that, he opened his trails to bicycles. I went to an event he put on to promote the trails and got the benefits of visiting a trail with someone who loves it and knows every rock. The riders got to share in all the knowledge your average park ranger has about his facility, then we got to see him bust his rear end in a small gully. Right near the clearing at its far end, the trail passes over a small creek. Mr. Ranger hits a hole and goes OTB (Over the Bars). Poor guy—his flashlight and gear flew in all directions. One sprained wrist later, we were on the trail again. This trail is easy, maybe too easy; it puts you off your guard and you forget sometimes that this *is* a dangerous sport. Stay focused and THINK at all times. It could happen to you.

Rescue index: Since this trail is a point-to-point, it is possible for you to strand yourself at the point farthest from the parking area. That would leave you slightly more than 3 miles out. Start walking, because there is no shortcut.

The Big Brown Creek Primitive Area Trail is a great way for the short members of your tribe to start learning to love trail rides.

Once you get back to the parking area, you are right by the main park road and headquarters building, and an extraction could be easily arranged, if necessary.

Land status: Can you say "Texas State Park"? No state could possibly have a better system of city-bustle escape-pods.

Maps: Ask at the headquarters for trail maps. They are free and will show you in good scale where you are along the trail. The quad for this trail is Young.

Finding the trail: From Interstate 45 where it passes through Fairfield, turn east at Exit 197, coming from the south, or Exit 198, if you approach from the north. Follow the main drag through town (stopping for supplies if you need any) for about 2 miles, to northbound Farm to Market 488. Turn and follow FM 488 until you reach FM 2570, where you will turn east and proceed about a mile to Park Road 64. Turn right on PR 64 and drive about 3 miles to the park headquarters. Right before you get there, a road to the left (north) heads a short distance to the trailhead parking area. Hit the trail.

Sources of additional information:

Fairfield Lake State Park
Route 2, Box 912
Fairfield, TX 75840
(903) 389-4514

Texas Parks and Wildlife Department
4200 Smith School Road
Austin, TX 78744-3291
(800) 792-1112 for information only

TPWD Reservation Center
P.O. Box 17488
Austin, TX 78760-7488
(512) 389-8900 for reservations only

Notes on the trail: There is always something interesting going on around here, so give the office a call and find out if any special activities are on the calendar while you will be in the area. Tell the ranger that Chuck from DORBA said "Hi," and ask him how that wrist is healing.

RIDE 16 *HUNTSVILLE STATE PARK TRAIL*

"DO NOT FEED OR HARASS THE ALLIGATORS"
—sign at the park headquarters

Okay, you are in your car driving from Dallas to Houston. As always, your trusty steed is inside or attached to your vehicle, and your helmet is in the back seat. You see a sign, and you know the time is near. Huntsville State Park is coming up, and they have trails. Time for a break.

When you ride at Huntsville State Park, you are in the midst of a beautiful forest of tall pines. There are two sets of trail here; one is "unsurfaced bike trail" and the other is "surfaced bike trail." The former is easy, sandy single-track that winds lazily among the trees for just over two miles. This part is absolutely beautiful, I mean to die for. Then you hit about three miles of double-track that carries you back to the main park road, near Interstate 45. Not crappy double-track, but nothing as cool as what you just left behind. From where you hit the pavement you may ride about a mile back to where you started, near the Interpretive Center. Or you may turn around and ride the five or so miles back the way you came. That way you get to hit the cool single-track again. Oh boy!

As I mentioned above, the park also provides some other trails. There are also about three miles of easy "surfaced bike trail" that starts right across the road from where you start the trail to the spillway, right behind the Interpretive Center. The surface of this "surfaced bike trail" is just about gone, kaput, finis. But it has not completely reverted to nature, so it's not the sandy forest loam of the "unsurfaced bike trail" but more like a real hard-packed clay, loose and gravelly in places but mostly providing very firm footing. This trail winds

RIDE 16 *HUNTSVILLE STATE PARK TRAIL*

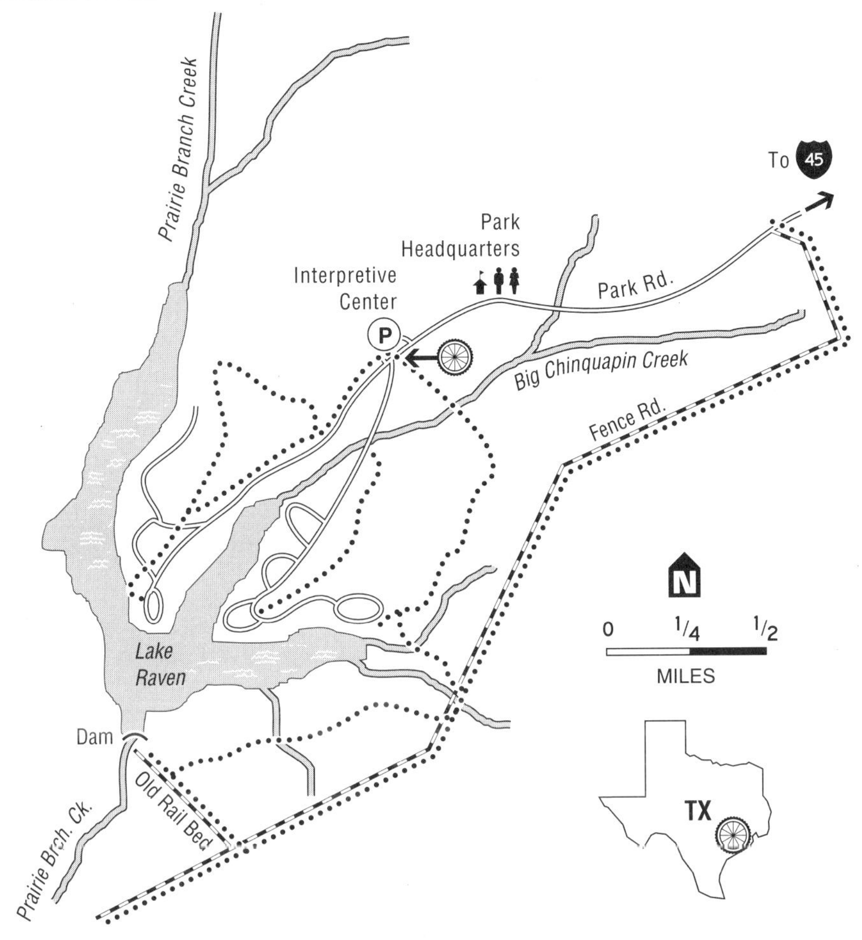

around the campground's tent and RV areas, so it might be a little more of a "kid's trail" than the trail to the spillway. Really, this trail is like a forgotten piece of the park. I don't know if anyone bothers to explore it these days, because the time I rode it there were no other users except a lady pushing a baby in a carriage. Practically deserted.

Fish, camp, picnic, ride, and relax. Take the family, and maybe even pack your hiking boots so that you can explore the farthest reaches of the trails shown on the map, the miles that are closed to bikes. Turn the kids loose on the trails around the campground while you and the marital unit wander over to the spillway and back. Enjoy another fine Texas Parks and Wildlife Department facility. Stop and tell the ranger how much you enjoyed the trail and how much you would like to see the park open the rest of its single-track to bikes.

General location: Roughly an hour north of Houston, just west of I-45.
Elevation change: Lake Raven Spillway is 285´ above sea level, and the highest point on the trail is listed on the topographic maps at around 375´, so you will vary about 90´ from the lowest to highest points.
Season: I have ridden here shortly after heavy rains, and only the double-track was slimy. The single-track trail was very rideable.
Services: The city of Huntsville is only a few miles to the north, and you will find all sorts of eating places and convenience stores within the city limits. There is a small store within the park, but the hours of operation vary, so it might pay to check with them before you make a trip down there expecting to buy a bag of ice. There are pay phones at the main entrance and several rest room/shower facilities.
Hazards: Watch for hikers on the trail, because if the weather is anything like nice, there will be several. Watch for obstacles such as tree roots and spots where the surface of the trails might be a little loose. Don't try to pick up any snakes you might see lying around. They have rights as trail users too, you know.
Rescue index: As is the case on many of the trails in this book, you are not in anything like a remote location, so getting help in the event of an emergency is simply a matter of getting back to the blacktop. This is best achieved by following whatever trail offers the most direct route according to the map. You will never stray more than a few miles from the pavement.
Land status: Thank you, Texas Parks and Wildlife Department, for another marvelous state park with bicycle trails.
Maps: The maps available from the ranger at no cost are very good. They have topographical information and are clearly marked with all pertinent points of interest, and each of the various trails in the park is delineated and described. They even have some brief descriptive information on local flora. The quads for this trail are Huntsville and Moore Grove.
Finding the trail: This one is extremely easy to find, since the main entrance is right by I-45 and you can practically see the trailhead from the headquarters building. About 3 or 4 miles south of Huntsville, there will be a sign telling you to turn west into the park. Just past the headquarters you will find the Interpretive Center. The dirt bicycle trail starts right across the park road from there; look for the "Bicycle Trail" sign on the south side of the road. Follow the single-track over to the spillway, then turn around and follow the double-track back to the paved park road. Turn left there, and you will ride pavement a mile or so back to where you parked. If you decide to explore the "surfaced

Hunstville State Park Trail has some beautiful single-track and some quiet dirt roads for you to enjoy. Alligators are optional.

bicycle trail," you will find its trailhead on the west side of the parking area, behind the Interpretive Center. This trail splits in two and winds around campsites near the lake. The northern section is roughly a loop, while the southern section splits again into two separate point-to-point legs.

Sources of additional information:

Huntsville State Park
P.O. Box 508
Huntsville, TX 77340
(409) 295-5644

Texas Parks and Wildlife Department
4200 Smith School Road
Austin, TX 78744-3291
(800) 792-1112 for information only

TPWD Reservation Center
P.O. Box 17488
Austin, TX 78760-7488
(512) 389-8900 for reservations only

Notes on the trail: Please stay off of the sections that are not open to bicycles. If we cooperate, someday they might be. The map I got from the rangers indicates that the trail is lined with distance markers, but I think I missed most of them when I was there. Fill your water bottles before hitting the trail, because there are no facilities anywhere on the unsurfaced bike trail. On your way out, stop by and mention to the ranger how much you enjoyed the trails. If we display the right attitude, I think someday we might be able to enjoy the back sections. I'll bet they are beautiful.

Central Texas and the Texas Hill Country

Every time I drive to the Austin area, I am overwhelmed by a flood of memories from recent trips and from the old days. When I lived here in the mid-1970s, Austin was still more of a big town than the big city it is now. It used to be so country here that it was like another world compared to places like Dallas and Houston. It is still the mecca for Texas musicians, and almost any night of the week you can find a range of live entertainment. If you like hard mountain biking and good chili, you have come to the right place. I will not attempt to guide you through the Austin nightlife, so if it is entertainment you seek, check out the local newspapers or ask the people you meet.

Austin has many good bike shops, being the major college town it is. I have listed only one as a contact for local cycling needs, because it is the only one I know and my club has real good relations with the owner, Hill Able, and his crew. For roadies, this is a good Texas city. Many streets have bike lanes, and because of the school the residents have a general attitude of acceptance toward cyclists. The school is the University of Texas, located just off Interstate 35 in North Austin. Many other sights and historical places abound, and the state capitol lies just south of the campus. Austin also has a closed-loop bike path called the Veloway where many local road bikers train. The Veloway is a 3.2-mile paved loop, mostly flat, with one fairly sharp hill. Ask at local bike shops for directions.

There is way more to Central Texas than Austin, and Austin is only the beginning of the Texas Hill Country. That actually lies to the west of Austin and San Antonio, and there are hundreds of mountainously excellent places down here. Mountain bikers will reel at the possibilities. As in many other areas of Texas, the trails here are hugged by floral hazards. Prickly pear cactus, yucca plants, and a host of other biting and stinging plants and bugs are the order of the day. There is a lot of hunting done in these Texas regions, so you may be cautioned away from certain trails because of their proximity to popular hunting locales.

Some of the most beautiful swimming holes and hidden beaches you will ever find ANYWHERE dot the landscape, though you may have to bribe the locals to get good directions. Ask around when you meet other riders or stop by a bike shop. If you have a free afternoon, you too may find a part of this Texas that captures your heart.

RIDE 17 *CEDAR BRAKE TRAIL*

Welcome to Dinosaur Valley State Park. Don't miss the dinosaur footprints in the river, and there is also an awesome photo-op with REAL dinosaurs. Well, they look real, except for the fence that keeps the happy couple under control. It seems that a while ago the Atlantic Richfield Oil Company gave the park a couple of dinosaur models they had lying around after they bought Sinclair. The models were made for the New York World's Fair in 1964, and they seem right at home here.

Since you brought your bike, you may get a chance to see some other critters as well. The last time I was here, the trails led us right by a fence that was being used as a back-scratcher by a herd of Texas longhorn cattle. These things are monsters; I cannot span the width of their horns with my arms. Big old "hamburgers-on-the-hoof."

When I rode here, we did ten miles of single-tracking and did not see every trail. What we have here is a place to wander unfettered on trails of loose limestone, some with considerable hills, and maybe never see the same piece of single-track twice. It is loose to the point of being almost gravel in places, and it is in the middle of a bunch of cactus, but it is a good place for one of those fun wasted afternoons where all you do is ride your bike. Am I the only person who does this? Hey, if I am not watching old westerns on a Saturday afternoon because it is raining, then I am out somewhere with a bike, hiding from beepers and telephones and cars. And I know a cool place when I see it. This is a cool place.

You are in the valley of the Paluxy River while you are here. None of it is real difficult, but there is some of what you could call your technical mountain biking—roots, climbs on loose gravel, and some slick limestone and bedrock outcroppings that are like ice when wet. The single-track weaves back and forth across an old gravel road, and you get to swap some elevation around. You know, trade some up for some down, etc. Unless you go real hard, you will not get beat up too bad by these trails.

And what is even better is that the boss ranger is a mountain biker. He gave me and a few friends a guided tour of the trails one Saturday, and that way we got to have the benefit of a park ranger's knowledge. They know every inch of their territory, all the history and all the local wildlife. Stop by the office anytime you are in a Texas state park, and ask who the boss is. You will walk away with a whole new respect for state employees. I promise.

Be sure and check out Glen Rose. It is a pretty good example of a neat little town on the banks of a beautiful little river. Another nearby point of interest is the Fossil Rim Park, but more on that later.

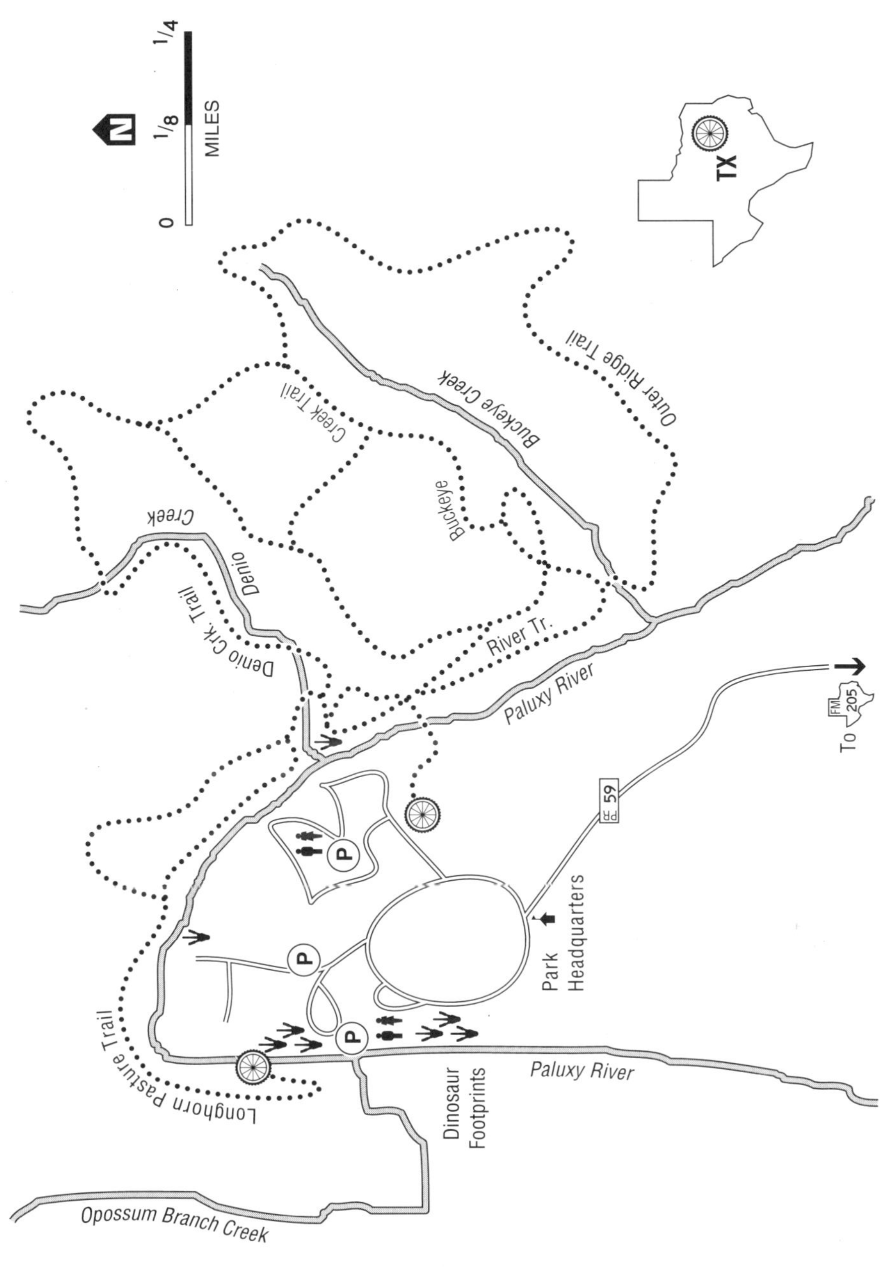
0
1/8
1/4
MILES
TX
Outer Ridge Trail
Buckeye Creek
Creek Trail
Buckeye
Creek
Denio
Denio Crk. Trail
River Tr.
Paluxy River
To FM 205
PR 59
Park Headquarters
Longhorn Pasture Trail
Dinosaur Footprints
Paluxy River
Opossum Branch Creek

This part of the Cedar Brake Trail is between the dinosaur and the footprints. You'll get your feet wet reaching this spot.

General location: Dinosaur Valley State Park is just outside the small town of Glen Rose, about 45 miles southwest of Fort Worth. I call it part of the Texas Hill Country.

Elevation change: Whoo boy. The Paluxy River is around 620–630´, and the tops of the big hills where the trail goes punch up to over 850´. I don't think you will quite reach 900´ anywhere on the trails I rode, but you will get close.

Season: Hey, it's Texas. Unless a tornado hit yesterday you can probably ride. Call old Billy Paul Baker and ask him for an update on trail conditions and status if you are in doubt.

Services: There is a small store in the park, but hours and days of operation vary, so it might be wise to grab what you need in Glen Rose before heading over to the park to ride, or else call ahead. A pay phone is located at the main entrance headquarters building. Glen Rose has several convenience stores and gas stations that are open every day of the week, as well as restaurants and the ubiquitous barbecue stands by the road. The nearest bike shop is probably in Fort Worth, so don't break any pieces off your steed.

Hazards: There are thorny things and plenty of trail sections where a misplaced front-braking maneuver will put you on your head. You will, I trust, not need to leave skin on anything to believe what I say. I heard the poison ivy is not too bad here, but then I am not real allergic. Watch for hikers, because there are usually plenty of them on the trail if the weather is nice.

Rescue index: Be careful, take your patch kit, and get lost. You could starve to death out here only if you fasted and hid from the rangers. If you got hurt, you would probably not have to wait too long before someone came along. Just keep in mind that you need to get down to the river to get back to the parking areas. The Paluxy River makes a big upside-down U-turn right here, and if you just go downstream you will either find the dinosaur prints exhibition or a road. If you hit a road other than the park road, it is either gravel or fenced-off. The gravel road will carry you between the fenced road and the headquarters area.

Land status: Texas state parks are a wonderful resource, and one of the best parts of living in Texas.

Maps: As usual at a state park, excellent maps can be had for free just by asking. Texas Friendly is spoken here, like the brochures say. The quads for this trail are Glen Rose West and Hill City.

Finding the trail: Glen Rose is in Somervell County, which is probably one of the smallest counties in Texas. Take US 377 south from Fort Worth to Granbury, then go south on TX 144 to Glen Rose, then go west on US 67. Or take US 67 west from Dallas to Glen Rose. Once you're in Glen Rose on US 67 West, go through the town to Farm to Market 205 and go right (north) to Park Road 59 (about 3 miles). Hang a right, and there you are. Show them your Conservation Passport or pay the $5.

Sources of additional information:

Dinosaur Valley State Park
Box 396
Glen Rose, TX 76043
(817) 897-4588

Texas Parks and Wildlife Department
4200 Smith School Road
Austin, TX 78744-3291
(800) 792-1112 for information only

TPWD Reservation Center
P.O. Box 17488
Austin, TX 78760-7488
(512) 389-8900 for reservations only

Notes on the trail: What more can I say except the ranger loves mountain bikes? The river has some good places to swim, sort of little blue-holes. "The trail" I keep talking about is actually about three different trails: the Denio Creek Trail, the Buckeye Creek Loop, and the Outer Ridge Trail. All may be tackled either as separate entities or used as a whole. Grab a map, fill your water bottle, maybe pitch a praline or two into your pocket, and have fun. Tell Billy Paul I said "hey."

RIDE 18 *FOSSIL RIM RIDE*

Specializing in family weekend adventures.
—park brochure

The day I rode here, I had such a good time that I could hardly wait to get home and write this chapter. Nowhere else I have ridden compares to this exotic game preserve. Not because of technical impact or scenic beauty—the trails here fall somewhere in the middle of the road for the Texas Hill Country. I was enthused because of the experiences I had that were of a non–mountain biking variety, so to speak. I got to take a look at the behind-the-scenes activity that goes on here, because a buddy of mine is one of the animal handlers. He had taken me and another pal on a guided tour of stuff you do not get to see if you take the standard jeep tour of the facilities.

There are over ten miles of single-track, rocky and somewhat technical, that you may enjoy if you take a mountain bike tour. The guides will show you things the average tourist does not get to see—pens where animals with special needs are kept, and places where new additions stay until they are acclimatized and ready to go on display, and lots of other schmoozy behind-the-scenes stuff. You will also get to ride along the pens where the cheetahs live, and if they are in the right mood, you may have spotted companions loping along next to you as you ooze past their area. You will get to see where the wolves are kept; Fossil Rim has several varieties, and each is on the endangered species list. You'll have an opportunity to get up close and personal with at least two types of rhinoceros, but they scare me, so I don't like to get real close. To make a long story short, this place is really special, and so are the people who work here and care for these animals.

There are thousands of critters running free here; you won't believe your eyes. Some of these things have huge racks. They are docile enough, but an addax or scimitar-horned oryx could give you a whole new respect for the continent of Africa. Man, those horns are wicked.

Take a ride on the wild side; spend a morning or afternoon relaxing and learning about animals whose natural habitats are being consumed by expanding humanity. The rhinos are two of only ten pairs that Zimbabwe has released to be raised in captivity. Their brothers and sisters now live all over the world, because they are not safe from poachers in their home country. There is no place else like Fossil Rim—not for many miles, at least.

General location: Fossil Rim Wildlife Center is located just south of the small town of Glen Rose, about an hour or so southwest of Fort Worth. It may be a stretch, but I call this the Texas Hill Country.

RIDE 18 *FOSSIL RIM RIDE*

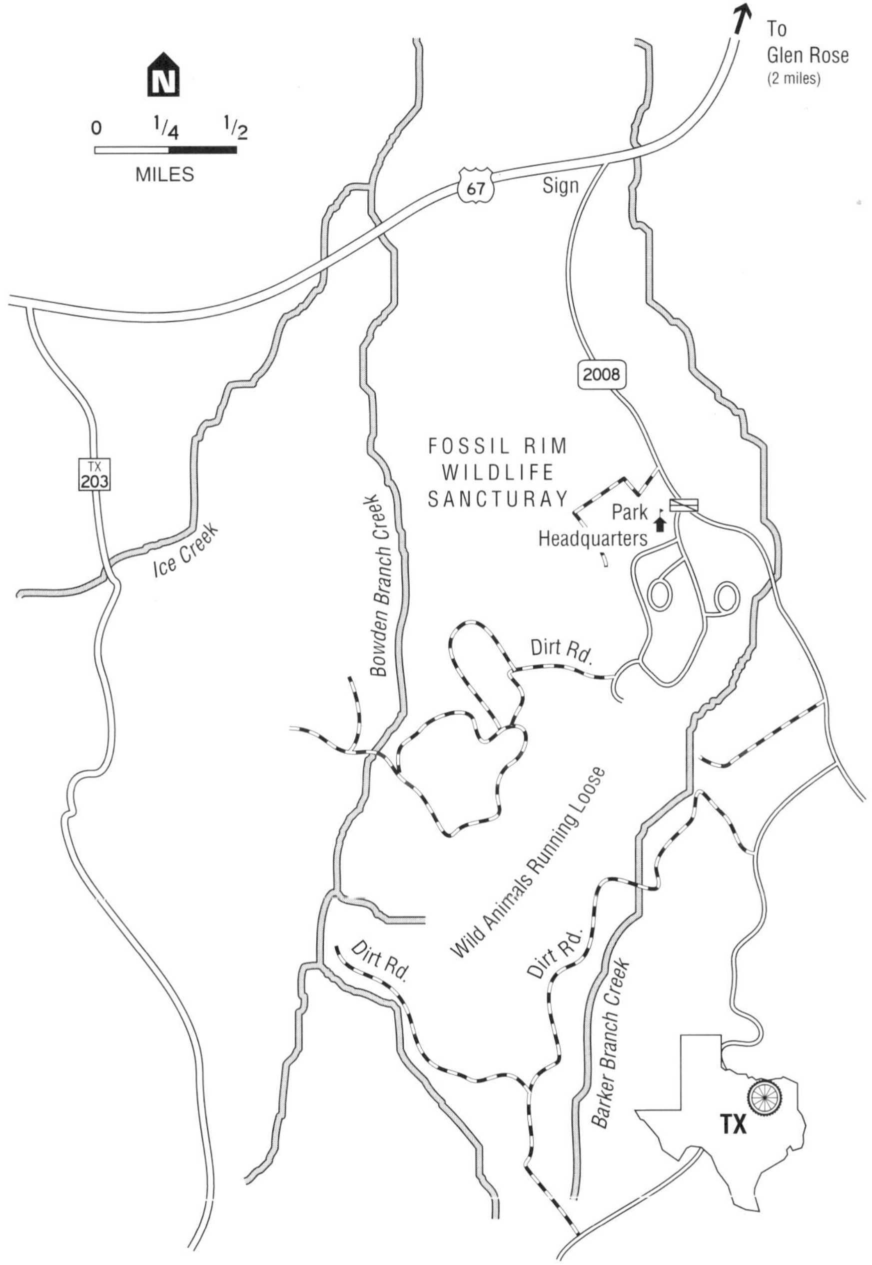

Note: *The riding here is by guided tours only so the single-track is not shown.*

Elevation change: There are several places in this neck of the woods that are over 1,200′ above sea level. There are others that sink to 900′. You can do some climbing and you can do some falling down. Don't get carried away.
Season: Unless some particular event should preclude a tour, you should be able to ride here anytime. The weather can have a bearing on trail conditions or tour guide enthusiasm, but this is a year-round facility. Be smart and call ahead.
Services: There are no pay phones in the park, but the headquarters has a concession with munchies and soft drinks. Rest rooms and water are available in the same location. The nearest place to do a serious resupply is Glen Rose, only a few miles away. Plenty of convenience stores, gas stations, and restaurants are just waiting for your wallet to walk through their doors. The nearest bike shop is far away; Fort Worth is probably the closest place for any kind of serious bicycle repair or support.
Hazards: There are tons of wild animals here, but all the REALLY dangerous ones are inside fenced pens. The trails themselves could be called hazardous, because their surfaces are typically loose and gravelly, and the native plants along the trail will not make for good landing pads if you do an OTB launch of your corporeal self. Otherwise, this is not as dangerous a ride as many. I only say that because you will be with somebody who has a lick of sense. There are active dirt roads, but the only traffic on these will be employees. You will also ride on some of these roads to get to the animal holding areas.
Rescue index: Since you will not be allowed to ride these trails without a guide, getting rescued is highly likely. I have to give this ride one of the best rescue indices, because the guides will take care of you if you get hurt or have bike problems.
Land status: This is private property, and you will be expected to obey the rules. They are not stupid rules, and you will be given the whole orientation before you take the tour.
Maps: The only maps I was able to get my hands on were the 7.5 minute topographic quadrangles I buy at One Map Place. Since then I have heard rumors that the park is building some pocket maps for people to carry on the tours. Ask your guide. The quad for this trail is Glen Rose West.
Finding the trail: From Glen Rose go west on US 67 to County Road 2008 and turn left (south) until you see the signs for the park, not far away (a mile or so). Drive through the gate and park by the Visitor Center.

All of the mountain bike tours are customized, and you may ride at any technical level you can handle. You will not be allowed to roam at will, since there are a higher than average number of ways to get hurt, maimed, eaten, or killed here. The guides are pals of mine, so treat 'em right; they are good people, and they really love these animals.

DORBA members Adam Eyres (left) and Steve Patterson (flatted) on the trail at Fossil Rim. Steve is a guy with a member number in the low single-digits, a real behind-the-scenes force in mountain biking in Texas and a major contributor to our club. They broke the mold after that guy. Thanks for all the hard work, Steve.

Sources of additional information:

Fossil Rim Wildlife Center
Route 1, Box 210
Glen Rose, TX 76043
(817) 897-2960

Notes on the trail: Mountain bike tours here are still in the experimental stages, and the marketing folks have not worked all the bugs out yet. Give the administrators some feedback on how you feel about what is being provided; I think you will find them to be very receptive to your suggestions. Since this is still a fairly new addition to the activities at Fossil Rim, I suggest you call ahead and ask about the availability of guides before driving far to get to the park. My pals have the day off sometimes, and I don't want you to be disappointed.

There is also a very nice selection of primitive tent camping, cabins, and a lodge. This is a top-shelf place, and the facilities are definitely above average. Plus, they are extremely well maintained. All of this costs money, of course, and it ain't cheap. In 1995 the cost for a half-day tour was $30.

RIDE 19 *TOWN LAKE HIKE AND BIKE TRAIL*

Gosh, it was so easy to skip class and ride down here from campus. I used to do it just about every day. Sorry, Dad.

Town Lake Hike and Bike is the granddaddy of urban Texas bike paths and cannot be ignored by anyone writing a book on Texas trails. It is almost tabletop flat and makes an easy loop along the shores of the Colorado River as it runs through an Austin area known as Town Lake. The trail's surface is smooth gravel, and it can be ridden on a road bike. I started riding it about the time those guys on Mt. Tam were inventing mountain biking.

The trail runs along both sides of the river and has many access points. Parking areas may be selected almost at will, but I would suggest parking in Zilker Park or near Barton Springs so that other points of interest are nearby (more on this later). You ride very near the bike shop listed below, and practically right by some awesome Tex-Mex places. Starting at Zilker Park and riding west to the footbridge puts you in the position of being able to ride up the northern side, by the bats, by the power plant and graffiti, across another bridge, by an area the Austin Fire Department uses for training their crews, down the sidewalk for a ways, back along the water just in time to offer a nod of loving respect to the statue of Stevie Ray Vaughn, then back to the park. Add another 15 miles to your total for the year.

I probably should offer an explanation of at least part of what I described in the previous paragraph. Living under the Commerce Street Bridge are about a thousand Mexican free-tailed bats. Just north of the bridge on the north side of Town Lake, you will find the "Bat Facts" kiosk. Stop and get acquainted. Also check the area known as Barton Springs Pool. Some of the state's coldest, clearest water and *muy attractivas señoritas* inhabit this finest of Texas swimming holes.

There is so much to do in this city that I cannot possibly tell you all of it. Try Chuy's 911 Hotplate, my personal favorite. Go for the green sauce.

General location: A stone's throw from downtown Austin, right down the street from THE University of Texas and the state capitol building (a lovely structure of Texas pink granite, I might add, something like four feet taller than the capitol building in Washington, D.C.).
Elevation change: The trail varies in elevation, but not very much. I would say this whole trail is within 30′ of the normal pool elevation of Town Lake, about 428′ above sea level.
Season: This is one of the year-roundest of trails. Ride here any time you have a hankerin', partner. Unless the trail is closed for some event or something out of the ordinary, only the severest of weather will keep you away.

Services: Name your poison. Anything you will need is within a few feet of the trail. Keep your eyes open and phones, rest rooms, food, water, bike shops, gang graffiti art, or anything else you might desire will pass by as you ride along.
Hazards: This is one heavily traveled trail, and you will encounter about a million other trail users as you ride here. Don't let the local tendency to ride with no helmet influence you; wear your brain bucket and live.
Rescue index: The odds of getting rescued from here are about as good as they get anywhere. This trail is in the middle of a large city, and people will be passing by on the trail almost constantly.
Land status: The park and trail are maintained by the City of Austin, though the lake belongs to the Lower Colorado River Authority (LCRA).
Maps: The City of Austin Parks and Recreation Department will send you a very nice packet of information about all of their trails if you just write or call and ask. The quads for this trail are Austin West, Austin East, and Montopolis.
Finding the trail: Go to Austin, find where the roads cross the lake/river, and start riding on the trail you will see there.

From Interstate 35 take Riverside Drive west until it turns into Barton Springs Road. Keep going until you see signs for Zilker Park. Turn right into the park and head back toward the trees to the north. Park in one of the parking areas—maybe the one by the Porta-potties, if nature calls. There is sort of a trail-thing there by the water. Hang a left and ride west until you find the pedestrian bridge at Mo-Pac Boulevard. It's not far. Cross the lake and head back east, toward downtown in the distance.

Ride east past the Commerce Street bridge and the Bat Facts signs. This is very near downtown. Keep going, past I-35 and up to the area of the power plant. Go around the power plant on the north side, checking out the graffiti along the way. Somebody put in some real time to paint this. I guess the city figured it was better to try and get some high-quality stuff by inviting it instead of trying to eradicate all the bandit bombings. Just past the power plant you will cross the lake at Pleasant Valley Road, because this is the end of the trail.

Just across the bridge you will pick up the trail again and pass the fireman school, then head west again by the lake. Soon the trail ends again and you must ride the sidewalk along Riverside all the way past I-35 again and down to where you turn north, back toward the lake. There are signs indicating where to turn for the trail, but they can be hard to notice. Look for signs directing traffic toward the *Austin-American Statesman* newspaper, right by a Stop-and-Go store just east of Congress Street. Turn right and follow the signs. You will pick up the trail again and ride by some big buildings. (One has a nice waterfall by the trail.) Soon you will see Stevie Ray.

Keep going until you are back near Zilker Park. There is a pedestrian bridge across Barton Creek; cross this bridge to the other side and turn right. You

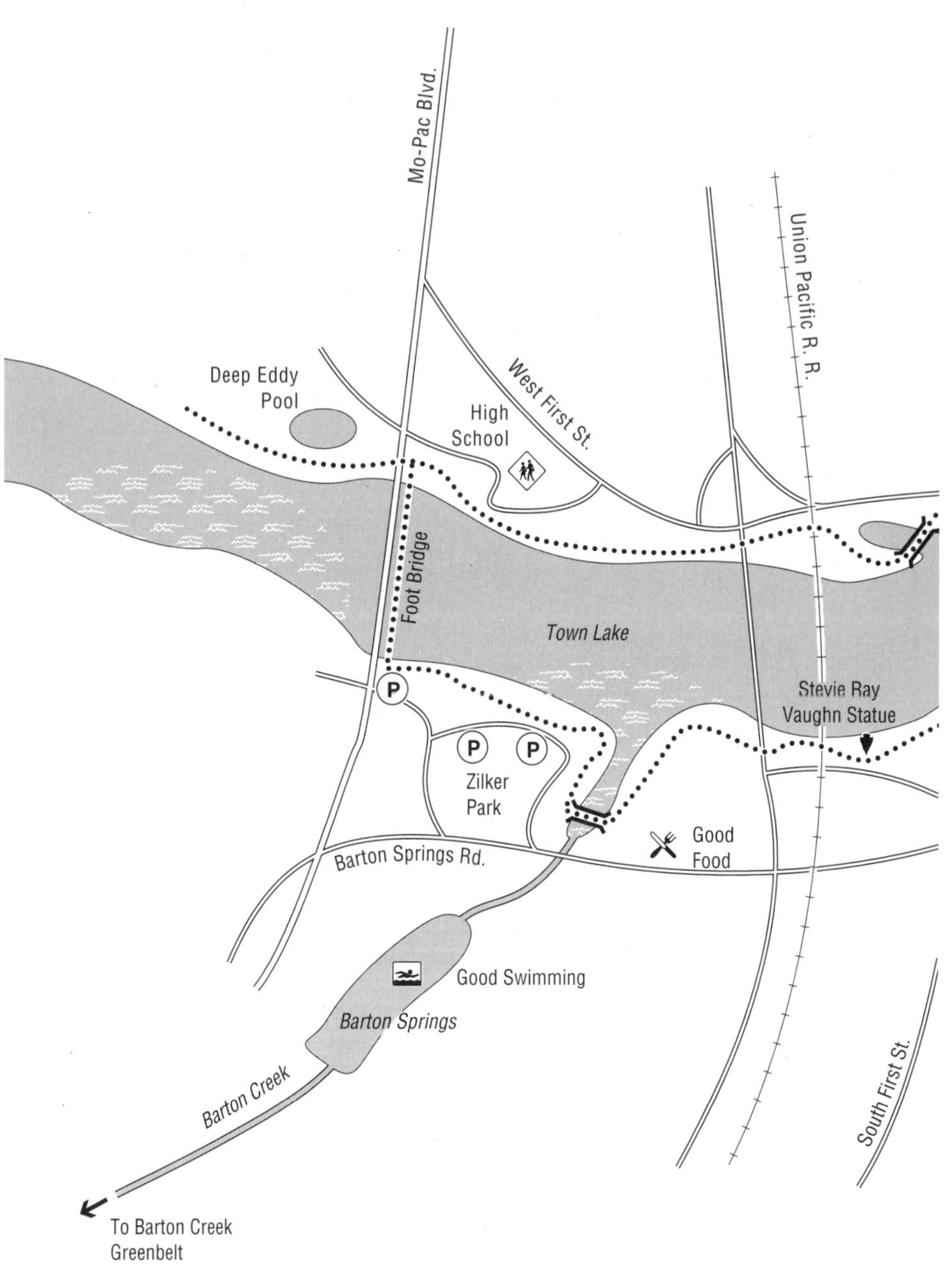
Mo-Pac Blvd.
Union Pacific R. R.
Deep Eddy
Pool
High
School
West First St.
Foot Bridge
Town Lake
Stevie Ray
Vaughn Statue
Zilker
Park
Barton Springs Rd.
Good
Food
Good Swimming
Barton Springs
Barton Creek
South First St.
To Barton Creek
Greenbelt

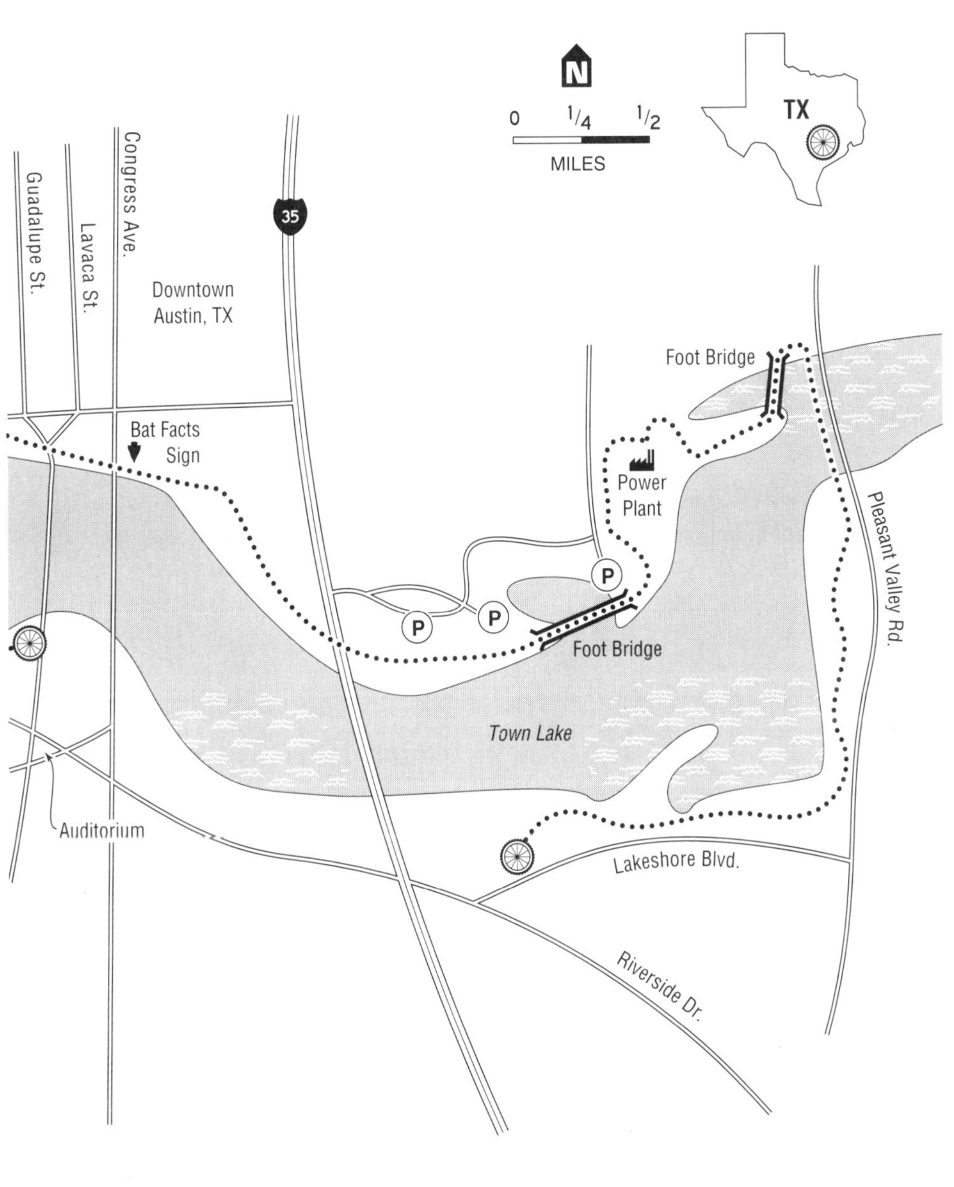
N
0
1/4
1/2
MILES
TX
35
Congress Ave.
Guadalupe St.
Lavaca St.
Downtown
Austin, TX
Foot Bridge
Bat Facts
Sign
Power
Plant
Pleasant Valley Rd.
P
Foot Bridge
Town Lake
Auditorium
Lakeshore Blvd.
Riverside Dr.

A beautiful place among many beautiful places, these fountains are beside the Town Lake Hike and Bike Trail in Austin. A good place to study or skip class.

will see miniature-gauge railroad tracks after you cross. Follow the trail again until you start seeing stuff that looks familiar; soon you will be ready to hang a left and get up onto the fields of Zilker Park and look for your car. If you miss the bridge at Barton Creek, you will soon hit Barton Springs Road and you will know to turn around. This is very near Bicycle Sport Shop.

Sources of additional information:

Austin Parks and Recreation Department
200 South Lamar Boulevard
Austin, TX 78704
(512) 499-6700

Bicycle Sport Shop
1426 Toomey Road
Austin, TX 78704
(512) 477-3472

Bicycle Sport Shop
13376 North Highway #183
Suite #512
Austin, TX 78750
(512) 258-7278

Notes on the trail: This place is packed on a nice Sunday afternoon, so I would recommend riding early if you plan to do anything like a steady pace. If you want to ride hard and fast, go somewhere else. This is not that kind of place.

Zilker Park is right across the street from Barton Springs Pool, the finest swimming hole in the state of Texas. The water is cold year-round, so the hotter the weather, the more folks there will be at the pool. They charge for admission, but there are real rest rooms and a concession area with a playground for the kiddies nearby. The railroad also has its depot near the pool. Have a nice day.

RIDE 20 *BARTON CREEK GREENBELT TRAIL*

Get out and ride this trail, but only if the weather is right. I am pushing you because you need to hurry. It is only a matter of time before bicycles are banned from the Barton Creek Greenbelt because of past and present abuses by riders with a "don't care" attitude—ignorant dweebs who have disregarded "Trail Closed to Bikes Due to Wet Conditions" signs for too many years. One day the signs will go up for good. A sad situation getting sadder.

This is the granddaddy of Austin mountain bike trails, sort of like the Town Lake Hike and Bike is the granddaddy of area jogging paths. It offers an out-and-back distance of about 15 miles, running roughly in a large L. Most of this is fairly flat single-track that winds along both sides of Barton Creek. Many places are highly technical because of outcroppings of rock and stretches of loose gravel, but there are also long sections of fairly smooth and easy riding. Near the western end of the trail, if you are interested, is a place called the "Hill of Life." This is a roughly half-mile climb of about 200 feet to the Camp Craft Road trailhead. A lot of the trail is hard-packed dirt that gets very muddy from rains. Damage to these areas and perceived reckless behavior are the reasons we bikers WILL someday be banished.

The last time I was here I elected to hike instead of bike, because the "Wet Conditions" signs were up. I passed probably 50 cyclists riding in the mud, most with no helmets. These jerks do not care about the future of our sport and will cause the rest of us to be removed from one of the most beautiful trails in the Austin area. It is indisputably shameful that so many riders feel so comfortable about disregarding logical and necessary trail rules. People often find it convenient to think they know better than the folks making the rules. These "one-percenters" often spoil things for responsible trail users. Enough whining already, let's get it while the getting is good. Soapbox mode off.

This trail is heavily used by hikers and joggers. Several spots are gated, and bikes are required to cross the creek to the other side to avoid sections of the

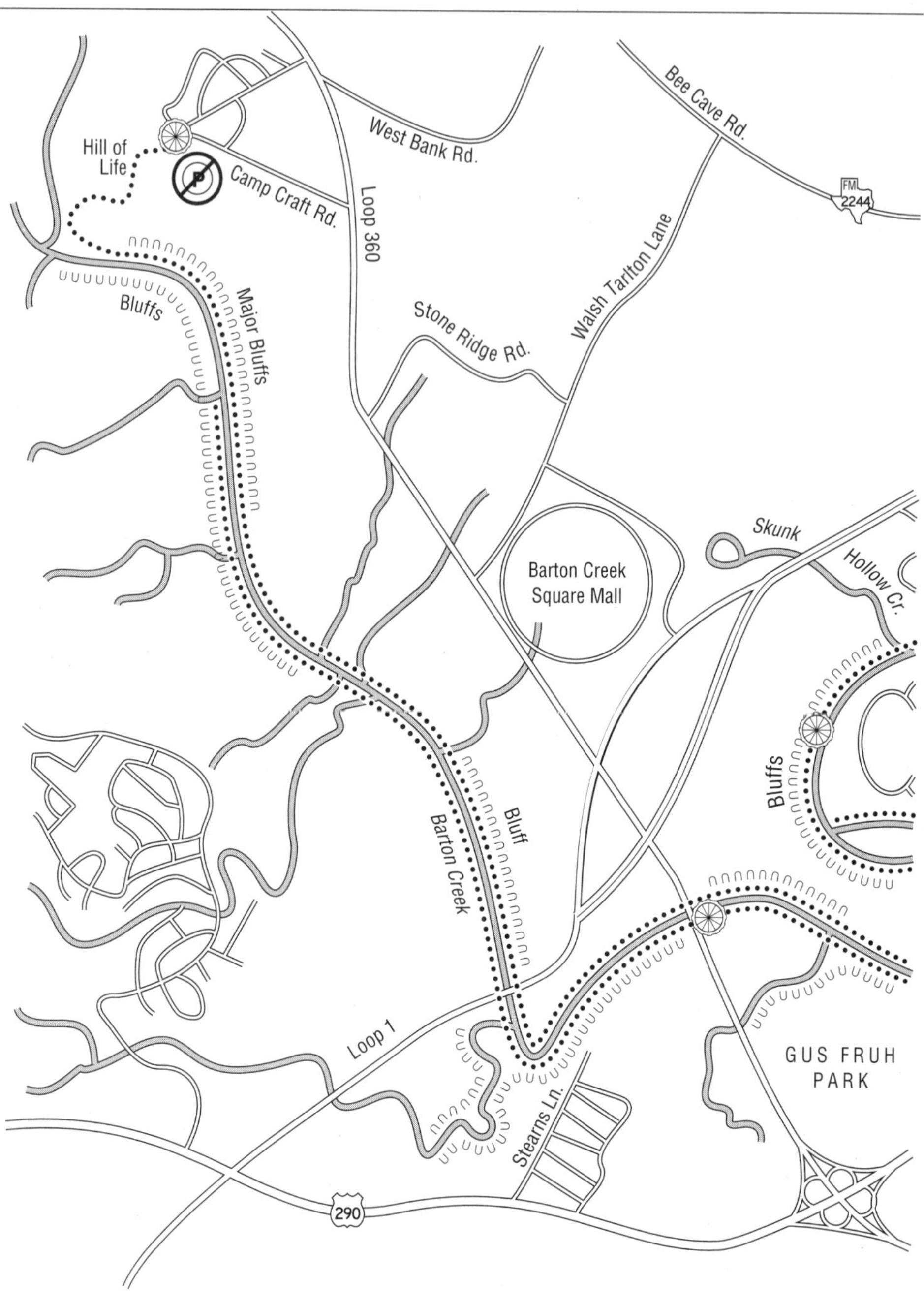

Hill of Life
Camp Craft Rd.
West Bank Rd.
Loop 360
Bee Cave Rd.
FM 2244
Walsh Tarlton Lane
Stone Ridge Rd.
Bluffs
Major Bluffs
Skunk
Hollow Cr.
Barton Creek Square Mall
Bluffs
Bluff
Barton Creek
Loop 1
Stearns Ln.
GUS FRUH PARK
290

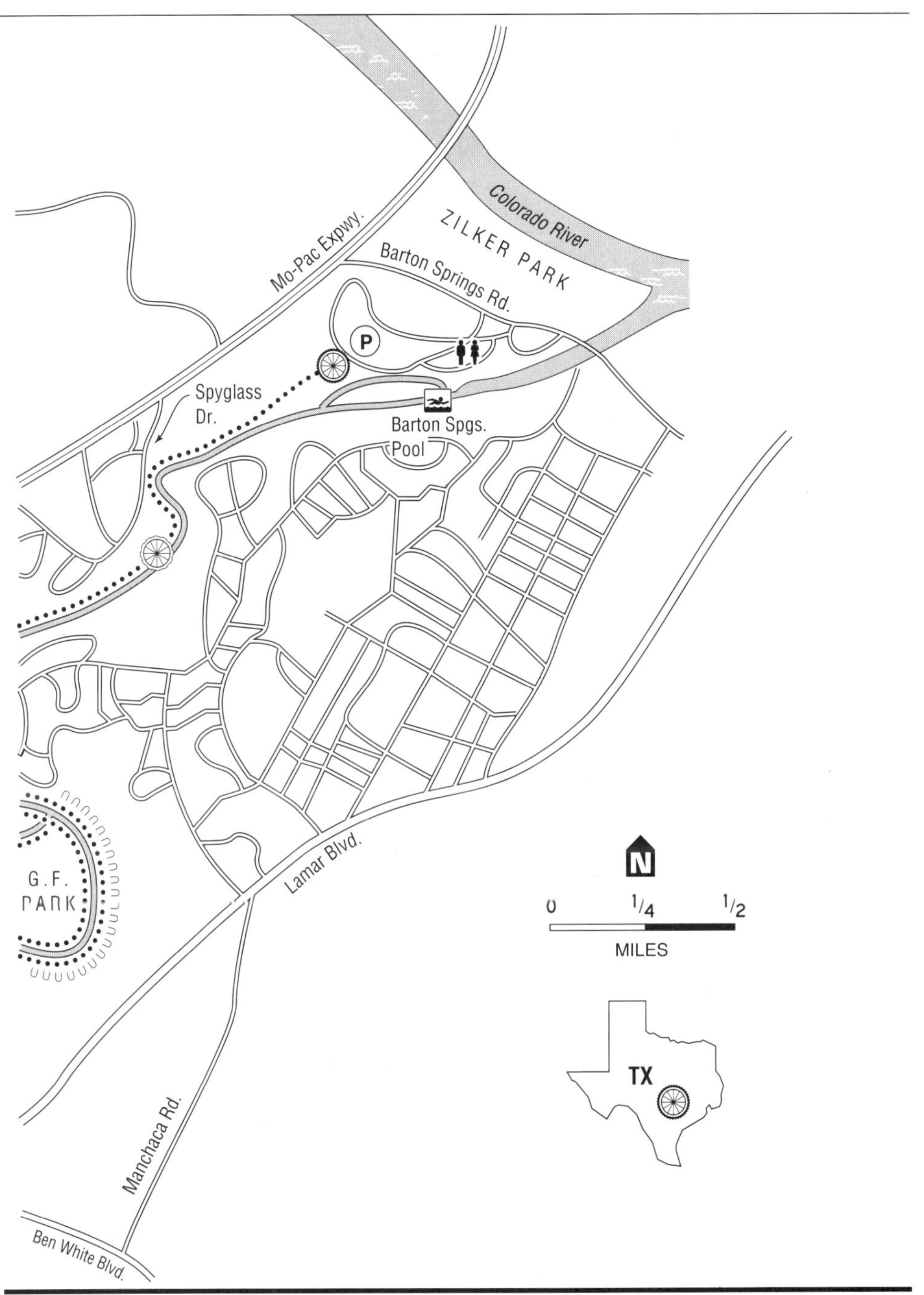

Colorado River
ZILKER PARK
Mo-Pac Expwy.
Barton Springs Rd.
P
Spyglass
Dr.
Barton Spgs.
Pool
G.F.
PARK
Lamar Blvd.
Manchaca Rd.
Ben White Blvd.
N
0
1/4
1/2
MILES
TX

The Barton Creek Greenbelt and a rider ignoring signs that the trail is closed due to wet conditions. Naughty boy.

trails where only foot traffic is allowed. A couple of places along the route are popular for rock climbing because of the tall bluffs bordering much of the trail. This is a popular ride, very scenic, and it is easy to forget you are in the middle of a quarter million people as you cruise through the delightful and dense woods along Barton Creek. Appreciate the greenbelt while it is available to us; this privilege will not last forever.

General location: In central Austin, near Barton Springs Road and Mo-Pac Boulevard.

Elevation change: The Barton Springs trailhead lies around 460′ above sea level, and the highest point, the Camp Craft Road trailhead, is pushing 800′. It is pretty much a steady climb from the former to the latter.

Season: PLEASE don't ride here if the trail is muddy.

Services: There are rest rooms, pay phones, water, and concessions near the Barton Creek trailhead. There are many eating places, an excellent bike shop, and many stores on the way to the trailhead, on Barton Springs Road and Riverside Drive.

Hazards: There are plenty of technical dangers here—tree roots and loose rock, invasive limbs and slippery conditions—but the biggest hazard, in my opinion, is people who ride here when it is wet. Did I mention that yet?

Rescue index: You are in the middle of a lot of folks, and this trail gets a lot of traffic. Unless you are somewhere you should not be, you could quite easily

The trained mountain bike eye will spot enough technical challenges in this photograph to instantly grasp the level of skill required to clean sections like this part of the Barton Creek Greenbelt.

be rescued here if you had an emergency. Or you could easily walk back to your car if you broke the bike. High marks for rescue index.

Land status: This is one of the finest Austin Parks and Recreation Department facilities, thank you very much.

Maps: There must be good maps somewhere, but all I have ever found is part of a packet of hike and bike trail information I got in the mail from the Austin Parks and Recreation Department. The quads for this trail are Austin West and Oak Hill.

Finding the trail: From Interstate 35, exit at Riverside Drive and go west until this street becomes Barton Springs Road. Keep going until you see signs for Zilker Park and Barton Springs Pool, as above for the Town Lake ride. Instead of exiting at Zilker, keep going and turn left into the parking areas for Barton Springs Pool. You will pass all of the pool stuff and go to the end of the paved road. This is where you will see the signs for the trailhead for the Barton Creek Greenbelt. Start riding up the trail.

You will see green and white arrows and mile markers as you ride, and from time to time you will receive instructions in the form of signs telling you where to cross and what sections to avoid. Just generally mosey along and enjoy the scenery. When you see the first highway bridge over the trail, you are at Loop #360. The next large bridge you will encounter is Mo-Pac Boulevard. Soon you will start riding sections that are obviously old roads instead of single-track.

You are nearing the picnic areas and the "Hill of Life." Ride it if you dare. Otherwise, rest a few, maybe, and head back the way you came.

There is such a network of trails along the greenbelt that you will have plenty of opportunities to wander around, but you cannot get extremely lost, because the greenbelt is only so wide. As long as you are following the creek, you will eventually find the place where you started.

Sources of additional information:

Austin Parks and Recreation Department
200 South Lamar Boulevard
Austin, TX 78704
(512) 478-0905

Bicycle Sport Shop
1426 Toomey Road
Austin, TX 78704
(512) 477-3472

Bicycle Sport Shop
13376 North Highway #183
Suite #512
Austin, TX 78750
(512) 258-7278

Notes on the trail: Do not even think about parking at the Camp Craft Road trailhead and riding from there. The residents of that area take a real dim view of people parking in front of their houses, since there is nothing but a gate and sign to mark the trailhead.

RIDE 21 *EMMA LONG PARK TRAIL*

Please do not miss Emma Long when you come to Austin. You would be making a big mistake. This place is way too good to be left to the grip-twisting-throttle-jocks. Way too fun.

I am talking about an Austin city park with a four-and-one-half-mile loop of rocky, technical single-track, often used for organized mountain bike and motorcycle racing. Though the trail is not extremely difficult, you should expect to work up a pretty good sweat, because it is demanding. There are even a few places where you will have to walk. Emma Long will definitely keep you awake as it snakes through the cedar trees and swoops up and down the sides of the hills. You will encounter ledges that drop one or two feet, and if you are unsuspended you might want to carry an extra front wheel or two. You will find lots of loose rocky conditions and several spots that could be

RIDE 21 *EMMA LONG PARK TRAIL*

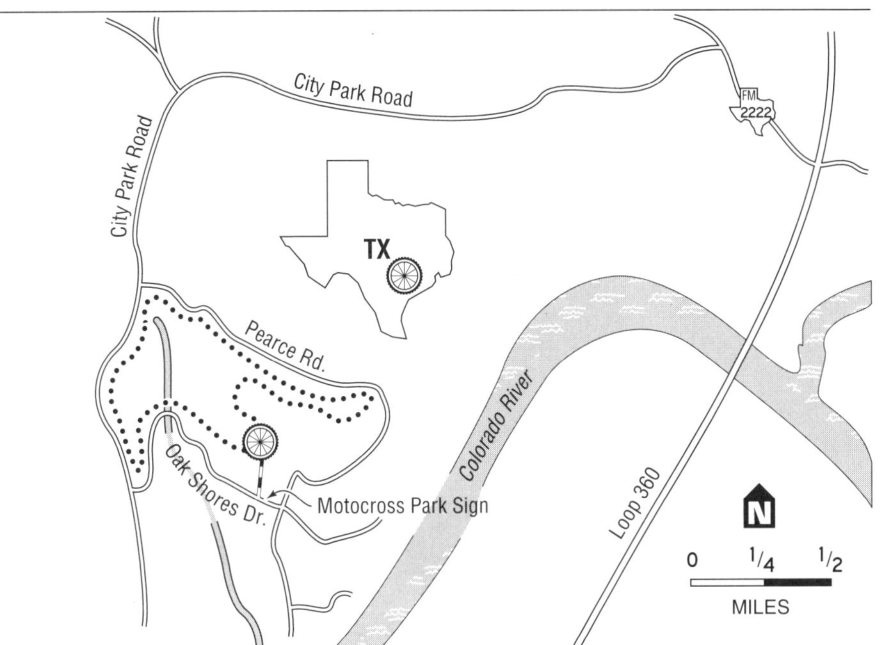

concealing a certain Mister Bustyerass. As you circulate clockwise, you will be guided by arrows and mileage markers every one-half mile.

Ahhh, I love the smell of castor-bean-oil motorcycle exhaust in the morning; it smells like victory. Get on your bikes and ride.

General location: Emma Long Metropolitan Park is located in far west Austin, near Farm to Market 2222 and Loop #360.

Elevation change: The lowest point in the park is near 620´, and the highest pushes 840´, so there is potentially 200´ of vertical work as you make a lap. You will find that the trail covers at least 150´ of that, the higher sections to the west and the lower back east.

Season: Unless there is an event that prevents you from doing laps, this park is open year-round.

Services: There is a litter barrel at the trailhead parking lot. If you require anything else, you will have to load up before you head out. The nearest pay phone is back toward town on FM 2222. There are closer bike shops, but I have listed my pals at Bicycle Sport Shop as a source for information on this park.

Hazards: There are at least a dozen ways to get maimed/mortally wounded/ killed while riding here. The loose trail conditions and steep terrain combined

Emma Long Park is a good place for front suspension and big air.

with the short line of sight while approaching many or most of the turns offers you a multitude of mangling methods. There are plenty of sharp-ended tree limbs along the trail—certain eye-pokers. I would not faint if I saw a snake out here, especially early in the year. There is an archery range nearby, but it is across the paved road, so don't stray far off the trail. The normal rider follows the arrows that lead you clockwise, but how many normal mountain bikers do you know? 'Nuff said.

Rescue index: I saw something here that I have never seen at another trail—perhaps it's because this is a motorcycle park—and that was signs for Emergency Medical Services (EMS) entrances. Several tracks into the trail area have alphabetic markers identifying each one. That means absolutely nothing if you are riding here alone and get stranded. The buddy system is the best guarantee of a clean rescue from this area. You are in a fairly remote location while riding here, and the nearest pay phone is miles away. If it was needed, a cellular phone would in no way be a waste of the few ounces one weighs.

Land status: This is a parcel of Austin Parks and Recreation Department land, specifically set aside to be used by motorcycles and other two-wheeled traffic, nothing else.

Maps: The only map I have located is the 7.5 minute quadrangle Austin West.

Finding the trail: From FM 2222 and Loop #360 in far west Austin, go west on FM 2222 to the traffic light at City Park Road. Turn left and follow City

Park Road for about 4 miles to Oak Shores Drive, then turn left and go about a mile to the sign for the motocross area. Pull all the way in and park in the large open area at the end of the road. At the west end of the large open area you will see the trailhead and where the trail heads off into the trees. Follow the trail until you pop out of the trees at the eastern end of the open area, near where you drove in. There are signs every one-half mile marking your distance and many arrows to keep you on track. There is supposedly a shorter loop than the "Main Loop," but all I ever saw were signs for the main one.

Sources of additional information:

Austin Parks and Recreation Department
200 South Lamar Boulevard
Austin, TX 78704
(512) 837-4500

Bicycle Sport Shop
1426 Toomey Road
Austin, TX 78704
(512) 477-3472

Bicycle Sport Shop
13376 North Highway #183
Suite #512
Austin, TX 78750
(512) 258-7278

Notes on the trail: Good trail. Fun, fast, tricky. One of the best in the area for most skill levels of riders. This place gets raced sometimes, and I can promise you that after three or four loops around Emma Long, you're gonna be cooked if you are doing anything like a race-pace. One interesting thing I saw while riding here the last time was some "splat" players. You know?—the paintball shooting game. I saw and heard them doing rapid-fire off in the trees. Crazy game. I like to shoot, but that just looks like too much fun. I think I read about combining "splat" with mountain biking; that could be good for a few laughs.

RIDE 22 *FOREST RIDGE PRESERVE TRAILS*

If you love miles of extremely difficult and treacherously intense trails, you will feel very satisfied when you ride here. Though this park has been declared a protected area by the local authorities, there has not been a lot of money or effort expended to clean up places along the lower regions where various morons dumped truckloads of trash before the land was secured.

RIDE 22 *FOREST RIDGE PRESERVE TRAILS*

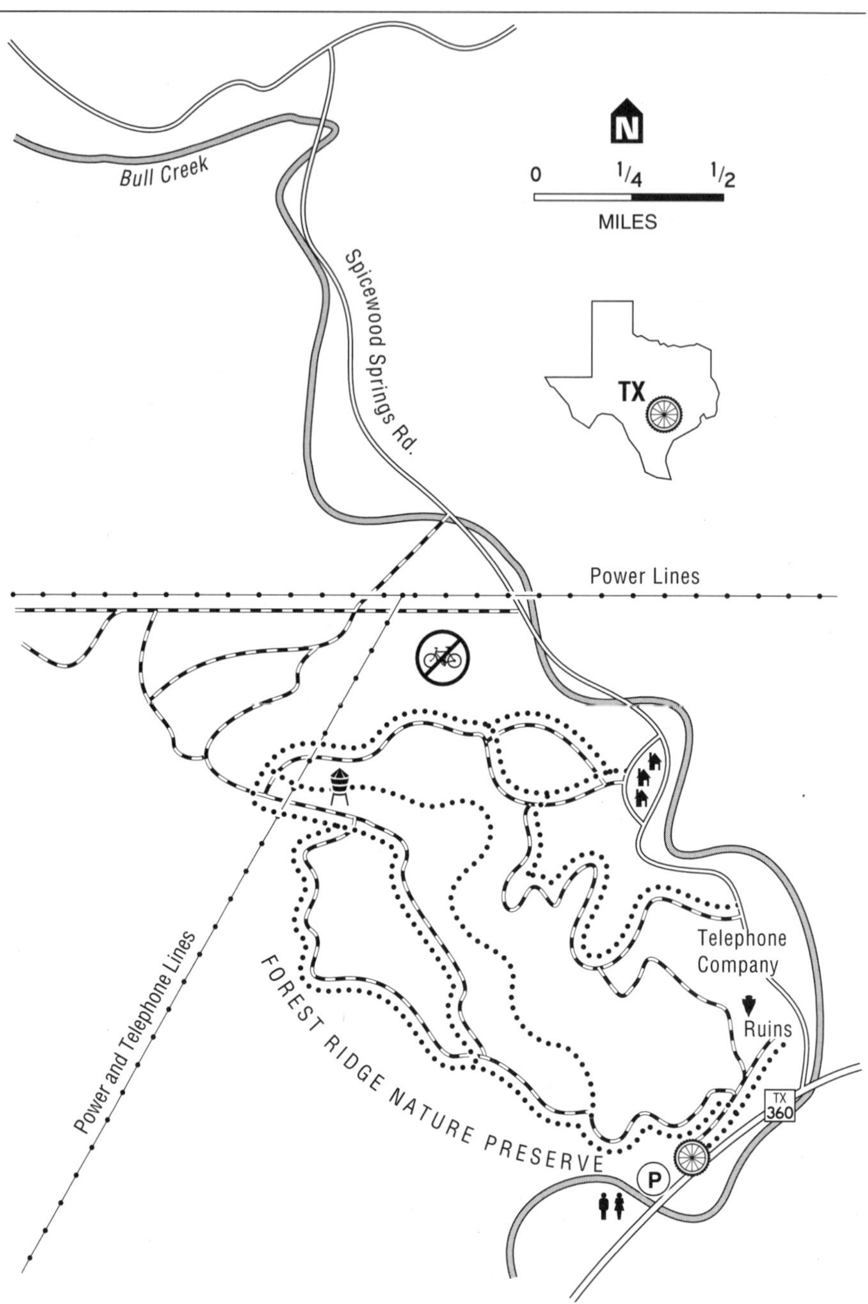

Note: *There are many more trails than shown. Ride only established trails and do not make new ones.*

This is another area park where mountain bikers are threatened with exclusion because of what the land managers perceive as destruction by abusive riders. One gal I talked to on the phone while chasing maps was very rude and felt certain that we are at work destroying as much as possible every time she turns her back. She left me with no doubt that she firmly believes mountain bikers should be removed from this park forever because of our uncontrolled behavior.

I am unconvinced that there is a lot of foundation for this belief, because to quote a local cyclist, "This place is bomb-proof." There has certainly been someone cutting trails here with no organization or care for the land, but I personally think it was motorcycles. I mean, look at this steep rocky terrain. These wide single-tracks appear to have been here for some time and are so thoroughly established that it would have taken a lot of mountain biking to have caused this damage. Still, we are blamed and are heavily scrutinized for our behavior in this park, so if a trail is signed as "Closed," please stay off of it and do not go cutting your own trails. There are plenty of miles of stuff already in place, so there is no need to get creative. Hell, you probably cannot ride half of what is there right now; I know I can't.

You can pretty easily ride ten miles around this park on the old jeep roads and single-track and not hit all of it. There is no way for me to provide you with an accurate map of all the trails without an aerial photograph. If you ride here—and you should if you are any kind of advanced-level rider—remember how delicate our privileges are. Show some respect. And don't run over any golden warblers; they are the reason this area is protected. Their habitat is being severely threatened by commercial and residential development in the Texas Hill Country. In my opinion, the heavy development in this area is the real danger, not cyclists. It wasn't cyclists who carried all this trash into the park. Somebody else has been messing around in here.

As you wind around the trails, you will be climbing toward the top of the main hill. From the higher reaches you will have some exceptional views of the surrounding area, and you may discover that you are mesmerized by the rugged beauty of the Texas Hill Country. This area IS Texas, and it is what Texans think of when they try to describe their state to people from elsewhere (i.e., foreigners).

General location: This trail is in northwest Austin, near Farm to Market 2222 and Loop #360.

Elevation change: Bull Creek lies around 550′ to 560′, and the highest point in the park probably exceeds 980′ above sea level. When you finally get to that large flat area on top of the hill, you will feel 400′ of climbing, I promise you.

Season: I know of nothing seasonal that will prevent you from enjoying this park any time of year. I probably would not recommend riding here in the wet, because this place is dangerous enough without being slippery. Wet weather would probably make it deadly.

As I recall, this rider goes OTB in about one second, courtesy of the trails at the Forest Ridge Preserve in Austin. He looks good to here though.

Services: There is a chemical toilet across the creek from the trailhead parking, but the nearest real rest rooms are over at Bull Creek Park, south of the trailhead at Loop #360 and Lakewood Drive. There is water at the same location. The nearest pay phone I am aware of is north of the trailhead and across Loop #360 at Old Spicewood Springs Road and Adirondack Court.

Hazards: Unless you ride with someone who knows the way around, you will spend most of your time here lost, with no idea of your exact coordinates. There is such a labyrinth of single- and double-track that getting lost is normal behavior for new visitors to Forest Ridge. Until you get your bearings and learn most of the trail, I would recommend carrying everything you will need to survive for several hours each time you ride here. Of course, it wouldn't kill you to ask someone for directions if you need them. Or to ask someone to show you around as you prepare to ride. Check out the other riders in the parking lot. Be friendly; it pays.

I might caution you that though there is no hunting season in this park, there are likely several bird-watching seasons every year, and I would strongly recommend not running over any hikers or critters. Anyone on foot could potentially be the president of the Sierra Club, and making them mad should be avoided like the plague.

The condition of the trail is enough to guarantee a battle between your riding skills and Mister Bustyerass. He's gonna win unless you are good, very good. Ride here like it might be your last, and maybe it won't. Ride here like you mean it.

Rescue index: The rescue index here is not good. As Murphy's Law will show, you always get hurt or stranded at the farthest point possible from where you parked. That would put you in some pretty rough terrain, possibly inaccessible to anything but helicopter or pedestrian rescuers.

Land status: The Austin Parks and Recreation Department is going to keep this place just like it is or better for a long time. Hopefully forever.

Maps: Resort to your source for quads and get Jollyville. I know of no other maps.

Finding the trail: Go north on Loop #360 from where it meets FM 2222 for about 1.5 miles, and you will cross Bull Creek. A pair of turns to the left here form sort of a frontage road and lead down to a water crossing on Bull Creek, almost under Loop #360. The parking areas for Forest Ridge and the Bull Creek Greenbelt are here on either side of the creek. As you pull into the northern parking area, you will see a gravel road that appears to parallel Loop #360 for a short distance. This is the start of the trail, and a sign and arrow here indicate the direction for bicycles to travel. Follow the road until you see an interesting branch. Investigate. Follow that until you find another interesting diversion. Ride that until you are tired and/or totally lost. Try to find your way back. Have fun.

Just remember that you have the creek on your southern boundary, Loop #360 to the east, Spicewood Springs Road to the north, and several miles of open country and rugged terrain between you and anything to the west. If you reach some big power lines, you are about 2 miles (as the crow flies) from the parking area. There is a large water tank on a high spot west of the parking area, and this marks the western end of Forest Ridge Park. There are more trails beyond this, but they are of questionable legitimacy. Do not ride them.

Sources of additional information:

Austin Parks and Recreation Department
200 South Lamar Boulevard
Austin, TX 78704
(512) 327-5437

Bicycle Sport Shop
1426 Toomey Road
Austin, TX 78704
(512) 477-3472

Bicycle Sport Shop
13376 North Highway #183
Suite #512
Austin, TX 78750
(512) 258-7278

Notes on the trail: Adjacent to the preserve area is the Bull Creek Greenbelt, another Austin park. There is a 4-mile trail along Bull Creek that you might be interested in exploring. It is mostly flat and rocky single-track, though the eastern reaches have a couple of significant double-track climbs that reach up toward the houses visible along the ridges in the distance. A worthy trail, and it will expose you to some excellent swimming holes along the creek. Check it out.

RIDE 23 *OLD HOMESTEAD TRAIL*

McKinney Falls State Park is a really cool place. There are two sets of falls along Onion Creek with *muy bueno* swimming holes. Ask the ranger for information on swimming and fishing in the park. For you mountain bikers, there is an easy single-track loop winding around the mesquite trees for about four miles. The trail is almost all hard-packed dirt, smooth and enjoyably fast.

The Old Homestead Trail has only minor technical challenges, almost no climbing, few strenuous sections, and little danger. There is an "up-side," however. Near the trailhead are the ruins of the old McKinney homestead (hence the trail's name) and gristmill, as well as the lower falls and a nice swimming spot. The homestead was constructed from limestone blocks hewn by hand. Take a close look at these and gain respect for what our forefathers were capable of doing using only hand tools. Pretty impressive.

Do not be surprised if you see several deer here; they will just about knock you down as they bound around among the trees. Watch out for Bambi and Company.

General location: McKinney Falls State Park is located in far southeast Austin, a few miles east of Interstate 35.
Elevation change: The falls on Onion Creek are at about 480′, and the highest point on the trail is probably 560′ above sea level. The trail seems much flatter, and most of it is pretty level.
Season: If muddy, most of this trail would probably not be usable, but unless significant rain has fallen recently you will find nothing seasonal to keep you off the single-track. If in doubt, call ahead. Sometimes there are events in state parks, and sometimes these are on the trails. They probably won't tell you not to ride, but it might be a little crowded.
Services: The headquarters has a soft drink machine, pay phone, water, and rest rooms. Any other supplies you need should be acquired from one of the convenience stores you will pass on your way to the park.
Hazards: Hikers on the trail might be considered an obstacle, but most of the year the visibility is good and you will have a respectable line of sight. This

RIDE 23 *OLD HOMESTEAD TRAIL*

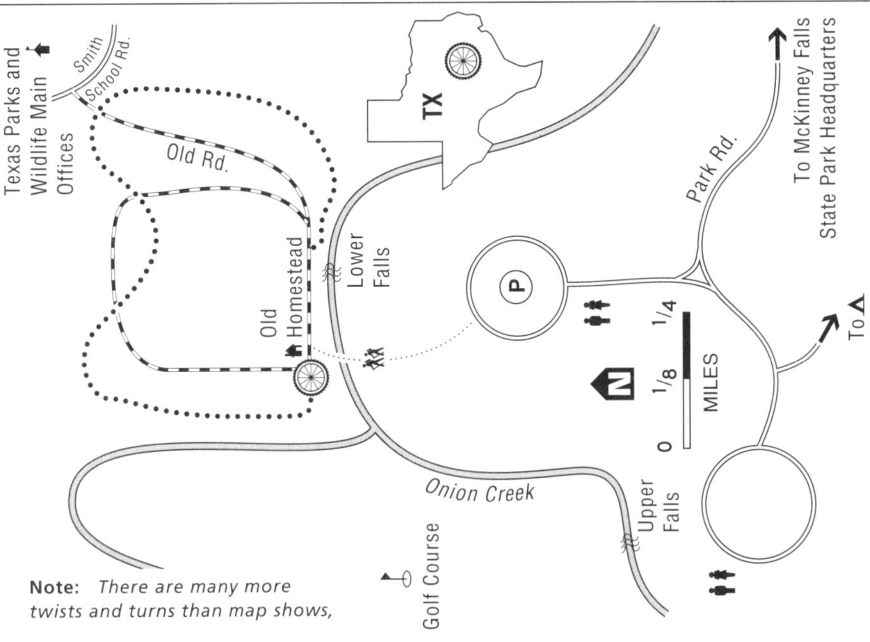

trail is mostly mild, but there are a few fairly technical sections. These swoop through the trees, and the danger of connecting with a tree at high speed is always one to be aware of. Many of the plants along the way have ways of getting your attention. The mesquite and prickly pear cactus will give you a less-than-warm welcome if you forget they are near.

Rescue index: You have a good chance of getting saved if you get in trouble here. It is a popular trail, and I am sure the Texas Parks and Wildlife Department will do anything they can to help you if you need saving, given that the trail runs right by their big headquarters complex.

Land status: Another gem of a park brought to you by those fine folks at the Texas Parks and Wildlife Department. Hurrah!

Maps: Even the ranger does not have maps of this trail. I think mine is pretty good; I drew it from memory. The quad for this trail is Montopolis.

Finding the trail: From I-35, exit onto East William Cannon Drive and proceed east. Cannon will gradually shrink until there is nothing but a two-lane country road. Getting to the park will be much easier someday, once the city has built Cannon all the way out to Scenic Loop Road, but for now you have to turn right off Cannon onto Running Water Drive. Turn and follow Running Water Drive to Bluff Springs Road and turn left. Follow Bluff

Springs Road to where the road forks. Bluff Springs Road goes to the left. Follow it and continue until you pass where Bluff Springs Road goes to the right. You will go straight on what is now Scenic Loop Road until you see the entrance for the McKinney Falls State Park on the left.

I know it is complicated; also, the city is presently building some new roads through this area, so all this may have changed by the time you head over here to ride. Call the park and ask for a current set of directions if this sounds confusing to you. It was to me.

Once you have reached the park, you may proceed to the picnic area near the lower falls. The old homestead and trailhead are just across Onion Creek from the parking circle at the end of the road into the picnic area. Start riding at the trailhead sign and follow the loop in a clockwise direction. The trail will wind all the way around, and you will find yourself near the TPWD headquarters complex and a gravel road. If you turn right on the gravel, it will lead you back to the trailhead. Or you can continue on the single-track and enter the technical sections of the trail. This winds around and dumps you at the old gristmill, near the trailhead and in sight of the falls. Have fun.

Sources of additional information:

Park Superintendent
McKinney Falls State Park
7102 Scenic Loop Road
Austin, TX 78744
(512) 243-1643

Texas Parks and Wildlife Department
4200 Smith School Road
Austin, TX 78744-3291
(800) 792-1112 for information only

TPWD Reservation Center
P.O. Box 17488
Austin, TX 78760-7488
(512) 389-8900 for reservations only

Bicycle Sport Shop
1426 Toomey Road
Austin, TX 78704
(512) 477-3472

Bicycle Sport Shop
13376 North Highway #183
Suite #512
Austin, TX 78750
(512) 258-7278

The Old Homestead Trail at McKinney Falls is a leisurely place to ride. Of course you have to make yourself keep going past the falls to get to the trail, and that is not always easy on a hot afternoon. I have seen riders make it this far only to drop their bike by those trees and dive in, all thoughts of mountain biking erased by cool water.

Notes on the trail: Notice the address for the Texas Parks and Wildlife headquarters. When you are at the northernmost reaches of the trail, you can toss a rock and hit these buildings, if you desire. Tempting, I know, but save your ammo. Just don't try to park over by the headquarters to gain access to the trail, even if personnel at McKinney Falls State Park recommend it; the rangers will run you off. I found out the hard way.

I camped here, and shortly before dawn I kept waking up to weird loudspeaker sounds. It sounded like they were calling people's names. I was freaking out until I finally made out part of a message about somebody's tee-time. There is a golf course next door to the park. Whew—I thought it was UFOs or something.

RIDE 24 *BLUFF CREEK RANCH TRAIL*

Man oh man, I love it here. This place is pure fun in the form of eight miles of custom mountain biking single-track that winds around and around in the general area of a buddy of mine's ranch. This is a pay-per-use facility and belongs to "the Bike Doc," a mountain biking doctor named Paul Nolan.

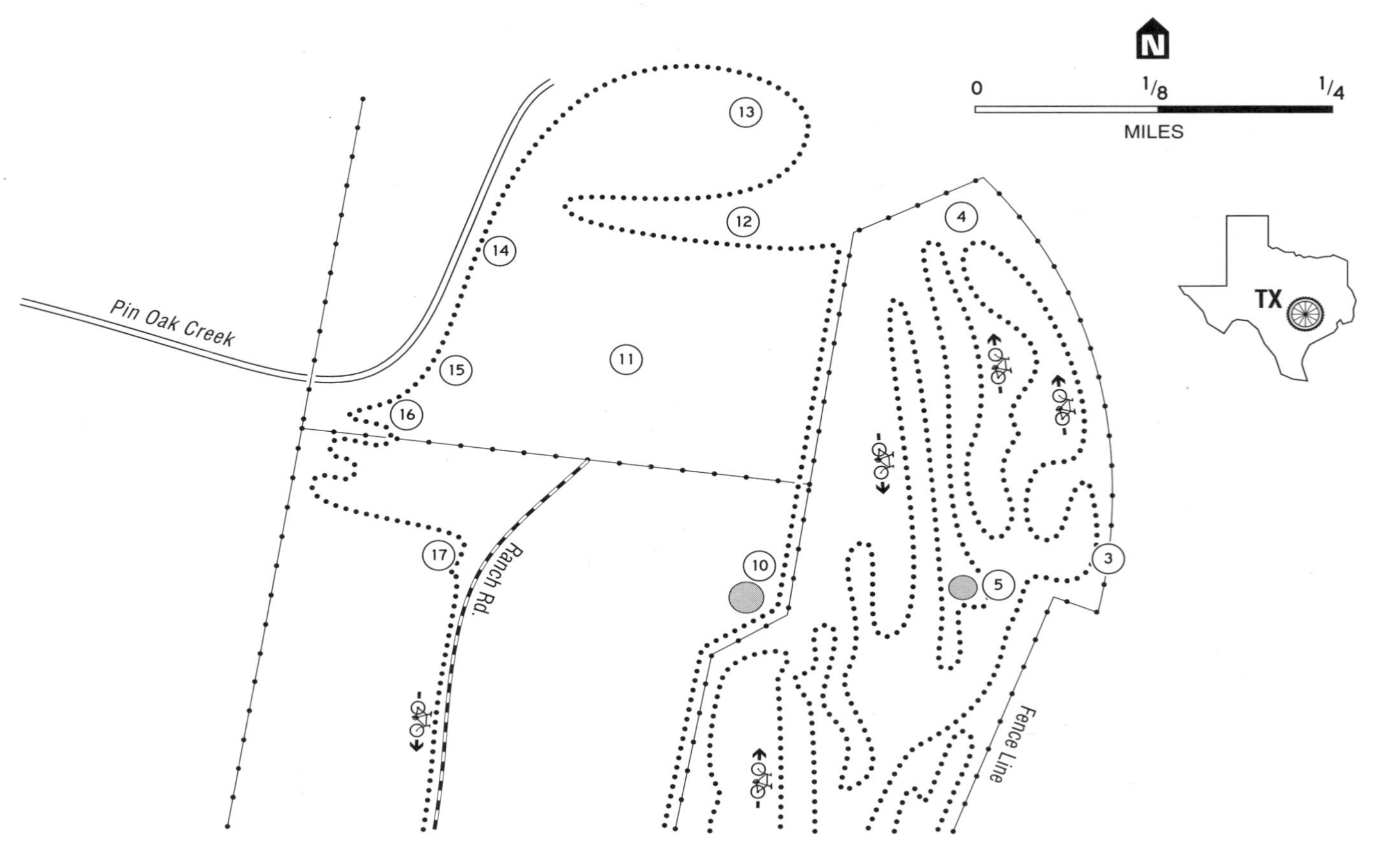
N
0
1/8
1/4
MILES
TX
Pin Oak Creek
Ranch Rd.
Fence Line
3
4
5
10
11
12
13
14
15
16
17

Key to numbered features

1. Entry Point
2. Twin Pines
3. Oh Shit!
4. Limestone Ridge
5. Billy Pond
6. Spaghetti Bends
7. Side Winder
8. Robert's Railing
9. Cattle Chute
10. Medack Tank
11. Outback
12. Gas Pass
13. Hay Meadow
14. Phew View
15. The Pass
16. The Plateau
17. Hanging Trees
18. Roller Coasters
19. Turkey Tank
20. The Bidet
21. The Barn
22. Race Start
23. Deer Park
24. Green Gate

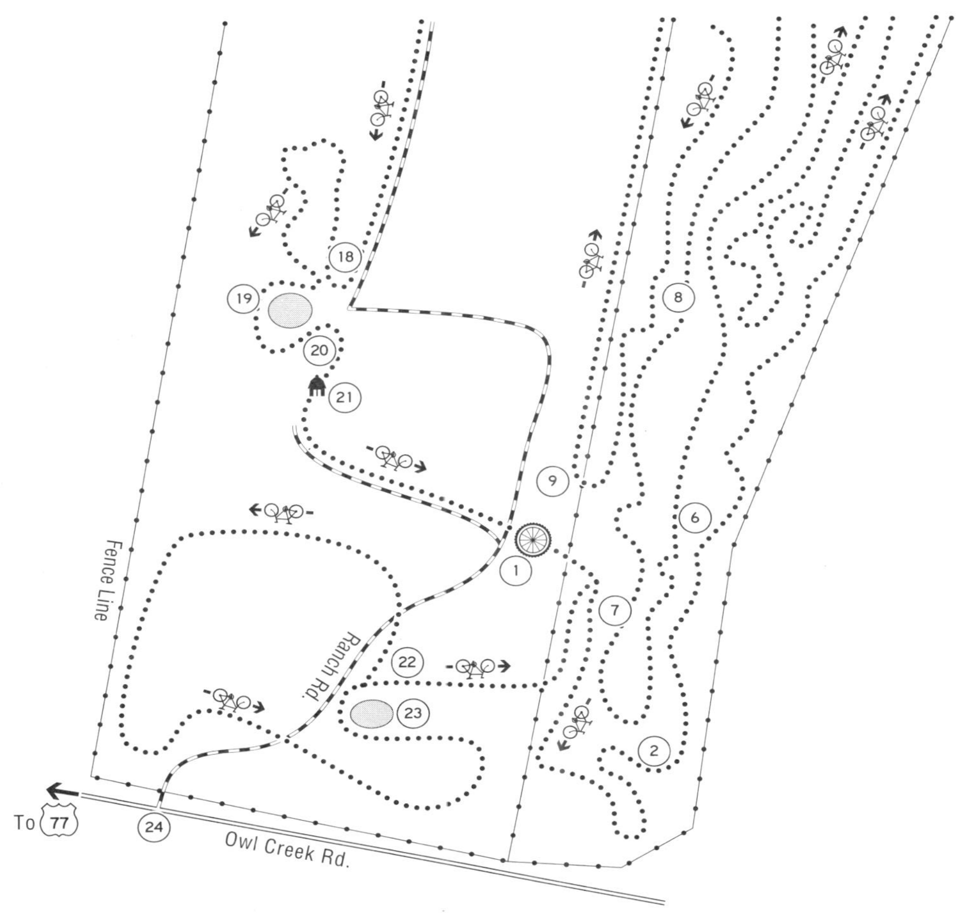

Nothing here is real tough. I have heard several racers I know call this an easy course, and I would be hard-pressed to disagree. It's not real technical, no hard climbs and nothing that cannot be done. But it is tight and it is sandy and it is fast. Very fast.

The way I met the Bike Doc is a pretty good story. I am driving along Old Maverick Road in Big Bend National Park, and way up ahead I see some bikes, two guys. It is Dr. Paul and a pal of his, just oozing along enjoying the downhill run to Santa Elena Canyon, fighting the sand and washboards. It was one of those weird things where you think you are seeing bikes ahead but it is like a Twilight Zone episode or something. I had just run out of film, so I was bumming heavily that I could not snap a picture of them, the first bikes with clipless pedals I had seen in a week that seemed to last a month.

The Bike Doc's trail is sandy and smooth most of the way, but there are a few loose rocks on one or two of the corners. Watch yourself here, because you can go hard, and the ground will hold your tires really well for a place so loose, but you can wash those tires out if you lean it too hard on some of the turns. Still, you can fly through here and carry two-wheel drifts through the turns if you have the *cojones*. Just remember: The short descents usually lead to a tight corner or fast sweeper-type curve. There is only one drop that really deserves to be called a downhill—a place called Pass Gas Pass. You scream down some tight single-track at the highest speed your nerve will allow. This place will keep you hopping, and you WILL have a blast, guaranteed. We have ways of making it so. Just let the bike do its thing and hold on when you try to nail one of the sweepers. It will make you feel just like the guys on the Formula One motorcycles, but don't drag your knee.

You can camp here, let the kids fish in one of the tanks, and enjoy the woods, but you can't get in without your mountain bike. The Bluff Creek Ranch doesn't take non–mountain biking guests, and neither do the bass in the tanks. Don't leave home without it.

The trail here is usually on the menu for the Texas State Mountain Bike Championships Series, and this race always draws several hundred mountain bikers. Check it out sometime; the folks around here are really good people. And you already know how I feel about Central Texas.

General location: The Bluff Creek Ranch is located about 9 miles south of Giddings and just north of Warda. This is about 60 miles east of Austin and about 110 miles west of Houston.

Elevation change: The land here has no great amount of relief. The lowest point is around 320´ above sea level, and the highest (near the entrance to the ranch) is up to about 370´. Fifty feet of variation definitely sounds about right, as my legs recall.

Season: You would be well advised to call ahead and check the conditions if there has been rain in the area. That is the only time the trails are closed.

The Bluff Creek Ranch is home to a mountain biker's mountain bike trail. Literally. Thanks Bike Doc, see you at the races.

Services: Dr. Paul will probably let you have a drink of water if your tongue is hanging out, but he can't offer you much more. Grab what you need in Giddings or Warda before heading to the ranch. There are no pay phones or Coke machines. There is a pretty good bike shop nearby, however. Bicycle Country in Giddings belongs to a pal of mine named Myron Brown, a good guy and bearded redhead.

Hazards: The tires on your bike will hold the ground fairly well here for such a sandy place. Nevertheless, you will find many opportunities to lose it in one of the short braking zones and slide off the trail into the cedar trees or a creek bed. Try and scan the trail as far ahead as possible, especially around all the corners, and be ready. I noticed several sharp turns that have a dozen or so sabers, in the form of cedar trees that have had limbs trimmed, poised on the outside apex. The trimmer failed to take them all the way back to the trunk to prevent this danger, so watch out.

Pass Gas Pass is another place to be careful. It starts as a steep drop off the backside of a hill, and about every 5 feet there is a step. I have never stopped to look, but I think they are water bars and not roots. Makes a fast descent, a scary, bumpy, fast descent. About halfway down it jukes to the right a little, and then the bottom has a hard right turn. Keep a finger or three on the brake levers, or have your life insurance premiums current.

Also watch out for the many small bridges that lie in the bottom of the creek beds you fly into. They are one-for-one; every creek has a bridge. Some are slightly to one side or the other of the line, and some have almost diagonal approaches from the trail. You may need to enter one edge of a bridge but exit another, requiring a diagonal run across the thing. Be careful.

Rescue index: Bluff Creek Ranch has one of the higher rescue ratings of any trail around, simply because of how the trail continuously wanders back up by the main barn at the ranch and then away into the trees. If you need to escape, stay on the trail until you reach the high pasture and can see the barn. If there are many riders around you during your playtime on the trail, you will notice them through the trees again and again, because the trail often passes near itself. This might allow you to skip some sections and make a faster trip to the parking area.

Land status: This is private land and can be used only with permission from the owners, which is easy to obtain if you display the secret sign (a mountain bike strapped to your car). Pay the attendant ($6 in 1994) and go have fun.

Maps: Sorry, not a chance. I have done the best I can with topographical maps of the area to give you a vague idea of where the trails run, but they are only an approximation and should not be considered perfectly accurate.

Finding the trail: From Giddings go south about 9 miles on US 77 to Warda. Just before you reach Warda there will be a sign for Owl Creek Road. Turn left (east) and follow Owl Creek Road about one-half mile to the green gate on the left (north) side of the road. Pull in and park at the top of the hill. Just past the first cattle guard, turn right over the mini-cattle guard/bike crossing and dive into the trees. Rotation is counterclockwise, and you will end up on the opposite side of the field, behind the barn.

Sources of additional information:

Bluff Creek Ranch
Paul or Susan Nolan
Owl Creek Road, Box 110
Warda, TX 78960
(409) 242-5894

Bicycle Country
1199 East Austin (US 290)
Giddings, TX 78942
(409) 542-0964

Giddings Area Bicycle Association
(409) 542-0964

Notes on the trail: Dr. Nolan will let you ride here just about anytime, but if you have far to drive, you might want to call ahead and check the conditions. Don't blame me if you drive 200 miles and then find out it rained like crazy the night before and the place is a marsh. There are two or three small tanks that harbor a reasonable selection of game fish, but check with the ranch before loading your fishing rod on your bike and starting out. They might prefer for you to use one over another or something. I don't fish anymore; I don't have the patience for it.

RIDE 25 *ROCKY HILL RANCH TRAILS*

The last time I went out to visit the fine folks at the Rocky Hill Ranch, one of the state championship races had just been held there the month before. Many of the markers for the race loop were still in place. Plus, the map I was offered described a 13-mile loop that corresponded to what was laid out for the race. For those reasons, the description that follows mirrors this configuration. There are, however, several more miles of riding available here, most of it is double-track. If what you find marked does not satisfy, ask at the café what other single-tracks are open to bikes.

The ranch is located in the Lost Pines section of the state on over 1,200 acres of prime terrain. The riding here is some of the most fun you can have with such minimal exposure to poison ivy. About half of what you will ride here is sandy single-track with some stretches of loose rock. The other half is double-track with the same surface.

Nothing here is extremely hard or dangerous, but there are some invigorating climbs and some challenging twisty-turnies among the trees. I would say that all of the beginner and intermediate sections can be ridden by most riders, but some walking may be necessary for those who are beginners or not heavily conditioned. Plus, there are one or two gullies in the expert sections that I always have to walk; they are just too steep and too sudden. Each section is shown on maps available at the café, and each is rated according to difficulty. Their estimations are realistic; the easy parts are mostly double-track, and if you try the expert-level stuff and then change your mind, you can take the dirt road instead of the single-track.

The trail is a winding loop that doubles back upon itself repeatedly and crosses several roads that could be used as bailouts to speed your return to the parking area. In many places the trail snakes through a mile or so of the forest and then returns you to one of the roads only a few hundred feet from where you passed by earlier. Some of the single-track is very tight, and in a few places the trail almost disappears as it passes over a bed of seemingly undisturbed pine needles. It is fast and loose and can be a lot of fun, if you can avoid contact with trees or the ground.

As you enter the grounds, you will park near the café and pay the nice man to let you ride here. In 1994 the rate was $5.50, about the same price as going

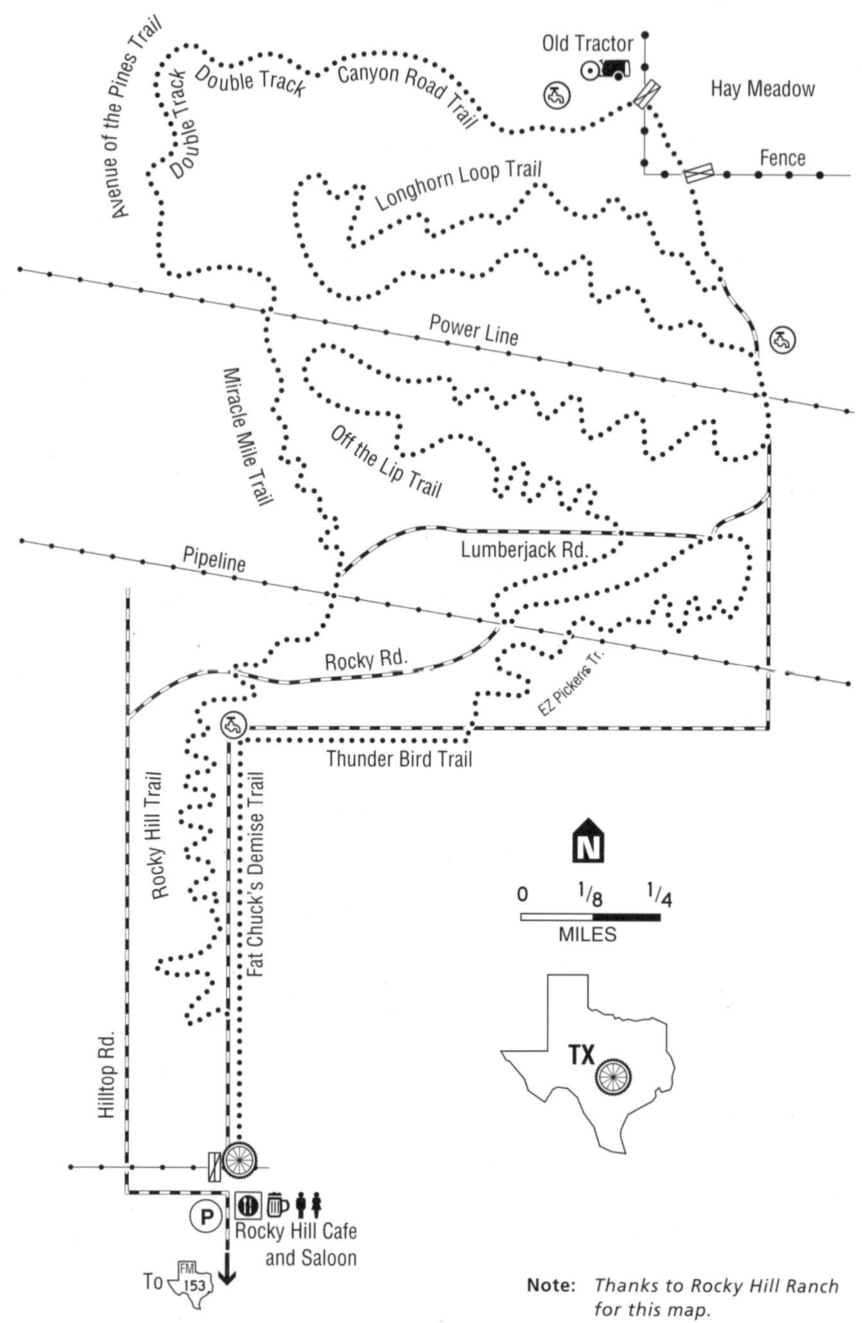

Note: *Thanks to Rocky Hill Ranch for this map.*

out to see a movie. From the café you begin your assault on the ranch by creeping up the first set of hills, marked on maps as "Fat Chuck's Demise." The guys who built this brought a friend out here once, telling him how much fun mountain biking is. He quit on the first set of hills—hence the name. Each section of the trail has a colorful name, and you will find them all well marked. At three spots along the way you will find water jugs to refill your bottles, and these water stations make nice spots to lounge awhile and take in the scenery. Maybe snap a few shots of your bike, like I always do.

There is allegedly a field here where Confederate troops camped and trained for the War for Southern Independence, and Harrison's Waterhole on Gravelly Creek was a longtime Indian camp and watering spot for early wagon trains traversing this part of Texas. The brochure for the ranch also says they can give you information on many road rides that loop through the area, so take your skinny tires if you have an inclination. Another interesting story says that one of the trails, Fofenique, is named for an Indian tribe that formerly inhabited this area. These folks shot a small round cactus out of slingshots to try and convince early settlers to keep moving. The cactus nearly went extinct (there were a lot of settlers) but has undergone something of a resurgence here on the ranch. Ask at the café if they can show you a specimen of said cactus.

When your day is done, stop by the café and visit with Grey and the rest of the folks who hang around here. There are some real salts among the locals, and they have some interesting junk hanging on the walls. Try one of their world-famous hamburgers and a Shiner Bock beer; you won't be disappointed. If you play darts, bring yours and pitch a few at the board. Have fun and enjoy the fine Texas hospitality and excellent Texas Hill Country single-track.

General location: The ranch is just outside of Smithville, which is about 40 miles east of Austin and around 120 miles west of Houston.

Elevation change: The highest spot on the ranch is over 500′ above sea level, and the lowest is down to nearly 300′, so you have quite a bit of relief here. Plus, you are up and down so much that cumulatively you are going to crank out way more than 200′ of variation. There is some ascending and descending to be done here.

Season: This is another typical year-round trail. The only constraints might be that days of heavy rain will likely make much of it slippery. Since much of the single-track is sandy or gravelly, it drains well and should be usable within a day or so of heavy rain. Call and ask for trail conditions if there is any doubt.

Services: Water and chemical toilets are available in the café area, but if you need any supplies you had best stop in Smithville before heading out to the ranch. Buescher State Park is only a couple of miles shy of the ranch (you go right by it on Farm to Market 153), and the camping there may be more inviting because they can offer showers and all the normal facilities of a state park. There are usually at least three water stops at locations shown on the maps, so there is no need to carry a whole lot in with you. Again, ask at the café.

Some places are flatter than others at the Rocky Hill Ranch. Some places aren't. Some places are downright hilly.

Hazards: Ha ha ha. Mister Bustyerass and many of his cousins live on the Rocky Hill Ranch, and they are especially fond of city boys and girls who like speed. When he finds you, he will make you pay. All of the loose rocks and inclined surfaces conspire to add to their collections of human skin, seeking a donation from each visitor. If a section of trail looks dangerous to you, then pay attention, because you are starting to understand. If they rate a trail here as "Expert," you had better believe it will tax your skills.
Rescue index: There is a phone in the café, so if you have an emergency, your only hope is to make it back to the entrance area—which could be a real challenge, since getting stranded or injured at the farthest part of the course would put you about 6 or 7 miles from help. It would be very easy to bail out and ride Rocky Road back from the power line or pipeline all the way to the café, but it would still be several miles.
Land status: This is all private land, so respect the wishes of the owners. And enjoy coming here to ride for years.
Maps: The nice folks at the café will give you a very good map for free. Just ask.
Finding the trail: About 1 mile north of Smithville, FM 153 will split from TX 71 and go east. Follow FM 153 about 3 miles, and on the north side of the road you will see the main gate for the ranch. It is notable because of a bent bicycle hanging from the center section. This is it. I have been told that there are nearly 20 miles of trail possibilities on the ranch, and I am nowhere near familiar enough with all of it to be your guide. Explore, take a side trail,

look around. Each trail is marked for identification where it splits from another, and you are on private property with only one or two gates to cross, so you can only get so lost. Along the way you might find a spot or two you want to run through again and again, and this is pretty easy, since they are nearly all interconnected with a gravel road, a pipeline, or a power line. This makes it easy to double back or take a shortcut out of the trail area.

Sources of additional information:

Rocky Hill Ranch
P.O. Box 655
Smithville, TX 78957
(512) 237-3112

Bicycle Sport Shop
1426 Toomey Road
Austin, TX 78704
(512) 477-3472

Bicycle Sport Shop
13376 North Highway #183
Suite #512
Austin, TX 78750
(512) 258-7278

Notes on the trail: The ranch is only open Thursday through Sunday, 9 A.M. to sunset. Also, there is a fee for using the trails here, so come prepared to pay. They do not have an ATM machine or take checks. The café is a good place to eat and hang out, so bring a little extra cash and hang out for awhile after your ride. The people there are typical down-home Texas types, so spend some time visiting. Camping is allowed on the property, but it is all of the primitive variety, so bring your tent and plenty of mosquito repellent. If you come to spots where letting the gate down is necessary to get to the next trail, PLEASE PLEASE PLEASE be sure to close it after you are through so none of the cows get out. The owner loves us and wants to improve the ranch steadily to make it more attractive to mountain bikers. There is a slalom course planned, as well as cabins and bike rentals. And the best part is, NO MOTORCYCLES OR HORSES ARE ALLOWED!

RIDE 26 *HILL COUNTRY RIFLE RANGE TRAIL*

Richard is the guy who runs the place. He usually has a holstered weapon at his side. He has some dogs hanging around that almost look like they might bite. You may hear automatic weapons fire while you ride here. The terrain is evil. The indigenous flora are not friendly. It sounds like a terrific place to ride, huh?

RIDE 26 *HILL COUNTRY RIFLE RANGE TRAIL*

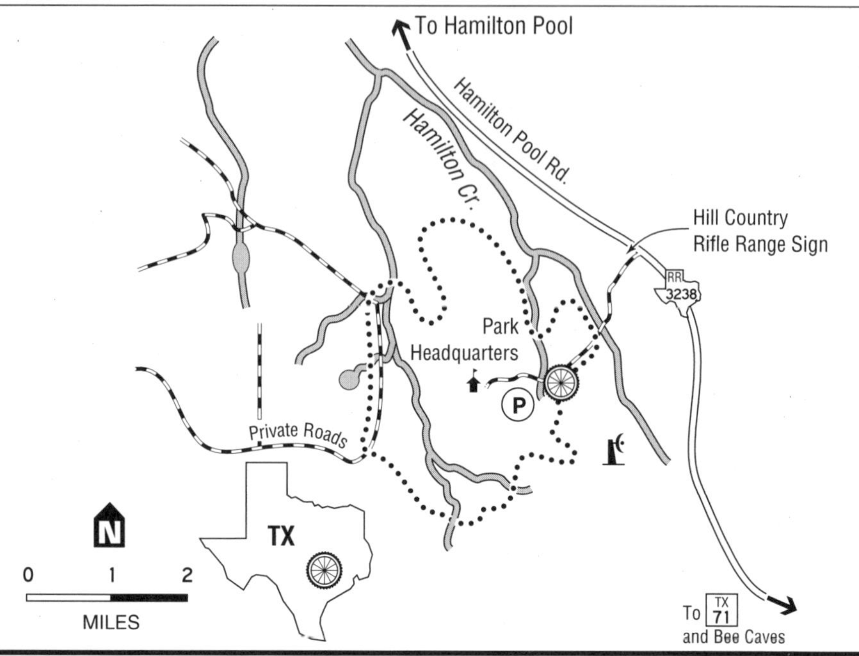

As you drive in along the washboard gravel road, you will pass a medley of small buildings, trailers, and vehicles. You will know you are in the country, and you will see how rugged the Texas Hill Country is. Then you will pass all the firing ranges. There are normal "sight-in-your-deer-rifle" ranges, plus some silhouette pistol ranges for honing your combat skills. There are some serious folks in this part of the country, and they take their shooting very seriously indeed.

That said, I will now give you reason to relax a little, but not too much. The trails here are hard, technical, rocky, steep, and dangerously intense. The gravel double-track that connects them into a seven-mile loop is mostly gentle, compared to the rest of the ranch. Area mountain bikers like riding here. They do not mind paying the $5 Richard will ask, because mostly they are just glad to have a place to ride their bikes and exercise their skills where they won't get hassled.

When you ride at the Hill Country Rifle Range, you will often hear people practicing with weapons. If guns make you nervous, don't go. The loop wanders all over Richard's ranch and carries you past several deer stands and across a creek with a fairly nice swimming hole (sometimes). It goes by a camp that I guess is either some cowboy or deer hunting stuff. The cedar trees may hide a few cattle at times, and I suspect you will see signs of their existence. In short, the Hill Country Rifle Range will be a ride like no other and one you will never forget. Especially if you get Richard started talking about survivalism.

General location: About half an hour west of Austin, on the way to the town of Bee Caves.
Elevation change: The highest point you reach along the trail is about 1,300′ above sea level, and the lowest is down near 1,000′.
Season: Don't even joke about riding here during deer season; the worst thing you could do is spook some hunter's eight-pointer. Other than hunts, the range is operated by a private individual, so days and hours of operation may vary. Call ahead and save yourself a wasted drive.
Services: There is a soft drink machine, and if you are not afraid of the dogs you can get a drink from the hydrant near the "office" building. Anything else you might need, including but not limited to awesome barbecue, should be acquired along the way before you turn off Bee Caves Road and head toward the range. In the event of an emergency, Richard has a phone, but the nearest pay phone is at a convenience store by the turn from Bee Caves Road.
Hazards: The trail alone is hazardous enough, in typical Texas Hill Country fashion. The surface is loose rock and gravel in many places, very steep and technical, and the location is fairly remote. There may be cattle running loose on this land; don't mess with them. There are snakes in this part of the world; leave them alone, too. The normal "vicious plant warning" is in full effect here.
Rescue index: You will be rescued here if you crack up, but it could take several hours before someone finds you and drags your body to the road. This is not a real popular trail—I mean, it is ridden, but nothing like every day. If your vehicle is still sitting in the mountain bike parking area at the end of the day, Richard will have to come find you, so at least the buzzards won't get a shot at you.
Land status: The Hill Country Rifle Range is all located on private ranch land, therefore you are subject to the code of the hills according to Richard Sievers, the owner.
Maps: Nonexistent. The quad for this area is Shingle Hills.
Finding the trail: Go west from Loop #360 on Bee Caves Road (Farm to Market 2244). Follow Bee Caves Road about 8 miles, until it ends at TX 71, and turn right onto TX 71. Follow this highway about 2 miles west, until you see signs for Ranch Road 3238 (Hamilton's Pool Road), and turn left (south). Follow RR 3238 for about 9 miles, until you see the entrance for the Hill Country Rifle Range at Rifle Range Road. Follow this gravel road until it ends right in front of the range office building. Pay the nice man and he will show you where the trailhead is and where he asks mountain bikers to park. Follow the single- and double-track marked with yellow flagging tape around

Welcome to the Hill Country Rifle Range. Home of big dogs, automatic weapons fire, single-track, and more.

the ranch until you are back at the gravel road you entered the property on. This will be about half a mile past the cowboy camp and is the only wide and well-traveled active road you will cross. Turn right onto this road and follow it back to where you parked. Go home or to Hamilton's Pool.

Sources of additional information:

Hill Country Rifle Range
(512) 264-1693

Bicycle Sport Shop
1426 Toomey Road
Austin, TX 78704
(512) 477-3472

Bicycle Sport Shop
13376 North Highway #183
Suite #512
Austin, TX 78750
(512) 258-7278

Notes on the trail: This is another pay-per-use facility. A world-class swimming hole called Hamilton's Pool is nearby, about 3 miles past the range on RR 3238. Definitely try to visit that while you are in the area. As long as you are at the range, bring some ammo and some weapons and blast a few targets. Now if I can just figure out a way to combine guns and mountain biking, I will never leave the saddle. Maybe I need to find some of those splat players from Emma Long and form a team. Cool.

RIDE 27 *WOLF MOUNTAIN TRAIL*

Pedernales Falls State Park—such a beautiful place. I always loved this park. When I went to school in Austin, we used to skip class regularly to go hiking or swimming here. As far as state parks go, this place is really special.

Yes, I know how it is spelled, but the locals insist on pronouncing the name like "Perd-in-allis." The word *pedernales* means "flint rocks" in Spanish. So in Texas we have Fred and Wilma Pedernales instead of the more usual variety. People still find flint arrowheads along the river from time to time. I don't think the state takes too kindly to folks carrying off artifacts, so I am definitely not encouraging anything unsavory.

There used to be some beautiful swimming holes around the falls, but nowadays only the beach areas downstream of the falls are open. I think a record number of people drowned the year I went to college here, and the falls have been closed ever since. I remember a sign showing how many people had drowned year-to-date; now only the signposts are there. But I digress. Plenty of marvelous places to just generally hang out and chill are still available. The bike and hike trail is well executed and offers both a few miles of double-track gravel road for the kiddies to enjoy and some miles of technical singe-track and steep gravel road to leave your lungs burning.

The trail starts as a double-track at the parking lot for the primitive camping area, and this out-and-back spur connects you to the full loop. The loop then winds down to Jones Springs, a nice spot to take a break and a photo or three. From there you join the single-track and ascend to near the top of Wolf Mountain. There are two routes around the top of Wolf Mountain, but neither is significantly more difficult or longer than the other. The descent on the double-track is blindingly fast and leads you back to the spur that brought you in. Making a full loop from the parking lot will put about seven miles on your odometer.

Though the trail is not real difficult, there is some significant climbing that would be unsuitable for a single-speed cruiser. Multi-geared bikes will give you the ability to clean any portion of the trail, including the single-track. The most difficult sections are made so by rock ledges and the loose surface in many areas, which require proper gear selection and some technical skills. I still say that this is a trail you could take a kid on, provided the child has intermediate technical skills and a real bike. Otherwise, you should expect to portage from time to time.

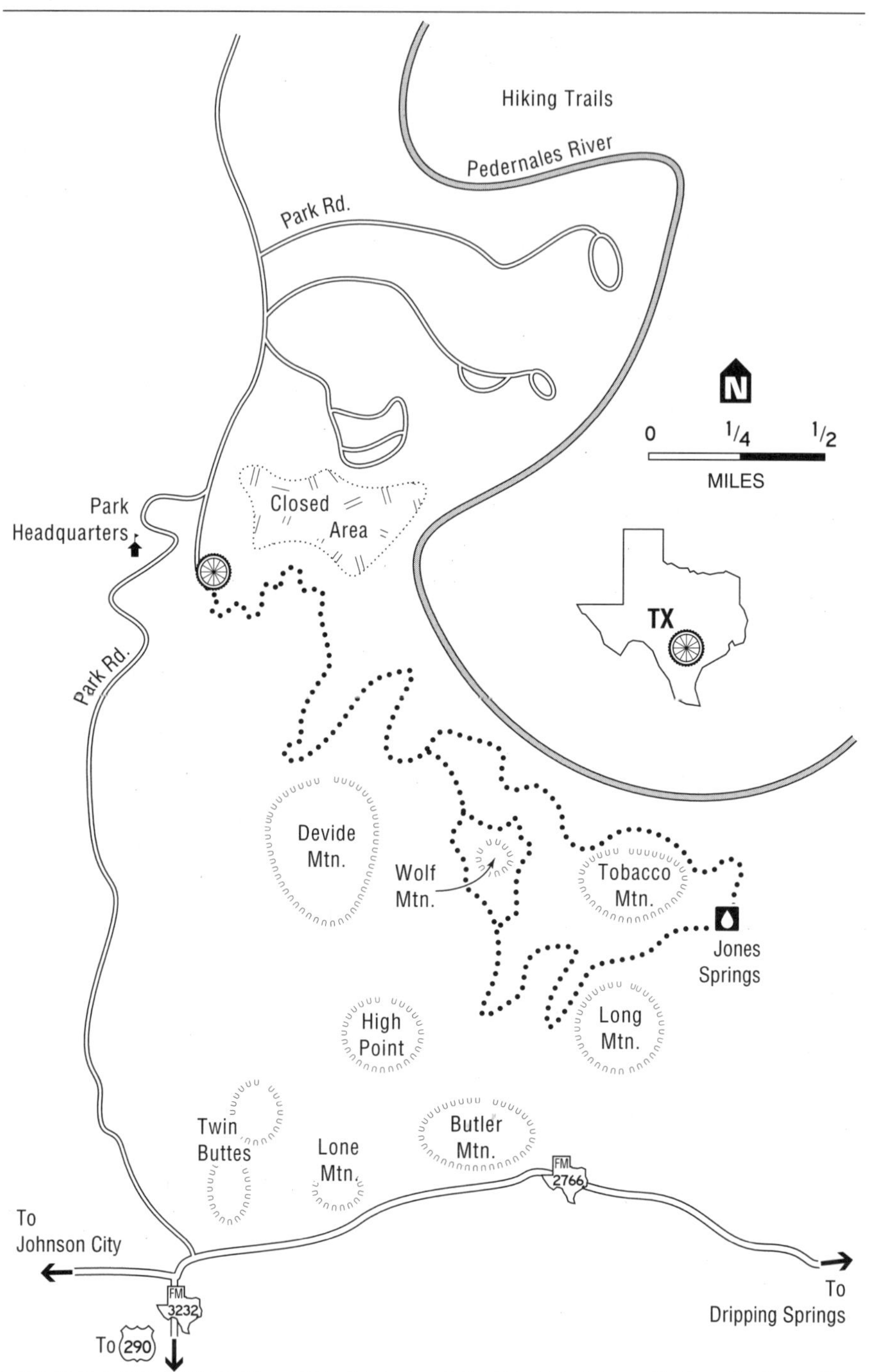

Hiking Trails
Pedernales River
Park Rd.
N
0 1/4 1/2
MILES
Closed Area
Park Headquarters
TX
Park Rd.
Devide Mtn.
Wolf Mtn.
Tobacco Mtn.
Jones Springs
High Point
Long Mtn.
Twin Buttes
Lone Mtn.
Butler Mtn.
FM 2766
To Johnson City
To Dripping Springs
FM 3232
To 290

The double-track portions are what could be called "improved surface," as the road has been covered with crushed caliche. The single-track, on the other hand, is a natural surface of mostly limestone outcroppings and loose rock and will become VERY slippery in the event of local rainfall. I have raced on stuff like this during a rain, and it ain't pretty.

There are some beautiful vistas from the higher points in the park, and sunrises and sunsets can be breathtaking. There is also a wide variety of wildlife—white-tailed deer, armadillos, snakes, and many types of birds. Many spots along the Pedernales River have a rustic beauty unequaled anywhere else in the area, and some of the swimming and ex–swimming holes are absolutely gorgeous. This is a very satisfying place to visit, and if you can make it during the summer you will be very pleased with the swimming, though fun can be had here year-round.

Within the park confines (and along the trail) are old ranching homesteads and rock fences that will give you fine examples of how things were built in the Old West. If you are a rock hound, you will find plenty of opportunities to see (and then say good-bye to, don't take) fossilized remains of various sea creatures and to observe interesting geological features. In any case, you will be able to experience Central Texas nature at its finest and most pleasing. Remember what General Sheridan said about Texas? He was a jerk.

General location: Pedernales State Park is roughly 45 minutes southwest of Austin, near Johnson City.
Elevation change: There is significant relief to the terrain within the park. The Pedernales River is around 800′ above sea level, and the top of Wolf Mountain takes you past 1,200′. The trail only wanders through about 200′ of elevation change, though.
Season: You can enjoy the trail here year-round, though sometimes the park closes during hunting season to allow the rangers to "harvest" their deer population. I would say this course is rideable (but dangerous) when wet, since the surface is mostly rock, but check with the rangers for trail conditions.
Services: There is a small store in the park, and it is open year-round. Water is available from a drinking fountain at the headquarters building, and a pay phone is also located there. The nearest bike shops are in Austin or San Marcos. The nearest town is Johnson City, about 10 miles away on Farm to Market 2766.
Hazards: The biggest hazard here takes the form of heavy pedestrian traffic during weekends. This is a popular hiking trail, and many nature groups have their walks here. Other hazards would include the trail surface's loose construction and the elevation changes, which can help you build so much velocity that bike control can be a challenge. Also, watch out for snakes and scorpions, either of which would love to get intimately acquainted with you.
Rescue index: There is a good chance of rescue here. Typically there are enough trail users in the park that you will generally be in no danger of being

alone if you break or are injured, though an equipment failure at the top of the mountain could result in a walk of 3 or 4 miles. In studying the map, you will see that the trail is a loop, with a spur of about 1.5 miles connecting the loop to the parking lot area. The parking area is not far from the headquarters, giving you a maximum of maybe 5 miles to walk from the farthest point on the trail to the ranger station if you break.

Land status: Another fine state park managed by the Texas Parks and Wildlife Department.

Maps: Excellent maps are available at the headquarters, though there is a slight charge for the best ones. (Topographical data and all points of interest are marked on the ones that are NOT free.) The quads for this trail are Pedernales Falls and Hammett's Crossing.

Finding the trail: From Austin go west on US 290 about 35 miles to the junction with FM 3232. Go north on FM 3232 about 7 miles, following the signs for Pedernales Falls State Park. When you reach the main gate, follow the park road to the headquarters and ask for directions to the bike trail.

Sources of additional information:

Park Superintendent
Pedernales Falls State Park
Route 1, Box 450
Johnson City, TX 78636
(210) 868-7304

Texas Parks and Wildlife Department
4200 Smith School Road
Austin, TX 78744-3291
(800) 792-1112 for information only

TPWD Reservation Center
P.O. Box 17488
Austin, TX 78760-7488
(512) 389-8900 for reservations only

Bicycle Sport Shop
1426 Toomey Road
Austin, TX 78704
(512) 477-3472

Bicycle Sport Shop
13376 North Highway #183
Suite #512
Austin, TX 78750
(512) 258-7278

Austin Ridge Riders
Tom Delany
Austin, TX
(512) 453-1955

I know riders who could probably clean these rocks along the Pedernales River. Kids mostly. More relaxed riders will prefer the Wolf Mountain Trail when visiting Pedernales State Park.

Notes on the trail: This is another facility where a day-use fee is charged, so have your Conservation Passport or $6 ready. The local mountain bike club, the Austin Ridge Riders, has access to some private land adjacent to the park. Tom and Ryan and friends have constructed an excellent 10-mile loop at the Flat Creek Crossing Ranch. The ranch is owned by Child, Inc., a nonprofit organization catering to the needs of children who have problems with their parents. (Don't they all?) If you plan to be in the area any length of time, I would suggest that you try to locate one of the members of the Austin Ridge Riders and see if they can help you get onto the ranch property. Volunteering to help maintain the trail is usually the price of admission. The trail there is tough single-track and will exercise your technical skills to the maximum.

RIDE 28 *WALTER BUCK WILDLIFE MANAGEMENT AREA TRAILS*

Although it is not one of my hobbies, a growing segment of the mountain bike community loves to hunt. Several of the popular hunting equipment outfitters are vending rifle-rack-equipped mountain bikes through their mail-order catalogs. If you are a hunter-biker, you may have already found places

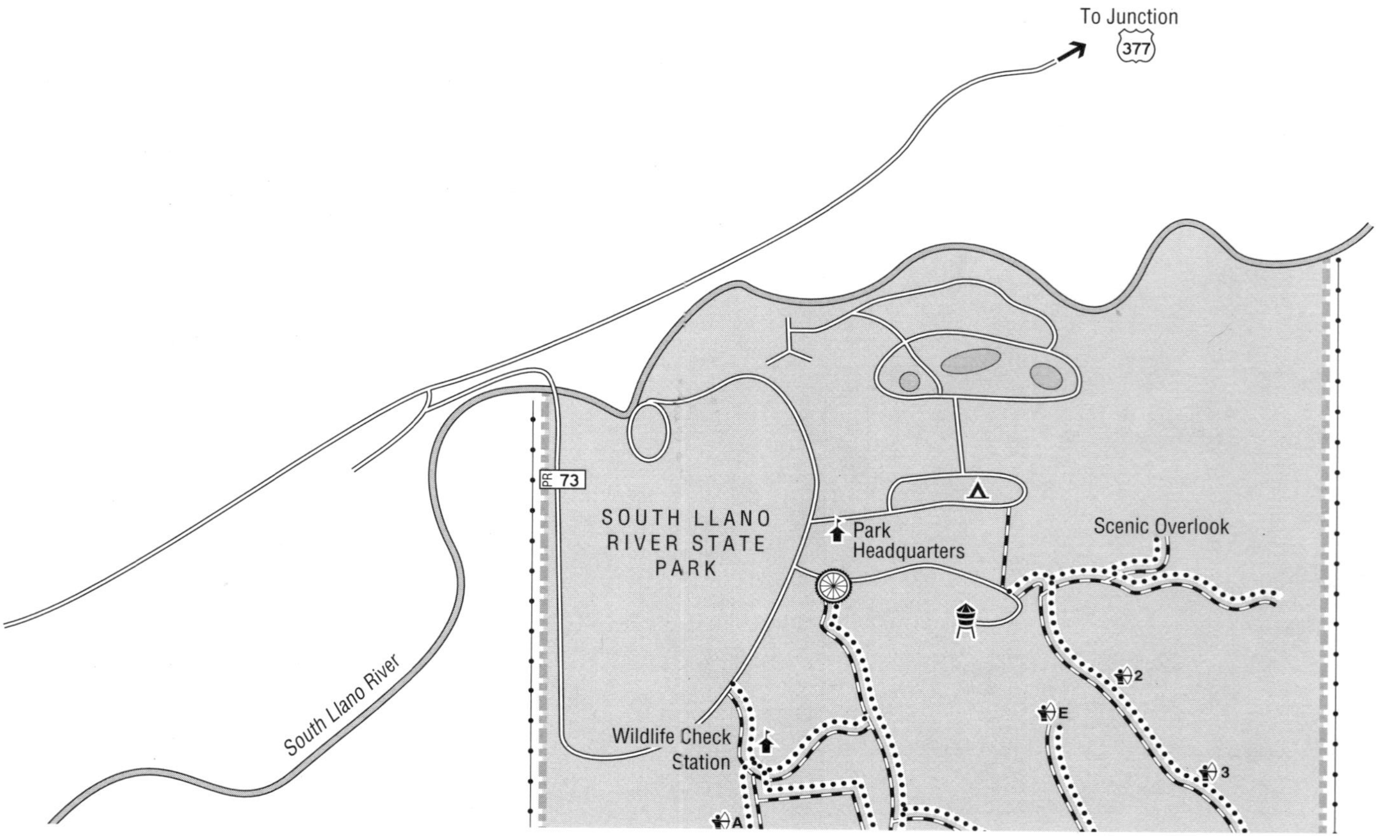

To Junction
377
PR 73
SOUTH LLANO RIVER STATE PARK
Park Headquarters
Scenic Overlook
Wildlife Check Station
South Llano River
2
3
E
A

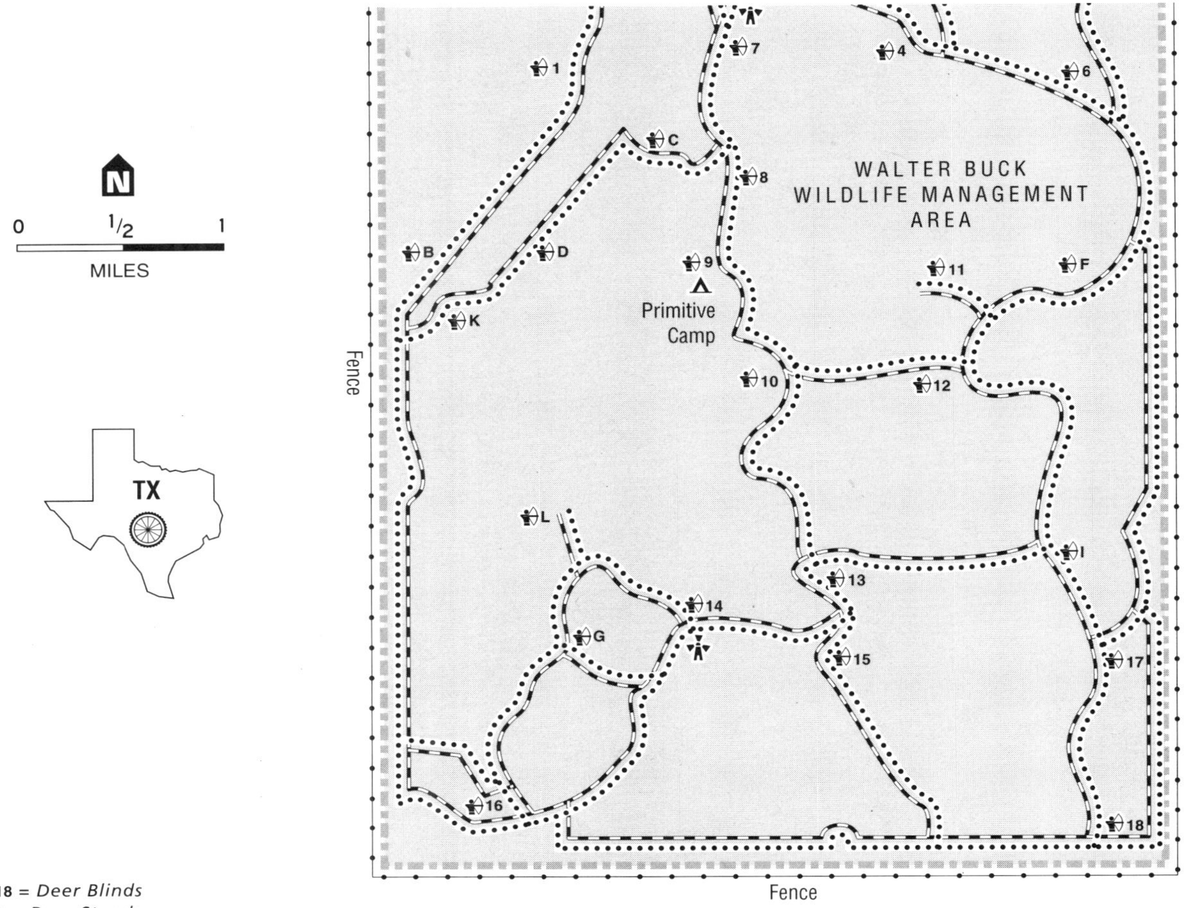

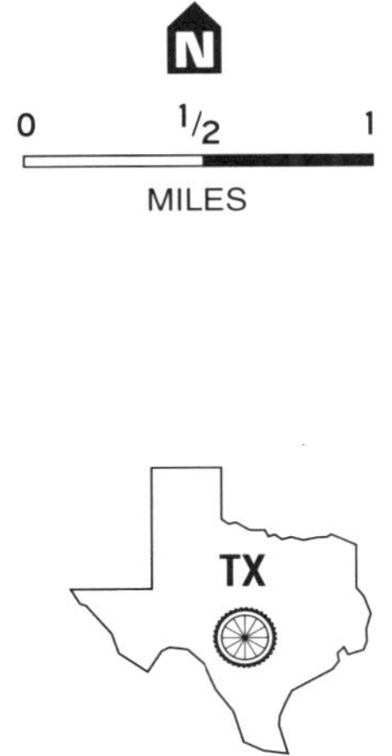

WALTER BUCK
WILDLIFE MANAGEMENT
AREA

Primitive
Camp

Fence

Fence

1 7 4 6 C 8 B D 9 11 F K 10 12 L I 13 14 G 15 17 16 18

Note: 1–18 = *Deer Blinds*
A–L = *Deer Stands*

that will allow you to combine both hobbies into one camping trip. All your life, you have probably been hanging out every October in beautiful places to ride. The Walter Buck Wildlife Management Area may interest you, because not only do they have nearly 15 miles of trails open to bikes, but they also close the place off nearly half the year for permit-only hunts.

The trailhead is all located in South Llano River State Park, a relatively new facility just outside of Junction, Texas. The South Llano River is another beautiful clear river that winds through the Texas Hill Country. The park sits adjacent to the wildlife area, which in turn is where all the trails are. If it is not hunting season, you are welcome to explore rocky rolling hills via the jeep roads that form a web across Walter Buck WMA. If you are an explorer, there are several pieces of double-track called "secondary roads—(rough)" that branch off from the main road and ramble. Don't worry about getting lost; all roads lead to Rome. Just don't cross any fences with closed gates.

Deer stands till you puke. You may feel like you are in the middle of the killing fields. You will be. You will see blinds and tall chair-type stands, each marked with a numeric or alphabetic designation that corresponds to a mark on the map. If you get "geographically challenged," it is easy to determine your location by referring to the map every time you pass one of the deer stands, which are many. *Many.*

The ride I am describing here is a loop of double-track and jeep road totaling about eight miles. It will lead you from the park headquarters area all the way out to the back of the property, around and up on top of one of the highest points accessible, and back again to where you parked. It is almost all loose caliche gravel, blinding in the summer sun, fairly demanding technically and physically. (Where the park maps say "hill," you better believe it.) These trails are a little more advanced than what runs through most state parks, but not so hard that average people will croak trying to ride a lap. The lowlands sections are mostly under the trees, but the sections with more elevation are very exposed, so take your sunglasses and plenty of sunscreen. Let's ride.

General location: The old Buck Ranch is southwest of Junction a few miles, roughly 2 hours west of San Antonio, in the beautiful Texas Hill Country.
Elevation change: The trailhead is the lowest point, at 1,750´ above sea level. The highest part of the trail is pushing 2,050´, and you will have loose gravel for the first 290´ of that. The last 10´ are okay. Catch your middle ring.
Season: Riding is only allowed here from May until September. October through January are various deer hunts, and turkey are hunted from the end of deer season until late April. In fact, South Llano River State Park is closed completely during turkey season, because the area near the picnic grounds is all hardwoods, a protected nesting area. Call ahead and check the trail status before you go if there is any doubt. Hunting seasons are variable.
Services: The overnight camping area has a soft drink machine, a pay phone, and a rest room building with showers. Just as you exit US 377 at the park

I would definitely not recommend riding through here with antlers on your head. Deer hunters wait years for luck to bring them a winning number in the lottery for hunting permits at Walter Buck Wildlife Management Area.

entrance, you find Buck Crossing Store; they have the usual supplies. The town of Junction is only about 5 miles away and offers gas stations and laundromats and all that sort of stuff. The nearest bike shop is in San Antonio and is listed below in the "Sources" section.

Hazards: There is not a lot of traffic along these trails, so one hazard is how lonely it is out here. Other dangers would include the loose and rocky conditions of the trails. Prickly pear cactus, mesquite, and cedar are the predominant flora and can also be considered hazards. I would not be shocked to see rattlesnakes in these hills, but they are about the only critters that might be a threat. Except for the armed variety, of course.

Rescue index: Since this park is staffed during working hours, it would be possible to get emergency help if you needed it. But only if a healthy rider is around to reach the headquarters and alert the authorities that an injured person is stranded in the field. Don't ride alone.

Land status: The park and wildlife area are owned by the citizens of Texas and are protected by the Texas legislature from ever being turned into anything but what you and I love, a (well-managed) wilderness area.

Maps: The staff at the headquarters will gladly offer you good maps of the trails, well marked with landmarks and prominent features, and free of charge. Be sure and tell the girls the guy writing the mountain bike book said hello.

Finding the trail: From Junction go west on US 377 about 5 miles until you see the signs for the state park and WMA. Turn left (by Buck Crossing Store) and follow the park road to the headquarters building. Behind the headquarters building you will find the trailhead to the double-track that leads into the outback. Follow this gravel jeep road according to the directions on the map in this book, or if you are feeling bold, take a different route and follow the directions on the map provided by the state park. You cannot get too lost, because there are signs on the fences indicating the boundaries.

Sources of additional information:

Park Superintendent
South Llano State Park
HC-15 Box 224
Junction, TX 76849
(915) 446-3994

Texas Parks and Wildlife Department
4200 Smith School Road
Austin, TX 78744-3291
(800) 792-1112 for information only

TPWD Reservation Center
P.O. Box 17488
Austin, TX 78760-7488
(512) 389-8900 for reservations only

Cenna's Cycles
2132 Northwest Military Highway
San Antonio, TX 78213
(210) 340-5845

Notes on the trail: You are in the middle of nowhere in a big way when you visit here. This part of Texas preserves a real western flavor. The Hill Country is Texas with a capital "T." Kerrville, to the east, is home to the Kerrville Folk Festival (every Memorial Day weekend) and also the locale of the Easter Hill Country Ride, a very popular road bike event. Kerrville-Schreiner State Park is a nice place to camp, right on the outskirts of Kerrville (more on this in the chapters on Hill Country State Natural Area). Welcome to Texas; now go ride.

RIDE 29 *HILL COUNTRY WILDERNESS TRAIL*

For a true taste of Texas riding you have to visit the Texas Hill Country, and for the ultimate Hill Country experience it has to be the Hill Country State Natural Area (or the SNA, in acronym parlance). This park contains at least 30 miles of trails, and you may ride almost all of them if you have the

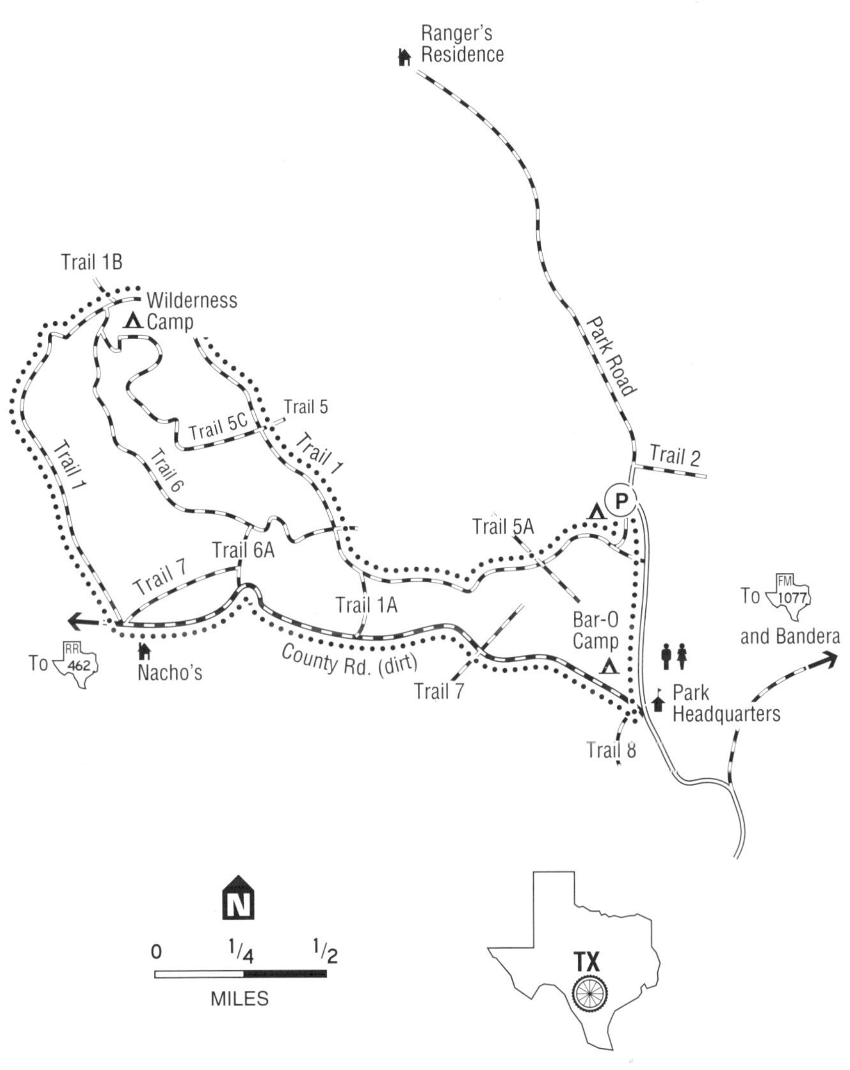
Ranger's Residence
Park Road
Trail 2
P
Trail 1B
Wilderness Camp
Trail 5
Trail 5C
Trail 1
Trail 6
Trail 1
Trail 5A
Trail 6A
Trail 7
Trail 1A
Bar-O Camp
To FM 1077 and Bandera
To RR 462
Nacho's
County Rd. (dirt)
Trail 7
Park Headquarters
Trail 8
0 1/4 1/2
MILES
N
TX

legs. Some are old jeep trails or double-track, but plenty are butt-kicking single-track. A few of the single-tracks are closed to bikes, typically because of line-of-sight limitations that make sharing them with the main trail-use group (horses) a sticky subject. It ain't no thang, though, because what we are allowed to ride is enough to make mountain bikers of any skill level glad they came.

The trail in this chapter is the easiest of the lot. It is all old gravel double-track, sometimes almost triple-track, where the bikes and horses have cut a groove on the crown of an old roadbed. This ride is not going to take you over the tops of any major hills (there are one or two on the property), it is only about six miles long, and it has a return on level gravel park road. The Wilderness Trail begins at the parking area for mountain bikers (how convenient) and makes a loop out and around a place called Wilderness Camp. Nontechnical and fairly flat, this is a ride anyone can handle, so take your fat friends.

Most of the way you are riding in exposed areas, so if you have sensitive skin it might be a good idea to slop on some 'screen. If you take a few pecan pralines, an orange, and an extra bottle of water, you might find a good place to relax by the trail for a minute or two. The Wilderness Camp is nothing more than a horse feeder/hitching post, so don't expect any picnic tables or rest rooms. But it is identified, and on some trails I have ridden, that is a definite plus.

There are no developed facilities of any kind in this park—not even a little barrel. I usually camp in Kerrville or stay in Bandera at one of the hotels. There are several dynamite barbecue houses and honky-tonks along the main drag, so get ready to spend some money. The natives will tell you this is the "Cowboy Capital of the World." Of the whole world, not just Texas or the West. You really are a dip if you drive all the way out here and don't take in some of the local culture. It has a western flavor unknown anywhere else this side of Dodge City. *Yeehaw and yippee-ki-yay, partner!*

General location: This trail is located 10 miles southwest of the "Cowboy Capital of the World" (drum roll, please)—Bandera, Texas. West of San Antonio about an hour for regular people.
Elevation change: The trailhead lies at about 1,540´ above sea level. You will then climb steadily to just over 1,600´ at the Wilderness Camp. Then a quick drop and finally the lowest point, at around 1,400´, where you meet the gravel county road. Climb gradually back to the trailhead on good roads.
Season: The seasonal references that follow apply to this ride and the next three. The Hill Country SNA is closed completely on Tuesday and Wednesday and to overnight camping on Monday. Unless the trails are muddy, you are welcome to ride here just about any other time from March to September. You will work for it in the wet on anything here except the roads. The deer hunters rule October through January or February, depending on what hunts are scheduled. Since most of the horse riders cannot handle the midday heat in summer, you

The Hill Country Wilderness Trail is well marked, just like all trails at the Hill Country State Natural Area. This place drips rustic old-west atmosphere. Try not to get any on your bike.

will likely find the place just about deserted and will have the whole thing to yourselves. Bring a couple of gallons of *agua* per *cabeza* if you try it.

Services: Water and a pay phone can be had at the headquarters anytime, plus ice when it is open (8 A.M. to 5 P.M.). Other than that, one chemical toilet is it. Any other supplies will have to come from Bandera or other small area towns. Bandera is it, dear hearts. The nearest bike shop is Cenna's in San Antonio.

Hazards: The equestrian traffic you may meet on the trail should be considered a hazard. Horses leave land mines behind that you will have to dodge, and they will freak out if you blink your eyes at them wrong. Snakes can be found here year-round, so they are number two on the list of troublemakers. Cactus, mesquite, and greenbrier are about the nicest of the indigenous plant life, so carry a patch kit and extra tube.

Rescue index: The rescue index of this trail is dependent on one thing; luck. The remoteness of this park makes a rescue entirely dependent on a good Samaritan wandering by and finding your broken body and then obtaining help. This is not likely to happen, since only a few folks ride these trails during the week and in summer. Take a buddy, someone capable of applying first aid in an emergency, or at least capable of finding their way out for help and then back in to save you. There are good bailout possibilities if you need them. Check the map.

Land status: Though undeveloped, this is another Texas state park and can be expected to be protected for our grandchildren's enjoyment.
Maps: These guys spent some bucks on keeping you found. This park has some of the best trail maps I have seen, and the trails are some of the best-marked I have ever ridden. Every intersection, EVERY INTERSECTION, with another trail is identified. Maps are free for the asking, and you will usually find them stuffed in a box on the bulletin board outside the park headquarters. The horse crowd gripes that they spent too much money on trail markings. You do the math. The quads for this trail are Tarpley Pass and Twin Hollow.
Finding the trail: From Bandera go south across the Medina River on TX 173 and turn west on Farm to Market 1077. Go about 10 miles. Keep going past where the pavement ends and follow the dirt road. Turn right where the signs say "The road ahead is closed," and cross the low water crossing. Don't haul ass, because that thing is always covered with algae and is slick, very slick. Proceed a short distance to the park headquarters. After stopping at the headquarters (for maps and to be neighborly), go north on the gravel road past the chemical toilet, and about a half mile or so up the road you will find the parking area on the west side of the road. It's the only one, and there is a sign for Hill Country Wilderness Trail. Park. Ride out of the lot past the sign that says Hill Country Wilderness Trail. This is Trail #1 on the maps. Are you okay so far? Follow the signs and stay on #1, past the Wilderness Camp, all the way around to where it hits the gravel road. Turn left on the road and follow it back to the headquarters building, then turn left and proceed to where you parked. If you are feeling bold, you may follow #1B where it cuts off to the right and goes around a hill and returns to #1. This side trail is single-track, rough and rocky, with one fairly good climb. No kidding.

Sources of additional information:

Hill Country State Natural Area
Route 1, Box 601
Bandera, TX 78003
(210) 796-4413

Texas Parks and Wildlife Department
4200 Smith School Road
Austin, TX 78744-3291
(800) 792-1112 for information only

Cenna's Cycles
2132 Northwest Military Highway
San Antonio, TX 78213
(210) 340-5845

Notes on the trail: If you are looking for something REALLY different to do the next time you are in Bandera on a honky-tonk Saturday night, be sure and visit Arkie Blue's Silver Dollar Saloon, a true Texas landmark. Elvis liked it. Kennis loves it. Mark says it is worthy. Just don't say anything nasty about how well old Arkie sings, hehehe.

The best "developed" state park in the vicinity is Kerrville-Schreiner State Park in Kerrville. Kerrville is about a half-hour drive to the north and makes an excellent place to camp or unwind after a day of riding here. Right on the banks of the beautiful Guadalupe River, it is worth checking out if you are in the vicinity. Kerrville-Schreiner also has a short set of trails the kids might enjoy, but only under adult supervision. Or adults under kids' supervision, whatever.

RIDE 30 *HERMIT'S TRACE RIDE*

The Hermit's Trace is just about all easy, some single- and some double-track. Several of the places that are slightly uphill will be loose, so the climbing can be energetic but never dramatic. Where you pass signs that say "No Bikes," you may be certain you are being cheated only of the privilege to walk your bike up and down a few hills. Stay on the old gravel road and you will pass an old residence, the Boyle House, after about two and one-half miles. Don't even think about entering, because I heard what sounded like a large hive of bees. People die from being stung by bees in Texas. We have those "africanized" suckers that are better known as the Killer Bees (apologies to John Belushi and friends). Let it lie there.

You gradually wind around to a point where you can take side trails from the main loop and see the Cougar Canyon Overlook or the hermit's house, if you like. Then it will be time to cruise back to where you parked, clocking around eight miles. You must park in the primitive camp area by the trailhead for the Hill Country Wilderness Trail. The ranger likes knowing how many mountain bikers he has out there, and that's how he knows who is who—by where you park.

The trails in this park are extremely well marked. Thank you, Mister Ranger. I have spent so much time wandering back and forth wondering if I was lost. You will be required to make turns at specific points along the route in order to follow the exact ride I am listing. If you get lost, it is not on me. On the other hand, it is never necessary to follow me 100% while in this park, not if you have the map. Experiment. Just stay off the trails that are closed. Easy as 1, 2, C.

Let me jump on my soapbox here, for just a moment. I do not care if you think you are John Tomac, Ned Overend, and Kung Fu all rolled into one:

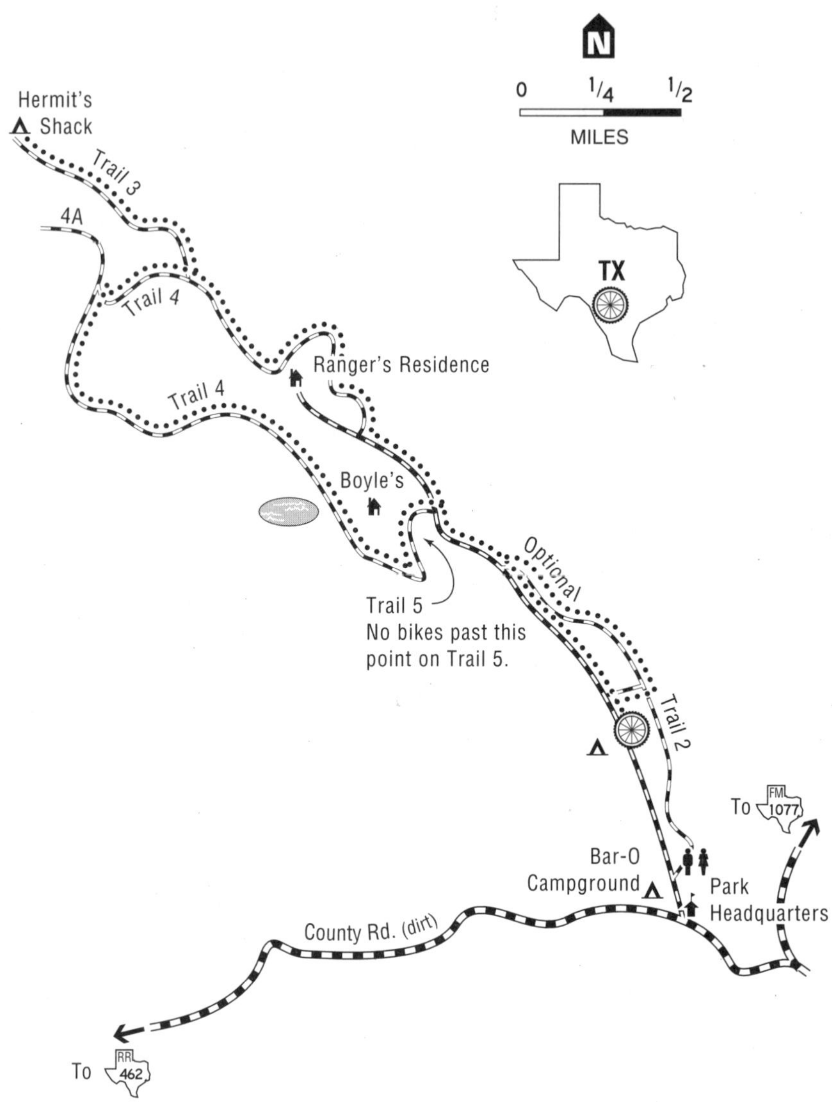

N
0
1/4
1/2
MILES
TX
Hermit's Shack
Trail 3
4A
Trail 4
Ranger's Residence
Trail 4
Boyle's
Optional
Trail 5
No bikes past this point on Trail 5.
Trail 2
To FM 1077
Bar-O Campground
Park Headquarters
County Rd. (dirt)
To RR 462

YOU ARE NOT. When you ride here, or anywhere, when it is muddy, you are just being an ass. When you refuse to dismount on steep/loose hiking trails and instead descend by locking and skidding your rear wheel, you are not doing our sport any favors. When I was here I saw some real trail damage, caused by what I describe above, on a trail bikes have no business riding. If you have any problem with what I am saying, then you look me up, anytime, and we will roll around in the backyard for a little while and settle our difference of opinion. I am easy to find. Don't be a jerk; make it work.

General location: Like above, 10 miles southwest of the "Cowboy Capital of the World" in the beautiful Texas Hill Country. Just an hour west of San Antonio.
Elevation change: You start at 1,540′ of elevation above the Gulf of Mexico (about 100 miles southeast). Then you work your way up and down and up again to about 1,750′ or so near the shack, and back down again to the parking area.
Season: Don't come here to ride during deer season. See the explanation for this park in the chapter for the Hill Country Wilderness Trail. It is mighty hot in summer, so bring something cold to drink. Have fun.
Services: Nothing, not even a litter barrel. No showers, no flushing toilets, no cabins, no beer on tap. Load up on grocery store stuff in Bandera before you head over to the park. You'll find a pay phone, water, and ice (when open) at the headquarters.
Hazards: Take special care if you meet any four-legged travelers. This sort of started out being their park. Them and the guys with the high-powered rifles. Oh yeah, don't come here during deer season. Most of this trail is fairly easy—not real tricky, as they go. Now that I have said that, be sure and wear your helmet. I can get hurt on the easiest trails. Stay out of private property and in the park.
Rescue index: I have to reiterate what I said in the previous chapter: You will need luck to be rescued from here. Though well-marked, this trail is nothing like ridden every day. Disaster would leave you wishing to hear a "neigh-whinny" or another bike. It ain't gonna happen unless you take a partner. Practice safe wrecks.
Land status: This is a state natural area—a state park without all the amenities. That means a managed wilderness area. Obey the rules. Thank you, Pat Neff.
Maps: The headquarters building has a pay station/sign kiosk with great maps, some of the best I have ever seen for free. The quad for this trail is Tarpley Pass.
Finding the trail: See the directions for getting to the Hill Country SNA in the previous chapter. Once you have found the parking area for the trails, you will park and unload, fill your bottles, and blast off up the dirt road you just parked near. Proceed in the same direction you were going before you stopped to park (roughly north). Ride the dirt road for about 1.5 miles until

Traffic jam along the Hermit's Trace.

you see a sign showing Trail #5 splitting off and heading into the trees on your left. Follow single-track #5 until #4 splits to the right. Bikes are not allowed any farther on #5, so you will turn right onto #4. You will now be on old double-track. Follow this to and past Boyle's old house and keep going. After a few miles you will see a split for #4A. Bear right and stay on #4. Soon you will be at the intersection for #3. Turn left onto #3 and follow it a mile or so to the old shack. Take a break, and when you are ready to ride again, retrace your steps southward on #3. Follow #3 until it reaches the dirt road, then hang a left and ride the dirt road back to the trailhead parking lot.

Sources of additional information:

Hill Country State Natural Area
Route 1, Box 601
Bandera, TX 78003
(210) 796-4413

Texas Parks and Wildlife Department
4200 Smith School Road
Austin, TX 78744-3291
(800) 792-1112 for information only

Cenna's Cycles
2132 Northwest Military Highway
San Antonio, TX 78213
(210) 340-5845

Notes on the trail: The hermit's shack is a primitive camping area, and you may like the vicinity enough to pack in a tent and the stuff you need to camp for the night. You won't find many places more secluded. Just remember that you have to pack in whatever you will need and pack out whatever you bring; there are no facilities of any kind. Not even a litter barrel. Please leave the area the way you found it, or cleaner. I have noticed that the horse-heads have no compunction about tossing cigarette butts anywhere along the trail. Don't follow their lead. If you pack it in, pack it back out again.

RIDE 31 *SPRING FALLS/BANDERA CREEK RIDE*

Let's move on to some tougher terrain. How about the following: five miles of very technical single-track, nothing real steep, but many creek crossings that will keep you on your toes? This ride put blisters on my hands, through my gloves. All the creek crossings were very taxing; I had already ridden some miles that day.

You start in the usual place, the primitive camping parking lot. You ride one-half mile of the Hill Country Wilderness Trail and then turn onto a loop of some REAL single-track, and from then on you are working your ass off. You pass by a nice quite spot called Spring Falls, one of the primitive camps. Stop and take a few pictures, have a pecan praline and think about your author, out there in the hot sun, sweating, in pain, so self-sacrificing . . . NOT! It was a beautiful day when I last graced these premises. I think I had barbecue for lunch. I love barbecue. And pralines.

Get back on the bike—it is time for the blisters. Take a nice deep breath as you exit the Spring Falls area and ride down to cross the road; the creek is next. As you switch to the Bandera Creek Trail, you will pass a sign indicating that the Corpus Christi Off-Road Bicycle Riders Association has joined the Adopt-a-Trail program. Its members drive all the way up here to help keep a place for you and me to ride. Thank you. Helluva a cool trail.

General location: Hang a right on the first road past Medina River going south from the "Cowboy Capital of the World." This trail finds you in the center of the fantastic Texas Hill Country.

Elevation change: Starting at the parking area, you are at 1,540′ above sea level, give or take. Then you work your way up to about 1,700′ and gradually drop down to about 1,380′ when you first hit Bandera Creek. Then, a little at a time, you rise as you ride the creek, and soon you are back at the start.

Season: Ride somewhere else during deer season, which varies from year to year. Call and ask about trail status during the cold months. Otherwise you may enjoy the trails here just about any other time of year. They don't grow over, are very well maintained and marked, and are usually very vacant.

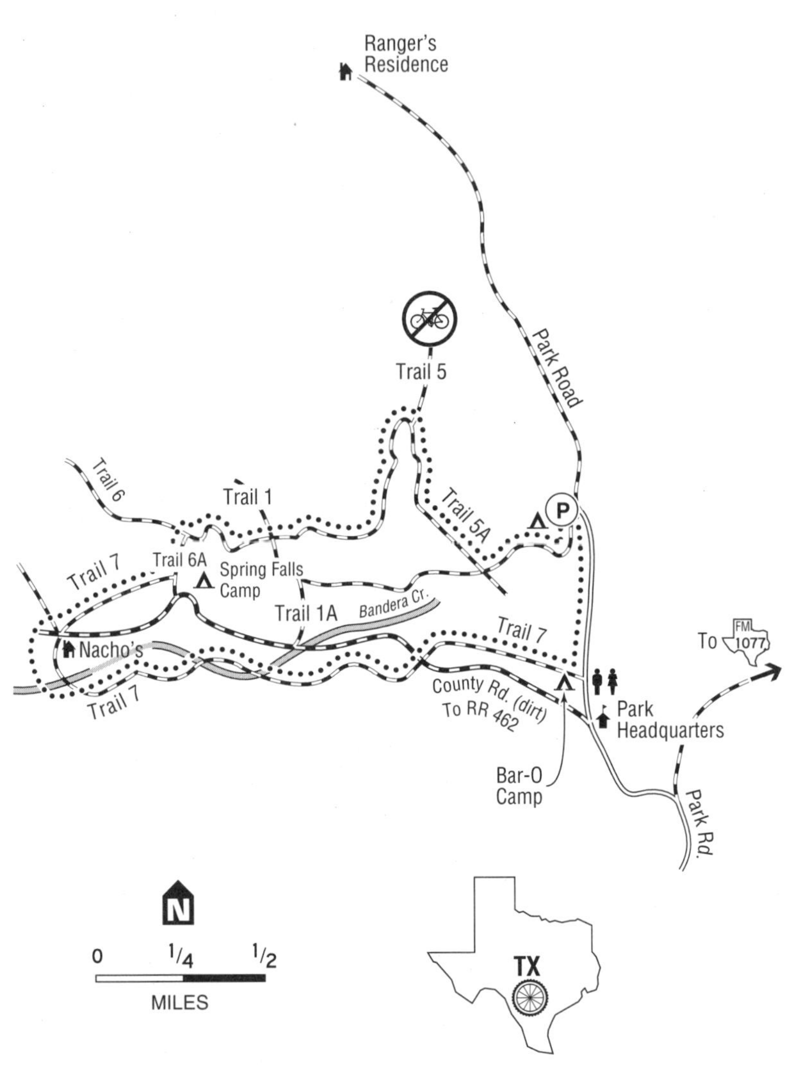
Ranger's Residence
Trail 5
Park Road
Trail 6
Trail 1
Trail 5A
P
Trail 7
Trail 6A
Spring Falls Camp
Trail 1A
Bandera Cr.
Trail 7
Nacho's
Trail 7
County Rd. (dirt) To RR 462
To FM 1077
Park Headquarters
Bar-O Camp
Park Rd.
N
0 1/4 1/2
MILES
TX

Your author on the approach to Bandera Creek. You were all surviving another Monday morning when this photo was taken. Sorry, cheap shot.

Services: Water, a pay phone, and a chemical toilet are available near the headquarters, and ice is too when the building is staffed—normally 8 A.M. to 5 P.M. The nearest bike shop is in San Antonio. The nearest full-facility camping is Kerrville-Schreiner State Park in Kerrville.

Hazards: There is nothing friendly about this place except the people. The trails are treacherous, the flora is stickery, the summer heat is terrible, and the other trail users are predominantly four-legged. The roads you cross are all active, so examine them for automobile traffic before you cross.

Rescue index: You might wait a while to be rescued from the trails here, because this park is usually not real well populated. If your car sits at the trailhead for a few days, the ranger will probably get suspicious and start wondering about you, but the only guarantee of being rescued is to have a partner to send for help if you get hurt or stranded. If someone can get back to the park roads, they can run to the headquarters and grab the pay phone and call for help. The nearest ambulance is at least 10 miles away, and the same holds for a hospital. Also, there are several good bailouts along the way if you need one; see the map.

Land status: This trail is all on land contained within the Hill Country State Natural Area, owned by the lucky citizens of the State of Texas and managed by the Texas Parks and Wildlife Department. They will keep it like it is now forever if we let them.

Maps: The ranger will give you an excellent map of all the trails for free. If he is not there, grab one at the pre-pay station next door. The quads are Tarpley Pass and Twin Hollow.

Finding the trail: Park in the primitive camping area trailhead parking lot. If you can't get that far, then refer to the chapter on the Hill Country Wilderness Trail for directions to the park. From the parking lot, ride the Wilderness Trail (Trail #1) for just over one-quarter of a mile, until you see the sign for Trail #5A. Turn right onto #5A and follow the single-track until you see the fork where Trail #6 joins #5A. Turn left onto #6 and follow the single-track. You will cross #1 after a short ways. Stay on #6. Soon you will pass the Spring Falls Camp primitive area. Turn left onto #6A for a short stint until you see the sign indicating where Trail #7 branches off to the right. Follow #7 until it hits the dirt road (identified on the maps as County Road), and cross over it. The old house you will see there is called Nacho's. Follow the trail around behind the house and down into and across the creek. Follow the single-track as it winds back and forth across Bandera Creek, and eventually you will again cross the dirt road. From there you will follow #7 until it enters the Bar-O Camp area, near the headquarters building. Turn left on the dirt road (identified on the maps as Park Road), and return to the parking area, a short distance north.

Sources of additional information:

Hill Country State Natural Area
Route 1, Box 601
Bandera, TX 78003
(210) 796-4413

Texas Parks and Wildlife Department
4200 Smith School Road
Austin, TX 78744-3291
(800) 792-1112 for information only

Cenna's Cycles
2132 Northwest Military Highway
San Antonio, TX 78213
(210) 340-5845

Notes on the trail: This is really good riding. Not extremely difficult, but sufficient to make you feel like you have done something. Plus, the scenery is about as good as it gets for this area. If you feel bold, there are some other possible routes using Spring Falls and Bandera Creek as a base. Explore at will. Be sure and stop by and say "hey" to the ranger when you leave, and tell him or her how much you liked the trails. The horse-heads never do anything but gripe, and I want us to leave a much better taste in the ranger's mouth than they do. Be nice, give 'em a pat on the back. What goes around comes around.

RIDE 32 *COMANCHE BLUFF/CHAQUITA FALLS RIDE*

We are moving back onto the double-track now, for the most part anyway. This ride is a good finish to our visit to the Hill Country SNA. If you have a penchant for swimming holes, then bring your suit, because you will pass two good ones along the way. If it is a hot day, you will be glad you came prepared.

This six-and-a-half-mile loop will give you a few miles of loose jeep road followed by some difficult technical ledge-work and then cap it all off with some mild single-track that will dump you by one of the swimming holes. Nothing on this route is extremely difficult, but I think you will agree that some of it is pretty tough. The whole route is scenic and secluded, and don't be surprised if you see a deer or ten.

The area known as Comanche Bluff will let you look down over a lovely small valley by the equestrian camp of the same name. Here the road crosses West Verde Creek and is just about guaranteed to give you wet feet and/or seat, year-round. Good swimming hole #1 is just below the bluff.

Farther along you will find some huge live oak trees that shield Chaquita Falls from view until you are about to drive into the pools above and below the falls. This is good swimming hole #2 and probably the best of the two if it contains enough *agua*.

Have fun, be very careful, and enjoy some more fine Texas Hill Country scenery along the way. Don't run over any deer.

General location: Go to the "Cowboy Capital of the World" and go southwest 10 miles. This puts you in the middle of the famous Texas Hill Country, a real Texan's Texas.

Elevation change: Starting at 1,540′ above sea level, the trail gradually winds around and up to about 1,670′ and then down again to about 1,450′ where the road crosses West Verde Creek under Comanche Bluff, then back up to around 1,600′ and down again to about 1,480′ and then back to the starting elevation.

Season: I've said it before and I'll say it again: Don't come here expecting to ride during the winter, because hunting seasons will probably conflict with your plans. If in doubt, dial it out. It pays to call ahead if there is any doubt about the status of the park.

Services: No facilities at all for disposing of trash. Water, a pay phone, a chemical toilet, and ice (during office hours) can all be obtained at the headquarters building near the main entrance. The nearest bike shop is in San Antonio, and the nearest full-service state park is Kerrville-Schreiner State Park in Kerrville.

RIDE 32 *COMANCHE BLUFF / CHAQUITA FALLS RIDE*

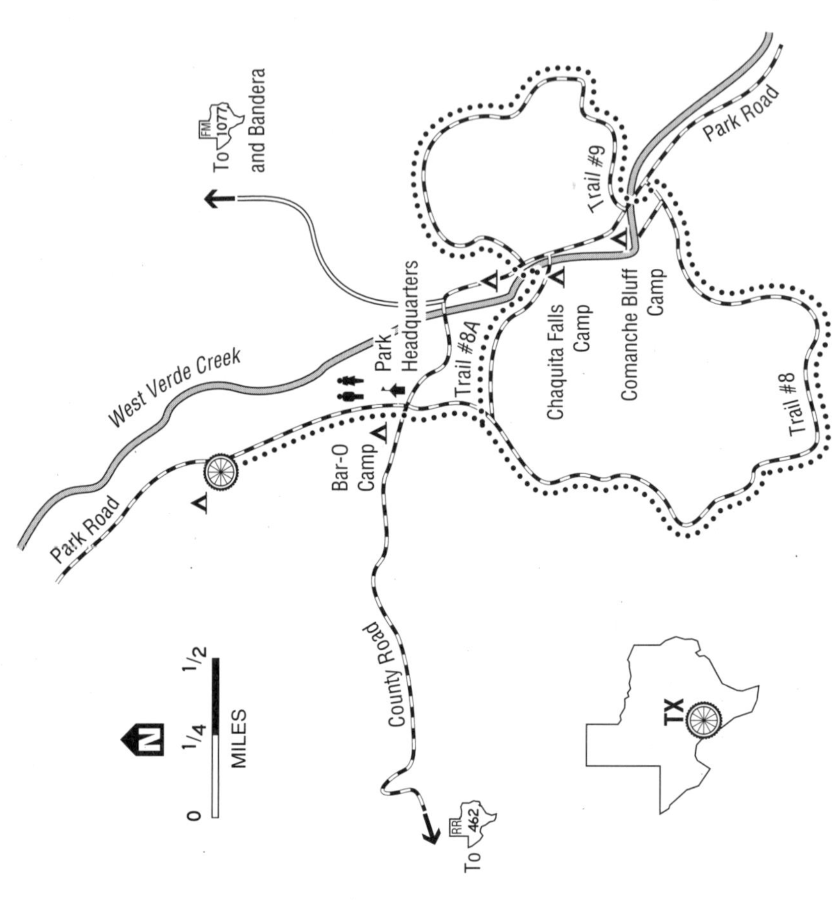

Hazards: You could buy the farm pretty easy while riding this trail. There are several ledges that drop at least 12 inches, so your technical skills will be tested. The trail is all loose gravel, and some stretches are fairly steep. There might be a snake or two in the vicinity, so look around before stepping on any sticks. Also watch for horses (and their backwash), since they are the main trail-use group in the park. Other dangers include just about every plant along the way. They have huge gnashing teeth. Run away.

Rescue index: It is feasible that an ambulance could be driven into most of the areas you visit on this trail, but only if someone knew you were stranded there. Your only hope of rescue is to have a healthy partner to go fetch help if you crack up. Just don't crash into your partner and get both of you wounded. There are several good bailouts if you need them; see the map.
Land status: The Hill Country Natural Scenic Area is another excellent state park managed by the Texas Parks and Wildlife Department.
Maps: The quads are, for the last time, Tarpley Pass and Twin Hollow, and the ranger has REALLY GOOD FREE maps.
Finding the trail: Always park in the primitive camping parking area about one-half mile past the headquarters building on the dirt road identified in the maps as Park Road. Ride back the way you just came. When you hit the intersection with the other road, identified in the maps as County Road, look across, and you will see a trail marker distinguishing Trail #8. Follow #8 all the way around as it becomes single-track and then double-track again and eventually hits the dirt road called Park Road. You just passed the left turn to the bluff. Hang a left on Park Road and splash through the creek and good swimming hole #1. Just past the creek, Trail #9 jumps off to the right. Follow that. If you are already beat or have a need, you may keep going on Park Road back to the parking area. Assuming you are still alive, I say turn left onto #9 and follow it around as it loops out and then comes back to Park Road. Cross the road, go through the trees, and cross the creek again. This is good swimming hole #2. Across the creek you will pick up Trail #8A and go right on the single-track. This will carry you back to where you passed by earlier on #8. Turn right on #8, and soon you will be back at the intersection of all the roads and the trail. Go past the headquarters to where you parked.

Sources of additional information:

Hill Country State Natural Area
Route 1, Box 601
Bandera, TX 78003
(210) 796-4413

Texas Parks and Wildlife Department
4200 Smith School Road
Austin, TX 78744-3291
(800) 792-1112 for information only

Cenna's Cycles
2132 Northwest Military Highway
San Antonio, TX 78213
(210) 340-5845

Looks like a good place for an ambush doesn't it? It's too quiet out there. A sunny section of the ride to Comanche Bluff.

Notes on the trail: This completes our visit to Hill Country State Natural Area and the historic Texas Hill Country. If you like barbecue, you need to spend some time in Bandera, because there are a few good places. If you like local culture, you need to do the Bandera thing, too, because this is about as flavorful as it gets for down-home Texas hospitality. Have fun and take your time. There is lots to do in the Hill Country, and the people are about as salty here as anywhere you will ever go.

The Texas Panhandle

Now we enter the Llano Estacado, or Staked Plains, an area of Texas that covers the southern end of the Midwest's High Plains. These lands make up most of the Texas Panhandle and average over 3,000 feet of elevation. Many years ago this land was covered with bison and nomadic bands of Indians. After the introduction of cattle and the elimination of the bison by the white settlers, the Indians retreated. Farming and ranching quickly helped increase the population of Americans of European extraction, forever ending the way of life that many tribes of indigenous peoples had enjoyed since the dawn of time.

This is the part of Texas where I kissed my first girl, went to high school, learned to drive, and saw my first sandstorm. In the spring, when the wind blows 70 to 80 miles per hour three or four times a month, it kicks up the dust in New Mexico and brings it east with a vengeance. If you have never seen it, you will not understand what I am talking about. It is an unbelievable nuisance. Large plate-glass-window storefronts have been known to shatter from the pressure of the winds. It is hard to walk around—the wind shoves you and pushes you, and opening doors can be a dangerous event.

Still, I have some real good memories of camping along the Cap Rock and in Palo Duro Canyon. We always took these things for granted, but most people would probably think the "flatlanders" live in an inhospitable wasteland. The High Plains is almost tabletop-flat for as far as the eye can see in every direction. During the day you can see huge grain elevators 10 miles away, and at night you can see the lights from other towns up to 15 miles distant. This is a place you really have to learn to love.

The trails here are all along or fairly near the Cap Rock areas that form the edge of the High Plains, separating them from the rest of Texas. And there are some good trails—one of my favorites in the whole book is coming up. Let's play.

RIDE 33 *COPPER BREAKS STATE PARK TRAIL*

Copper Breaks State Park is another of those places that wants visitors so badly that they will let you ride just about anywhere you want. Anywhere that is an existing trail, that is. The equestrian area offers about six miles of old ranch roads, sandy/gravelly double-track that is almost all flat and easy. This out-and-back ride consists of the main trail and two spurs that branch from

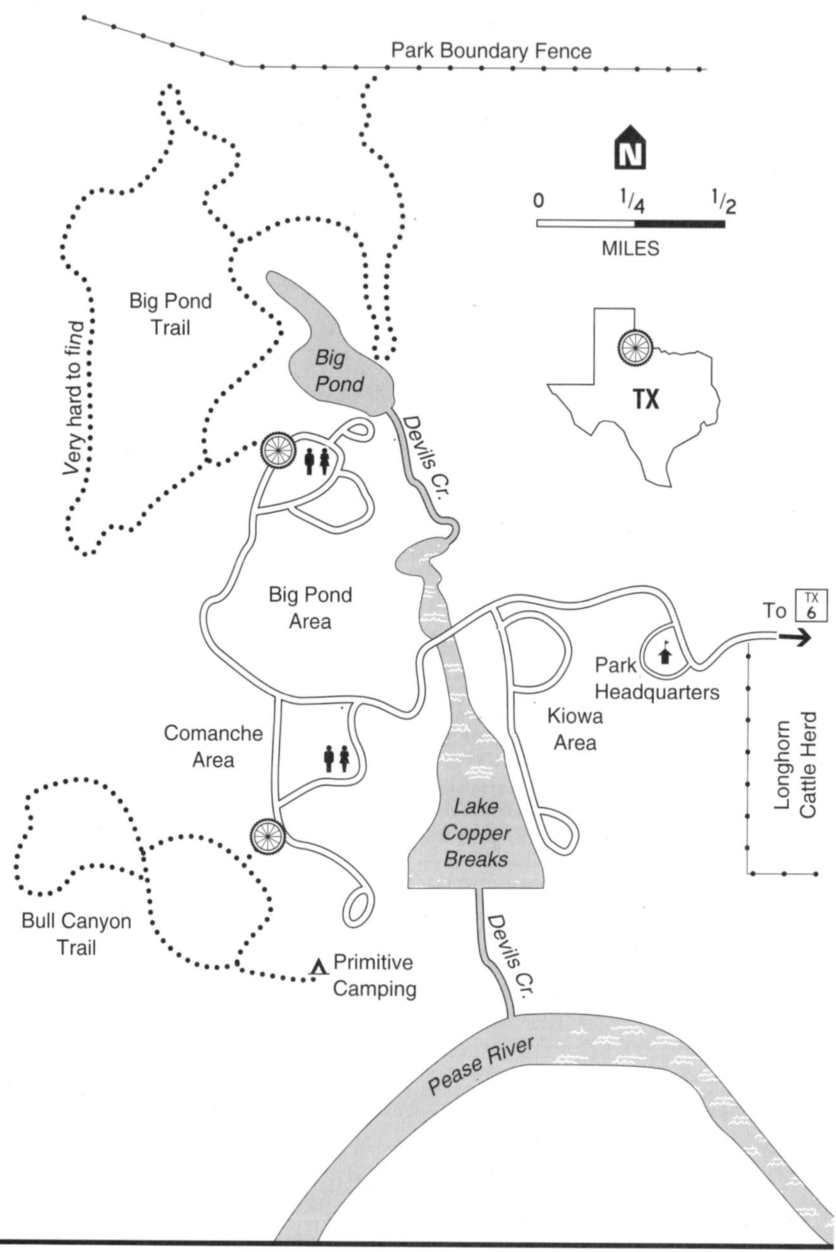
Park Boundary Fence
0
1/4
1/2
MILES
TX
Big Pond Trail
Very hard to find
Big Pond
Devils Cr.
Big Pond Area
To TX 6
Park Headquarters
Kiowa Area
Longhorn Cattle Herd
Comanche Area
Lake Copper Breaks
Bull Canyon Trail
Primitive Camping
Devils Cr.
Pease River

it and run short distances into the "breaks," the broken land formations that give the park its name. The "copper" part of the name comes from chunks of raw copper ore that you can find lying around on the ground.

This is rugged terrain; it possesses a natural beauty that a few of us can appreciate. It is an area of gullies and badlands, where ranching is the main industry. Nearby, a few miles to the east, is a prominent point of land known as the Medicine Mound, a popular holy place for the Indians that once inhabited this area. In fact, there is a lot of history around here that involves the red folks of old. The town of Quanah, 13 miles to the north, is named for Quanah Parker, famous Comanche war chief and son of a kidnapped white woman, Cynthia Ann Parker. And as we will see as we move farther west, many of the last great battles between the cavalry soldiers and the Indians occurred in this part of the state.

Copper Breaks State Park is one of the best-kept secrets in the Texas Parks and Wildlife system. This park was almost closed a few years ago, but the locals got together and lobbied to save it. Be sure and take a walk through the Visitor Center at the headquarters to get the full effect. There is not much else in this area, so sightseeing is mostly limited to the immediate area of the park. Take advantage of the resources and paraphernalia the Texas Parks and Wildlife Department have pulled together for your enjoyment.

General location: Roughly halfway from Amarillo to Wichita Falls in the northwestern part of the state.

Elevation change: The small lake near the trailhead is home to the lowest point along the way, at around 1,400′ above sea level. The far north end of the trail, where you meet the fence, is nearly 1,500′.

Season: Unless it is raining, you can ride here anytime. Summer brings horseflies that bite like fire, but the riding is very consistent.

Services: The headquarters has an emergency phone (credit card or collect calls only). There are showers in the Kiowa camping area, and rest rooms and water are near the trailhead in the equestrian camping area. That's it. The nearest place to get supplies is the town of Quanah, 13 miles north. The nearest bike shops would be in Amarillo or Wichita Falls.

Hazards: This is really a fairly safe place to ride. That does not mean you would never see a Western diamondback rattlesnake if you looked around. They live here but are very shy. The biting flies will drive you crazy in the summer, and if you camp here, you should sleep in a tent, because the skunks are about the boldest I have seen anywhere. Keep an eye peeled for horseheads, because this is their trail.

Rescue index: If you can get word back to headquarters that you need help, they could get to you fairly easily; the terrain is not real severe. Still, in an emergency that could be the least of your worries, because the nearest hospital is miles away. Having a riding partner that could go fetch help is always a good insurance policy for mountain bikers.

Your author, a man who knows his bull, riding near Bull Canyon at Copper Breaks State Park.

Land status: The trails are all within the boundaries of a state park and therefore protected from development.
Maps: The headquarters has maps for free, but they are very limited in the information they present. The quads for this park are Margaret, Teacup Mountain, Maybell Canyon, and Big Mound.
Finding the trail: From the town of Quanah on US 287, drive south 13 miles on TX 6. The entrance to the park is on the west side of the highway. Follow the park road past the headquarters and around toward the Big Pond Equestrian Area. The trailhead is located near the campsites at Big Pond. Park by the windmill and trail signs. Follow the double-track all the way to where it ends at the fence that marks the boundary of the park. If you can locate them (they are fading from lack of frequent use), follow the two side trails to where they disappear, and then head back to the main trail.

Sources of additional information:

Park Superintendent
Copper Breaks State Park
Route 2, Box 480
Quanah, TX 79252
(817) 839-4331

Texas Parks and Wildlife Department
4200 Smith School Road
Austin, TX 78744-3291
(800) 792-1112 for information only

TPWD Reservation Center
P.O. Box 17488
Austin, TX 78760-7488
(512) 389-8900 for reservations only

Notes on the trail: Another trail exists in this park, and it is also open to bikes. The Bull Canyon Hiking Trail is about 2 miles of single-track that winds around the mesquite and juniper, drops into Bull Canyon briefly, then loops around and returns you to the point you started from. A fairly easy ride, worth checking out if you have a few minutes. The trailhead is plainly marked on maps available from the headquarters.

RIDE 34 *QUITAQUE CANYON/LOS LINGOS RAILS–TO–TRAILS*

Welcome to the Cap Rock, an area of canyons in many ways similar to the Grand Canyon area of Arizona. To my mind this may be the best trail in the whole book. It is 25 miles of easy point-to-point railroad bed (formerly the Fort Worth and Denver line), mostly smooth gravel with a 1% grade, downhill much of the way. Some stretches are hard-packed dirt that could get muddy during the spring rains. The scenery of the Cap Rock area of Texas is some of the best the state of Texas has to offer, and the history of this area is some of the most fascinating of any ride we will attempt.

The first half of the trip, the Quitaque Canyon Trail (pronounced like KITTY-KWAY), is an interesting and beautiful ride that will let you combine your big chainring with a small cog to blast along at speeds approaching 20 miles per hour, veritably flying the whole way. If you camp at nearby Caprock Canyons State Park, you can buy a lift to the South Plains Trailhead from the ranger for $5. This makes the trip an easy one-way ride that anyone of any skill level can enjoy.

About halfway along the ride you will pass through the oldest and longest wooden railroad tunnel in Texas. Built in 1920, the Clarity Tunnel is now home to thousands of pigeons and Mexican free-tailed bats. If you pause at one end and walk in slowly enough to allow your eyes to adjust, you may be able to see a bat or two as they swoop around from roost to roost. You will almost certainly hear their squeaking calls and smell the musky scent of their

RIDE 34 *QUITAQUE CANYON / LOS LINGOS RAILS-TO-TRAILS*

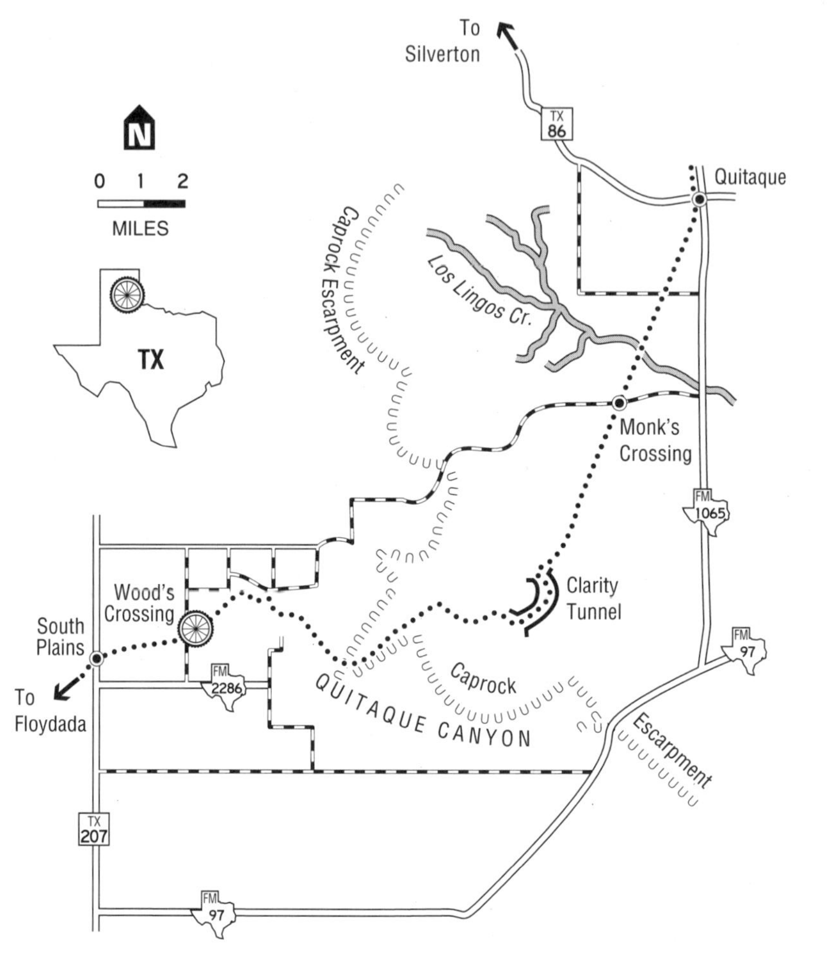

droppings. The rangers keep a water jug at the southern end of the tunnel, so you can recharge your bottles here instead of carrying extra ones on the trail with you.

Long before you reach the tunnel, you will begin to see Quitaque Peak, just a few miles to the south. Winding through the Quitaque Canyon, you follow Quitaque Creek, crossing small bridges over it and other area creeks about every mile or so. There are large piles of railroad ties every so often from when the rails were pulled up a few years ago, just before this was turned into the Caprock Canyons State Park Trailways System. If the weather is hot, you will smell the creosote as you pass the piles of old timbers. Along the way you will also see evidence of an old telephone line. Nothing is left but the poles, and just about every one of these will have a vulture sitting atop it, giving you the eye like they wish you would stop moving long enough for them to have a bite of lunch.

After the tunnel the trail is called the Los Lingos Trail. Those of you with a knowledge of Spanish will recognize *los lingos* as "the tongues." It is the name of a creek that roughly parallels an area known as the Valley of Tears. Perhaps you are familiar with the Trail of Tears? In the 1800s, the federal government gathered all the southern Indian tribes and forced them to relocate to reservation lands in Oklahoma, then called Indian Territory. One of the routes they had to take passed through this area. Many of these indigenous peoples did not survive the trip and were buried along the way. Unknown numbers of them found their last resting places in the canyons you will pass as you ride down from the tunnel toward the Quitaque Depot Trailhead. Look around you and get a feel for how unhappy it must have been to travel through this area on foot, under the conditions of a forced march, as cavalry soldiers hurried them along with little feeling for their hardships. If you feel a chill run through your spine as you ride along enjoying the day, it might be the spirits of long-dead warriors watching you from their graves in the canyons. If you are the religious kind, say a silent prayer for the lost souls who wander these canyons and arroyos.

General location: This trail runs from South Plains to Quitaque in the eastern part of the Texas Panhandle, about 80 miles southeast of Amarillo.
Elevation change: The South Plains Trailhead lies at about 3,200′ above sea level. The Quitaque Depot Trailhead is down around 2,500′.
Season: Great riding any time of year, but cooler times such as spring and fall are probably slightly more enjoyable than high summer. During the hottest months biting flies are so bad they will keep you slapping and swatting, trying to wave them away.
Services: The only facilities associated with the actual trail are a water jug at the Clarity Tunnel, about half the distance from South Plains to Quitaque. The town of South Plains has a gas station, and the town of Quitaque has a 24-hour convenience store with pay phones. Camping, shuttle service, rest rooms, water, and showers are available at Caprock Canyons State Park. Bike rentals and a shuttle service are also available in Quitaque from The Bike Depot. The nearest bike shop is far away, like in Lubbock or Amarillo.
Hazards: This is not a real dangerous trail, but it is very remote. Snakes may be seen from time to time and should be offered a wide berth. Biting flies can be a problem during the summer. This is harsh terrain, so carry what you will need to survive any difficulties that might arise. (Patch kits, tools, and a pump should be considered a necessary part of your equipment if you tackle this trail.) The roads you cross are few, but all of them are active, so take care to watch for automobile traffic.

Since there ain't a lot of shade in this part of Texas, we sometimes have to build our own. The Clarity Tunnel, half-way point from Quitaque Canyon to Los Lingos Creek.

Rescue index: The rangers have four-wheel-drive vehicles and they regularly drive the trail, so getting rescued from here is possible, but, as always, there will have to be a healthy person to ride out and fetch help if an injured person gets stranded out here in the middle of nowhere. Your only recourse if you need emergency help is to follow the trail to where it passes near inhabited ranch houses along the way and beg one of the residents to call the authorities for you.

Land status: This trail lies on old railroad easement that is held and managed by the Texas Parks and Wildlife Department as the Caprock Canyons State Park Trailways System.

Maps: Good maps of the area are available from the state park headquarters, free of charge. The quads for this area are South Plains, Wilson Creek, Edgemon Lake, Quitaque Peaks, Quitaque, and Lake Theo.

Finding the trail: The Wood's Crossing Trailhead actually lies a couple of miles or so outside the small town of South Plains. From TX 207 about 16 miles north of the town of Floydada, go east on Farm to Market 2286 about 2 miles, and turn left on the second dirt road. Go north about a mile, to where the railroad bed crosses the dirt road. Go through the gate and ride east, toward the canyons in the distance. After about 15 miles you will reach Monk's Crossing Trailhead, a pair of gates where a dirt road crosses the trail. About 3 miles later, another pair of gates and another dirt road cross the trail. About 2 miles after that, you will be in Quitaque and crossing TX 86. After crossing the highway, continue along the railroad bed until you reach the next paved road, FM 1065 (a distance of only about one-half mile). If you were shuttled from Caprock Canyons State Park, head north on this paved road until you reach the entrance to the state park, about 4 miles north of the town of Quitaque.

Sources of additional information:

Park Superintendent
Caprock Canyons State Park
P.O. Box 204
Quitaque, TX 79255
(806) 455-1492

Caprock Bike Club
P.O. Box 475
Quitaque, TX 79255

DFC Cycles and Fitness
3501 50th Street
Lubbock, TX 79413
(806) 792 8501

Notes on the trail: This rails-to-trails project actually extends for nearly 65 miles, another 40 miles past the town of Quitaque. The plan is to build campgrounds along the railroad bed about every 10 miles and open the whole thing up as a multi-use trail facility. You cannot ride all the way over to the town of Estilline right now, but to me the area from the South Plains Trailhead to the Quitaque Depot Trailhead is the most interesting. I grew up out here and have always been in love with this part of the state.

All of the land on either side of the railroad corridor is private. DO NOT cross over fences and get on these private lands unless you want to attract the angry attention of landowners along the way. They will DEFINITELY prosecute trespassers.

This trail is a multi-use facility, so it is not unusual to meet equestrian or pedestrian traffic along the way. Be polite and offer them the right-of-way. I even saw some farmer in a tractor cruising the trail the day I was here. Enjoy the trail; it is one of the best in this book.

RIDE 35 *CAPROCK CANYONS STATE PARK TRAIL*

This trail is easy double-track in places and almost nonexistent single-track in others. It varies between old ranch roads and cattle trails, hard-packed dirt and red sand sprinkled with white gypsum deposits. You start from the trailhead near an old corral and then proceed along a spur to a point where the trail splits and becomes a loop that leads you down into a canyon, along a

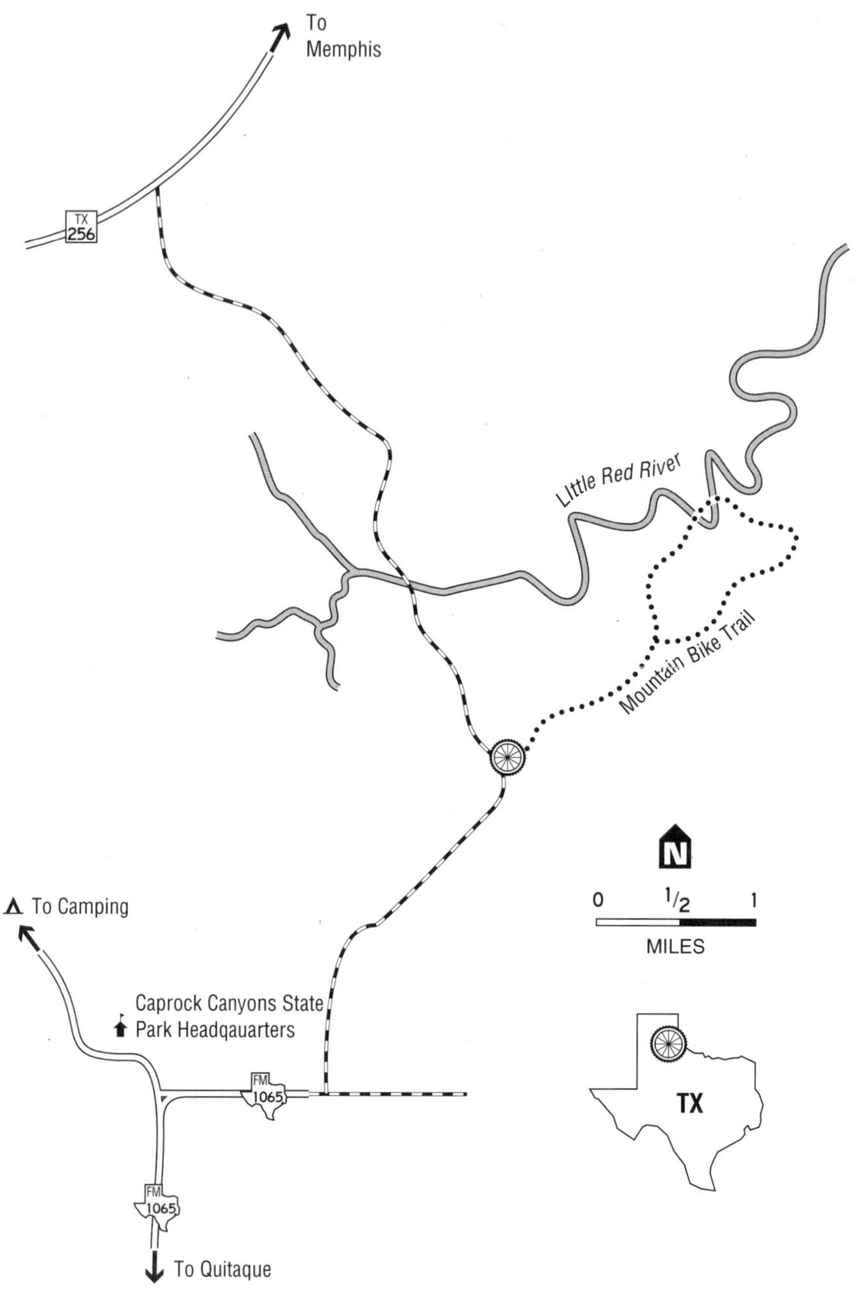
To
Memphis
TX
256
Little Red River
Mountain Bike Trail
To Camping
N
0
1/2
1
MILES
Caprock Canyons State
Park Headqauarters
FM
1065
FM
1065
TX
To Quitaque

riverbed, then out of the canyon and back to the split that goes back to the trailhead. All together you will have gone over five miles when you get back to the parking area.

The trail is to date the only one in Caprock Canyons State Park where mountain biking is welcomed, but there are several others that are very worthy hiking trails. Bring your boots and explore some of the other singletrack in the park. The red canyons in this area are beautiful, and their natural beauty can be breathtaking at dawn. The mesquite and cactus that cover this area are home to a surprising collection of wildlife. Mule and white-tailed deer will bound from behind every stand of bushes as you walk along, and raccoons and skunks will plague your campsite after dark. Don't try to sleep on the ground without the benefit of a tent—the critters will bug you all night and you will get no sleep.

This trail may not be for everyone. It is marked by signs where it begins and where it splits to form the loop. Other areas are unmarked and may all but disappear at certain times of year. Once you complete the steep rocky descent and reach the Little Red River at the bottom of the canyon, you will have to follow the winding riverbed to locate the section of old road that leads up the side of the canyon and returns to the split. The climb out of the canyon is on loose rock, very difficult and challenging. At one point as you climb out, you will be offered a nice long view of the area you have just ridden through, and this in itself may be justification for exploring the mountain bike trail at Caprock Canyons State Park.

General location: Caprock Canyons State Park is in the eastern central section of the Texas Panhandle, an area of eroded canyons known as the Cap Rock.
Elevation change: The trailhead is near the highest point, lying around 2,460′ of elevation, and the lowest place you go along the basin of the Little Red River is situated near 2,150′.
Season: This trail should be rideable unless very wet, in which case it would be a mess. I would say it is enjoyable year-round unless the weather is severe.
Services: The only services are near the headquarters: A pay phone, rest rooms, and water are available there. The nearby Honey Flat Campground has showers and a soft drink machine. The town of Quitaque, 4 miles south, has a 24-hour convenience store with gas pumps. The nearest bike shops are in Lubbock and Amarillo.
Hazards: Boy, getting lost or injured on this remote range could be dangerous. Snakes are always a threat in terrain such as this, and biting flies will plague you in the summer. The descent into the valley of the Little Red River is steep, rutted, and covered with loose rocks and must be respected and ridden with care. The equestrian trails are near, and though this is identified by a sign as the mountain bike trail, you could run into some horses. Remember your manners.

Rush hour on the Caprock Canyons State Park mountain bike trail. Since this chapter was written, much more prime single-track in the park may have become available to mountain bikers, thanks to the Texas Parks and Wildlife Department and the personnel at the Caprock Canyons State Park.

Rescue index: It is just barely possible to get rescued from here in an emergency, but only if you have a healthy partner to send back for help. Most sections of this trail would be accessible by four-wheel-drive vehicles if needed, but the ranger would have to come unlock the chain across the road at the trailhead.

Land status: The trail is all located on land that is part of a fine state park, managed by the Texas Parks and Wildlife Department.

Maps: The park headquarters has very good topographical maps available at no cost. The quads for this trail are Lake Theo and Turkey.

Finding the trail: Quitaque is about halfway between US 287 at Estilline and Interstate 27 at Tulia, on TX 86. Caprock Canyons State Park is north of Quitaque about 4 miles on Farm to Market 1065.

From the park headquarters, head south on the main park road out of the gate at the entrance and turn left onto the pavement of FM 1065. Proceed east past where the pavement ends and turn left on the first dirt road. Follow the dirt road north for about 2.5 miles, until you see the signs indicating the trailhead on the east side of the dirt road.

Park by (but do not block) the gate and follow the double-track to the left of the corral to where the sign shows it splits. Follow the left branch and take the single-track (old cattle trail) down into the canyon and over to the riverbed. There you will turn right and follow the gradual left-hand bend in the Little Red River (yes, that Red River) as best you can for about half a mile, until you see the double-track climb out of the riverbed to your right and wind toward the side of the canyon to the east. This will be after the river has doubled back and started heading north again, and just before it makes a bend to the east (in 1995, right past some trees). In the distance to the east you will see the old road leading up the side of the canyon. Follow the double-track out of the canyon and around to where it carries you past the spot where you split off earlier. Continue on the double-track, returning to the parking area near the corral.

Sources of additional information:

Park Superintendent
Caprock Canyons State Park
P.O. Box 204
Quitaque, TX 79255
(806) 455-1492

Caprock Bike Club
P.O. Box 475
Quitaque, TX 79255

TPWD Reservation Center
P.O. Box 17488
Austin, TX 78760-7488
(512) 389-8900 for reservations only

Notes on the trail: This trail needs to be ridden more, and it also needs for mountain bikers to exhibit more interest in it. That might someday cause more miles of the excellent single-track trails in this area to be opened up to mountain bikes. Just use it responsibly and yield to other users if you meet any. Have fun and enjoy the rugged natural beauty of this part of my state.

To the north, on the far side of the John Haynes Ridge, is a Boy Scout camp called Haynes Canyon. This is where I had my first experiences with backpacking and primitive camping and where I developed my love of the canyons in the Caprock section of Texas. It is my favorite part of the state, next to the Big Bend Country. I wish you some serious quality of experience.

RIDE 36 *CAPITOL PEAK TRAIL*

When I was in high school, I made a bet with some friends that I could pedal out of this canyon on my ten-speed. We hauled our bikes to the headquarters from Plainview in the back of my pal's jeep. Then we unloaded them and both of us coasted down the hill and turned around, and I rode out. You know, I don't even remember it being that hard to do. Youth is definitely wasted on the young.

RIDE 36 *CAPITOL PEAK TRAIL*

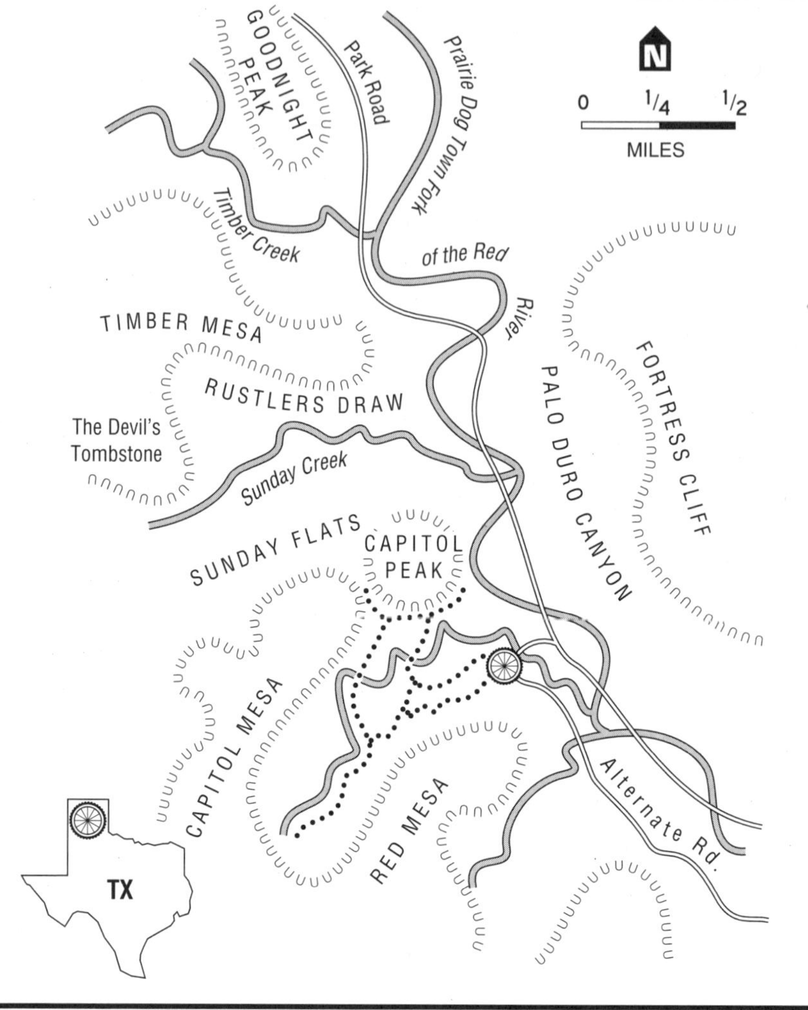

In 1989 I had a wild hair to fly to Amarillo and pedal to where my mom lives in Fort Worth. I packed my touring bike in a box and fixed my panniers up as carry-on luggage. I planned to camp at state parks along the way and take a few days to enjoy rural Texas. I got to Palo Duro late in the day, took a few shots of my bike and the canyon, and threw camp. The next morning I packed my stuff, drew a deep breath, and headed up the road toward the headquarters at the top of the hill. *I thought I was gonna die!!!* I had to stop four times on the way out and rest, leaning against a rock or a road sign and puffing like a locomotive. The canyon road's grade seemed to have grown a few percentage points in the 15 or so years since the last time I had ridden it. Of course, the 40 pounds of gear on my bike and extra 20 or so pounds on me since high school could also have had an effect.

As you stand at the trailhead and look at the canyon walls surrounding you, it will seem obvious that some killer mountain biking could most certainly be done somewhere in the vicinity. Well, here it is. The Capitol Peak Trails are a looping maze of single-track, in the neighborhood of five miles or so, that let you explore part of Palo Duro Canyon State Park. They are marked with signs of three different colors to indicate their difficulty. Like at ski slopes, green will mean the easiest level, blue is intermediate, and black is the hardest and most dangerous of the three. None are deadly, and the climbing and technical requirements are a nice mix of the skills most of us flatlanders already have. Several of the short quick drops you will have to negotiate along the trail are very abrupt, especially on the black trail, so don't get going so fast that you surprise yourself with any trips over the handlebars. You might fall for several feet before the ground cushions your fall. The soil ranges from red sand and hard-packed dirt, very easy to ride, to loose softball-sized rocks almost impossible to pedal over.

Gosh, I could go on for hours about the history of this area. First of all, you should know that *palo duro* is Spanish for "hard wood," a name derived from the Spaniards' experiences with the local juniper trees. An army colonel named Ranald Mackenzie sneaked down into this canyon one moonlit night and massacred the wives and children of a bunch of Comanche Indians who were elsewhere doing that old war party thang. The next day Colonel Mackenzie and his men slaughtered about a thousand horses that belonged to the same band of braves. Needless to say, these two actions took the wind out of the Indians' sails, and they were captured and imprisoned shortly afterward. A lot of blood has been spilled in this canyon. The ghosts of dead warriors are thick as pea soup late at night on a full moon when the coyotes are howling the way they are prone to do. You'll feel it, too, if you let your imagination wander a little. Welcome to the "Grand Canyon of Texas."

General location: Located in the northern portion of the Texas Panhandle, about 10 miles east of the town of Canyon and about half an hour southeast of Amarillo.

Elevation change: Though the elevation gain from the deepest part of the Prairie Dog Town Fork of the Red River to the area near the headquarters is almost 700´, the park areas you will ride your mountain bike on are all within 10´ or 20´ higher or lower than 2,840´ above sea level. If that is so flat it embarrasses you, then you need to ride the big hill on the park road leaving the canyon. It has a short piece rated at 11% of grade. That is 11´ rise in 100´ of run—700´ of climbing in about 5 or 6 miles.

Season: Definitely a write-off if it has been raining. This place is all made up of red sandy clay and rocks that will be a mess when muddy (voice of experience).
Services: There are a couple of small concession facilities in the vicinity—the Sad Monkey Railroad and the Goodnight Trading Post. The railroad depot has soda machines, a pay phone, and food and drink when they are open. The trading post has soda machines, gasoline, and a café. Rest rooms with running water are located in each camping and picnic area in the park; the ones in overnight areas have showers.
Hazards: The local flora and fauna are the most likely source of hazardous conditions. Juniper, mesquite, and cactus are prevalent and will tear a jersey or flatten a tire in a second. Western diamondback rattlesnakes are a common item at certain times of year. Be careful riding here in the spring and fall, when they may sun themselves by lying across the trail any time of day. The biting flies are hard to ignore in the summer, and skunks are a critter to be avoided all year. Pesky little varmints will not let you sleep without a tent.
Rescue index: You have a good chance of being saved here if you need a rescue, because this is a popular place almost year-round. Plus, you are never real far from the paved park road, so getting out to seek emergency help is much easier in this park than in many I have described for you. Of course, and once again, it really helps to have a healthy partner riding with you if you do a header off one of the small bluffs. Dragging yourself out with your fingers can get old if you get hurt often, especially if you are in a hurry. Remember the buddy system!
Land status: One of the jewels in the Texas Parks and Wildlife Department's state parks system.
Maps: The only maps I have discovered are available from a bike shop in Amarillo. Hill's Sport Shop is responsible for building and maintaining the trails and also for organizing mountain biking events that take place here throughout the year. Definitely go by and visit them if you can, since the park headquarters is often out of maps. The quad for this park is Fortress Cliff.
Finding the trail: Palo Duro Canyon State Park is 8 miles east of Interstate 27 at Canyon on TX 217.

Drive down into the canyon and turn right on the Alternate Park Road just past the second water crossing. The trailhead and parking are on the right, marked by signs, and each loop in the trail has a sign where it splits from the main trail. Meander around and try to hit them all. Go exploring. You cannot really get lost here (if you stay on the bike) because the trails are contained in a relatively small area bounded by pavement on one side and sheer canyon walls on all others. It is possible to wander into one or two of the canyons and ride up the small creeks, but you will soon reach areas of loose rock and deep sand that are not really bike-friendly. Check it out, though, if you are so inclined.

Life is good, slow down and smell the bluebonnets. Palo Duro Canyon State Park and the Capitol Peak Trail.

Sources of additional information:

Park Superintendent
Palo Duro Canyon State Park
Route 2, Box 285
Canyon, TX 79015
(806) 488-2227

Texas Parks and Wildlife Department
4200 Smith School Road
Austin, TX 78744-3291
(800) 792-1112 for information only

TPWD Reservation Center
P.O. Box 17488
Austin, TX 78760-7488
(512) 389-8900 for reservations only

Hill's Sport Shop
4021 Mockingbird
Amarillo, TX 79109
(806) 355-7224

Notes on the trail: This is another park you can expect to find locked up if you arrive after about 10 P.M., so plan to get there earlier than that if you need a place to camp. There is a lot to see and do here, so try to plan a long enough stay to enjoy some of the touristy stuff: ride the railroad, do some hiking or road biking, or take in the stage show *Texas,* which is performed on summer evenings. On your way to the trail, you will go right by the amphitheater where the show happens. Because of the show *Texas,* the office hours at this park are unusually long—from 8 A.M. to 10 P.M.

The Gulf Coast

Hurricanes, anyone? Floods, mosquitoes, snakes, cool single-track? Despite the name of this section, this book leaves the Gulf Coast of Texas largely unexplored. I know there is more stuff out there, but I focused mostly on the Houston area because the trails there are famous statewide. And deservedly so.

The Texas Gulf Coast stretches 400 miles, from Brownsville and the Rio Grande in the south to Port Arthur and the Sabine Pass battleground in the east. There are limitless rides possible along the beaches, but I am allergic to sand, so I am keeping you inland. Feel free to explore any of the beach-type rides listed in the "Honorable Mentions" chapter.

When I was working on this manuscript, I had a friend living in Houston. It was a perfect setup for me: When Cheryl would come home to Dallas for the weekend, I would drive to Houston and stay at her apartment, which was very near Barker Dam and the Ho Chi Minh Trail. That way I had a nice base-camp to launch my explorations of this area, and everything would have been perfect except that every time I went to Houston it rained. But somehow I managed finally to get all the trails studied and move on.

There are a ton of mountain bikers in this area, and just about any trail you attempt will be crowded with other riders. Stay awake, stay alive, stay cool, and use lots of mosquito repellent.

RIDE 37 *HO CHI MINH TRAIL*

I had heard of this place for ages before I ever made it here to ride. It lived up to its reputation as "cool single-track," and I was thoroughly pleased with what I found. Here in the heart of one of the nation's largest cities is one of the area's best (and busiest) mountain bike parks. And one of the muddiest, if the weather has been wet recently.

The area behind the baseball and soccer fields, all the way over to Buffalo Bayou, is like a spider's web of single-track. Some of the trails are flat and very easy, but most crisscross gullies and creeks in a challenging flow of short, steep climbs and drops. The ride I am going to describe for you is a loop of about five miles from the parking area trailhead to and across an area called simply "The Gully" and from there to and along Buffalo Bayou all the way east to the end of the park. From there you may return along Memorial Drive (opposite from the jogging trail, which is strictly OFF LIMITS TO BICYCLES) or retrace your path through the trees on the single-track, whichever you desire.

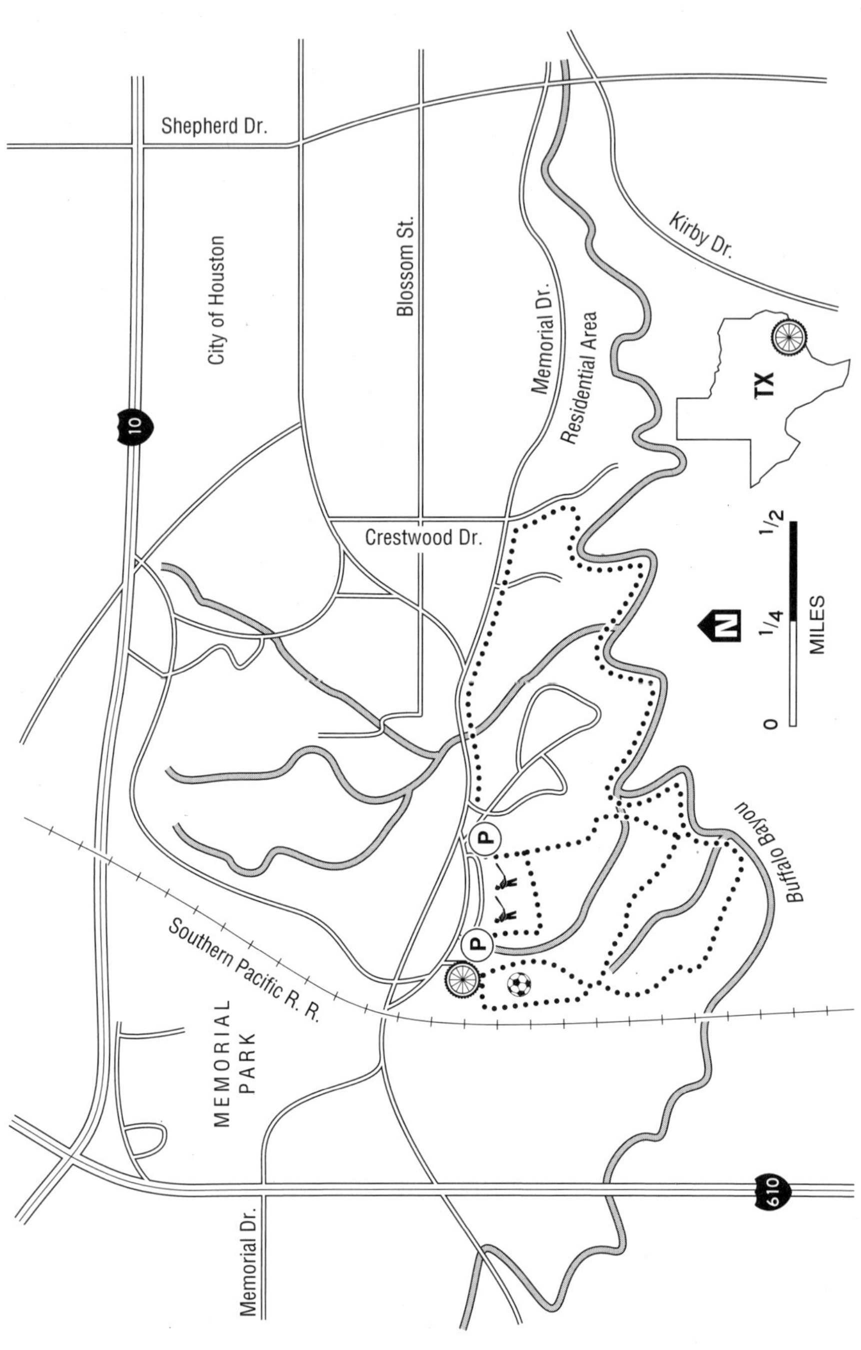
Shepherd Dr.
City of Houston
Blossom St.
Memorial Dr.
Residential Area
Kirby Dr.
TX
10
Crestwood Dr.
N
0
1/4
1/2
MILES
P
P
Buffalo Bayou
Southern Pacific R. R.
MEMORIAL
PARK
610
Memorial Dr.

Due to the effects of erosion, you will be using your technical skills to hop tree roots and negotiate washed-out sections. Quick judgment and gear selection is necessary as you swoop up and down the small hills and gullies. Since there are so many mountain bike enthusiasts in this area, you will be sharing the trail with lots of other riders, so keep your eyes peeled and pay attention to your surroundings. This is a trail where you will not need sunscreen, because the whole area is densely covered with hardwoods, providing a leafy canopy of green; you will seldom see the sky.

This is yet another park where mountain bikers have been threatened with banishment because of repeated abuses by people riding in the mud. Don't be a squid-pie—let the dirt dry. The local mountain bike club, Houston Area Mountain Bike Riders Association (HAMBRA), has established an information line for you to call to find out if the trails are closed due to wet conditions, and they have installed signs at the trailhead to show when it is smart to stay out of the park due to muddy trails. Responsible actions like this are exactly what is called for in many areas where sensitive ecological conditions exist. Hurrah!

General location: Practically in the middle of Houston.
Elevation change: Overall elevation changes are minimal, but repeated short stints of up and down are the order of the day. Look for the whole trail to be between 60′ and 100′ above sea level. I mean, the topo maps for this area have contour lines every 5′. Spooky.
Season: Nothing like a happy ride will ever happen here if it has been raining. Any other time you are more than welcome to enjoy the trails.
Services: The trailhead parking area has nothing but that. The park roads that form the "picnic loop" just east of the trailhead have pay phones, drinking water, and rest rooms. The nearest bike shop is West End Cycles, very nearby.
Hazards: I think there might be a few hundred tons of poison ivy along this trail; I am guessing so because it is such a densely wooded area. The heavy level of traffic, as well as the many severely eroded sections of the trail, could be considered a hazard. There are a few technical challenges, mostly tree roots and low limbs, but some sections of the trails can be loose and quick enough to make tires slide if a lot of speed is carried into a curve or turn. And last but certainly not least, the mosquitoes here have been known to fly away with children and small pets. Carry and use your repellent.
Rescue index: I will rate this ride high on the rescuability counter, because it is in such close proximity to such a large urban area. Also, you will find many other riders on the trails, so getting word out for emergency help should not represent a major effort.
Land status: The riding here is all on trails contained within a City of Houston park and, as such, should be protected as long as the citizens of Houston stay awake to potential threats, if these ever occur.

HAMBRA has busted some major butt keeping the Ho Chi Minh trail at Memorial Park open to bikes. Thanks mountain bikers.

Maps: The only map I have found for this is a quad, namely the one called Houston Heights.

Finding the trail: Houston's Memorial Park is located in the southeastern quadrant of the intersection between two major highways, Interstate 610 (West Loop #610 South) and I-10 (Katy Freeway). The trailhead is on the south side of Memorial Drive and just east of Loop #610 a short distance, between Loop #610 and the baseball complex. Park, then ride south past the sign kiosk, through the small creek, along the east side of the soccer field, and back into the trees. Follow the trails in a gradually southward direction until you find Buffalo Bayou, then roughly parallel the bayou all the way east, to where it crosses Crestwood Drive. This will dump you near Memorial Drive once again. Follow the trail on the south side of Memorial Drive back to where you parked, about a mile or so to the west.

Sources of additional information:

Houston Area Mountain Bike Riders Association (HAMBRA)
4912 North Highway #6
Houston, TX 77084
(713) 856-9732

West End Bicycles
5427 Blossom Street
Houston, TX 77007
(713) 861-2271

Notes on the trail: A lot of activities and events take place in this park, and a lot of people count on it for their recreation. If you are a Houston-area mountain biker, I strongly urge you to become involved with HAMBRA so that you can take part in trail maintenance days and become aware of the politics of keeping this park open to bikes. There are a lot of people out there who do not like us, and only a positive approach to the issues will preserve our opportunities to enjoy these trails. Get in tune and take action soon.

RIDE 38 *BARKER DAM RIDE*

Western Houston is home to the Barker Reservoir, constructed in the 1940s after severe flooding in 1935, which devastated parts of the city and claimed several lives. The dam that impounds this part-time reservoir is roughly U-shaped, and it is possible to ride all the way around the park by following the dam until you reach the end of one arm of the U. There you may either turn around and return the way you came or follow paved and gravel roads that will let you cut across to catch the other leg of the U. Most of your riding will be off-road, however, and the very flat and almost rural surroundings make the dam popular with joggers and recreational riders who want to escape the hustle and bustle of the big city for a short while.

By starting at Cullen-Barker County Park on Barker-Clodine Road, you will have an opportunity to fill water bottles and visit rest rooms with indoor plumbing, then do your ride and return to the same facilities. Since the Houston area is typically very flat, the riding is easy unless the weather provides strong winds, which it does sometimes. In this case you should choose whether to ride the dam in a clockwise or counterclockwise direction based on whether you want to ride the soft gravel into or with the wind. It would probably be advisable to have the wind at your back while on the gravel, since this would give you a hard, paved surface when fighting headwinds. Your choice.

If you make a complete circle, you will clock around 14 miles. Roughly 8 of these miles will be on the sandy gravel of the dam. If you choose you may continue to ride the dam to the west of Barker-Clodine Road for another 5 miles of out-and-back trail.

If the Houston area has been visited with rain during your visit, the dam may be your only hope of an off-road ride. I made a circuit here the morning after

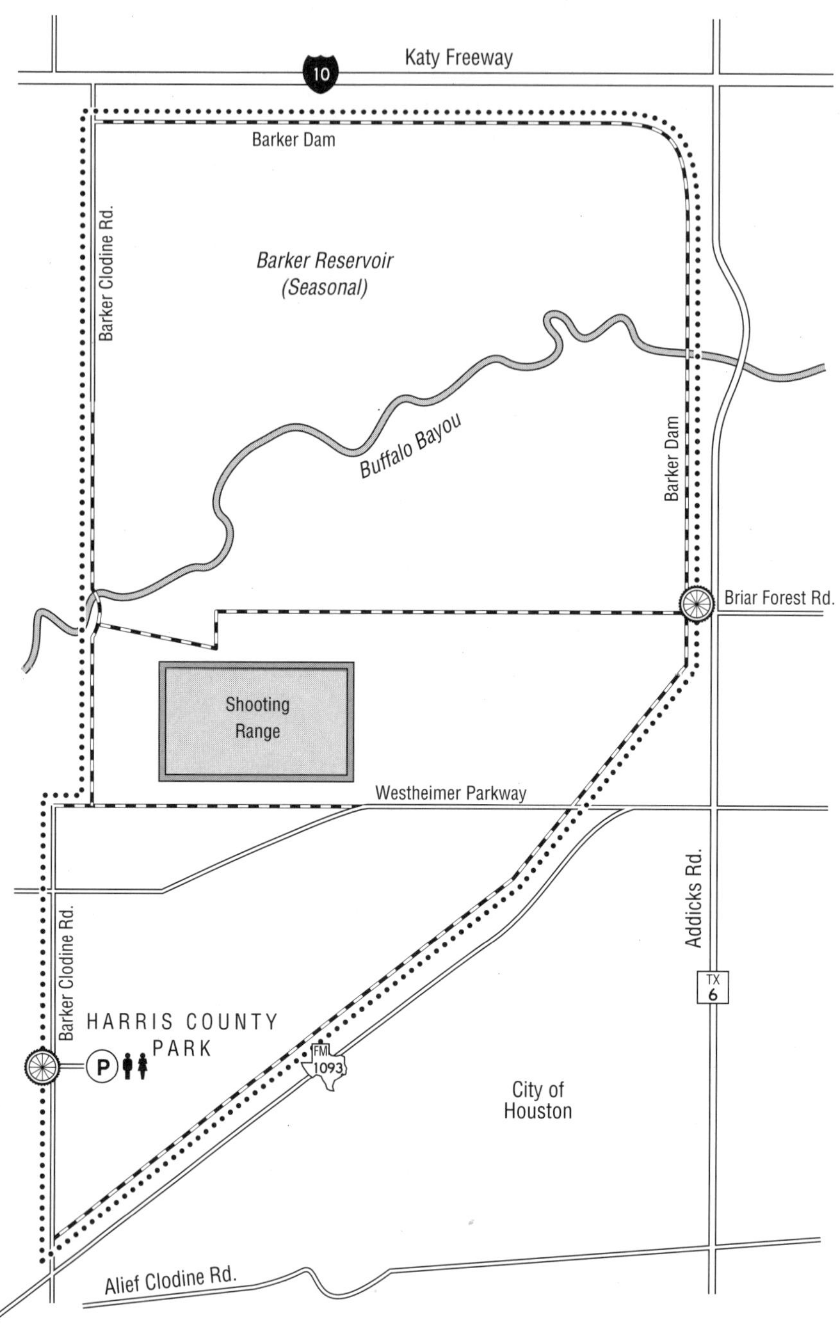
Katy Freeway
10
Barker Dam
Barker Clodine Rd.
Barker Reservoir
(Seasonal)
Buffalo Bayou
Barker Dam
Briar Forest Rd.
Shooting
Range
Westheimer Parkway
Addicks Rd.
TX
6
Barker Clodine Rd.
HARRIS COUNTY
PARK
P
FM
1093
City of
Houston
Alief Clodine Rd.

an inch fell, and though I plowed through a bunch of puddles of standing water, it was very rideable and there were very few stretches of sloppy mud. My bike was a mess afterward, but it cleaned easily with a garden hose.

The area enclosed by the dam is almost all wooded. It was originally planned for development as a golf course and military training area, but this plan never materialized. It is very common to see equestrian, foot, and other bicycle traffic, but automobiles are not allowed. If you see one, it will likely be city or county workers performing their job duties within the boundaries of the reservoir area.

General location: Barker Reservoir is on the west side of Houston, about 17 miles west of downtown, and about one-quarter mile south of Interstate 10, a.k.a. the Katy Freeway.

Elevation change: The dam is around 30′ above the surrounding terrain, which is all tabletop-flat and between 85′ and 105′ in elevation.

Season: The dam may be ridden all year, even during a heavy rain if you do not mind getting somewhat muddy. Nobody cares if you plow through the puddles here, unlike on single-track trails in the state. The reservoir only exists after heavy rains; it empties and is drained most of the time.

Services: TX 6, a.k.a. Addicks Road, runs north and south along the eastern part of the dam. There are many convenience stores, gas stations, and other commercial establishments along Addicks Road. The nearest bike shop I know of is West End Cycles, near downtown.

Hazards: There is a shooting range near the southern end of the loop, so you may hear shots in the distance, but this should provide no danger to riders. Be very careful at the spot where the dam road crosses Westheimer Parkway, since traffic on the pavement is usually substantial. There are really no other "dangers" to speak of, unless one should happen across a poisonous snake. I strongly suspect that the mosquitoes in this area tend toward gargantuan.

Rescue index: Getting rescued from anywhere on the dam would be a fairly straightforward affair. All along the eastern leg you will generally be within sight of numerous commercial areas, including convenience stores and gas stations with pay phones. While you are out on the western leg, you will be somewhat more isolated, since you will have to climb through a few gates that restrict the area to pedestrian and bicycle traffic. In an emergency it would be necessary to go north or south to one of the city streets to obtain assistance.

Land status: This land is owned by Harris County and is maintained as a public park.

Maps: The only maps I have seen are in the form of USGS topographical maps that may be purchased from map stores. The quads for this ride are Clodine, Addicks, and Richmond NE.

Finding the trail: From I-10 and TX 6 proceed south on TX 6 to Westheimer. Turn right (west) on Westheimer and proceed to Barker-Clodine Road. Turn

Barker Dam is as flat as the day is long.

north and go over the dam (that's the trail) and continue about one-half mile to the county park on the east side of the street. Park here and ride back south on Barker-Clodine Road to the dam. Going west will take you about 5 miles to the end of the dam. Going east will lead you around in a loop until you are back at Barker-Clodine Road just south of I-10. This will be the second paved road you encounter. Turn south (away from the freeway) and continue until you reach the gate at the point where Barker-Clodine becomes a gravel road. Cross through the gate and follow the gravel road until you reach another gate where Barker-Clodine again becomes a paved road. This will be where the trail crosses Westheimer Parkway. Soon you will see the buildings at the county park again, on the east side of the road.

Sources of additional information:

Houston Area Mountain Bike Riders Association (HAMBRA)
4912 North Highway 6
Houston, TX 77084
(713) 856-9732

West End Bicycles
5427 Blossom Street
Houston, TX 77007
(713) 861-2271

Notes on the trail: As mountain bike trails go, Barker Dam is sort of a last resort. If it is too muddy to ride Memorial Park, chances are the dam is usable. Since it is flat and nontechnical, cyclists of almost any skill level will be able to ride here without busting a gut or scraping a knee. There are some gates to cross, but they are constructed in such a way that you can slip your bike through the ones that are too tall to pass over. If you brought your fishing gear, you may find enough water in Buffalo Bayou to justify getting a hook wet. A bicycle is the optimum way to visit the spots where fishing is available, since automobile traffic is not allowed.

RIDE 39 *JACK BROOKS PARK TRAIL*

Jack Brooks Park was named for a famous Texas politician. Originally it was Camp Wallace, a training area for artillery and infantry troops departing for theaters of operation during World War II, circa 1942. After the war it was used as a mustering point for navy veterans returning from overseas. The land was purchased by Galveston County in 1973 and opened as a public park. There are some lovely wooded areas, small ponds, a bayou, picnic pavilions, and a field for radio-controlled airplanes.

This is another location popular for local and state races. The park contains about six miles of single-track and a few miles of dirt roads that may be enjoyed by the off-road cyclist. You will find some easy parts that anyone could ride, flat and straight and hard-packed, and then you will find sections that are much more technical, with tight turns and root-covered climbs that will have you testing your handling and weight-shifting skills.

The trails here are mostly divided into two major loops. The loop to the east of the parking area goes by a pond and is mostly a network of interconnecting trails under a hardwood canopy. To the west of the parking area are the more difficult sections, which wind around and pop out onto one of the gravel roads in the park. Both loops have long sections that parallel the bayou, and from these sections you will see many opportunities to catch side trails into the trees. Most of the trails under the trees have a surface of good old black gumbo, though some of the exposed single-track is sandier and slightly looser.

Located within the city limits of Hitchcock, just a few miles from Galveston and the Galveston Island Seawall, and within easy side-trip distance of NASA's Johnson Space Center, this area offers you many recreational opportunities. The park has excellent facilities for picnicking and would be a good place to take the family for a day trip. Turn the kids loose to fish in the pond or play in the playground, then head for the trails.

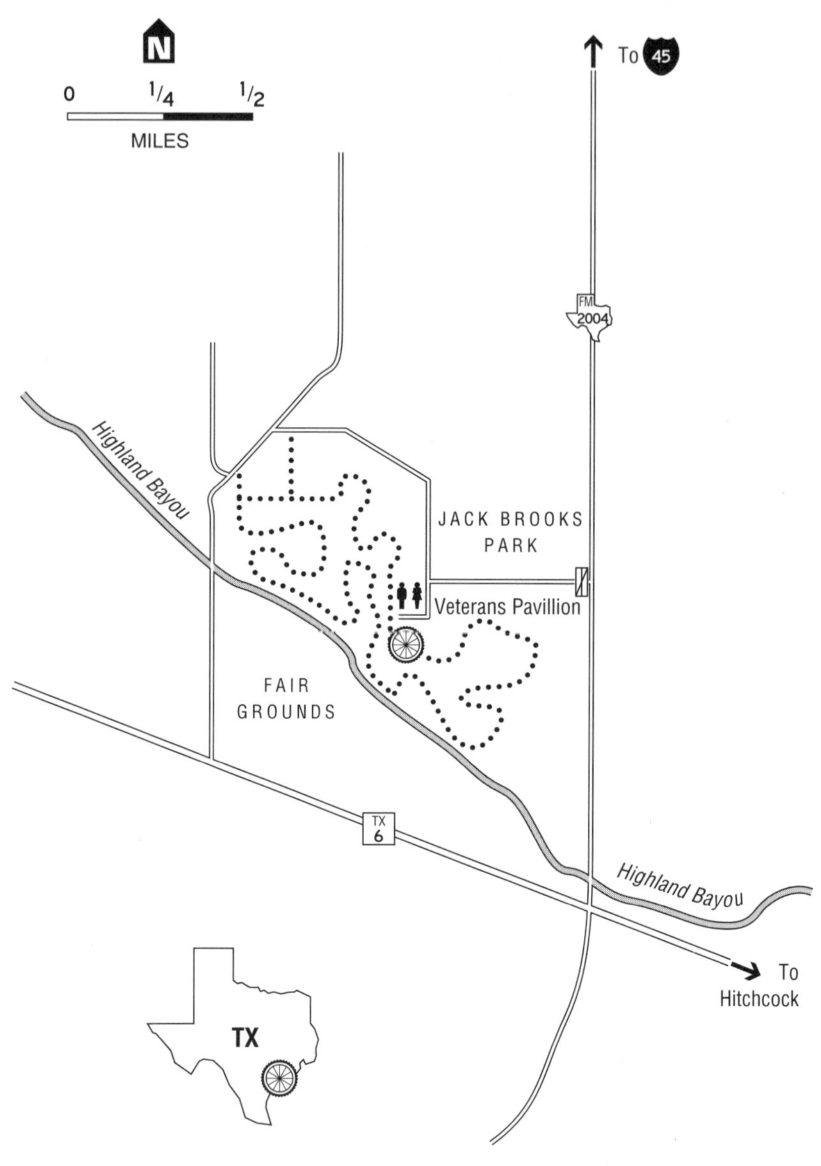
N
0
1/4
1/2
MILES
To 45
FM 2004
Highland Bayou
JACK BROOKS PARK
Veterans Pavillion
FAIR GROUNDS
TX 6
Highland Bayou
To Hitchcock
TX

General location: Southeast of Houston about half an hour; very close to Interstate 45, the Gulf Freeway.

Elevation change: Don't laugh, but you cannot really call the minuscule amount of variation here an "elevation change." According to the topographic maps, the whole area lies around 15′ above sea level.

Season: It often rains enough to make the trails here so muddy and sloppy that riding is highly impractical. Within a day of moderate rains, however, the trails can be very inviting, since the soil here drains very well. If an event is going on at the nearby dog track, you may find unbearable traffic. It might pay to give the track a call before heading down to Jack Brooks—it might save you a lot of aggravation.

Services: Rest rooms and drinking water are available in the park, but any other requirements you may have should be attended to before you enter the grounds for a ride. The town of Hitchcock is just a mile or so past the entrance to the park and has pay phones and places to get ice or munchies.

Hazards: The mosquitoes are formidable—no joke. There are also many places where wooden shipping pallets have been laid over low spots that get muddy. These can surprise unwary riders as they blast up and down the many short hills in the technical sections. Hit them square in the middle and you will live to ride another day. Take care over exposed tree roots (there are many), because these things are slippery even when they are bone-dry, and deadly when they are slightly damp from rain.

Rescue index: Getting rescued from anywhere along the trails would require no major effort once authorities were notified of an emergency. Making that 911 call represents much more of a challenge, since the county park board has not been able to arrange to have pay phones installed in the park. Drive to Hitchcock if you need a phone, or carry a cellular phone into the park with you. There are usually quite a few people riding here, so other traffic can probably be counted on for help.

Land status: The land in Jack Brooks Park belongs to the citizens of Galveston County, thanks to the Galveston County Beach Park Board.

Maps: The map I have included is about the best you will find; it is far better than anything I was able to acquire while working in this area. The quad for this trail is Hitchcock.

Finding the trail: Proceed southeast on I-45 from Houston. About 35 miles out of Houston you will find the exit to Gulf Greyhound Park on Farm to Market 2004. Go south on FM 2004 about 3 miles past the dog track, and on the right (west) side of the road you will see the main gate to the park. Turn right onto the grounds and follow the park road until you find the Veteran's Pavilion. Park there and look to the south of the pavilion. There you will see the trailhead and bike trail markers. The trail appears to the right and left. Going to the left into the trees will allow you to make a full loop of the property. From there just follow the signs and arrows.

Welcome to Jack Brooks Park. The mosquitoes here have been known to fly away with pets and small children.

Straight south of the pavilion, immediately alongside the trails, you will find Highland Bayou. The trails lie between the bayou to the south and the paved park road to the north, back there in the trees on either side. You can't get real lost, but when you hit the gravel road at the end of the trail on the western side of the park, turn right to go back toward the parking area on the gravel road. Soon you will see the trail plowing back into the trees on your right, next to a sign prohibiting horses.

Sources of additional information:

Galveston County Beach Park Board
(409) 766-2411

Jack Brooks Park Keeper
(409) 986-5533

Bike Barn Bicycle Shop
2425 Bay Area Boulevard
Houston, TX 77058
(713) 480-9100

Notes on the trail: The gates to the mountain bike trails are locked around dark each night and opened again about 8 A.M. the next day, or whenever the park keeper arrives, because he has to open the gate to get into the county's maintenance area. Another issue worthy of mention is that new trails are added here from time to time, so it might be beneficial to check with one of the bike shops in the area to find out if anything interesting has been added since I compiled the information in this chapter. If the weather has been bad, Jack Brooks will be a swamp. Drive to Galveston and ride the Seawall.

RIDE 40 *LAKE SOMERVILLE TRAILWAY*

I loved this place. I thought it would be great fun to get a pace line of my pals on mountain bikes, maybe a tandem or two, and try to do this out-and-back in the best possible time, a distance of about 27 miles round-trip. It is nearly all fast sandy double-track that is flat as a pancake and smooth as Elvis's version of "Silent Night." Oh baby, I'll have another peanut-butter-and-nanner sammich over here, raht now, for The Kang. And maybe take a shot at a TV set.

The reservations I have about hauling buns here are that the trail is heavily used by the equestrian set and you would deserve a whipping if you blasted ANY OF THEM off the trail. Okay, instead of being screaming technoweenies, we will do that old family thang and take the kids. If you have some that are getting a little big for their britches in the endurance category, bring them here and let them roll until their legs will not pedal another revolution. Or—and here is an even better idea—bring the tandem and the Burley. A two-seater could be the way to go here, if the added weight doesn't dig too deep into the sand. It was fine on a single.

Speaking of digging in, I thoroughly enjoyed riding here in spite of the deep sand. The northern sections of the trail were *no problema,* but the areas nearer Nails Creek were almost too powdery to traverse. I think either the horses are more prevalent on the south side of the lake or the soil is less durable to their hooves. It was sandy near Birch Creek, too, but very good riding. The terrain near Nails Creek certainly has more relief, and that may contribute to the erosion.

This is a major-league bird-watching area, in case you are so inclined. In the spring the wildflowers will knock your eyes out, and in the fall the colors of the trees will do the same. In the summer carry plenty of sunscreen, because many miles are exposed.

General location: Roughly halfway between Austin and Houston in the central section of the state. Near US 290 in Brenham.
Elevation change: Pretty flat. The whole trail lies between 240′ and 260′ of elevation.
Season: Variations regarding seasonal use follow the rains on this trail. There is no hunting except for mosquitoes hunting warm-blooded animals and hawks

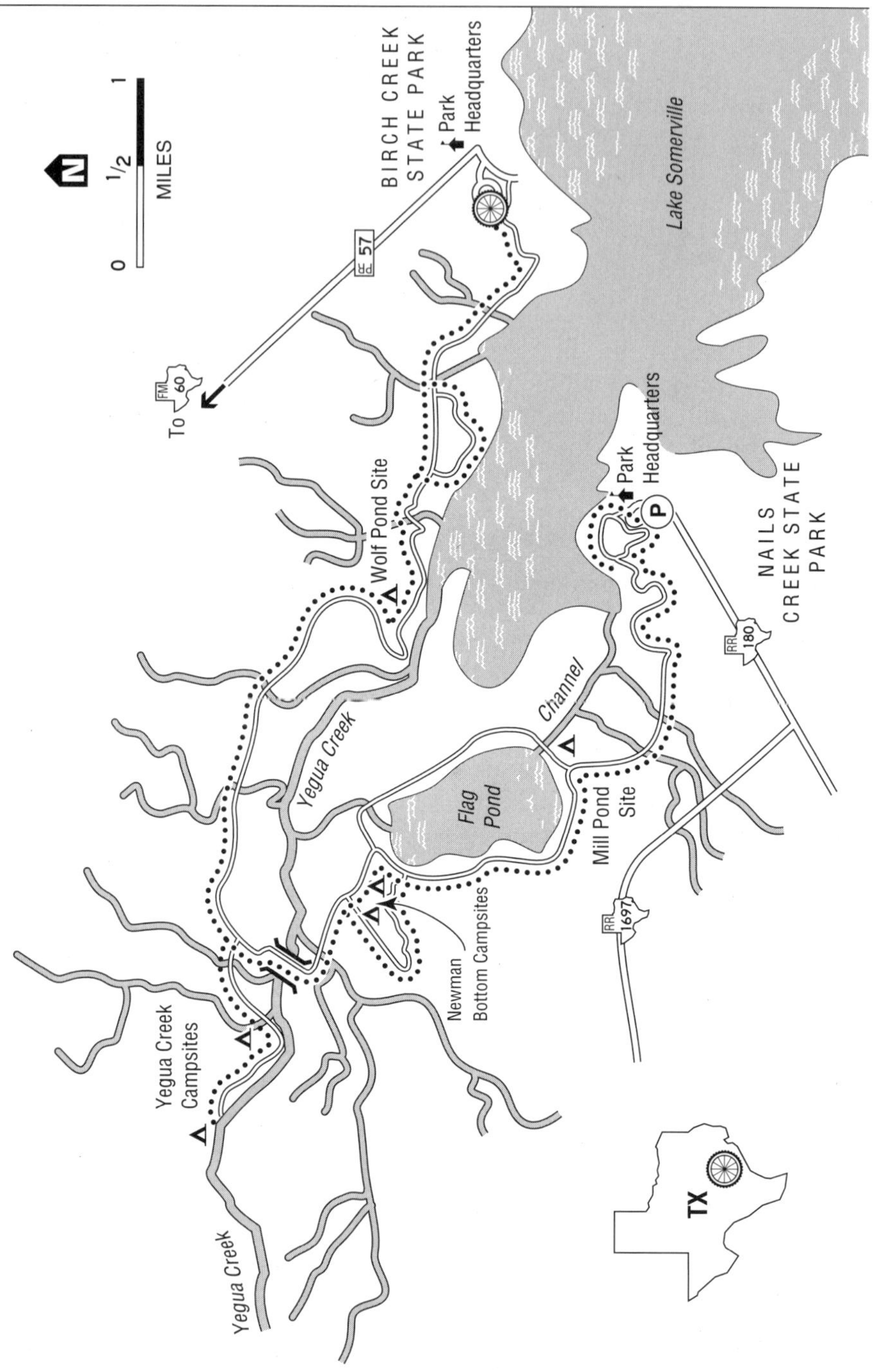

0
1/2
1
MILES
BIRCH CREEK
STATE PARK
Park
Headquarters
57
To
60
Lake Somerville
Wolf Pond Site
Park
Headquarters
NAILS
CREEK STATE
PARK
180
Channel
Yegua Creek
Flag
Pond
Mill Pond
Site
1697
Newman
Bottom Campsites
Yegua Creek
Campsites
Yegua Creek
TX

The bridge over Yegua Creek, Lake Somerville Trailway. If your destination from here is Nails Creek, I'll clue you in: it gets pretty soft after this, real talcum powder if those tall four-legged critters have been through there much.

hunting small rodents. Some sections might be firmer or softer, depending on "nice" weather, because of traffic volume. Horses really chew the snot out of a good piece of dirt.

Services: The headquarters building has water, a soft drink machine, and a pay phone. Other needs will have to be satisfied before your arrival in the park, in Lyons or Brenham. The nearest bike shop is Bicycle Country in Giddings.

Hazards: The water along the trail is for animals only—specifically, the large, meaty, four-legged things that are the predominant trail-use group at this park. Other hazardous concerns are the mosquitoes and the snaky looks of much of this territory. The trail offers no other dangers than its loose surface in many locations. Take plenty of sunscreen, because most of this is open, exposed land.

Rescue index: The whole trail is easily within the driving accessibility of a normal ambulance, but its remoteness and low traffic rate mean you could get pretty lonely waiting for another human being to pass by here. Carry or drag a partner and get rescued, that's my motto.

Land status: This land is another fine Texas Parks and Wildlife Department property.

Maps: The rangers will provide you with an excellent map for free. Thank you very much. The quad for this trail is Flag Pond.

Finding the trail: We start our quest at the town of Brenham, where US 290 and TX 36 cross. Go north on TX 36 to the intersection with Farm to Market 60 in Lyons, about 20 miles. Turn left and follow FM 60 to where it meets Park Road 57 and turn left. After a few miles you will pass the park entrance sign and headquarters building. Turn right on the first road and park on the right by the pavilion. The trailhead is there, near the west end of the parking area. Follow the signs as far as you want and turn around. Follow the signs back.

Some places have forks where decisions must be made. Refer to the maps or wander. Either way, your destination will be the same, and the distance will only vary by a few miles. Continue to the Nails Creek Unit trailhead and get a drink from the hydrant near the corral. Explore the area, try a different route on the return, and have fun.

Sources of additional information:

Park Superintendent
Lake Somerville State Recreation Area
Birch Creek Unit
Route 1, Box 499
Somerville, TX 77879
(409) 535-7763

Park Superintendent
Lake Somerville State Recreation Area
Nails Creek Unit
Route 1, Box 61C
Ledbetter, TX 78946-9512
(409) 289-2392

Texas Parks and Wildlife Department
4200 Smith School Road
Austin, TX 78744-3291
(800) 792-1112 for information only

TPWD Reservation Center
P.O. Box 17488
Austin, TX 78760-7488
(512) 389-8900 for reservations only

Bicycle Country
1199 East Austin (US 290)
Giddings, TX 78942
(409) 542-0964

Giddings Area Bicycle Association
(409) 542-0964

Notes on the trail: Like I said earlier, this is a good family-type trail. Flat, easy, variable in assault level distance-wise, so take the kiddos. Single-speed cruisers are welcome here. Just take plenty of drink, film, and partners.

RIDE 41 *BRAZOS BEND STATE PARK TRAIL*

Good, smooth, easy, crowded, pretty . . . NEXT!

Now hold on a minute, partner, we need to linger a little. This is one of the best family-type trails in this book. It is what I wished my parents would have turned me loose on when I was about 10 or 11 years old. A kid could have a day full of big fun and only get into minor trouble, if he or she is smart enough not to mess with any alligators. More on this later.

I offer up eight miles of wide graveled path, flat as if it were laser-planed, along some of the prettiest of Texas terrain. The trees are full of Spanish moss and the lakes are full of lily pads. On a nice afternoon you will find plenty of other trail users, so expect to make it a nice relaxed afternoon or evening cruise down gentle lanes with lots of company.

For bird-watchers, this park is a great experience; check out the nature observation tower. Seeing binoculars and foot-long cameras is not unheard-of, and if the birders have their tripods set up, give them a wide berth, because THEY are sharing THEIR trail with us technoracerhead weenies. Take it easy, smell the flowers—it's a beautiful day. Do I sound like Mister Rogers? There is also an astronomical observatory replete with telescopes, so you might be bold and stay in after dark, like the song says. People will think you are crazy, too.

If you see any alligators, leave them be. They eat Dobermans, German shepherds, and pit bulls for breakfast. I think they mostly hang out in Elm Lake and 40 Acre Lake.

General location: Southwest of Houston, about an hour.
Elevation change: Another easy flat trail. The lowest spot is at around 50′ above the Gulf of Mexico and the highest is at about 65′.
Season: This trail is good during meteor showers and eclipses. And just about any other time of year, including the wet ones.
Services: Near the trailhead are rest rooms with water and a pay phone but nothing else. If you need any other supplies, you should load up in Rosenberg or Richmond before you get to the park. The nearest bike shops are in Houston.
Hazards: Do not mess with the alligators and snakes, or you will be breaking the law and taking a big chance. Don't try to do 100 miles per hour through

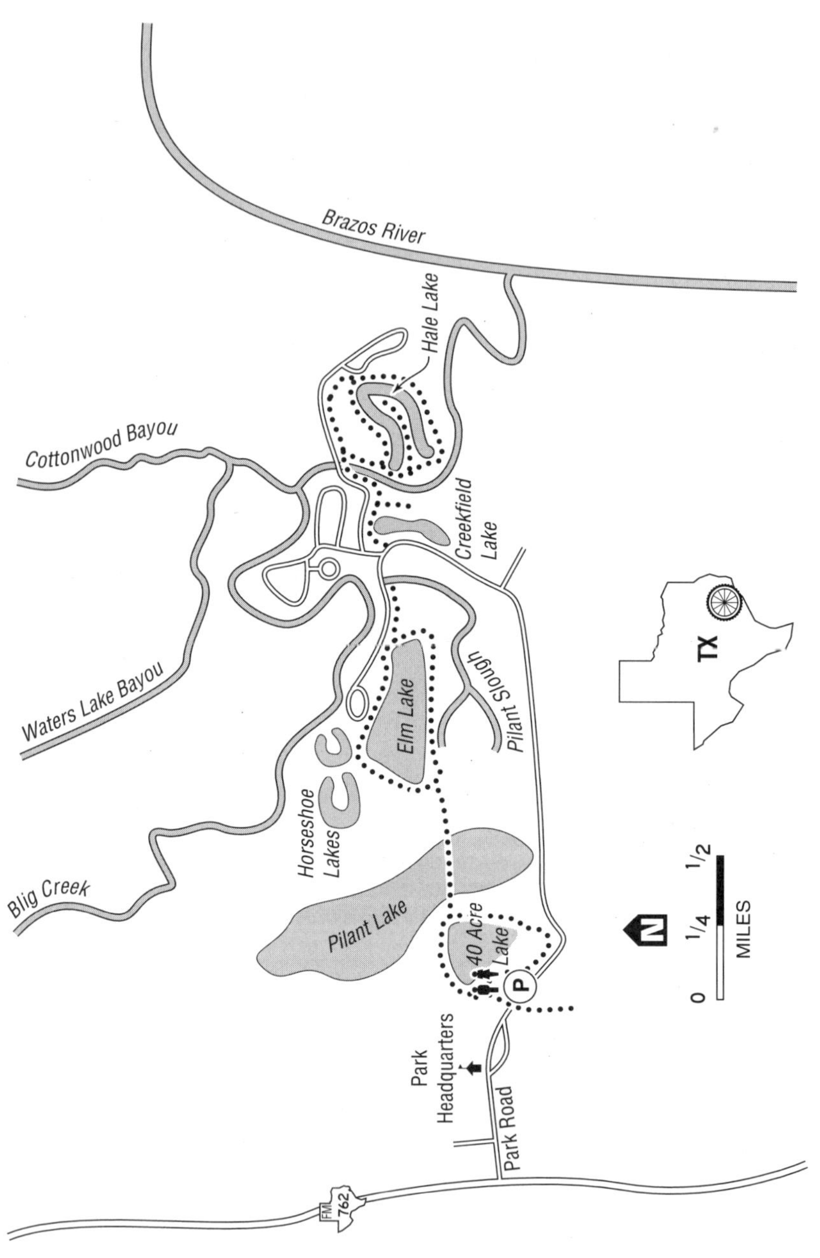
Brazos River
Hale Lake
Cottonwood Bayou
Creekfield Lake
Waters Lake Bayou
Pilant Slough
Elm Lake
TX
Horseshoe Lakes
Blig Creek
Pilant Lake
40 Acre Lake
P
N
0
1/4
1/2
MILES
Park Headquarters
Park Road
FM 762

This place is a multi-course meal of different settings. From quiet woods like this to lily pad ponds to tall birding platforms you will ride through a myriad of different scenes.

here, because there will be too many people pushing baby carriages past the alligators and snakes. Mosquitoes are a concern here, and you will need sunscreen on the mostly open trails during high summer.

Rescue index: The chances of being saved here if injured give this trail one of the best rescue indices. There are so many users here on a nice day that you will assuredly not be alone. Also, just about any section of this trail would be accessible to emergency crews if an extraction were necessary.

Land status: Since this is a Texas state park, you need never fear that it will ever be anything else—not without major advance warning, anyway.

Maps: The headquarters will provide you with excellent maps showing all major trail features. The quads for this trail are Otey, Damon, Smithers Lake, and Thompsons.

Finding the trail: From US 59 in Richmond, go south on Farm to Market 762 about 20 miles to the park road, where you will see a large brown sign. Turn left into the park and stop at the headquarters and say your hellos. Proceed past the headquarters to the stop sign and turn left, and then turn left again into the first parking area you see.

You will see a sign kiosk and single-track behind the rest rooms. Turn right and follow the trail, taking your pick of various forks as suits your mood, checking references on the map. All roads lead to what was once called Hale Ranch State Park. A bunch of easy cruising with the one you chose as a cycling partner for the day. Get bold, take that side trail. Nothing on the way home today will hurt you or your pals.

When you get to the paved road and trailhead past Elm Lake, you may turn right and ride the other half of the park by following the trail along the road until you reach Hale Lake. From there you may choose your tour by referring to the map again and doing extra mileage if you feel the need. There are various routes possible on the ensuing single-track; just check your maps.

When you are ready to return, the route promises no hassles except the need to weave between the peds. Go west, young mountain biker. Soon you are back at the trailhead, ready to load up and go home.

Sources of additional information:

Park Superintendent
Brazos Bend State Park
21901 FM 762
Needville, TX 77461
(409) 553-3243

Texas Parks and Wildlife Department
4200 Smith School Road
Austin, TX 78744-3291
(800) 792-1112 for information only

TPWD Reservation Center
P.O. Box 17488
Austin, TX 78760-7488
(512) 389-8900 for reservations only

Notes on the trail: I can't say enough nice things about this trail. It is gentle, it is convincingly country, it is a worthy use of leisure time. *Wear a helmet. It looks good even while you're taking it easy.*

Far West Texas

Welcome to the Franklin Mountains, another historic part of the state. Lots of colorful people have passed through this region throughout its history. Right across the Rio Grande River from El Paso is Juarez, Mexico. I mean it is just right over there across the river, plainly visible from America.

This is high desert country, part of the Chihuahuan Desert, and the southern end of the Rocky Mountains in the United States. The State of New Mexico, the Carlsbad Caverns area, and the Guadalupe Mountains are to the north and northeast. Fort Bliss military reservation is nearby and is a very important part of the local culture.

The bulk of the half million or so people who live in this area are of Hispanic descent. You will notice this in the names of streets and towns and in the architecture of local buildings. Being able to *habla* at least *muy poquito español* would be very convenient. Have fun, ride hard, and stay out of the sun when you can.

RIDE 42 *TRANS MOUNTAIN TRAILS*

This is a hard area to define. The final version of what the Texas Parks and Wildlife Department is going to use to govern mountain bike use of this land is not yet finalized. Presently an area of old jeep trails on the eastern slopes of the Franklin Mountains is open and provides at least ten miles of intense rocky trails for your exploration. The jeep roads lead back into some of the canyons in what is known as the Castner Range (named for the old artillery range many of the trails cover). Northwest of Trans Mountain Road is a network of crisscrossing double-tracks that will shake fillings out of your teeth if you do not have suspension. Still, this desolate high desert terrain has a special beauty all its own. Though the Castner Range is not actually part of the state park, it is on the planned acquisition list.

I rode here in August and it was hot. Real hot, not a shade tree in sight, and no hope of a cooling rain shower. I struggled up and down the steep foothills of the Franklins in a large loop that carried me up high enough to see almost all of El Paso and Fort Bliss in the distance. I was not really having much fun and was feeling a little nervous about all the gang-type graffiti I had seen scribbled on every building in the area. I feared my white pickup truck would be tagged by mad spray-paint bombers while I was off trying to make sense of the tangle of trails in the area. My fears were unfounded; nothing bad

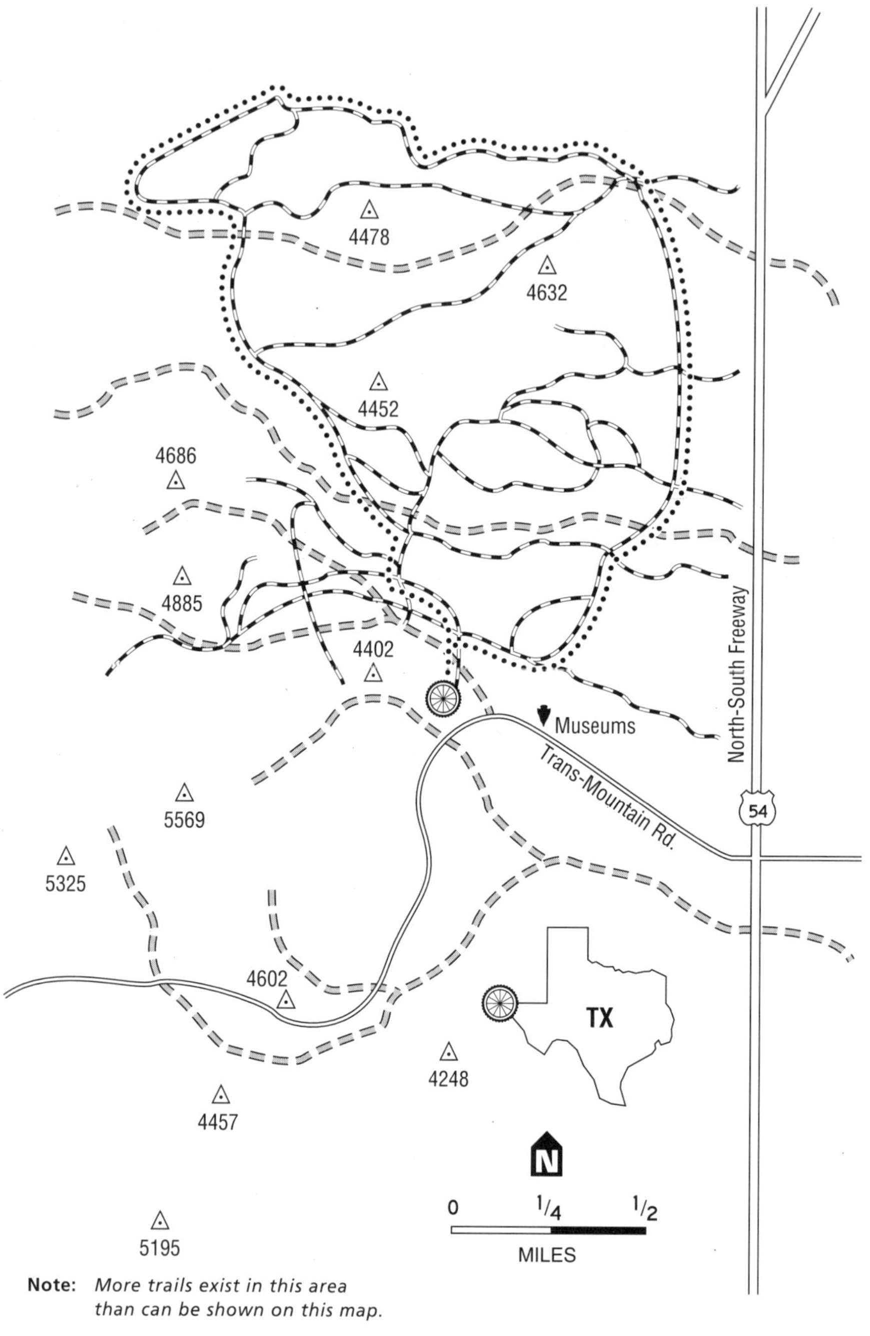

Note: *More trails exist in this area than can be shown on this map.*

happened. Still, this is a spooky place, fraught with tales of people killed for lost treasure and signs warning of undetonated munitions from when the army used this as a firing range for its artillery soldiers.

Make no mistake, this is harsh terrain and the riding is tough. As the state figures out what it intends to make available to mountain bikers, some of the single-track may be opened, and from what I have heard it would make very worthy riding. The information I can offer you at this point is limited to the jeep trails, but I strongly urge you to try and contact some of the locals to see if you can luck into getting a guided tour of the area. The El Paso Bicycle Club regularly holds mountain bike rides of varying degrees of difficulty and skill requirements, and at least one of the local bicycle shops is involved with off-road racing in the area. Check the information section for more data on finding these folks.

General location: Franklin Mountains State Park is the largest urban park in the Texas Parks and Wildlife Department system, weighing in at 24,000 acres. This fills in the open land between the city of El Paso and the New Mexico border—the very farthest western tip of Texas.
Elevation change: The topography of this area ranges in elevation from 4,100′ above sea level up to around 4,700′, but as best I can tell, the trails lie mostly between about 4,200′ and 4,600′. This is steep terrain with a lot of relief.
Season: The trails here will be slippery and dangerous if these rocks get wet, but I am aware of no real "seasonal" concerns here except for the searing summer heat. From June until September these trails would probably be most appropriately ridden from shortly before daybreak until 9 or 10 A.M., or possibly as a moonlight escapade.
Services: There are no facilities of any kind at or near the trailhead. There are convenience stores all along US 54, a.k.a. the North-South Freeway, so if you need anything, stop before you get to the park. The nearest bike shop is Ride On Sports.
Hazards: Innumerable dangers await you along these trails. The plants all have teeth, and the trails themselves are an obstacle course of cranium-sized boulders. There are untold miles of rugged jeep roads, and what is not rocky is ankle-deep sand and gravel. At a few points along the way you will be able to observe gang graffiti sprayed all over a big chunk of rock that juts from the ground. I'd keep an eye peeled for any low riders that might be in the area.
Rescue index: You have a good chance of being rescued here, but only if you stay fairly near the parking area. If you wander way off into the mountains, you could die and not be found for weeks. There is really a fair amount of traffic along these trails; joggers and mountain bikers are a common sight. The downside is, it would probably take a military Hummer ambulance to get in here to extract you if you got hurt. Or a chopper, and those Care Flight helicopter trips are an expensive hobby.

Land status: Right now this land is property of the Department of Defense. Don't be deterred—the Texas Parks and Wildlife Department plans to add this and several privately held parcels of land to Franklin Mountains State Park.
Maps: I managed to score a pretty good set of maps of the area from the park manager by requesting the Management Plan for the park. Otherwise, until the parks department decides what they are doing, the only other map of the area with any interesting details is the USGS 7.5 minute series topographic quadrangle North Franklin Mountain.
Finding the trail: From the intersection of Trans Mountain Road and US 54 (the North-South Freeway), go west about a mile. Just a short distance past the Wilderness Park and Border Patrol Museums (maybe one-quarter mile), there is a turnout and graded parking area alongside Trans Mountain Road, on the side away from the city. Park there and mount up—this is where it gets interesting. Hit the double-track, heading generally in the direction of the mountains. If you follow the jeep roads that roughly parallel the mountain range, you will gradually work your way up higher and higher until you are on one of several long ridges far above the city. This is not up in the mountains per se but more like riding along the base of the eastern slope, working your way to the north. Ride as far as the trails go or until you get tired, then head east on one of the roads that descend toward the highway and city in the distance. Go east until you are almost to the highway, then hop on the next jeep trail you find going south. You will probably not be able to see your parking area, but the Wilderness Park Museum will become visible in the distance, and you can use that as a reference for finding your way back to the parking area. Take your time. Explore. Somewhere up there are pieces of several single-tracks that lead up into and over the mountains. I never could find them, because if you start riding up into one of those canyons, you will run out of rideable trail before you get to where the single-track apparently lies.

Sources of additional information:

Park Manager
Franklin Mountains State Park
P.O. Box 200
Canutillo, TX 79835-9998
(915) 544-7184

Park Superintendent
Hueco Tanks State Historical Park
Hueco Tanks Road
Rural Route 3, Box 1
El Paso, TX 79935
(915) 857-1135

Have you ever heard that Marty Robbins tune, the one about old El Paso? Well, that's it down there. The view from the Franklin Mountains.

Texas Parks and Wildlife Department
4200 Smith School Road
Austin, TX 78744-3291
(800) 792-1112 for information only

TPWD Reservation Center
P.O. Box 17488
Austin, TX 78760-7488
(512) 389-8900 for reservations only

El Paso Bicycle Club
(915) 584-4455

Ride On Sports
6950 North Mesa
El Paso, TX 79912
(915) 585-1085

Ride On Sports
525 Telshor
Las Cruces, NM 88001
(505) 521-1686

Notes on the trail: There are presently no facilities for camping in the developed sections of the park, the Tom Mays Unit. If you want a truly one-of-a-kind camping experience, I heartily recommend staying at Hueco Tanks State Park. (*Hueco,* Spanish for "hollow," is pronounced hway-ko.) This place is a pile of house-sized boulders covering as much ground as a large industrial complex, located about 30 miles east of El Paso. It was once a watering stop on an old stagecoach line that crossed this part of the country and was the site of many gun battles between the white man and the red man in the days of the Old West. If you like rock climbing, the ranger at Hueco Tanks claims to have some of the best bouldering in the world. He insists that people come from all over the planet to play on his rocks. *No mountain bike trails,* at least not yet.

Another interesting note about the area is that Warren, the ranger at Hueco Tanks, has outlined a plan to have a multi-use trail built from Hueco Tanks over to Guadalupe Mountains National Park. This trail would follow the old stage route and could provide some of the most intensely enjoyable outdoor experiences imaginable. It would stretch for approximately 130 miles. Write the Texas Parks and Wildlife folks and lobby for this project if it sounds interesting to you.

If you visit the Wilderness Park Museum located one-quarter mile east of the trailhead area, you will get a chance to walk through their nature garden. They have one of just about every type of Chihuahuan Desert plant and can share with you a ton of information on local critters. Just don't take off through their garden on your mountain bike—they don't appreciate that a whole lot.

Right next to the Wilderness Park Museum is the U.S. Border Patrol Museum. I did not give it a try, but that catchy title sounds pretty intriguing, eh?

The Big Bend Country

It is a desert-mountain country whose qualities offer an allurement, a satisfaction of the soul, only if the visitor will put himself in the right mood, and will remain long enough to know it with some intimacy.

—*Freeman Tilden*

The Rio Grande is the only river I ever saw that needed to be irrigated.

—*Will Rogers*

Whoa Nellie, this is it. The Big Bend Country is THE most interesting and historic part of the state, and the most haunting. I saved the best for last.

Mountain biking here is the ultimate test of a rider's survival skills, endurance, and courage. The area I am leading you into is all within the confines of the Big Bend National Park, therefore all mountain biking is restricted to "anywhere you can drive your car," according to the park rangers. *All single-track is strictly off limits to bikes.* This might seem like a killer for fun riding, to the uninitiated, but not really. All of the "primitive" or four-wheel-drive gravel/dirt roads in the park are open to you and can provide some of the most picturesque and enjoyable riding you will find anywhere. While generally light on technical challenges, they are heavy on aerobic intensity. These roads still give you access to back-country areas never witnessed by most park visitors. And they stretch for miles.

It would be a mistake to visit Texas for mountain biking and not see the Big Bend Country, even though driving there is a day-long affair. The Spaniards called this region of the state *el despoblado,* "the uninhabitable region," and it takes its present-day name from the northward curve the Rio Grande takes on its route to the Gulf of Mexico. The Rio Grande del Norte or Rio Bravo, famed river of myth, legend, and movies, forms the 900-plus river-mile border between Texas and Mexico. The river is a popular destination for canoe and raft enthusiasts, and since you drove all the way here I would strongly suggest that you hire a guide and float part of it if at all possible. Especially if you might never come back to this area. That is the only way to see the fabulous canyons in the park.

The Big Bend Country is the land of razors and easy death. There are probably a hundred different ways to die within a mile of where you are standing. The dangerous-plant warnings issued for other parts of the state were just a warm-up. The plants here are vicious, and every one has thorns or needles. If you lean into a bush while negotiating a curve in the road, you will come away bleeding. And if you have been leaving the patch/tool kit and pump in the car until now, dig it out. This is no place to get stranded far from your car because of a flat or mechanical failure. Maybe cram an extra tube into your pocket too. Or water bottle or energy bar. *Es no caca.*

Carry more water than you think you will need, because the arid "high desert" air will surprise you. Sweat evaporates so quickly here that you will not even realize you are dehydrating, so force yourself into a habit of drinking constantly. Using a CamelBak is a real good idea, and keeping some bottles in your cages, too, will keep you out of trouble. I have a pal who has backpacked the Big Bend twice a year for 20 years. He and a friend decided to do the Glenn Spring Loop after reading an article in a popular cycling publication (data provided by yours truly) and thought a CamelBak would hold plenty of liquid for the 35 or so miles to the river and back. They ran out of water with over 15 miles of climbing ahead of them. In 100-plus degree heat. They were moving a tenth of a mile at a time and then resting. Not a drop of shade within 10 miles. Death in the Big Bend is quick, easy, and always at hand. Don't jack around—be a Boy Scout (be prepared) and be on your best behavior.

The terrain here is high desert, with mountain ranges thrown in to provide interesting scenery and varied climate zones. The area in the Chisos Mountains known as The Basin is very interesting. It is a hidden, protected, nearly circular valley in the center of the mountain range. The Chisos Mountains are where most of the wildlife lives, and also the site of one of the campgrounds you can go to if you want less-than-primitive camping facilities. There are no mountain bike trails in The Basin. Driving in, you will pass a sign that indicates the point along the road that is exactly one mile above sea level. And that is not anywhere near the highest point in the park. Pretty cool, huh?

The weather can be your enemy here like nowhere else. The rainy season is roughly from June to October, which is summer in the rest of the state. A storm you never saw coming can cause flash flooding that will strand you in the outback as it washes across (or away) the road in a mad torrent. DO NOT attempt to cross flooded water crossings. Several people have tried, and some of them died. The fall, winter, and spring are excellent times to ride here, because the summer heat is brutal. It is not uncommon for the desert floor to reach 115 degrees by noon, and shade is not a feature of the Chihuahuan Desert. Plan your trips accordingly, and take plenty of sunscreen and water. And inner tubes. Survival here is seldom by accident.

Make note of the fact that in the "Rescue index" section of each ride I mention that you will often be very isolated, hardly ever seeing automobile traffic on the dirt roads. Let me also point out that the nearest hospital is over 100 miles away and that the next ambulance up the road is probably 40 miles away. Let that frighten you if nothing else does. Wear a helmet when you ride, and ride like you mean to stay alive. Don't get to cooking along at top speed and pushing the envelope like an 18-year-old; it would not be a good idea to get hurt out here, even a little. Let your conscience be your guide, and use your best judgment. I have a dead friend who never came back from this part of the country. He was blasting down a hill with no helmet and something happened. No one knows for sure what.

In spite of this bevy of warnings, let yourself be enchanted. This place is intoxicating. I waited too many years to find myself looking out across the desert toward the Chisos Mountains. There are so many beautiful and interesting places here that you just have to keep coming back until you have found them all and decided which ones are special for you. It seems most folks who have fallen in love with the park will not tell you where their favorite camping spots are; they prefer to keep them secret to preserve the solitude of that special location. And they go every year, just like clockwork.

The best way to enjoy riding in the park is to bring what you need to survive unsupported in the desert for several days, camping at one or another of the primitive campsites. You will typically be able to reach miles of unpaved double-track from many good campsites. I cannot devote enough space here to describe all the campsites, because there are just too many. Don't be bashful—ask the rangers to give you pointers on the locations that are available. Make your selections based on their descriptions and on whether or not they advise you to try and drive to these locations.

The main park roads form an upside-down **T**, one crossing the park from east to west and the other forming the vertical portion of the **T** where it ends at Panther Junction. The east/west road will be called the main park road from here on, as it is the only one with any real bearing on our rides. It exits the park on the western side to become TX 118 and run through Study Butte, Texas, and it ends in Boquillas Canyon to the east.

The rest of the roads in the park are of the unpaved variety. Driving five miles on these "unimproved dirt roads" can take an hour. Successfully negotiating these roads is basically a matter of a) how much ground clearance your ride has; b) how much you value the paint job; and c) whether you have a good spare tire. Carrying two spares is a good idea. Sometimes four-wheel-drive and a winch will be required to get past washouts in the road, but this is just on the roads with "primitive four-wheel-drive" designations. Ask the rangers; they gave me excellent advice on whether I could reach certain spots in a full-size two-wheel-drive pickup truck.

There are so many cool places here that I will not attempt to take you to them all. The best way to find out where neat stuff is would be to ask. The rangers are extremely helpful and informative, and people you meet along the way can usually give you dependable information. Plus you might want to buy some of the guidebooks at the headquarters. That is how I found the derivations for place-names and where the interesting points along the roads are.

There are many fascinating stories in this area, especially those that explain the names of places in the Big Bend. In the early 1900s the army visited the region to map and catalog the area. The story has it that in 1903 a meeting was called by M. A. Ernst (of Ernst Tinaja and The Big Tinaja Store fame) to record the names of all the places in the Big Bend and the reasons they were so named. The inhabitants were concerned that the army guys would call everything Boquillas this or Boquillas that, since Boquillas was about the only name people outside the region knew.

Digging into the history of this area is going to turn up some fascinating stories. The famed Buffalo Soldiers spent some time in this area taming the Indians and *banditos* and helping the *norteamericanos* to settle the land. The *banditos* are responsible for a lot of the history here. They used to come across the river and raid villages in the area that now forms the park. They killed a lot of locals and raised a bunch of hell back in the late 1910s and early 1920s.

Judge Roy Bean, the famous "Law West of the Pecos," held his nineteenth-century kangaroo courts over in a place called Langtry, near the park. Many people passing through this area found themselves at the business end of the hangman's rope as a result of the judge's special form of justice. Not a nice man, but he loved his Lily Langtry painting.

Hiking is probably the ultimate way to see the best parts of the park. Take your hiking boots and try to take a day away from the bike to hit one of the many awesome trails. The South Rim Trail and Pine Canyon Trail both come highly recommended as "must-sees."

It should be noted that historically the hikers have been the off-road group most involved and interested in the Big Bend. That will change if I have anything to say about it. I think this place should be a mecca for mountain bikers seeking memorable off-road experiences. If you go and you like it, join the Big Bend Natural History Association and get involved with what is going on in the park. In spite of ourselves, we might someday have access to more than we do presently, and there are some places in these 800,000 acres that would make awesome destinations for mountain bike trips. Mexico keeps talking about a 1.5-million-acre biosphere preserve that might be a reality someday, just across *el Rio Bravo*.

When setting out to camp in the park's primitive areas, remember that special permits are required. You must complete an application at the headquarters before you pitch your tent. Consider how many potential "primitive campers" there are wanting to use this place, and balance that against how far into the future people will be coming here. You will see it is best to follow the code of these hills: Take nothing but photographs, leave nothing but footprints. Many people will follow you to share your campsite after you are gone. Please leave it the way you found it, or cleaner. Sanitation and litter are critical issues in the park. You are expected to carry a shovel to dig a hole to go to the bathroom in, and to pack used toilet paper out with you. The stuff takes forever to break down in the desert.

I think the thing I love the most about the park is that it is so isolated. The solitude is profound. The park is primitive, and the only conveniences are small gas station/convenience stores every 30 miles or so on the pavement. Bring what you will need to live, and bring your camera and lots of film. This place is unforgettably exciting and breathtakingly beautiful.

Some valuable phone numbers for Big Bend National Park:

General information: (915) 477-2251

Panther Junction Ranger Visitor Center: (915) 477-2251

Castolon Ranger Station: (915) 371-2253

Chisos Basin Visitor Center: (915) 477-2264 or 2392

Persimmon Gap Visitor Center: (915) 477-2393

Rio Grande Village Visitor Center: (915) 477-2271 or -2356

The nearest bike shop I am aware of is in Midland. El Paso would likely be the next nearest town with bike shops.

Peyton's Bikes
3327 West Wadley, Suite #3
Midland, TX 79707
(915) 699-1719

Ride On Sports
6950 North Mesa
El Paso, TX 79912
(915) 585-1085

RIDE 43 *HOT SPRINGS RIDE*

The Fountain of Youth that Ponce de Leon failed to find
—J. O. Langford, Hot Springs, Texas

I am going to start you out real easy. The rides get tougher the farther you go into this section of the book. This first ride is about the easiest one in the park and will give you a measuring stick for deciding on other rides you may want to tackle. If you think this one is hard, it is time to go home.

I like to use this one to unwind from a day or two of hard riding. It may also be claimed as a good bath after a few days of camping primitive-style. You can park just north of the pavement on Old Ore Road (about one-quarter mile north of the pavement on top of the hill, there is a small parking area) and then ride an easy mile or so of asphalt (speed limit is 45 mph, so it's okay). Then you pedal about two miles of real easy two-lane dirt road to the ruins

RIDE 43 *HOT SPRINGS RIDE*

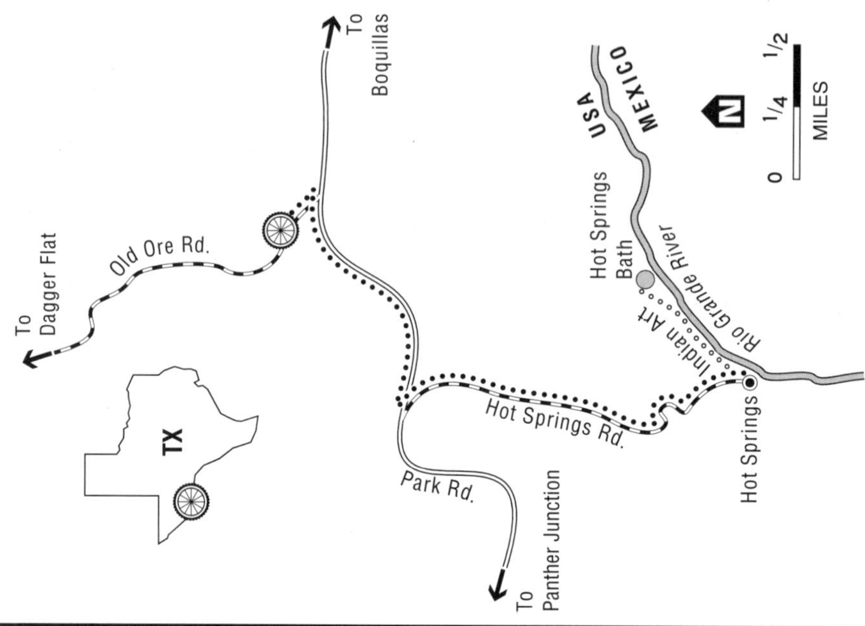

of Hot Springs, Texas. Very easy, no hard climbs, no loose rocks. So basic that I am stretching to include it as a ride. But you need to check out the spring, and riding there from a camp along Old Ore Road works nicely.

This ride offers no tremendous views unless you start it from Rio Grande Village and pick up Boquillas Canyon. That is another place you have to go. If you park and ride from there you can detour to the canyon overlooks and then ride through the tunnel and over to the cutoff to the hot springs and back. This trip will be a little over 20 miles by the time you get back to Rio Grande Village. And all but about four of that is paved.

Once you hit the cutoff from the park road onto the dirt, you only have about two miles to ride to the ruins of the bathhouse. There may be some washboarding, but no great climbs or dangerous areas. The road splits into two one-way pieces just before the parking area. This part is interesting, because if you are in a car you just about fill the whole thing up, and the curves around the edges of the hills can be a thrill. If you go over the edge of the road here, it is a fair drop to the bottom. Not hundreds of feet, but more than a few.

The remains of the town of Hot Springs, Texas, and the parking area are the signal that you are nearly there. Walk your bike from this point, past the ruined post office and bathhouse, and follow the arrow to the trail. Along the cliff to your left are markers with explanations that, except for some modern graffiti, the marks you see on the rocks are Indian hand-paintings and petroglyphs. This stuff is really cool. Look where someone long ago pecked little designs into the flat rock faces with a stone awl. People were a lot more patient back then.

Keep following the trail until it rounds the bend and you see the remains of another bathhouse, which has been turned into a large hot tub. Your body will thank you for an hour or so in the spring after you have been riding hard for several days. Just the ticket when it has reached that third or fourth day with no bath. Leave the shampoo at home, but bring your swimsuit or shorts.

General location: Big Bend National Park is that kink in the Rio Grande about halfway along the border between Texas and Mexico. This is about halfway between El Paso and Del Rio.

Elevation change: The hot springs are at about 1,850´ feet or so, right on the banks of the Rio Grande. The highest point along the road on the way to Rio Grande Village is around 2,100´ or a little more. Rio Grande Village is in the mid-1800s, since it is down on the river.

Season: This road is probably nasty when the rains are falling, but it should be fine any other time. Watch your thermometer in the summer; it will be blistering out here.

Services: There is a store at Rio Grande Village. That is your only option if you need somewhere to spend money—gas, pay phone, ice, camping, etc. The nearest bike shop is far away.

Hazards: Automobile traffic and washboarding on the road are about the only things to watch for. The dropoffs near the end of the road could be dangerous if some fool in a car tried to pass you, but I reckon you should be able to outrun any car that tried to overtake you through here.

Rescue index: Since there is a high level of traffic on this road (relatively), I have to give this ride one of the better rescue indices of any ride we will do in the park. You are about as close to civilization here as you will get during your stay in Big Bend.

Land status: Big Bend National Park will always be a protected area, safe from development and abuse. It is the hope of everyone who loves the park that the Mexicans will follow through with their plans to incorporate lands across the river into their own version of a national park.

Maps: Stop at the headquarters at Panther Junction and take your pick from the selection. The free ones will show you enough to find the spring, the turn to Old Ore Road, or the Rio Grande Village/Boquillas area. The quads for this ride are Boquillas and San Vicente.

Finding the trail: From Interstate 10 at Fort Stockton, go south on US 385 past Marathon to Panther Junction.

Boy, this mountain biking thing can be rough, eh? That is me suffering, ignoring personal misery, and it is all for you dear readers.

Drive toward Boquillas from Panther Junction, and just before Old Ore Road you will see a sign directing you to turn right for the road into the area of Hot Springs, Texas. Keep going. Right before the tunnel to Boquillas you will see a gravel road to the left that is the southern terminus of the Old Ore Road. Pull onto Old Ore Road and head north to the top of the hill, where you will see a small parking area on the left. Park and head back to the pavement the way you just came. Turn right onto the park road and backtrack toward the Chisos Mountains for a mile or so, then turn left (south) at the sign for Hot Springs. Follow the road; it only goes to the spring.

Sources of additional information:

Park Superintendent
Big Bend National Park, TX 79834
(915) 477-2251

Big Bend Natural History Association
P.O. Box 68
Big Bend National Park, TX 79834
(915) 477-2236

Desert Sports
Lajitas, TX
(915) 371-2602

Notes on the trail: This area of the park has a lot of history behind it. J. O. Langford envisioned it as a health resort and worked toward that goal. The post office was the mail stop for Texans and Mexicans alike from 1927 until 1942. Until about 1952, the springs were operated as a park concession by a lady named Maggy Smith. Old Maggy was another memorable Big Bend resident, and many tales about her survive to this day. Try to snag one of the brochures at the headquarters that lists the history of the springs. This area was a real hot spot (ugh) for a long time.

RIDE 44 *OLD MAVERICK ROAD*

Now we move up the scale into a full-blown ride. Old Maverick Road is an "improved dirt road" stretching from Santa Elena Canyon to near the town of Study Butte (pronounced like "stoodie," *not* the way it is spelled). It is 14 miles of two-lane graded road—no terrible climbs or technical challenges, but plenty of great scenery. And very rideable. The only problems come from passing automobiles, because they stir the dust up so bad. As difficulty goes, this is a "medium." I call it that because this ride is not technical, but it is long and it runs through harsh surroundings.

We have here a good point-to-point or out-and-back ride. If you can make arrangements to get picked up at Santa Elena Canyon, it makes for a fairly easy ride. If you intend to do it as a round-trip ride, you can park just off the pavement at the spot provided and take an afternoon to pedal over to the Sierra de Santa Elena and Santa Elena Canyon. This is the one canyon in the whole park you can walk right up to. You really have to see it. You can hike right to the spot where the Rio Grande pops out of the canyon and heads toward flatter terrain.

Then you have the Sierra de Santa Elena, one impressive chunk of rock. It jumps straight up out of the ground at river elevation (just over 2,100´) and tops out around 3,600´. Fifteen hundred feet of vertical wall that hypnotizes some rock climbing pals of mine. It is so mesmerizing you cannot pull your eyes away. All along the front edge are old waterfalls and crevasses that must be as big as canyons in their own rights.

Along the way you will find many great opportunities to take pictures: Alamo Creek and The Badlands lie to the east, while the Rattlesnake Mountains are to the west; the Cerro Castellan and the Chisos Mountains can be seen far to the east; and all along the way are various ruins, including a very interesting *jacal* (mud house). The long, low structure is about halfway between the pavement at Maverick and Santa Elena Canyon. It was once home to Gilberto Luna and his family. Gilberto herded goats around Alamo Creek and built this typical local structure.

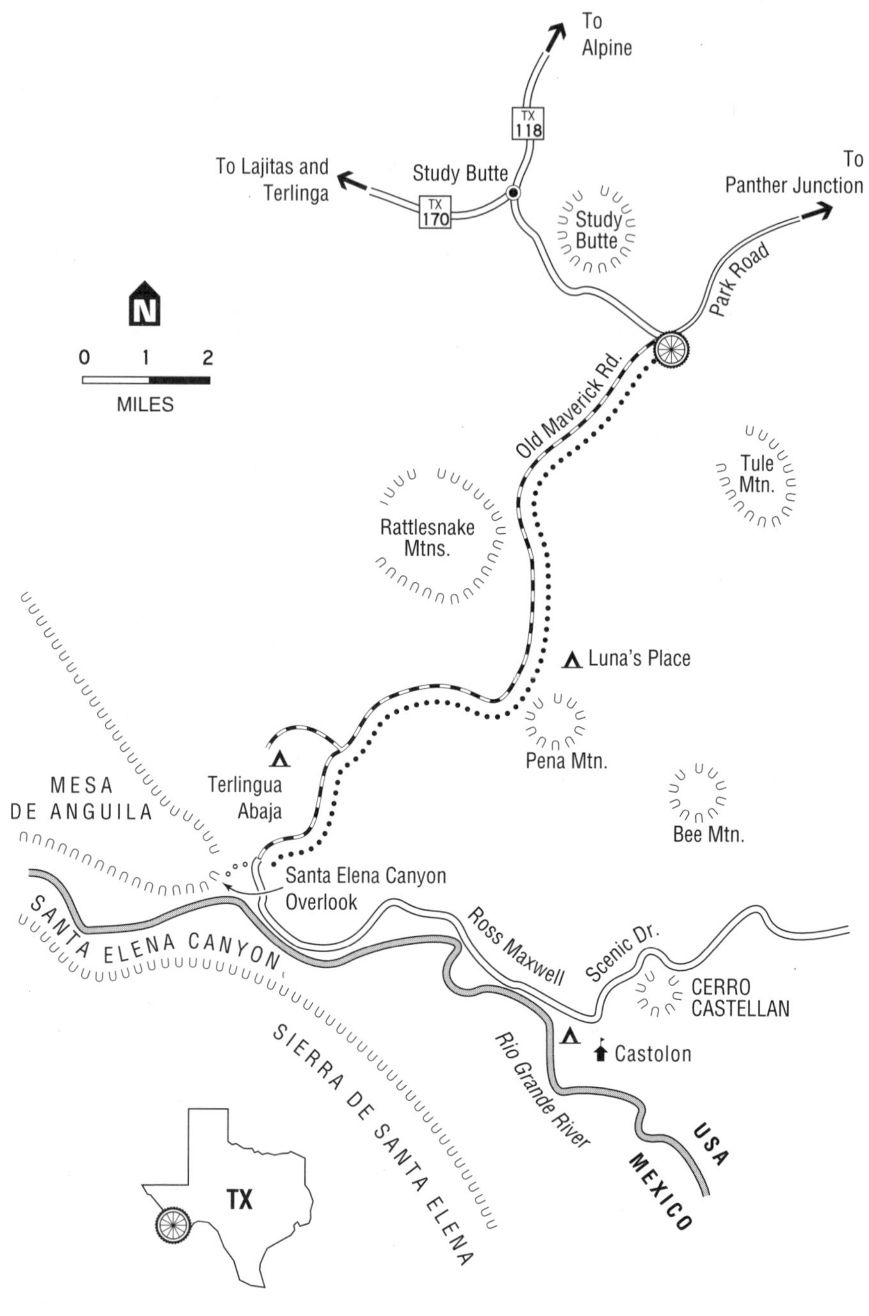
To
Alpine
TX
118
To Lajitas and
Terlinga
Study Butte
TX
170
Study
Butte
To
Panther Junction
Park Road
N
0
1
2
MILES
Old Maverick Rd.
Tule
Mtn.
Rattlesnake
Mtns.
Luna's Place
Pena Mtn.
Terlingua
Abaja
MESA
DE ANGUILA
Bee Mtn.
Santa Elena Canyon
Overlook
SANTA ELENA CANYON
Ross Maxwell
Scenic Dr.
CERRO
CASTELLAN
Castolon
SIERRA DE SANTA ELENA
Rio Grande River
USA
MEXICO
TX

General location: In the western part of Big Bend National Park, approximately 22 miles west of Panther Junction. The town of Study Butte is so close it can be used as a trailhead.

Elevation change: You start near Study Butte at about 2,750´ of elevation and drop to around 2,150´ right on the river. This 600´ discrepancy is fairly evenly spread over the 14 miles of travel.

Season: Unless it is pouring rain, you will be okay on Old Maverick Road anytime. I would get out here pretty early to start if you visit in any other season than winter. That way it is not so hot it fries your brain. I have seen pictures of Old Maverick Road being swallowed by Alamo Creek in a flash flood. Don't ride here if it is threatening to rain.

Services: There are no facilities of any kind at the trailhead. You are going to have to carry enough stuff to be out all day, so if you need supplies, stop in Study Butte before you get to the trailhead. The VERY small village of Castolon, east of Santa Elena Canyon, allegedly has a gas station, but I failed to find it the afternoon I passed through here.

Hazards: Dust storms will be your least favorite part of this ride, if automobiles happen to pass you. Get off the road if you like; traffic is light enough that it will not slow you down real bad. I bet a snake or two have slithered across this road since it was built, so keep your eyes open for sticks lying in the road, because there are no trees to produce sticks. Which brings us to the lack of shelter along Old Maverick Road. Do not attempt this ride if the weather is threatening, and take the proper precautions before planning a ride here if the summer heat is in full bloom.

Rescue index: You stand a fairly good chance of being helped out of this area if you need it, as Big Bend rides go. You will probably see people in cars driving Old Maverick Road, and lots of those souls will be tourists, just like you. Cycling has sort of a clean-cut reputation, and I think someone would stop to help you. I am tap dancing around this issue because you are getting near the river now, and folks are sometimes leery of people heading up from the river. More on that later. (See "Notes on the trail" for Ride 47—The Glenn Spring Loop.)

Land status: Still part of the national parks system. Thank you, Teddy Roosevelt.

Maps: Maps of Old Maverick Road can be obtained at the Panther Junction headquarters or in most bookstores that sell maps. It is plainly marked on every map I have seen that details Big Bend National Park. The quads for this ride are Castolon, Terlingua, and Tule Mountain.

Finding the trail: Drive west on the park road toward Study Butte from Panther Junction. About 22 miles from the ranger station, you will see the sign for Old Maverick Road and Santa Elena Canyon. Turn left off of the pavement, then pull into the small parking area located on your immediate left. Go south on the dirt road until you hit pavement again. Turn right and go to the parking area where the hiking trail into the canyon begins. Walk

When you see photographs like this one of the Big Bend it always looks distorted, like the shot is made of layer after layer of different pieces of scenery. That's the way it is here, it looks the same in person. Only in color.

your bike on the hiking trail if you decide to explore it, since you are now on single-track, OFF-LIMITS TO BICYCLES.

Sources of additional information:

Park Superintendent
Big Bend National Park, TX 79834
(915) 477-2251

Big Bend Natural History Association
P.O. Box 68
Big Bend National Park, TX 79834
(915) 477-2236

Desert Sports
Lajitas, TX
(915) 371-2602

Notes on the trail: A first-aid kit, plenty of sunscreen, food and water, and a map should definitely be in your pack when you start taking rides like this. You will be all alone in the middle of nowhere, and it is essential that you be able to operate in a totally self-sufficient way for half a day or more when you attempt outings of this level.

Buy some of the guidebooks. This ride will take you near lots of neat stuff that you will miss otherwise. I do not have the room to include all the sights here.

If you need to make a stop before the ride, try to hit the Study Butte store; this place is way cool. The two times I have been there, some of the locals were sitting around on the little veranda strumming guitars and blowing into flutes and such—it was really downhome. It is right on TX 118 as you pass through the town of Study Butte. Buildings are sort of sparse around here, so when you see some, you are there.

RIDE 45 *GLENN SPRING ROAD*

This ride totals about 18 miles round-trip—20 if you include the short side trip to Robber's Roost. Though there are no real climbs or technical barriers, I will give this a medium difficulty rating just on the basis of the desolate surroundings and challenging road surface. You will ride from the park road to Glenn Spring and back on an "unimproved dirt road." Much of this is loose rock and sand deep enough to keep you moving pretty slowly, so expect this to be a trip of at least half a day.

Glenn Spring gets its name from Mr. H. E. Glenn, who settled there sometime around the 1880s. He excavated and walled the largest spring to provide drinking water for himself and the horses he was raising. Later the area became home to nearly 80 residents as it grew to be a candelilla wax camp. Candelilla is a native plant that is the source of the wax used in some car and shoe polishes.

The ride is best conducted as an out-and-back from the parking area near the park road to the cut-off for Black Gap Road and back. On your ride you will pass a couple of interesting peaks: Nugent Mountain on the Chisos (west) side of the road as you start, and Chilicotal Mountain on your left (east). Both have names derived from local settlers who lived in their vicinities.

Along the way you pass turns for Pine and Juniper Canyons. Do not turn right from Glenn Spring Road; bear left at each of the intersections. Each has

RIDE 45 *GLENN SPRING ROAD*

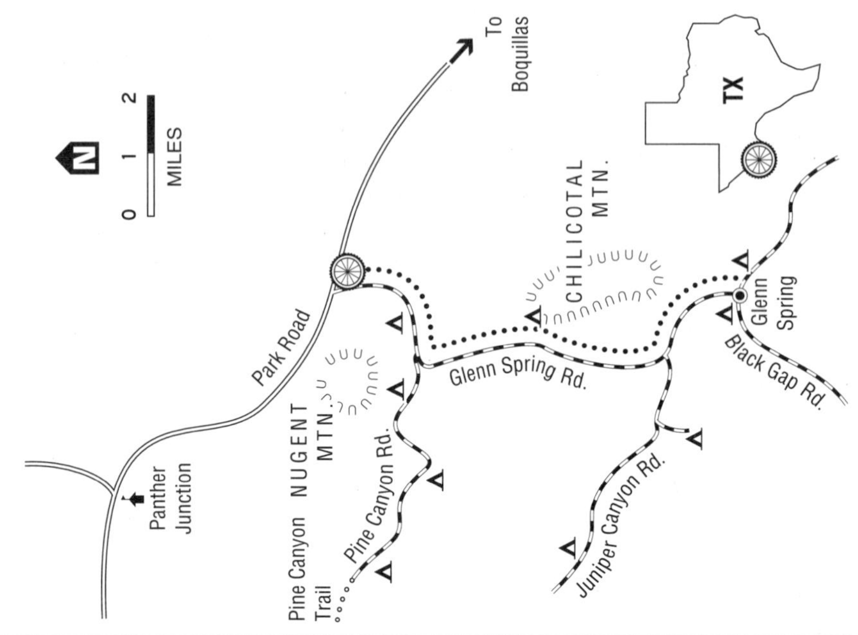

a sign denoting its destination, but signs disappear in the desert. Keep left and you will be able to get to Glenn Spring, *no problema*.

This area has a couple of significant tourist attractions. Rice Tank is a primitive camping area located beside an old earthen stock tank. It was built by a Mr. John Rice on land that was part of his ranch in the 1920s. Just about a mile west of Glenn Spring Road on Juniper Canyon Road is another primitive campsite called Robber's Roost. The name comes from the fact that a bunch of bad guys used to camp up there long ago. There were also a couple of noteworthy gunfights in that area. They fought the law and the law won.

Be sure and ask for the Glenn Spring brochure at the headquarters, because it gives you a map to the ruins of Glenn Spring village and all the other points of interest in the vicinity. It also tells the history of all the more notable sights along Glenn Spring Road.

General location: This ride is in Big Bend National Park. The trailhead lies about 6 miles east of Panther Junction.

Elevation change: The lowest spot along the road is 2,600′ above sea level. This would be where the creek through Glenn Draw crosses Black Gap Road—the turnaround point for this ride. The highest point on Glenn Spring Road is at the cutoff for Pine Canyon Road, marked on the topos at 3,470′.

That truly is nearly 900′ of overall elevation change, and you have to grind it on both legs of the trip, so it adds up. Where Glenn Spring Road leaves the park road is rated at 3,130′.

Season: Watch out for heavy rains, as always. Dozens of small ditches cross Glenn Spring Road. They are easy to forget about, but all of them would be full of rushing water if it rained much. And as I mentioned elsewhere, if you are here in the summer you will be riding at night or EARLY in the day.

Services: *Nada.* Get what you need at the gas station by Panther Junction or at the store in Rio Grande Village.

Hazards: I cannot overemphasize how alone you will be out here. Glenn Spring Road is by no means driven from end to end every day. I would say someone might find you in a week or two if you died of a snakebite by the road, or an allergic reaction to a scorpion, or injuries sustained from crashing with no helmet on. Take your first-aid kit and plenty of food and water. Take a rain suit or warm clothes in the winter. Getting rained on for hours (you sure won't find a tree to get under) and then getting stranded on some high piece of exposed land while the water owns the road could mean death from hypothermia. An icy wind in these conditions would not make for happy campers. Be prepared (as any good Boy Scout) and have what you need to survive if things take a turn for the worse.

Rescue index: The likelihood of being saved from an emergency on this ride is not good. As I mentioned above, you might go for a day or five without seeing a car. Your only hope might be surviving on your wits and walking out of the desert if a catastrophe occurs. A signal mirror or smoke marker might get the attention of a passing plane (yeah, right), and a CB radio or cellular phone might be worth their weight in gold if you needed either. I don't think you will have much luck with a cellular phone here, but I don't have one, so I cannot say for certain. A portable satellite uplink station would be handy. The park information booklets say to make a large "X" or the word "HELP" out of piles of rocks if you have an emergency. Sure, if a chopper happens by you are cool. Best advice I can give you is to be EXTREMELY CAREFUL. Don't take any unnecessary risks, and don't attempt a ride like this alone. And live to ride another day.

Land status: We should all say a silent prayer of thanks that President Theodore Roosevelt had the foresight to make Yellowstone the first national park. Now we have Big Bend and so many more. Bully Ted, bully.

Maps: The park headquarters has lots of good stuff for sale. Topographic park maps can be yours for less than $10. The quads for this ride are Panther Junction and Glenn Spring.

Finding the trail: Drive east on the park road from Panther Junction toward Boquillas Canyon. Turn south after about 5.5 miles at the sign for Glenn Spring Road. Park a few hundred yards from the pavement at the small clearing on top of the hill. Start riding south and stay on Glenn Spring Road until you reach the cutoff for Black Gap Road. Turn right on Black Gap

That big lump of dirt in the center is Chilicotal Mountain, named after some early character who lived there. On the road to Glenn Spring time is in your mind, it ain't out there in the desert.

Road, go to the bottom of the hill (maybe one-quarter mile), and rest by the shade trees along the creek. When you are ready to return, head back toward the Chisos Mountains on Glenn Spring Road.

Sources of additional information:

Park Superintendent
Big Bend National Park, TX 79834
(915) 477-2251

Big Bend Natural History Association
P.O. Box 68
Big Bend National Park, TX 79834
(915) 477-2236

Desert Sports
Lajitas, TX
(915) 371-2602

Notes on the trail: This ride will give you a good taste of the backcountry and the desert, and it will get you ready for the next phase of rides—the hard ones. If you thought Glenn Spring was a nice warm-up, then you are ready to move on and do the loop down Black Gap Road to the Mariscal Mine ruins and the

Way tiny in the center of this shot is someone parked at the camp area at Nugent Mountain. This is the first campsite you pass heading south from the Park Road on Glenn Spring Road. Not a lot of trees, huh?

River Road. If you do not like the condition of Glenn Spring Road, you might want to go on home now and lose the mountain bike for a road bike. Bedrock, loose rock, gravel, and deep sand are the definition of mountain biking in the Big Bend, *el despoblado*.

RIDE 46 *GLENN SPRING LOOP*

Here you have a 35-mile loop that is one of the more popular mountain bike rides in the park. You are going to start from a remote location (Glenn Spring) and make a counterclockwise loop around the west side of Tally Mountain following Black Gap Road. From where Black Gap runs into the River Road, you will cut back to the east, by the ruined Mariscal Mines and Mariscal Mountain, over to the river at Solis Landing. From there you will pass the remains of a couple of dwellings made of piled stones, near the river, and then head away from the Rio Grande and back up to Glenn Spring.

This ride rates high on the difficulty scale. As usual, this is not due to technical challenges but because of the loose surface of the double-track and from the isolated nature of all the places you will visit. Plus, there are some areas

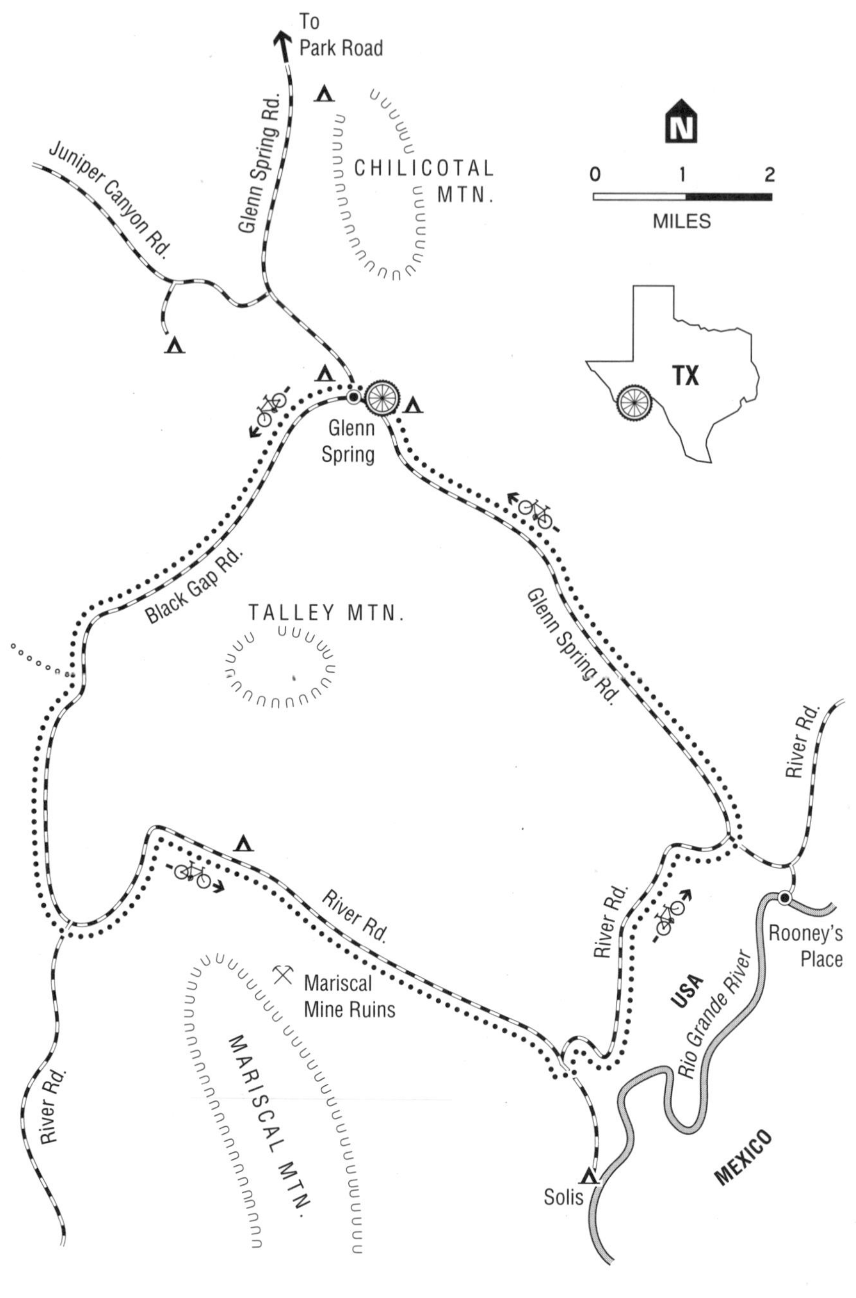
To
Park Road
Glenn Spring Rd.
Juniper Canyon Rd.
CHILICOTAL
MTN.
0 1 2
MILES
TX
Glenn
Spring
Black Gap Rd.
TALLEY MTN.
Glenn Spring Rd.
River Rd.
River Rd.
River Rd.
Rooney's
Place
Mariscal
Mine Ruins
USA
Rio Grande River
MARISCAL MTN.
River Rd.
Solis
MEXICO

made tough by the nature of the terrain and the significant elevation changes. We are riding on loose sand, gravel, and rock, and we are in the middle of the Chihuahuan Desert. There is no place to stop and get a drink or make a call if you get in trouble. And there are no 7-11 stores along the way, so you had better start this ride well prepared to be on the trail for several hours, like at least half a day. Maybe all day if you stop and waste time taking pictures the way I do. Carry extra water and food and your stainless-steel underwear, because this ride is for tough-butts only.

The Glenn Spring Loop will take you past more interesting stuff than any other ride in the park, except maybe the Old Ore Road. The scenery ranges from a really neat old water crossing made of poured concrete and local stone to old mining and residential ruins to a foreign country. Mexico is a stone's throw away across the muddy Rio Grande. The area around Glenn Spring is interesting to explore all by itself. The ruins of the village and the surrounding terrain make for a ruggedly beautiful picnic area, if you like, and the ride along Black Gap Road is fascinating. Be sure to get the Glenn Spring brochure from the headquarters at Panther Junction so you will be able to find all the historic stuff.

General location: East of the Chisos Mountains, south of the park road in Big Bend National Park.

Elevation change: The junction of Black Gap Road and Glenn Spring Road lies at just about 2,600´. From there you go up and down a little on Black Gap Road until you hit the open desert, then it is a big-ring cruise to the cutoff for the mine ruins. From there you gently descend to 1,900´ and the Rio Grande mud at Solis as the road winds around the mud holes. The jaunt over to Rooney's Place is easy, and when you turn left onto Glenn Spring Road you will climb gently through more open desert until you are back in Glenn Spring. This last leg gives you a 600´ climb spread like mayonnaise over roughly 9 miles of desert-floor wheat bread.

Season: Stay away from here if it is raining heavily or threatening to. The roads are all crisscrossed with runoffs, and these can make the road impassable if they fill with rushing *agua*. Again, as in the other rides here, the summer heat will keep all but the most insane cyclists hidden inside with their air conditioners on full.

Services: You're kidding, right? There is nothing out here, folks. If you need water or other supplies, you had better load up before you head to Glenn Spring to start the ride.

Hazards: As in every other ride in the park, the loose surface of the road is going to make for extremely dangerous cornering if you try to push the limits.

Don't just stop your bike and plop yourself down by the road without examining the area for unwanted neighbors like snakes and scorpions. Any other humans you see that are not on bikes should not be approached; they could be the bad guys. If they are wearing uniforms, okay, but otherwise stay far away from them.

Carry a tool kit, pump, patch kit, and spare tubes. This area is not driven on anything like a daily basis, and if you break down you are stranded a long way from any form of help. It will be just you and the candelilla plants and the javelinas.

If you take the side trip down to Solis Landing, you will be very near the actual "big bend" in the river. Mariscal Canyon, at the river end of Mariscal Mountain, is the namesake for the Big Bend Country. A canoe trip through Mariscal Canyon is about the only way to see the canyon, and it is definitely something worth trying. Take a day off the bike and ride a raft. You won't be disappointed.

Rescue index: Not good. Bad, in fact. If you need help, your best bet is to hike back to the pavement by Nugent Mountain, or if you break down farther down by the river, head on over toward Rio Grande Village. Carry a map for just such an instance. Remember the advice the park brochures give you about building an "X" or large "HELP" from rocks if you are stranded. Maybe in a year or two a helicopter will fly by and see your message. Don't hold your breath.

Land status: Once again, this is all Big Bend National Park. Nobody will ever turn this into discount stores and strip shopping centers.

Maps: Great maps can be had at the headquarters, or sometimes at bookstores in cities. Remember cities? The folks around here do, vaguely. The quads for this ride are Glenn Spring, Mariscal Mountain, Solis, and San Vicente.

Finding the trail: Go east on the park road from Panther Junction about 6 miles, to the turn for Glenn Spring Road. Turn right and head south on this "unimproved dirt road" for about 8 miles, until you reach the place where Black Gap Road splits off to the right. This is just past the southern end of Chilicotal Mountain, very near Glenn Spring. You may park near the road junction in one of the cleared spots along the road. Head roughly southwest on Black Gap Road until you reach another road that cuts off to the left and heads around the northern end of Mariscal Mountain. This will be about 3 miles past the trailhead for the Elephant Tusk Pack Trail, marked by a sign. This trail heads off to the north from Black Gap Road and into the Chisos Mountains.

After you turn toward Mariscal Mountain, you will be on the River Road and soon will be among the ruins of the Mariscal Mine. *Mariscal* is the Spanish word for "marshal" or "blacksmith," and it is believed that these areas got their name from a local resident, someone long ago in the forgotten past. You will stay on the River Road after exiting the mine area and soon will find yourself needing to turn left at the split for Solis Landing, about 5 miles past the mine. If you ignore the turn, you will find yourself at the river after about 1.5 miles. If so, you may want to take advantage of the shade around one of the more popular camping spots along the river.

In the opinion of many Big Bend mountain bikers this is the best piece of riding. This is a shot along Black Gap Road, the first leg of the Glenn Spring Loop. After this you gradually head over to the ruins of the Mariscal Mine and from there to the Rio Grande River.

After the turn at Solis, you will be heading roughly northeast, and in about 4 miles you will find the turn for Glenn Spring Road. If you stay on the River Road about half a mile past the Glenn Spring turn, you may take another road to the right and visit the ruins of some dwellings. Rooney's Place is what is left of an old homesite about a quarter of a mile from the River Road. Turning off the River Road onto the Glenn Spring Road will find you climbing steadily for 7 miles or so until you are once again at your parking spot near the ruins of Glenn Spring.

Sources of additional information:

Park Superintendent
Big Bend National Park, TX 79834
(915) 477-2251

Big Bend Natural History Association
P.O. Box 68
Big Bend National Park, TX 79834
(915) 477-2236

Desert Sports
Lajitas, TX
(915) 371-2602

Notes on the trail: I expect that you are smart enough to look at maps and see that it would be possible to ride the River Road from the east side of the park near Rio Grande Village to the west side of the park near the Cerro Castellan and the village of Castolon. The River Road would probably be a good ride for an overnight camping trip or a day ride for a couple of hammerheads, but there are reasons why I have not suggested doing the whole thing here. Most of the people you will meet along the river are not your friends. In fact, if you were riding there and saw a group of people crossing the river carrying garbage bags or brown paper packages, you had better be thinking about hiding and not being seen by them. I have heard too many horror stories of people disappearing along the river. Some speculate that they were killed by drug dealers coming across the river with a load of heroin.

I am not kidding around about this. Friends of mine who have spent years on the river say they have never seen anything they thought was suspicious, but people do disappear from the park occasionally, and no one knows where they go. There is illegal alien traffic across the river and through the park from time to time, and you may see Border Patrol vehicles or airplanes while you are riding. The illegals probably would not be a threat, since they are trying to get through here as fast as possible, but the druggies could be big trouble if they spotted you spotting them.

Be careful along the river—the dangers are not all of the snake/insect/crash-related variety. There have been cases of people (kids, I think) on the Mexico side of the river taking rifle shots at rafters running the rapids on the Rio Grande. As a result, I pretty much stay away from the river and will not advise you to ride along there any more than just to make this loop. There are no other reasons one could not make a nice leisurely camping trip out of the River Road ride. Just keep your eyes peeled, and stay out of sight if you see anything suspicious.

RIDE 47 *OLD ORE ROAD*

This is the hardest ride in the park, partly because of the distances and tough riding involved and partly because it must be done as an out-and-back. If possible, make arrangements to have you and your equipment shuttled to the Dagger Flats end and recovered at the Rio Grande Village end. Or vice-versa, depending on the direction of the wind. If you attempt this ride, you will be tackling 28 miles of, surprise, loose gravel and rock called a "primitive four-wheel-drive road." The Old Ore Road is exactly what the name says: the

RIDE 47 · *OLD ORE ROAD*

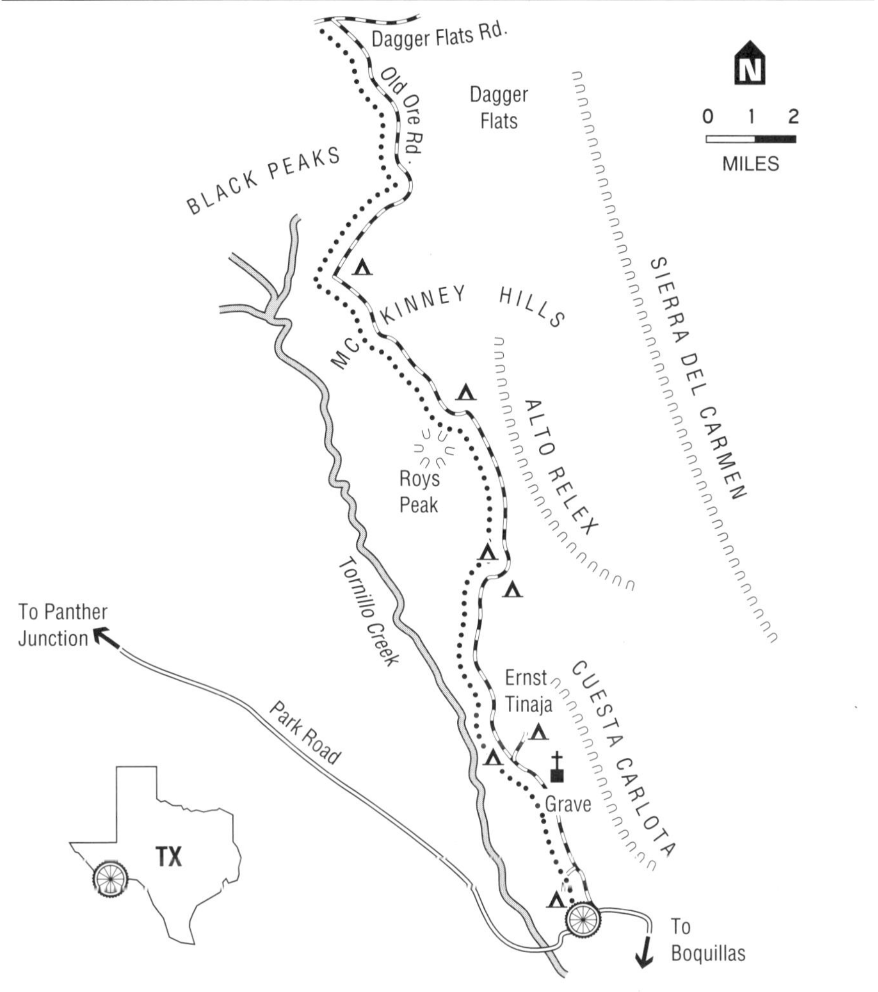

route used by wagon trains hauling quicksilver from Boquillas to Marathon, nearly 100 miles to the northwest.

The area known as the Big Bend Country was really booming around the turn of the century and until about the time World War II started. At one time there was ample grass for grazing cattle, until overgrazing wiped out this natural resource. The hot springs brought people from near and far, and the mining and candelilla wax factories had a relatively high number of workers living in the area. All this is gone now.

The Alto Relex is to your east for several miles along the Old Ore Road. The scenery here is nothing but eye-popping spectacular, absolutely breathtaking.

Around the turn of the century, Pancho Villa and his *banditos* raided local villages and generally made nuisances of themselves with the residents of the area, until finally the cavalry came to the rescue in the form of the U.S. Army's Buffalo Soldiers. This brought an end to the raiders and outlaws that had replaced the Indians as the enemies of settlers in the Big Bend Country.

Speaking of Indians, they used many of the *tinajas* and really good camping spots since the beginning of man's reign in the park area. Until they were decimated and replaced by people of European descent, they ruled this land; they were the true masters of the mountains and desert. Their horsemanship was unparalleled, and their expertise in survival skills will likely never be seen again. They could live here, really live here and love it. Think about that as you ride the Old Ore Road. You are just some of the many travelers who have passed through the Tornillo Creek/Ernst Basin/Dagger Flats area.

Like I said, this is probably the hardest ride in the park, but it's also one of the prettiest. You will be offered views of beautiful high cliffs and fields strewn with their boulders, and you will pass through areas of high desert that are bordered on one hand by strikingly colored badlands and on the other by far-away mountains that seem to float above the horizon in the distance.

A few of the places you will pass bear significant history. Dagger Flats is this huge wasteland of flat, open high desert country. It gets it's name from the numerous giant yucca plants, otherwise known as Spanish daggers. Another notable place is McKinney Spring, whose name came from a couple who settled this area and eventually discovered one of the richest quicksilver veins in the area. You will drop from the open desert of Dagger Flats into McKinney Spring and through a sheltered valley that forms the portal to the rolling hills you pass on your way to Roys Peak, named for Roy Stilwell, another early resident. South of Roys is the turn for Telephone Canyon, a hiking trail, and a primitive campsite. When the army was here defending the settlers from raiders, they built a telephone line from here back to headquarters, hence the name. At La Noria (Spanish for "the well") there was once a village, now in ruins. The village's name refers to the *tinaja* in Ernst Canyon, and the canyon and *tinaja* were named for M. A. Ernst. He lived there as postmaster, peace officer, and owner of The Big Tinaja Store until he was killed in an ambush a few miles north.

You should try to get an early enough start to allow time to explore some of the side roads. An even better idea is to camp at one of these primitive sites, if you have the ground clearance and do not mind getting a few scratches on your automobile. Without a winch and four-wheel-drive you should not attempt to go farther into the desert than maybe five or six miles from either end. There are places where the road barely exists, because, true to its word, the National Park Service does not maintain this to be driven by normal automobiles.

Of course, the ideal way to see this stretch of the park would be to camp it by bike. If you have the *cojones,* this would make an ideal two-day trip, starting at Dagger Flats and riding to Candelilla or Ernst Tinaja to spend the night. Carry enough water to outlast the time you intend to spend on the trail. Figure at least a gallon a day, because it is so dry here that you will become dehydrated in a few hours if you do not make a serious effort to drink constantly. Even in the winter. Dehydration leads to, at best, cramps and unhappy campers.

General location: The Old Ore Road runs from the park road near Rio Grande Village straight north, roughly paralleling the eastern border of Big Bend National Park.

Elevation change: Where the Old Ore Road meets the pavement of the park road, the elevation is almost exactly 2,050´. From there you will gradually work your way up to about 3,000´ at a point about halfway between Roys Peak and McKinney Spring. Then you drop to about 2,850´ going through McKinney Spring and wind back up to 3,150´ just before you hit Dagger Flats Road and turn around.

Season: Watch for conditions that might contribute to flash flooding; if the water gets over the road, you are stranded. The summer heat here can fry your brains, as well as burning your skin to a nice tomato-like color.

Services: The store at Rio Grande Village is only a few miles to the east of the southern trailhead, and it is open year-round, including Sunday. The 7-11 store at La Noria is closed, hahaha. Get it? There are no facilities of any kind at either trailhead or along the route.
Hazards: Take everything you have read in other chapters about this area and multiply it by ten. You will probably not see another soul through here, so traffic is certainly no concern. Desert plants, snakes, and insects are always a danger, so PAY ATTENTION. The surface of the trail is loose almost everywhere and could take you down if you lose concentration for a second.
Rescue index: You might want to get your affairs in order before coming here—as in, get your "Last Will" current. If you crash and burn, it will be days before you are discovered. The only way out is to go to one end of the road or the other. Under your own power. Period.
Land status: One more fine part of Big Bend National Park.
Maps: You would be smart to pick up a topographical map of this area. The headquarters has some excellent ones for less than $10. There are many spots you might miss without good information—information that is well worth "less than $10." The quads for this ride are Boquillas, Roys Peak, and McKinney Springs.
Finding the trail: This gets a little complicated, because we have choices, so choose based on prevailing winds.

South (Rio Grande Village) trailhead: Drive east on the park road from Panther Junction about 15 miles, to the sign indicating the left turn for Old Ore Road. Go north, to the top of the hill, and park in the small clearing on your left.

North (Dagger Flats) trailhead: Drive north from Panther Junction on the park road that becomes US 385 to the turn for Dagger Flats Road (about 13 miles) and go right (east). Go 2 miles and take the first road going south. This is the Old Ore Road.

Sources of additional information:

Park Superintendent
Big Bend National Park, TX 79834
(915) 477-2251

Big Bend Natural History Association
P.O. Box 68
Big Bend National Park, TX 79834
(915) 477-2236

Desert Sports
Lajitas, TX
(915) 371-2602

Notes on the trail: Take plenty of film, because there are numerous good photo-ops during this ride. Carry plenty of spare tubes and your tool kit, and do not start this ride if anything is out of order. It is too remote and too severe to be taken lightly. When you have ridden the Old Ore Road, you may consider yourself an expert on surviving rides in the Big Bend Country.

Between Ernst Tinaja and Candelilla there is a grave on the east side of the road. Stop and pay your respects. This guy's relatives still come over from Mexico to put flowers on his grave.

I don't know why, but I found this to be a real spooky ride. Perhaps I am just superstitious, but Dagger Flats gave me the creeps like nowhere else I have ridden. The Alto Relex area of cliffs is stunning visually, and the badlands between McKinney Springs and Dagger Flats can be absolutely beautiful in the light of the setting sun.

Take a pal, take the day, and take a deep breath. They quit making places like this when they broke the mold making this one.

OKLAHOMA

Oklahoma—where the wind comes sweeping down the plain. I was a kid here, and I grew up with all the cowboy and Indian stuff we were taught in school. The history of this state is fascinating, and the early settlers left a legacy rich in hard work and deep-seated values.

However, they were not mountain bikers. Only recently has there been much of an interest in providing trails suitable to off-road cycling. There have always been rides, but many are on private property or were "gray" in a legal sense. The popularity of our sport in the 1990s has opened the eyes of a lot of state and city land managers, as well as advertising executives. I suspect that by the time you read this, there will be some new places to ride—places that are only now in the planning stages. Check the bike shops in towns anytime you are nearby, because they always know where the trails are. Or at least who rides them.

Did you know Oklahoma was Indian Territory until the land was opened up to settlers? The name "Oklahoma" is derived from a Choctaw Indian phrase that means "red people." The state flag is a blue field with the buckskin battle-shield of an Osage warrior decorated with seven eagle feathers. I like this place. It became a state (our 46th) in 1907 after the famous Land Rush when the Sooner Boomers crossed the territorial lines and went deep into the interior before the official opening day for land-grabbing. People rode their horses and drove their teams as hard as they could to reach whatever land they could. Then they brought their families in to settle on those claims. The settlers who attempted to follow the rules governing land-grabbing arrived at their intended homes on opening day only to find squatters who had arrived a day or two earlier. There were some interesting verbal exchanges. Some of the Sooner Boomers were not dislodged until later, when the Buffalo Soldiers arrived.

The famous Buffalo Soldiers figure prominently in the past here and in many of the areas described in this guide. This is not the place to go into the entire history of the 9th Cavalry and 10th Cavalry, but let me mention that they were a regiment of freedmen and ex-slaves, soldiers who fought for the Union in the War for Southern Independence (a.k.a. the War Between the States, or the Civil War for you Federals). Their name derives from their thick dark hair. To the Indians it resembled that of the buffalo, and their ferocity in battle seemed as lion-hearted as the fight of a bison. They not only drove out many of the aforementioned illegal Boomers and helped settle the state but also built much of Fort Sill, where there are still a good many buffalo. So the next time you are down around Lawton, think about them men it took to tame this land. It is interesting to note that the Buffalo Soldiers went on to do some serious mountain bike touring—from a fort in Montana to St. Louis, Missouri! This was, of course, long before anyone had coined the phrase "mountain bike touring." There may have been better gunfighters, and possibly even better cyclists, but no one has been born who was more at home and better capable of surviving in our nation's wilderness areas. These guys still have not received the respect they deserve for their accomplishments.

Bonnie and Clyde hung out here. They robbed banks. Jesse Chisholm of Chisholm Trail fame lived here, though his partner Charles Goodnight was a Texan. Will Rogers was from here, as well as his best friend Wiley Post, with whom he died in an airplane crash in Alaska. They were a couple of interesting characters. Will, you may know, was a famous humorist and rope-trick artist during the Depression era, sort of an Oklahoma version of Mark Twain. Anita Bryant was from Oklahoma before she was Miss America.

There are some absolutely beautiful places in Oklahoma. Some of the reservoirs and the lands that surround them are going to provide many people with the best experiences they have ever had on camping trips. I have many fond memories of when my dad would take our family camping at Lake Tenkiller or Stanley Draper or somewhere equally cool.

I urge you to spend some time off the bike in order to take in as much local culture as possible. For instance, if you are in Oklahoma City you might want to check out the Cowboy Hall of Fame. They have some beautiful artwork and some real old saddles on display.

When I was growing up in Oklahoma, I was a Cub Scout. We used to make field trips to see Indian ceremonies, and we learned all about the famous warriors and the cavalry soldiers they fought it out with. If you have the time, seek some of this out, because you will travel a long way to find the beautiful Indian artwork and authentic ritual ceremonies that are available to you in Oklahoma.

The Oklahoma Highway Patrol has a "zero tolerance" policy concerning traffic violations. I mention this because most of the highways here have 55 miles per hour speed limits, and it is tempting to bend the rules at times. Take your time and arrive safely to enjoy your rides. And save money too.

The same cautions regarding poisonous plants and dangerous snakes that you will read over and over in the Texas sections apply here with equal intensity. I think poison ivy and water moccasins were invented in Oklahoma, and the biggest moccasin I have ever seen was here.

Trail etiquette is just as important here as anywhere else in America. Don't be one of the jerks that scares horses and hikers with their asinine riding behavior. Don't ride destructively, and stay off the trails when they are muddy.

Try to meet some of the locals when you ride. That is always the best way to score information on other trails in the area. I should tell you that I purposely left some places out of this book in an effort to force you into area bike shops to get information on them. Some obvious places. If I mention a certain bike shop crowd and refer you to them for the poop on other area riding opportunities, take heed. It might prove worthwhile to humor me from time to time.

Okies, as they sometimes refer to themselves, are a pretty hearty lot. They really know how to enjoy their state's outdoor areas, and they like to see foreigners do the same. The state tourist bureau will gladly send you a map of the best on- and off-road experiences to be had here. Just write them and ask. It's free.

Oklahoma Department of Tourism and Recreation:

Travel and Tourism Division: (405) 521-3981
Information and Brochures: (405) 521-2409 or (800) 652-6552
Camping and Resort Reservations: (405) 521-2464/-3988 or
(800) 654-8240

Division of State Parks
2401 North Lincoln Boulevard
Oklahoma City, OK 73105
(405) 521-3411

RIDE 48 *WHISPERING PINES TRAIL*

This northeastern Oklahoma state park has a little bit of everything. The facilities here include an airport, a golf course, stables, Fort Gibson Lake, the Western Hills Lodge, boat rentals, a heated fishing dock, three mountain bike trails, and little Bambi to boot. If you need some place to have your family reunion that would have a little something for everyone, this just could be the place for y'all.

Stop by the Nature Center for a map of the trails and a chance for the tikes to pat Bambi. When I visited Sequoyah State Park, the ranger had a pen with four fawns that were so obviously hand-raised you could walk up and scratch them behind the ears. A first for this reporter, I assure you.

People often find where Bambi's mom stashed him under a bush. They take him out and play with him. They pat Bambi some more and then drive home. Later Mom comes back and smells Mr. and Mrs. Human's scent on her baby. At that point Mom feels freed of the burden of raising her young, since Mr. and Mrs. Human have been here. Bambi wanders around lost and deserted and nearly starves. Enter Mr. Ranger to save the day and raise the children as a foster parent. If you see cute little Bambi, don't try to pick him up.

Our interest is of course off-roading of the two-wheel leg-launched variety. Sequoyah State Park lists three trails open to bicycles, designated by colorful names.

The Green Section is an easy double-track running from the Nature Center to where the Yellow Section begins, mostly within earshot of the road. Green has some smooth fast downhill sections, nothing technical or demanding

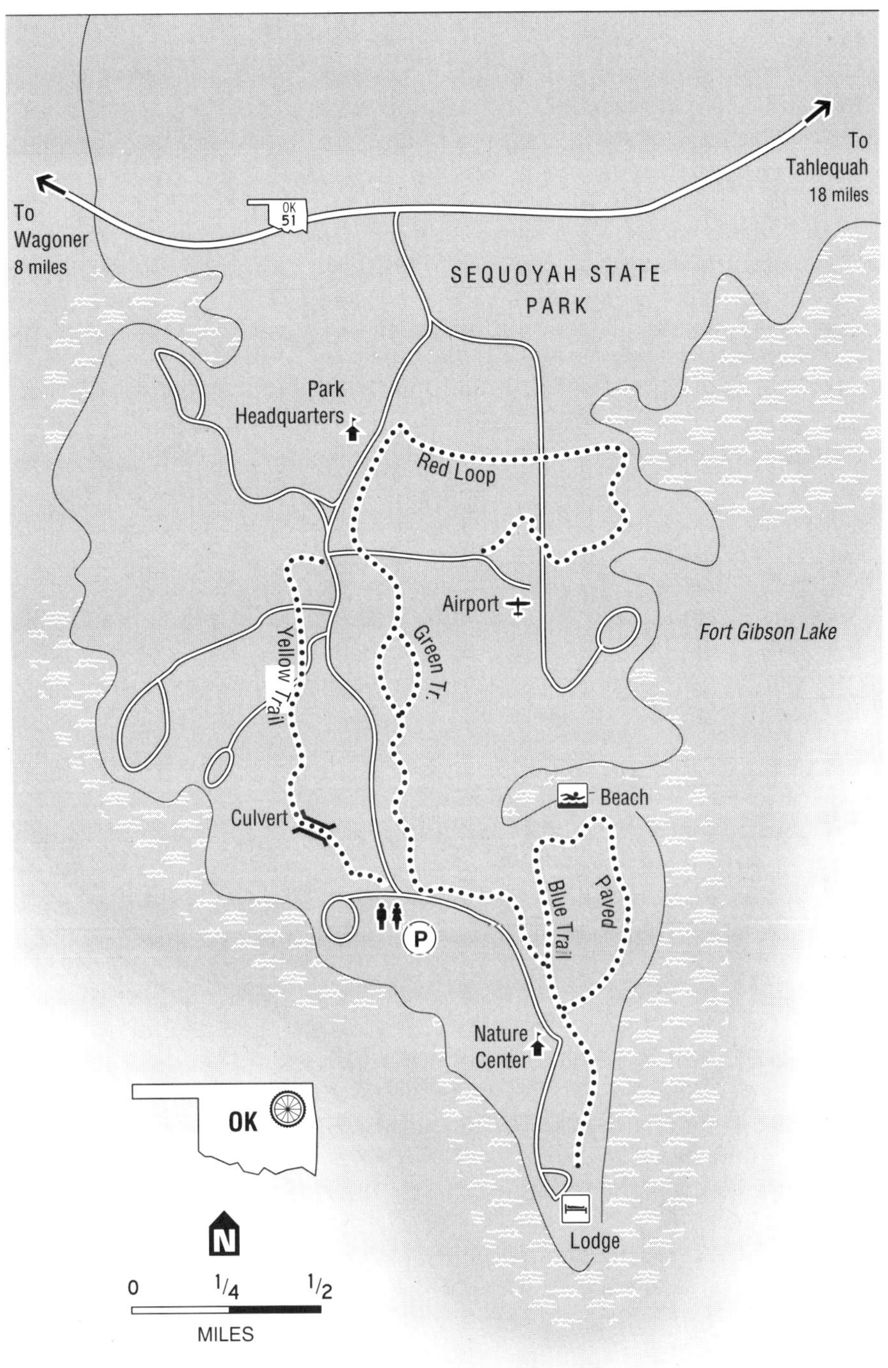
To
Tahlequah
18 miles
OK
51
To
Wagoner
8 miles
SEQUOYAH STATE
PARK
Park
Headquarters
Red Loop
Airport
Fort Gibson Lake
Yellow Trail
Green Tr.
Beach
Culvert
Paved
Blue Trail
P
Nature
Center
OK
N
Lodge
0
1/4
1/2
MILES

physically. It rates as a very easy ride. This point-to-point trail, with the short loop on the end, is about two miles in length.

The Yellow Section is similar to old Greenie but is more like single-track and crosses some active roads, requiring that definite care be taken of automobile traffic. It is an easy point-to-point of about two miles, with slightly more elevation change than the Green. This trail starts at what they call the golf pro shop and winds around to where the end of the Green trail is.

The Red Section takes you down near Fort Gibson Lake and back around by the airport, starting and ending near the Visitor Center. This is also easy double-track with a sandy, loose rock surface, and it crosses active roads. At these spots, care must be taken. The total distance of this loop trail is about two and one-half miles.

Most of the trails are sandy gravel. They drain well and are entirely rideable when wet. There are some short sections on the Yellow that are similar to black gumbo and might be gummy when wet, but the rest is firm. Two or three sections may be combined into one nonstrenuous ride. You will ride just less than seven miles total if all available trail is explored. All are signed very well, so there should be no getting lost.

There are a few slightly technical spots like tree roots and loose rocks, and a small creek crossing or two that you should be careful of if you are uncertain of your skills, or if you are just clumsy. I would say any portion of these trails could be ridden by 99% of mountain bikers on a hybrid bike. Another good place to turn the kids loose on the BMXers and let them run wild?

General location: About an hour east of Tulsa, Oklahoma, on Fort Gibson Lake.

Elevation change: The lake elevation is 554´ above sea level, and the highest point along the trail is about 644´.

Season: This place is a game refuge, so hunting is not a concern, and the trail is durable enough to be enjoyed in the worst of the wet seasons. No worries, mate.

Services: The Visitor Center has water and a pay phone, and the Nature Center and golf pro shop both have water and rest rooms. Bike rentals are also available at the Nature Center. The lodge has rooms and cottages for rent and a playground for the kiddies, and arrangements may be made here for horseback trail riding (yuck). The nearest bike shops are in Tulsa.

Hazards: The mosquitoes here are of considerable abundance in the warmer times of year, so take repellent. If you see any snakes, act like you did not. Leave them alone—you are a guest in their home. The trails are very safe as mountain bike trails go. There's not a lot of traffic, and though the surface is loose in many places, there are only a few spots where turns or technical obstacles might offer trouble.

Rescue index: These trails possess some of the best ratings for rescuability, since the trails all either cross or parallel active roads. Walk to the pavement and stick your thumb out.

Bring the kids and count Bambi and his pals as you ride the Whispering Pines at Sequoyah State Park.

Land status: The trails described here are located on the grounds of Sequoyah State Park.
Maps: Fairly good maps are available at the Visitor and Nature Centers. They are supplied at no cost. The quads for this area are Wagoner East and Hulbert.
Finding the trail: Sequoyah State Park is east of US 69 at Wagoner on OK 51.

The best place to park is the Nature Center. From there you simply go along the side of the road in the direction of the main park entrance, on the opposite side of the road from the Nature Center. After the golf course and just before the turn for Camping Area #6, you will see the sign identifying what you are riding as the Whispering Pines Trail. Follow the double-track past the sign, then follow the directions on the map for your trail of choice. If you ride the whole enchilada, you will return to this area, across the road from the golf pro shop.

Sources of additional information:

Sequoyah State Park
Route 1, Box 198-3
Hulbert, OK 74441-9725
(918) 772-2046

Oklahoma Tourism and Recreation Department
Division of State Parks
2401 North Lincoln Boulevard
Oklahoma City, OK 73105
(405) 521-3411
Oklahoma Tourism and Recreation Department

Literature and Information
Box 600000
Oklahoma City, OK 73146-6000
(405) 521-2409
(800) 652-6552

Notes on the trail: The camping is nice here, all sorts of nonbiking distractions are available, and the scenery is relaxing. What more motivation do you need? Be sure and take a walk through the Nature Center and check out all the snakes and other critters they have on display. It's free.

RIDE 49 *TURKEY MOUNTAIN PARK TRAILS*

This sprawling Tulsa trail network offers something for everyone. There are easy-going nontechnical areas, mostly flat and thoroughly negotiable, and there are intense, highly difficult technical areas with long, hard climbs. The exact length of the maze of trails in this park is somewhat uncertain and probably varies with season. I would say it will be easy for you to ride ten miles and never traverse the same section of single-track two times. Of course, it would also be easy to ride ten miles in circles and hit the same single-track a bunch of times if you get lost, which does happen here.

Turkey Mountain Park is an "urban wilderness" area within sight of downtown Tulsa. As you approach from the north, you will be able to see and identify Turkey Mountain, a peak that juts 300 feet above the Arkansas River. Most of the trails have the sand/gravel/rock surface common to this area and can easily be ridden the day after hard rains. Most sections are under the canopy of trees, but some areas are more exposed and will find you stopping in shady places to get out of the sun on hot days.

Since the park lacks any sort of facilities, you will need to fill your bottles and go to the bathroom before you head over to ride. The parking area is usually packed during nice weather, so you will likely have plenty of company as you ride here. Some people come out here with metal detectors looking for a cache of gold that Jesse James and his gang supposedly buried here. It has never been found—not that anyone has advertised, at least.

Several spots offer memorable views of the downtown area and the river, and these may be used to facilitate locating yourself when (not if) you become

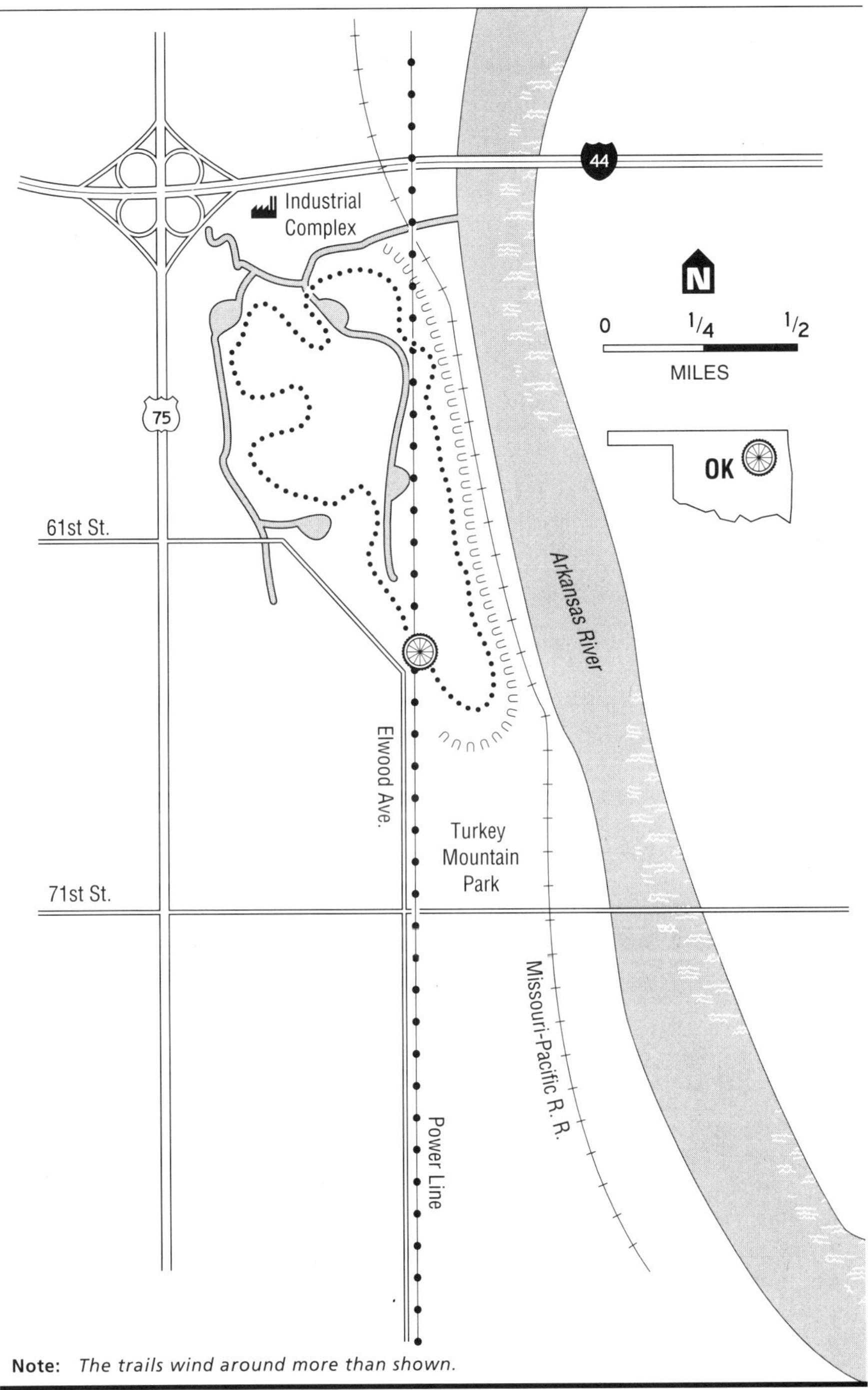

Note: *The trails wind around more than shown.*

lost during your wanderings. Don't worry. You can hardly travel more than a few miles from the parking area, because the park is bounded on roughly two sides by the roads that lead into and around the park—on one side by the river, and on one side by a YMCA and large industrial complex. There are three small ponds along Moser Creek that may also be used to offer some indication of your exact location within the park grounds.

Races are held here on a fairly regular basis, and this is the main mountain bike trail for people in the area, so finding a partner to help you get out of the park is usually *no problema.* Get on your bikes and ride.

General location: Turkey Mountain Park is located in the central portion of Tulsa, right on the western banks of the Arkansas River. This puts you south of Interstate 44 and east of US 75.

Elevation change: The parking lot is near the highest point in the park, about 920′ above sea level. The trails will lead you down almost all the way to the river, which lies just over 610′.

Season: There are no seasonal constraints I am aware of that might keep you off the trails. Hard rains will make part of this park very slippery, but it drains remarkably well and usually stays in good shape. Some parts may grow over slightly in summer.

Services: There are no services whatsoever at the trailhead. Across the river on 71st Street are all manner of convenience stores, gas stations, and a bike shop. If you need water, rest rooms, or any supplies, you will have to satisfy these needs before you head to the trail.

Hazards: The trails here can be very dangerous. They are typically covered with a variety of loose materials and may offer difficult footing in places. There are many major technical challenges, such as tree roots and large rocks and plenty of very fast downhills. You must be as level-headed as possible to stay upright and hold onto your uninjured status. You will meet pedestrian traffic and equestrian trail users, and you must offer them the right-of-way when they appear.

Rescue index: You could have a problem if you get hurt here, because the confusing maze of trails in this park will make discerning your exact location extremely difficult. Besides, there is no phone in the park, so acquiring emergency help is probably going to require a healthy and uninjured riding partner who knows the quickest route back to the parking lot and then to the nearest pay phone.

Land status: This is a city park and therefore a protected area that hopefully will always stay as such.

Maps: Hah. I did the best I could creating the one in this book. I had nothing more than my experiences and 7.5 minute quadrangles to go by. Formal maps do not exist, to the best of my knowledge. The quads for this park are Supalpa North and Jenks.

This is some guy, I can't remember his name, showing me around the trails at Turkey Mountain in Tulsa. I had such good luck as I wandered around looking for trails to write about. I kept running into people who offered to give me guided tours and asked for nothing. Many thanks to you all, a million times. I couldn't have done it without you.

Finding the trail: From I-44 go south on US 75 to the exit for 61st Street. Go east on 61st and follow it as it curves around and up to the top of Turkey Mountain. The trailhead is located right where 61st becomes Elwood Avenue and turns due south. You'll see a sign and small parking lot on the north side, and the road drops down a long hill immediately past the trailhead.

Go through the opening in the pipe fence and begin your ride by wandering to the right on the trail nearest the park sign. This will take you along the steep bluff to the east and then let you follow the perimeter. The trail will lead you around to the north and the fine mountain biking areas. Following the perimeter will gradually lead you down to the area around the YMCA. From there you may go south a little at a time. Soon you will be following trails back up the hill to the parking area. Ride the perimeter of the park to get the layout in your head before you attempt to explore all the side trails available. This might make it easier for you to find your way back to the parking area when you are ready to depart. Along the way you will pass some handy reference points: some ponds, a pipeline, a power line, a railroad, etc. Fix them in your mind and you will sort of know where you are.

Sources of additional information:

River Trail Bicycles
6861 South Peoria
Tulsa, OK 74136
(918) 481-1818

River Parks Authority
(918) 596-2002

Notes on the trail: Whew, good riding on exciting trails. Carry plenty of water and your tool pouch, spare tube, and pump. It can be a long hot walk if you have a mechanical problem. Try to make friends with someone along the way so maybe they can show you around and help you find the best sections of the trail. There is also an easy paved jogging trail along the east side of the river that might interest the less athletic. Ask at the bike shop (River Trail Bicycles) for directions and information on bike rentals.

RIDE 50 *OLD MILITARY ROAD*

When you have developed your mountain biking and survival skills and they are ready to be tested, it is time to visit the Winding Stair National Recreation Area in the Ouachita National Forest in eastern Oklahoma. The rides here are technically challenging, the climbs hard, and the conditions sufficiently difficult that you will need to be on your toes and have the body and bike well tuned. If you don't, you are going to suck wind.

The Old Military Road was built in 1832 to connect Fort Smith in Arkansas with Fort Towson near the Red River in Oklahoma. It was used to convey troops and supplies between military installations of the day and also saw the passage of various Indian nations being relocated by the government to the Indian Territories in Oklahoma. Built during the administration of President Andrew Jackson, it was traveled by several figures of historical significance. Along the road you could have met some people who went on to fame—people like the first president of the Republic of Texas, Sam Houston, and the 12th president of the United States of America, General Zachary Taylor.

The Old Military Road Trail is a tough, rocky hiking path connecting the Talimena Scenic Drive on Winding Stair Mountain with the trailhead on Holson Valley Road. It consists of approximately seven miles of point-to-point single-track, fairly well marked by white and/or blue rectangular blaze marks painted on the trees along the trail, every 100 yards or so. Keep your eyes in scan-mode, going from the trail to the trees and back constantly. That way you

RIDE 50 *OLD MILITARY ROAD*

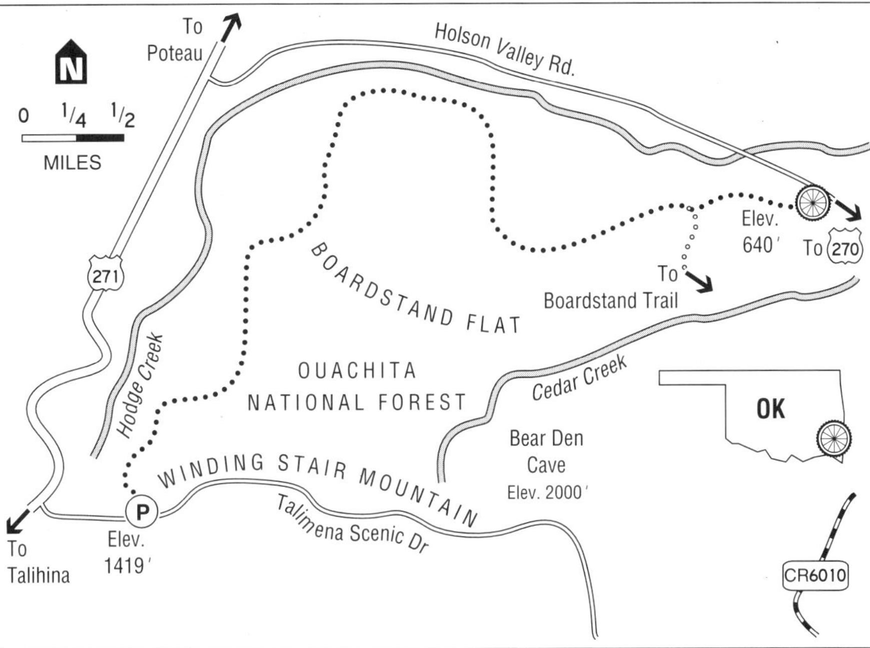

will not get lost, at least not too lost. I wandered a little the first time I rode here, but anyone with a lick of sense will be able to stay on the proper route.

The trail crosses several active gravel roads, so look carefully for automobile traffic before blasting across any of them. In several places you will be riding on old double-track. Take heed: This is very old double-track indeed, like 150 years old. These sections are pieces of the Old Military Road, and if you listen real close you can almost hear the sound of wagons bouncing and crunching along, ferrying bullets and beans to soldiers at Fort Towson.

The Ouachita Forest is huge, stretching far into Arkansas, all tall pine trees and sandy rocky soil. This trail is very rideable in all weather conditions, but treacherous when wet due to how slick the rocks get. You will spend some time walking your bike across loose, rocky creekbeds no matter how good you are technically, and you may meet cattle along some sections. When you reach the trailhead on Talimena Scenic Drive, hang a right and go a short distance over to Dead Man's Vista. The view is breathtaking when the area is blessed with clear weather.

General location: The trail is located in the Winding Stair National Recreation Area, Ouachita National Forest, in the eastern part of the state.

Elevation change: You are going to need some good legs to enjoy this trail. The highest point is the Old Military Road Picnic Ground trailhead on Talimena Scenic Drive. It weighs in at just over 1,410′ above sea level. The trail is almost all downhill from there, to the low point at the trailhead on Holson Valley Road, which lies at about 640′. This gives you nearly 800′ of elevation change to burn your legs and lungs.
Season: The summer is not a good time to ride here because of the ticks and chiggers, and from October through December, deer hunters roam around the trails armed to the teeth. The trail will hold you any time of year, but I would have to say the period from late winter to early spring probably offers the best conditions for mountain biking.
Services: There are no services at either trailhead. The Winding Stair Visitor Center, located at the junction of Talimena Scenic Drive (OK 1) and US 271, has water and rest rooms. Talimena State Park, about a mile south of the Visitor Center, has a pay phone, water, rest rooms, and showers. The nearest town is Talihina, about 7 miles south of the Visitor Center. It has services and at least one 24-hour convenience store. The nearest bike shop is far away.
Hazards: Take notes on my advice here. As the signs say, this is bear country, so make lots of noise as you ride. Put a bell on your bike, or do like me and sing bad 1960s rock songs as you plow along. Ticks and chiggers are thick in the summer and will chew your ankles like crazy. Copperheads and rattlesnakes are always a threat, so keep your eyes open in warm weather.

I would strongly recommend wearing full-fingered gloves, because there are a ton of spiderwebs stretched across the trail, and you may get a surprise hitchhiker attaching himself to your glasses or shirt as you blast along at full speed. The gloves will allow you to remove him with no fear of getting bitten.

The trail itself offers many opportunities to get hurt, so riding solo here is probably stupid. Take a partner. Deer hunters will blast anything that moves in season, so wear bright colors and, again, make lots of noise. This is a dangerous place to ride, full of hazards. Be careful and live to ride another day.
Rescue index: Do not get hurt here, because getting rescued will be quite an ordeal. You are in a fairly remote area, far from any sort of emergency support, in an area very difficult to reach or escape from. Your only hope for rescue would be to send another rider out for help. This person would have to reach the park's Visitor Center or a road and then have emergency personnel sent in to your location, provided he or she were able to *describe* your location. The nearest hospital of any measure is in Talihina, at least 15 miles away.
Land status: This trail is contained entirely by national forest lands, which are protected from development, kept in trust for citizens of the good old USA.
Maps: The Winding Stair Visitor Center has fairly good maps for free, but a topographic map of the Ouachita National Recreational Trail is available from the United States Forest Service for a few dollars at any good map store.

Within an hour the Old Military Road had just about devoured your author. He was a bad boy and did not bring enough to drink. Don't be a SQUID, bring lots of LIQUID.

This map clearly shows all trails in the area that allows mountain bikes, as well as their trailheads. The quad for this trail is Blackjack Ridge.

Finding the trail: The Winding Stair Mountain National Recreation Area is about 30 miles southwest of Poteau on US 271.

In my opinion, the best way to tackle this trail would be to park at the Holson Valley Road trailhead and ride uphill to the Old Military Picnic Ground trailhead. This will give you a downhill return leg. The Holson Valley Road trailhead is located about 3 miles east of US 271 on Holson Valley Road. At that point you will see a gravel road heading south from Holson Valley Road. Turn there. The trailhead parking area will be on your left just a short distance south.

If you prefer to ride this trail the hard way, then start at the Old Military Road Picnic Ground. Go east on the Talimena Scenic Drive (OK 1) about a mile from US 271, until you see the sign for the Old Military Road Picnic Ground on the north side of the highway. The trailhead is on the east end of the picnic area.

Sources of additional information:

Choctaw Ranger District
HC 64, Box 3467
Heavener, OK 74937
(918) 653-2991

Ouachita National Forest
P.O. Box 1270
Federal Building
Hot Springs, AR 71902
(501) 321-5202

Notes on the trail: This is a "hiking trail" with the following rules: No motorized or equestrian traffic. Always obey the IMBA rules concerning trail right-of-way by yielding to hikers when you meet them. It would only take a few foolish bikers to get us kicked out of this beautiful single-track. Take plenty of water, because you will not find anywhere to get a drink on the trail, and the going here is much slower than you might expect. If you have the Ouachita National Recreation Trail map, I have some other advice for you too: DO NOT attempt to start your ride from Talimena State Park by jumping on the Ouachita Trail. The Ouachita Trail is a HIKER ONLY trail, and NO BIKES ARE ALLOWED. Besides, it is way too rough and steep to be enjoyed. Take my word for it—you will be sorry. I found out the hard way.

RIDE 51 *BOARDSTAND TRAIL*

I have yet to figure out where the name for this trail comes from, except that there is an area marked on the topographics called the Boardstand Flats. There must be a story behind that one. This trail is about three and one-half miles of tough, technical single-track, almost overgrown in places, that will dump you onto a gravel road (County Road 6010) that you can ride about two miles up to the Talimena Scenic Drive and Dead Man's Vista. Since it amounts to another point-to-point type of trail, you will either have to ride from the trailhead to the top of the hill or shuttle to Dead Man Gap and ride downhill to the trailhead.

This is a hard trail; significant climbing is required to get to the vista at Dead Man Gap. The actual Boardstand Trail goes on beyond CR 6010 another three and one-half miles to meet the Ouachita National Recreation Trail, but the last mile or so is too steep and rocky to do anything fun with. You would have to walk anyway, so I recommend turning at CR 6010 and riding the gravel road to the Talimena Scenic Drive. It is steep but rideable—much more so than the single-track. Besides, you SHOULD NOT ride on the Ouachita Trail, which you would have to do if you continued on beyond CR 6010 on the single-track. The view from the top of the hill is worth taking the time to investigate, and the parking area there makes a good place for a break.

The soil here is rocky and sandy. It drains well enough to be ridden when wet, but the rocks get extremely slippery. You will be fighting for bike control

RIDE 51 *BOARDSTAND TRAIL*

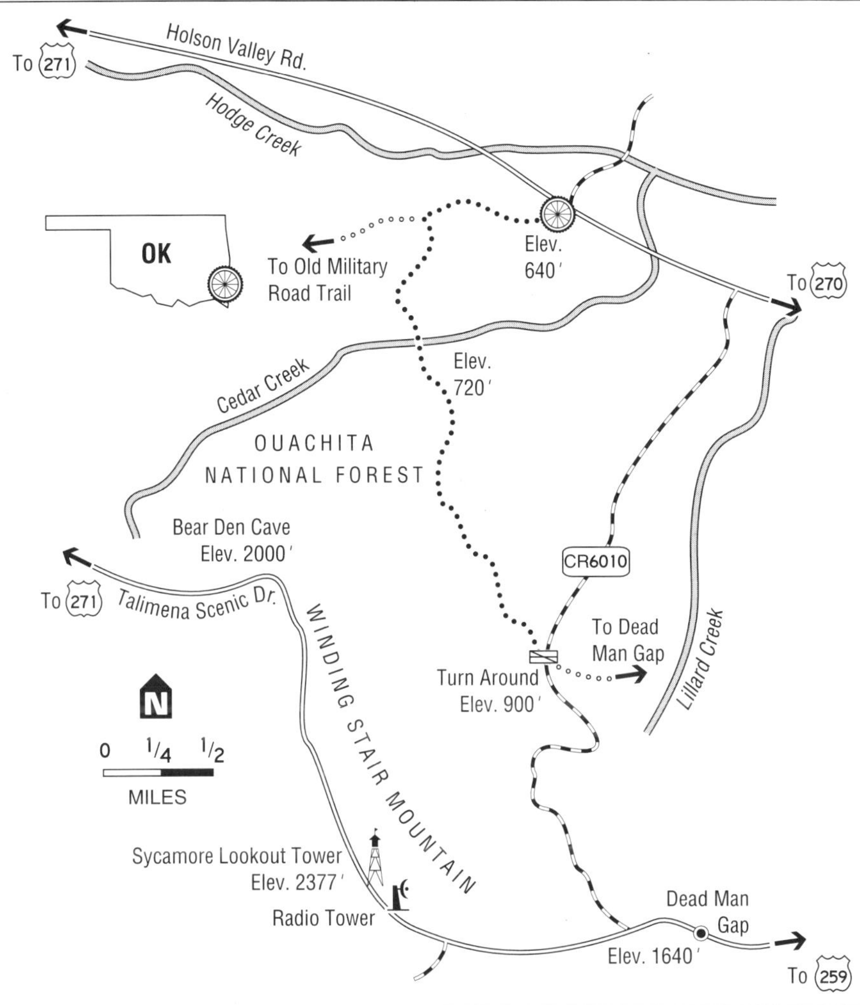

if you attack this trail in the rain. In addition to the technical challenges the Boardstand Trail offers, not getting lost will keep you busy.

Following the blue and white rectangular blazes painted on the trees along the way will prove you are on your toes. To impress your friends, be sure and stay watchful of the trail markers. When I rode here, it was so overgrown that I spent way too much time backtracking to relocate the trail. Still, it is nice for a city boy like me to get into the woods where the only sounds are the birds singing and the wheels turning. This trail will definitely offer you a secluded ride, far from the noises of the city.

One interesting thing to notice when you reach the pavement of the Talimena Scenic Drive is the hang glider launch point located near Dead Man's Vista. I saw the sign indicating the launch area, but I have to wonder, where do those knuckleheads land? There is nothing in sight for miles but trees and mountains.

General location: The trail is located in the Winding Stair National Recreation Area, Ouachita National Forest, in the eastern part of the state.
Elevation change: Another trail with significant climbing. The low point is the trailhead off Holson Valley Road at elevation 640´ above sea level. The point where CR 6010 meets the Talimena Scenic Drive and the parking lot for Dead Man's Vista are sitting at about 1,600´, so you are gaining about 1,000´ from bottom to top. Sort of makes saving the downhill leg for your return sound inviting, eh?
Season: The summer is not a good time to ride here because of the ticks and chiggers, and from October through December deer hunters roam around the trails armed to the teeth. The trail will hold you any time of year, but I would have to say the period from late winter through early spring probably offers the best conditions for mountain biking.
Services: There are no services at either trailhead. The Winding Stair Visitor Center, located at the junction of Talimena Scenic Drive (OK 1) and US 271, has water and rest rooms. Talimena State Park, about a mile south of the Visitor Center, has a pay phone, water, rest rooms, and showers. The nearest town is Talihina, about 7 miles south of the Visitor Center. It has services and at least one 24-hour convenience store. The nearest bike shop is far away—I can't say for certain where.
Hazards: I am going to repeat verbatim my cautions for all trails in the Winding Stair area. As the signs say, this is bear country, so make lots of noise as you ride. Put a bell on your bike, or do like me and sing bad 1960s rock songs as you plow along. Ticks and chiggers are thick in the summer and will chew your ankles like crazy. Copperheads and rattlesnakes are always a threat, so keep your eyes open in warm weather.

I would strongly recommend wearing full-fingered gloves, because there are a ton of spiderwebs stretched across the trail, and you may get a surprise hitchhiker attaching himself to your glasses or shirt as you blast along at full speed. The gloves will allow you to remove him with no fear of getting bitten.

The trail itself offers many opportunities to get hurt, so riding solo here is probably stupid. Take a partner. Deer hunters will blast anything that moves in season, so wear bright colors and, again, make lots of noise. This is a dangerous place to ride, full of hazards. Be careful and live to ride another day.
Rescue index: Do not get hurt here, because getting rescued will be quite an ordeal. You are in a fairly remote area, far from any sort of emergency support, in an area very difficult to reach or escape from. Your only hope for rescue

Take a good look at that wire gate and this dirt road because if you miss the turn here you will have a bad day. This is where to get off the Boardstand Trail.

would be to send another rider out for help. This person would have to reach the park's Visitor Center or a road and then have emergency personnel sent in to your location, provided he or she were able to *describe* your location. The nearest hospital is in Talihina, about 15 miles away.

Land status: This trail is contained entirely by national forest lands, which are protected from development, kept in trust for citizens of the good old USA.

Maps: The Winding Stair Visitor Center has fairly good maps for free, but a topographic map of the Ouachita National Recreational Trail is available from the United States Forest Service for a few dollars at any good map store. This map clearly shows all trails in the area that allows mountain bikes, as well as their trailheads. The quad for this trail is Blackjack Ridge.

Finding the trail: The lower trailhead is located about 3 miles east of US 271 on Holson Valley Road. Go east on Holson Valley Road and turn south at the sign, onto the gravel road. The parking area will be on your left.

The higher trailhead is located about one-quarter mile east of the intersection of Talimena Scenic Drive (OK 1) and County Road 6010 (the Dead Man's Vista parking area is right here, too), about 6 miles east of US 271, on the north side of the road.

About 3.5 miles along the trail from the Holson Valley trailhead, you will cross a gravel road. Across the road the trail passes through a wire gate with orange metal fence posts. This is CR 6010. Turn right onto this road to go up the hill to Talimena Scenic Drive. You will see to your right that the gravel road splits at a **Y** a short ways up the road. Bear left at the **Y**.

Don't continue on the trail past this road, because it gets extremely difficult and steep. It also becomes the Ouachita National Recreation Trail, a HIKER-ONLY trail; NO BIKES ARE ALLOWED.

Sources of additional information:

Choctaw Ranger District
HC 64, Box 3467
Heavener, OK 74937
(918) 653-2991

Ouachita National Forest
P.O. Box 1270
Federal Building
Hot Springs, AR 71902
(501) 321-5202

Notes on the trail: If you look at the maps, you will see that it would be possible to connect the Boardstand Trail with the Old Military Road and make a loop by riding the Talimena Scenic Drive back to the Old Military Road Picnic Ground. If you attempt this, you had better have eaten your Wheaties, because the pavement from Dead Man's Vista to the picnic area goes up a mountain or two, gaining roughly 700′ of elevation in the process. It can be fun, but your legs will pay for riding this loop of nearly 20 miles. And another thing—don't come here if you have squeaky brakes. Your friends will disown you after the first long descent.

RIDE 52 *HORSETHIEF SPRINGS TRAIL*

The Horsethief Springs Trail is another hard, rocky hiking trail through a forest in the Winding Stair National Recreation Area. There is a lot of Old West history around this area. The spring is where notorious outlaws would hide and ambush settlers and other travelers. They had a nasty habit of stealing these folks' horses, hence the name of the spring at the top of the hill. One notable figure that used the spring as a place to launch her escapades was the Dame of the Desperadoes, the Queen of the Bandits—none other than the infamous Belle Starr.

The trail starts at Cedar Lake and climbs steadily up to the pavement at the trailhead campground on Talimena Scenic Drive. This trail also crosses the Ouachita National Recreation Trail shortly before reaching the campground. It is a single-track of approximately seven miles in length configured as a point-to-point, so you will either need to start at one end and shuttle or just

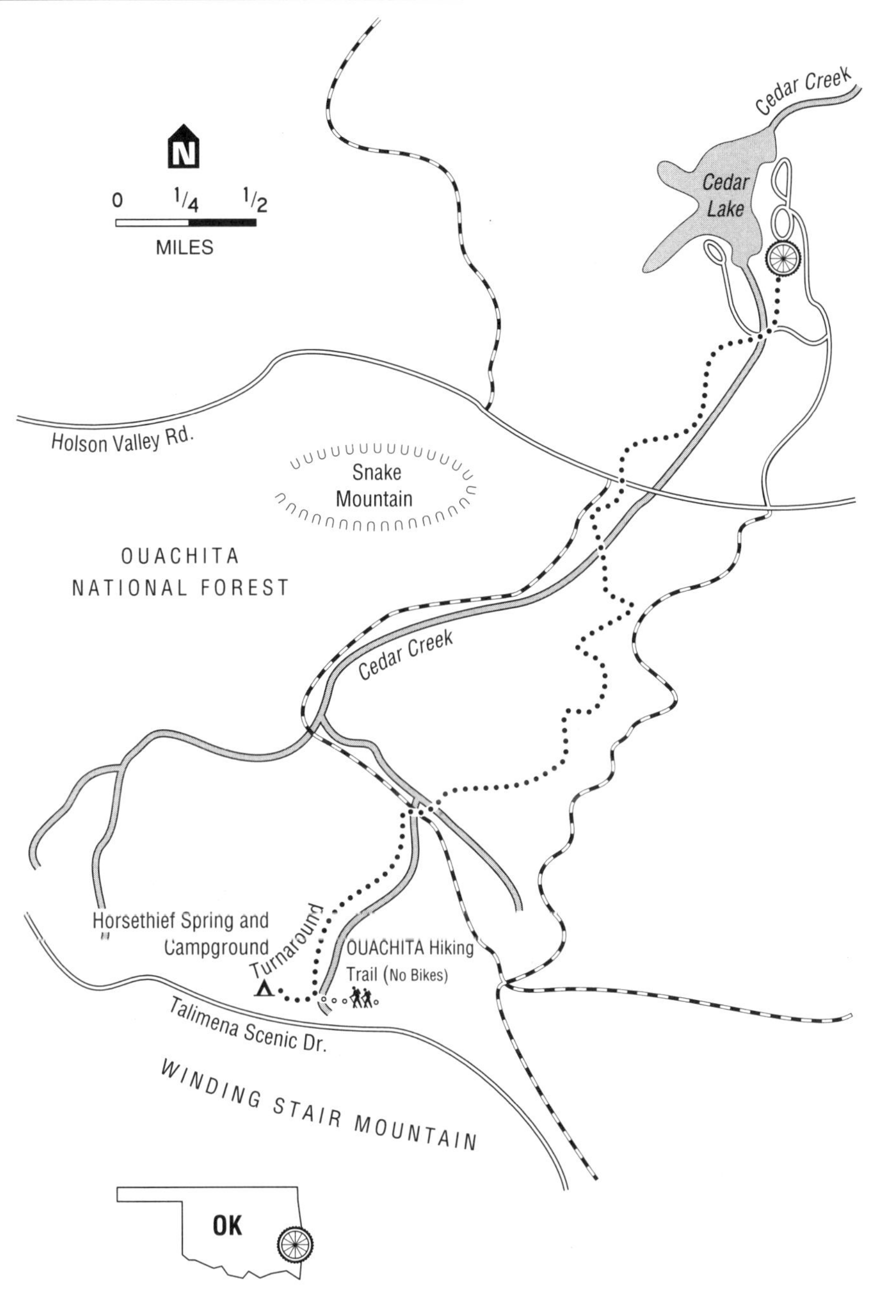
N
0
1/4
1/2
MILES
Cedar Creek
Cedar Lake
Holson Valley Rd.
Snake Mountain
OUACHITA NATIONAL FOREST
Cedar Creek
Horsethief Spring and Campground
Turnaround
OUACHITA Hiking Trail (No Bikes)
Talimena Scenic Dr.
WINDING STAIR MOUNTAIN
OK

do it as an out-and-back. If you ride out-and-back it is probably better (i.e., easier) to start at Cedar Lake and ride up the hill so that you have a nice downhill for your return.

This trail is open to equestrian traffic and is fairly severely eroded in places from heavy use by the horse folks. I strongly recommend that you take extreme care not to skid your tires and contribute to this erosion. There are many additional equestrian trails in the area, and our ride crosses several of these. You must take care to yield the right-of-way if you meet anybody riding these large hairy critters, since you have much better control over a bike than they will ever have over a 1,000-pound slab of solid muscle. Those goofy things scare so easy, and when they get scared they freak out. Especially if they are being operated by someone sort of unused to being perched way up there. Which is common here, thanks to the stables at the foot of the hill.

You will cross a few beautiful streams along the way, and these will probably require dismounting. There are several other technical obstacles along the way that will have you bailing off the bike and walking, so don't be bashful about that. A certain amount of hiking is nearly always required while cycling off-road in this area, especially near the higher elevations, where the trail is extremely rocky and tricky to ride.

Once you reach the trailhead on the scenic drive, you will find picnic tables, a chemical toilet (that stinks something fierce), and the springs. You can fill bottles here, but be careful not to jiggle the pipe where the water spills out, because you will stir up silt and rust and the water will not look very potable. If anybody in cowboy garb saunters up to you and tries to steal your mount, well, you've been warned. That is why it is called Horsethief Springs.

General location: The trail is located in the Winding Stair National Recreation Area of the Ouachita National Forest.

Elevation change: This place is another good chance to exercise your climbing muscles. The trailhead is the lowest point on the route, at about 720´ above sea level, and the Horsethief Springs Campground reaches up to about 1,770´. You can subtract, right? A nice, gentle 1,050´ climb in 7 miles. You better eat your Wheaties.

Season: With the summer bringing ticks and chiggers by the multitudes and the deer hunters shooting everything that moves from October through December, you may want to ride here late winter through spring. But only if you have good sense.

Services: The picnic area by the trailhead has water, rest rooms, and parking. The nearest pay phone is in the equestrian camping area at Cedar Lake, and there is a small store on the road into the lake grounds. There are no bike shops anywhere near here.

Hazards: A full menu of dangers awaits you on this trail. Snakes must always be watched for and expected. Chiggers and ticks live here by the billions, as

If you can ride by a place like this and not stop then you need to lighten up. A quiet moment along the Horsethief Springs Trail.

well as plenty of large spiders that string webs across the trail in densities that vary according to season. Summer is always the worst for pests. Wearing full-fingered gloves is always a good idea anyway and could be helpful with the spiders.

The rangers insist that there are bears in this area, and I for one am fairly certain that I have glimpsed at least one big black bear while driving on the scenic drive. Make plenty of racket while you ride. Talk, sing, mumble, or put a bell on your bike, and they will hear you before you see them, almost always insuring that they will hightail it the other direction and save you the embarrassment of being mauled.

Any rainfall will make the trail slick as ice and have you fighting to keep your machine rubber-side down. Respect the rights of hikers and horses, because they have the right-of-way over bikes, *always*. Also, be extremely careful while crossing the active roads along the way, because folks in this neck of the woods are not real accustomed to people on bicycles popping out of the trees and darting across the pavement.

Rescue index: The likelihood of getting rescued on this trail in the event of an emergency is probably better than on other trails in this area. This is simply because there is more traffic through here, since the equestrians are allowed. Still, you are in a fairly remote area, and if you find yourself in need of help, you have a major problem—unless you have a partner who can find his or her

way to the road and then flag down an automobile or reach Cedar Lake or one of the residences in that area.
Land status: This trail is contained within the Ouachita National Forest and is managed by the National Forest Service.
Maps: The Visitor Center near Talimena State Park has maps that describe the trail, but USGS topographic maps will show you a lot more detail about the area you are about to tackle. There are also National Forest maps; they're available for a fee from many bookstores and hiking equipment stores. The map in this book was generated from data on these and the USGS topographic quads Hodgen and Big Cedar.
Finding the trail: From Heavener go south on US 59/270 about 5 miles, to OK 1005 (Holson Valley Road), and go west on OK 1005. In a couple of miles you will see the signs for Cedar Lake and County Road 7269. Turn right (north) and proceed to the picnic pavilion. Park by the signs for the trailhead.

The trailhead for the Cedar Lake and Old Pine Trails is also the trailhead for the Horsethief Springs Trail and Ouachita Trail. Start your ride, following the signs and the white blazes on the trees all the way up the mountain to the Horsethief Springs picnic ground. In several spots you will be sharing single-track with equestrian trails, and staying on the proper trail will require watching your blaze marks. Anybody with as much good sense as God gave a rock has already figured out that they could get dropped off at the picnic ground and ride to the lake, just doing the trail one-way. Doing so would give you a ride that is downhill most of the way, so this option is recommended for weenies only.

Sources of additional information:

Choctaw Ranger District
HC 64, Box 3467
Heavener, OK 74937
(918) 653-2991

Ouachita National Forest
P.O. Box 1270
Federal Building
Hot Springs, AR 71902
(501) 321-5202

Notes on the trail: There are many equestrian trails in this area, and you should try to acquire maps of these, because exploring them can be as satisfying as riding any single-track anywhere. Ask at the Winding Stair Visitor Center or swing through the equestrian area at Cedar Lake and see if there are any maps in the map box by the rest rooms and pay phone.

There is also a 3-mile loop trail around Cedar Lake you might be interested in investigating. It shares our trailhead and is mostly flat and easy but has moderate technical challenges in the form of tree roots and large rocks in a few spots. You will see signs directing you toward the Cedar Lake Trail as you embark on your way to Horsethief Springs. Simply turn where directed; you will eventually return to the point you started from. Be extremely careful crossing any bridges you find on the loop trail, because they can be slippery when wet, and at least one is washed out on one side and has about a 4-foot drop-off. Not a pleasant wake-up call.

RIDE 53 *LITTLE BUGABOO CREEK/ WHISKEY FLATS RIDE*

There is a place in southeast Oklahoma where they are begging for you to come ride. It is a wildlife management area called McGee Creek Natural Scenic Recreation Area. There are miles of technically tough single-track and more miles of easy double-track to explore. I will combine both into the focus of this chapter. You will begin with a delightful piece of rocky single-track, then connect to another that winds down to McGee Creek Lake. This part is fairly hard riding. Then you will backtrack to find your return route, an easy gravel double-track back to the parking area.

The Little Bugaboo Creek Trail is two miles of rocky but mostly flat single-track "hike and bike" trail. It follows Little Bugaboo Creek from a point near the headquarters building to a clearing in the dense trees where several other trails meet. From there you will follow the sign that directs you onto the Whiskey Flats Trail, an old roadbed that meanders along the side of the valley for about one and one-half miles. The end is in the bottom of the valley—a stretch of McGee Creek Lake known as the Quiet Water Zone.

After you have rested for a moment, it is time to begin the climb out of the valley. Your return will not be dismount-free, because the loose rocks will guarantee the need to walk up a few steep sections. It is a pretty good grind up the hill to where the other trails converge, and when you get there you will be happy to jump on the South Rim Road for about two miles of easy downhill double-track back to the headquarters area. Once back you will have covered about seven miles or so.

I like it here. It is pretty, it is extremely quiet, and they love mountain bikers. This just might be an ideal place to go when it is wet and mushy in Texas. There is ample opportunity for recreating in this park. There are hiking trails, equestrian facilities, a lake for fishing, and plenty of room to roam.

General location: McGee Creek Lake is roughly halfway between Atoka and Antlers, north of OK 3, in the southeastern part of the state.
Elevation change: The trailhead lies at about 740′ of elevation. From there you climb fairly gradually up to around 900′, at the intersection of all the

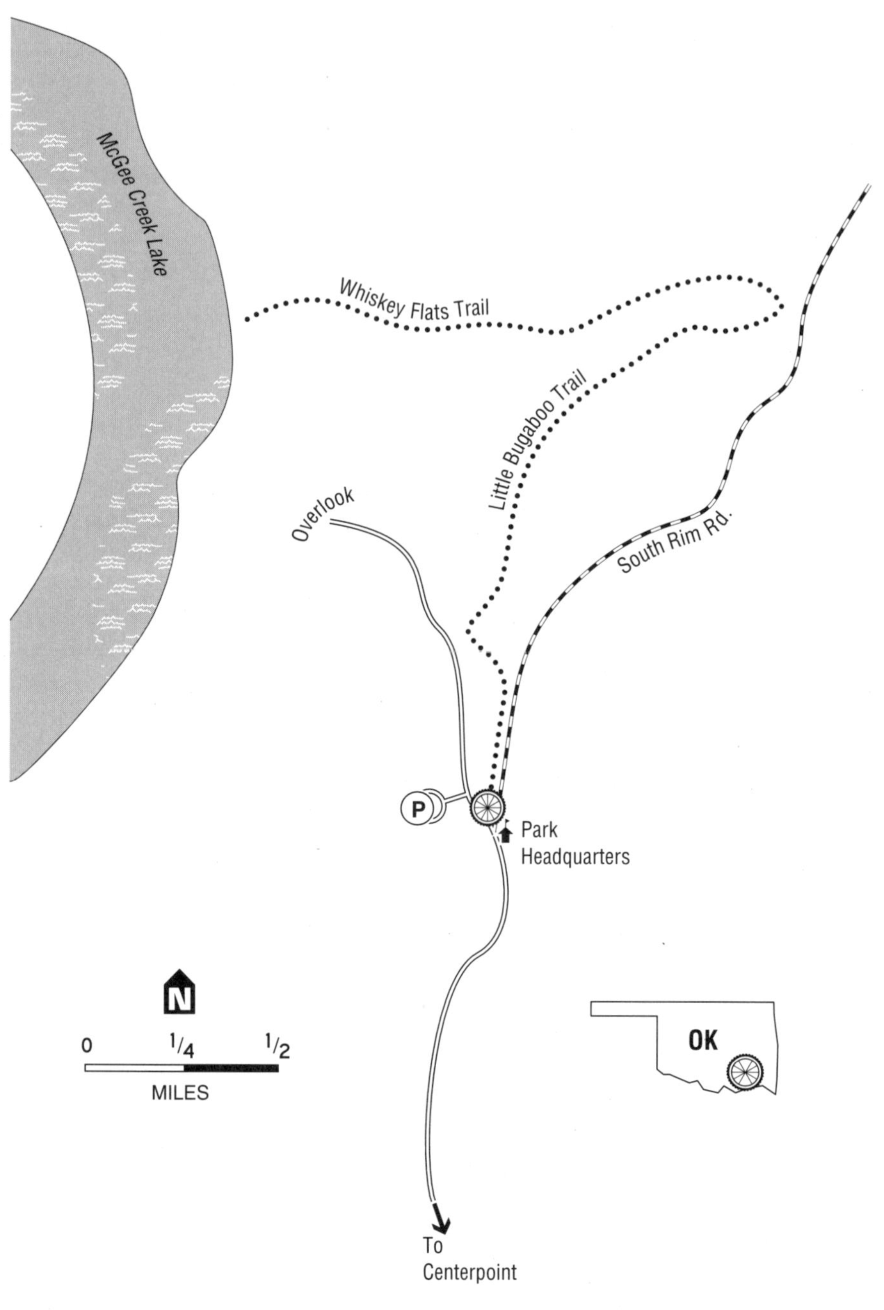
McGee Creek Lake
Whiskey Flats Trail
Little Bugaboo Trail
Overlook
South Rim Rd.
P
Park
Headquarters
N
0
1/4
1/2
MILES
OK
To
Centerpoint

trails at Whiskey Flats. You make a rapid drop to lake level after that, about 600´. Then you do the whole thing in reverse.

Season: Anytime is Whiskey Flats time, but summer is probably the worst choice, because the ticks and chiggers are at their strongest during the high heat. Hunting is allowed here, so stay away during deer season, typically October through December. Early spring is probably your best choice, before the trails start to grow over. Some almost disappear in the summer through lack of use.

Services: The headquarters building has rest rooms, showers, and drinking water. The nearest pay phone is at the store where you turn off OK 3 to drive to the park, about 10 miles south. The camping in the McGee Creek NSRA is all primitive at present, though plans for a full-service campground are being made. Picnic table sites in the state park campgrounds across the lake in the dam area offer a more cordial environment, if also more crowded. There is no bike shop in the area that I am aware of.

Hazards: The worst chiggers and ticks I have ever been infected with greeted me when I visited here. Even liberal coatings of repellent had no effect on them. I was covered with bites by the time I realized it was too late. You will see some other crawling critters too, like spiders bigger than you will believe, their webs stretching across the trails in many places. Summer is not a good time to be walking around in the tall grass along these trails in Lycra shorts.

Any time of year the loose gravel and rocks will challenge your bike handling skills, making careful riding mandatory if you value your skin. I think it is also safe to assume there may be a snake or two in the vicinity, and I strongly recommend paying very close attention to where you put your feet if you jump off the bike to take a break or to portage a difficult section.

Many of the trails in this park grow over in summer, so ask the staff about their condition before planning any major shortcuts into your route selection. You may get there and find no trail visible, only an occasional piece of flagging tape.

Rescue index: It would be possible to be rescued here, but only if you had a partner who could make it out of whatever remote trail you were on and find his or her way back to the headquarters to summon emergency personnel. This place is an awful long drive from the nearest hospital, probably at least 25 miles. Be careful when you ride, and live to ride another day.

Land status: This is all land owned by the federal government but leased to Oklahoma for 25 years.

Maps: The state of Oklahoma will offer you a good map with all the trails marked, free of charge. This document also contains all the rules of the park and information on camping. Ask at the headquarters. The quad for this park is Lane NE.

Finding the trail: From US 69/75 at Atoka go east on OK 3 about 20 miles to the Centerville Store. There is a sign at the store directing you north to McGee Creek NSRA. From there follow the paved road north for about 10

This photograph was taken somewhere between Little Bugaboo Creek and Whiskey Flats. Gee, I wonder why they called it Whiskey Flats? Duh.

miles, to where it enters the park. You must register with the officials at the headquarters and let them know your riding plans before starting. Park in the fenced area on the west side of the park road just inside the gate from the headquarters building. The trailhead is behind the headquarters and is marked by a sign. Follow the double-track until you find the sign showing where the single-track of Little Bugaboo Creek Trail splits off to the left. Follow the yellow flagging-tape markers and stay on the single-track until you reach the clearing where the signs indicate the South Rim Road and Box Spring Camp area. The Whiskey Flats Trail exits next to a sign on the west side of the clearing, near where you enter. Follow the blue flagging tape to where the trail ends at the lake. Turn around and go back the way you came until you are again in the clearing with all the signs. Go right out of the clearing onto the double-track and ride south on the South Rim Road until you are once again at the headquarters building.

Sources of additional information:

McGee Creek State Park
Natural Scenic Recreation Area
HC 82, Box 572
Atoka, OK 74525
(405) 889-5822

McGee Creek State Park
Park Office
Route 1, Box 6-A
Farris, OK 74542-0006
(405) 889-5822

Oklahoma Tourism and Recreation Department
Division of State Parks
2401 North Lincoln Boulevard
Oklahoma City, OK 73105
(405) 521-3411

Oklahoma Tourism and Recreation Department
Literature and Information
Box 600000
Oklahoma City, OK 73146-6000
(405) 521-2409
(800) 652-6552

Notes on the trail: There are many more miles of trails in the park than I can describe in a few short chapters. For a place to get away from it all and listen to the birds tweet, you will not find many that will be more hospitable and have more to offer than McGee Creek Natural Scenic Recreation Area (McGee Creek NSRA to those who prefer acronyms).

The area where the trails are is locked behind a gate from about 6 P.M. until about 8 A.M. If you do not plan to wrap up your riding until after hours, then you need to park outside the gate, near the headquarters building.

For now there are only primitive camping facilities here, but a campground with RV pads, water, and electricity is planned for the area near the entrance.

Equestrian use of the trails in this park extends into areas that are not officially sanctioned for horses. Be nice and offer them the proper courtesies. For the present, what this place needs more than rules is people using the facilities. Invite your friends.

RIDE 54 *HOG CAMP RIDE*

If you find the single-track around here a little more intense than you like, try some of the double-track. The South Rim Road connects with another called the Hog Camp Road, which will carry you up to the top of a ridge that runs through the park and then around to one of the equestrian camps. Then you will turn around and return on the same double-track, a fairly easy round-trip ride of about 12 miles.

RIDE 54 *HOG CAMP RIDE*

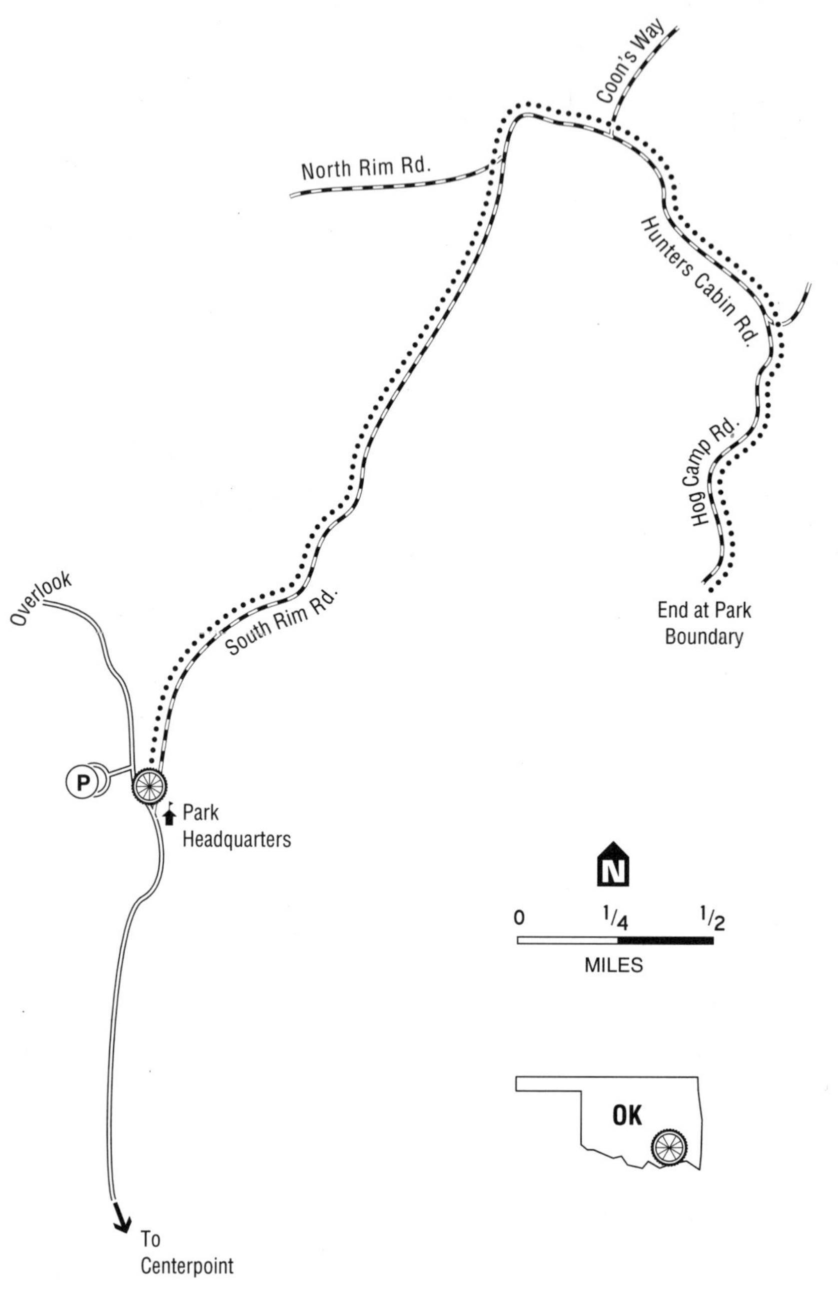

This ride is an out-and-back with some gradual climbing but nothing severe. It is almost all rocky but well within the capabilities of nearly every rider. I will venture to say it would make for a good picnic ride for the whole family. Leave Fido at home, though, because pets are not allowed on the trails. The chiggers and ticks would probably rip him limb from limb, anyway.

This ride passes through an area with some interesting history. Way back when, a cache of loot was supposedly buried somewhere around here by the early explorer Cortez and his pals. If you happen to notice a rock with the shape of a pistol carved into it, grab your metal detector and shovel and find that gold! As the legend goes, the treasure was discovered by a local resident, who marked it by carving a gun on a rock nearby. He died shortly after cashing in a chunk of gold he found, and the booty has never been heard from again. Several people have spent lifetimes digging around these hills looking for buried treasure, and speculation about the location of said loot continues to this day.

General location: McGee Creek Natural Scenic Recreation Area is about halfway between Atoka and Antlers, in the southeastern part of the state.

Elevation change: The trailhead is the lowest you go, at about 740´ above sea level. From there you climb steadily to about 1,000´ where you turn right onto Hog Camp Road. Then you have a gentle descent to around 860´ to cross a creek. Then you climb up to 900´ again right before the end of the road. Your return gives you all the same in reverse.

Season: The bugs are terrible in the summer, so cooler times of the year will make for better mountain biking. The soil conditions are such that the trail should be navigable in just about any weather, so I don't think the trails here will ever close for muddy conditions. Hunting is allowed in the park, so it would be advisable to call ahead for trail status before driving several hours to get here.

Services: The headquarters building has rest rooms, showers, and drinking water. The nearest pay phone is at the store where you turn off OK 3 to drive to the park, about 10 miles south. The only camping in the NSRA (in 1995, anyway) is primitive. They plan to build some more luxurious facilities in the future, but it hasn't happened yet. The nearest bike shop is not anywhere near here.

Hazards: Spiders, ticks, chiggers, and snakes are your main enemies here. Other interesting things to be wary of include the loose gravel surface of the road. Don't get your fingers too far from the brake levers as you approach turns—there are a few places along the way with significant grades, and your speed can exceed 20 miles per hour with little or no effort. Another trail concern is those large hairy critters called horses. They are very common around here. The side trails you will pass often grow over in summer, so even though you will see shortcuts on the map, you may not like what you find.

Rescue index: Since this is a trail that an ambulance could probably drive on fairly easily, if you got hurt way back in there, a rescue would be feasible. Don't ride alone, though. There will need to be somebody who can ride out to fetch help if you get in trouble.
Land status: This is federally owned land that the state manages as a state park under a 25-year lease agreement.
Maps: Maps showing all the trails in the park are available from the headquarters staff, free for the asking. The quad for this ride is Lane NE.
Finding the trail: The headquarters is located about 10 miles north of OK 3 and Centerville Store, about halfway between Atoka and Antlers. The parking area is across the road from the headquarters, just inside the gate. The trailhead is right behind the headquarters, marked by a sign. Start at the trailhead and follow South Rim Road north until it ends where North Rim Road and Hog Camp Road split and go left and right, respectively. Follow Hog Camp Road to the right until it reaches the fence that marks the state park boundary. Turn around and return the way you came. Easy as pie—very straightforward and direct. No chance of getting lost. There are one or two side trails you can explore if you want. Have fun.

Sources of additional information:

McGee Creek State Park
Natural Scenic Recreation Area
HC 82, Box 572
Atoka, OK 74525
(405) 889-5822

McGee Creek State Park
Park Office
Route 1, Box 6-A
Farris, OK 74542-0006
(405) 889-5822

Oklahoma Tourism and Recreation Department
Division of State Parks
2401 North Lincoln Boulevard
Oklahoma City, OK 73105
(405) 521-3411

Oklahoma Tourism and Recreation Department
Literature and Information
Box 600000
Oklahoma City, OK 73146-6000
(405) 521-2409
(800) 652-6552

If you take your dog with you on the ride to Hog Camp Road and he stops at every tree it will be a very long day.

Notes on the trail: The gate is locked at about 6 P.M. and does not open again until about 8 A.M. the next morning, so plan to get in and out before curfew. Or you may park outside, near the headquarters—just stick a note or something on your windshield that says who you are and what you are doing. Other considerations are the likelihood of meeting equestrian traffic and the lack of any facilities along the way. Carry what you will need, because there is nowhere to refill a water bottle once you get on the trail.

RIDE 55 *ARCADIA LAKE TRAIL*

Fast, smooth single-track that lies practically in the midst of the largest city in the state is hard to come by. And good every-rider appeal is even harder to locate. Here are six miles of advanced/intermediate/beginner offerings that will soothe your savage beast. Actually, Arcadia Lake covers part of what long ago was the famed Route 66 of myth and legend—old US 66.

Running around one end of Arcadia Lake, this trail winds from Spring Creek Park through Edmond Park to Central State Park. Though the signs claim that the trails are marked by difficulty rating, I found like two signs. But I think

RIDE 55 *ARCADIA LAKE TRAIL*

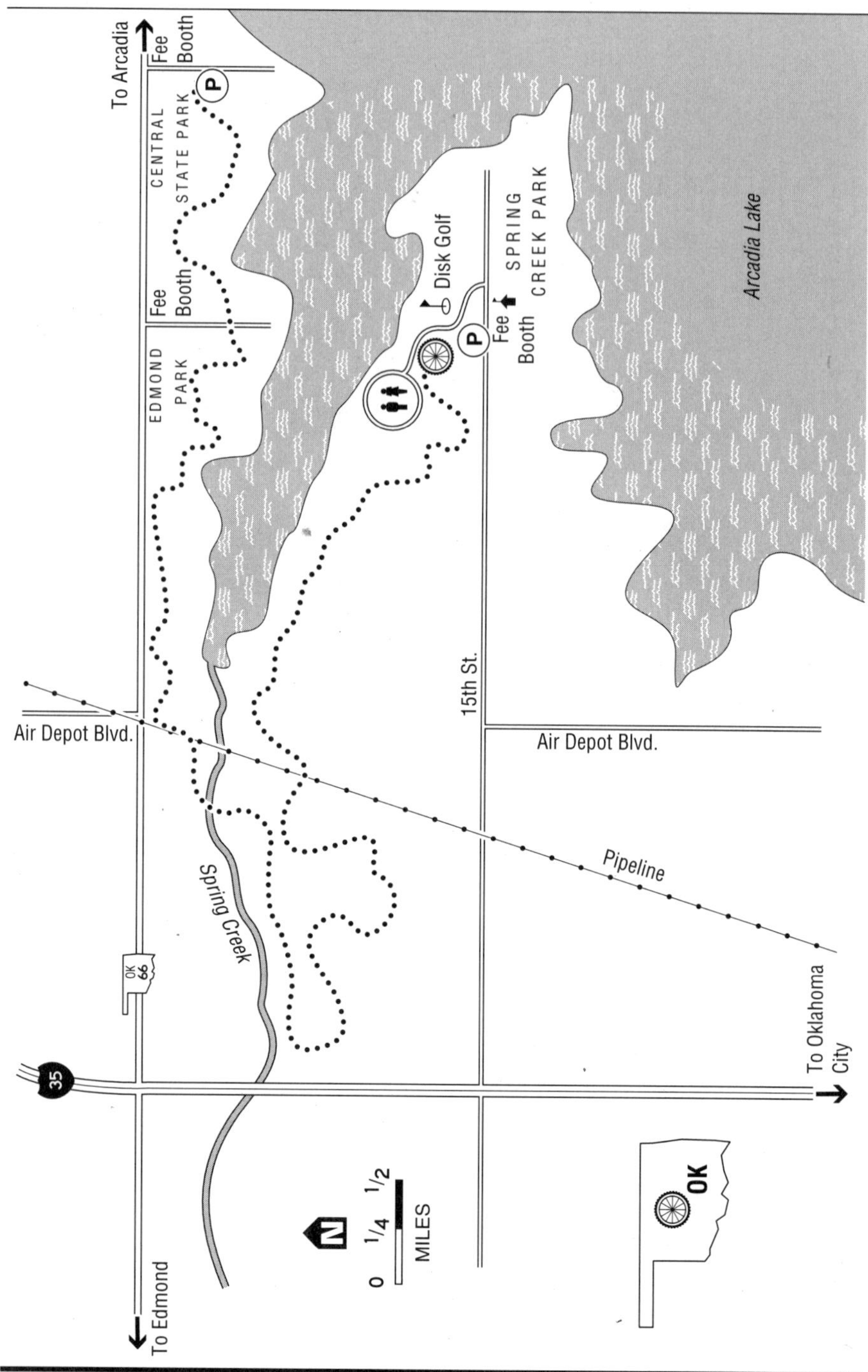

nearly all the riding here is within the skills of most off-road cyclists I know. If you desire the expert-level sections, just bear right at each fork in the road. If you prefer to bypass the hard stuff, stay on the wider and better-established trail. Someone has been building several interesting branches from the main trail. Thanks, whoever.

This is sandy soil, and many places can be ankle-deep when a lot of folks have ridden on it. It leans toward being better and easier riding after a rain, since the moisture will stick the red sand together somewhat and provide slightly more support for your tires. Much of the riding you will do in the western and Spring Creek sections is exposed. You will ride across fields where the ragweed towers on either side of the trail; it gets especially thick and crowds the trail in summer. The sections on the north side of the lake, Edmond and Central State Parks, carry you through a lot of tight single-track that weaves around between thickly forested areas. Starting at the trailhead by Spring Creek Park and doing the whole enchilada out-and-back is probably the preferred run. If you park on a dead-end road just outside the park gate, you pay only $1 for admission instead of the $6 that will be charged for a car.

While you are in the area, you might be interested in checking out some of the local sights. This area simply drips with history from the last 100 years. There are Indian villages, museums, the state government buildings, the Cowboy Hall of Fame, and lots of opportunities for recreating in one of the authentic Wild West parts of the country. YEEHAW, PARTNER!

General location: Arcadia Lake is located on the north side of Oklahoma City, just about in the middle of the state.
Elevation change: The lake lies around 1,000′ above sea level, and the highest point on the trail is up to maybe 1,100′.
Season: Some of the park facilities may only be operated seasonally, so call ahead if there is any doubt. It may grow up a lot in the summer, and it may be powdery sometimes. No hunting is allowed, so you are safe from gunfire.
Services: The trailheads all have rest rooms; ask at the fee booth or refer to your maps. There are pay phones at each beach, and showers at the campgrounds. There are no concessions in any of the parks, but many convenience stores are within a short drive in just about any direction or along the way. There are several bike shops in Oklahoma City.
Hazards: Pedestrian and cycling traffic present the biggest hazards along the trail. Poisonous plants are known to exist in the trail area, and anytime you are in the bush, you should watch out for snakes. Mosquitoes are another potential threat during their season, which is anytime but below-zero days.
Rescue index: As places to get hurt go, this would be a good place to pick. There are several spots where the trail passes near paved roads. Several residences, manned park buildings, and areas of human activity are in reasonable proximity to the trail, thanks to its urban nature and multiple access points.

I think this lady likes the trail at Arcadia Lake. I like the t-shirt.

Land status: Arcadia Lake is owned and operated by the City of Edmond. Part of the trail abuts private property, but as long as you stay in the park you will not be violating any boundaries.
Maps: Any of the manned booths at the park entrances can provide you with a very nice map of the facilities, though the detail offered for the trail is pretty limited. The quads for this area are Edmond and Arcadia.
Finding the trail: From Oklahoma City go north on Interstate 35 to Edmond and exit at 15th Street, going east. Follow 15th Street until just before it enters Spring Creek Park and turn left onto the dead-end dirt road. I like to start near Spring Creek Park, because you can leave your car on the old road just outside the park and pay the lowest entrance fee possible. They only charge a buck if you are on a bicycle. Ask for a map and directions to the trailhead at the fee booth.

Sources of additional information:

City of Edmond
Arcadia Lake
P.O. Box 2970
Edmond, OK 73083-2970

Lake Project Office
(405) 396-8122

Central State Park and Campground
(405) 340-7291

Edmond Park
(405) 340-7292

Scissortail Campground
(405) 340-7293

Spring Creek Park
(405) 340-7294

Notes on the trail: Do you like Frisbee Golf? There is a disk golf course very near the trailhead in Spring Creek Park. I personally prefer freestyle, but whatever.

American bald eagles visit Arcadia Lake every year, according to the park's literature. This may be the place I find mine. I hope.

RIDE 56 *STANLEY DRAPER LAKE TRAILS*

I was amazed at the quantity and quality of single-track on the north end of Stanley Draper Lake. Between Tinker Air Force Base and the water there are probably 15 miles or more of sandy trails, mostly single-track. Fast, smooth, fun trails that will satisfy your need for speed. The land in this area is laced with more trails than I could possibly ever put on a map or tell you how to follow, so take your time. Explore, ride around, take some side trails.

When I rode here I followed some Okie Dirt Riders arrow-signs that appeared to have been laid out to mark a motorcycle "enduro" race course. This provided me with a loop, easy to follow, of about ten miles. I know a leg of the Oklahoma State Mountain Bike Championships is held here—every year, I think—so there is a lot of riding history associated with this area.

These trails weave around under the trees, up and down across some small creeks, leading you along the southern edge of Tinker Air Force Base, right by what looks like an old obstacle course. There are many good jumps and a ton of quick drops that swoop through the creeks and wind among the trees. The terrain is not terribly hilly, but neither is it completely flat. It is not extremely difficult technically, nor is it completely lame. I think the harder stuff is across Douglas Boulevard to the west, but it is all stuff that the right rider can grease. These are fun trails, always good for a few laughs. And you will likely have some company—this is a very popular spot to ride one's mountain bike.

I grew up not far from here and came to this park often with my dad. While visiting the area I found several landmarks I remembered from my youth. The whole experience was one of discovery and rediscovery, learning and relearning

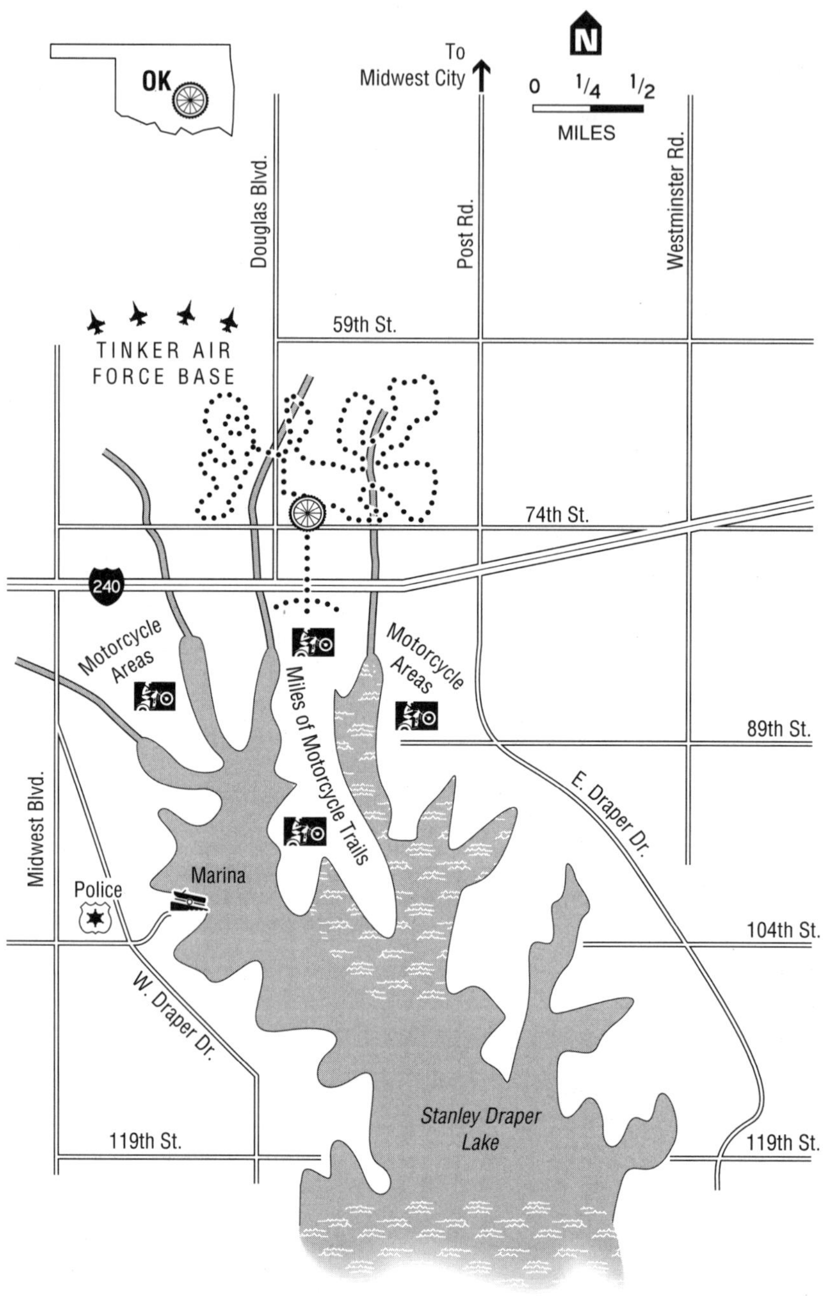
OK
To
Midwest City
0 1/4 1/2
MILES
N
Douglas Blvd.
Post Rd.
Westminster Rd.
59th St.
TINKER AIR
FORCE BASE
74th St.
240
Motorcycle
Areas
Motorcycle
Areas
Miles of Motorcycle Trails
89th St.
E. Draper Dr.
Midwest Blvd.
Police
Marina
104th St.
W. Draper Dr.
119th St.
Stanley Draper
Lake
119th St.

my old stomping grounds. It felt good, and I had a very enjoyable set of trips to the area while doing research for this book. Such was sadly not the case every time I packed up and left my home for travels. Oklahoma was good to me, now and then, and is even prettier than I remembered from the old days. Enjoy it—they don't make 'em like this any more.

General location: Stanley Draper Lake is on the east end of Oklahoma City, near Midwest City.
Elevation change: The lake level is said to be 1,191′ above sea level, and the highest point along the trails is about 1,300′.
Season: Anytime the weather is not RAIN RAIN RAIN, you will be okay riding here, because there is no hunting. As I mentioned above, several competitive events are held here during the year, both motorized and non-. From time to time, these events will keep you either off the trail or busy avoiding racers.
Services: There is nothing at the trailhead except a place to park. There is a convenience store at the southwest corner of the intersection of Douglas Boulevard and 74th Street. There are bike shops in Oklahoma City and Norman—good ones.
Hazards: The main hazard you will face is not having too much fun. But seriously, folks. The trail here offers some technical dangers, but the main thing to be wary of is other riders who might be circulating the wrong direction on the trail. Tree roots and tricky sections along the way can put you on your head pretty fast, but this trail is not as wild as many. Getting lost on the trail is a real possibility, but you can only get so lost. The many active highways and roads you pass under will give you reference to your location. The lake to the south and the air force base to the north are going to keep you from wandering those directions overly far. Fences rule the land to the east.
Rescue index: You are above-average in the rescue rating here. These trails get a lot of use, so you will seldom be alone. As long as you can get word to the authorities, I am sure emergency crews could extract you from this area with no major problems. Of course, they are probably going to send you a bill for said activity. The center of this area is roughly bisected by a dirt road. Bailouts and shorter loops are easily ridden here, because the trails offer many convenient shortcuts for reconnecting with the parking area.
Land status: Part of this land belongs to Tinker Air Force Base, and part belongs to the Oklahoma City Water Utilities Department.
Maps: I found no maps of the trails here, so I leave you with the quads Midwest City, Choctaw, Franklin, and Moore.
Finding the trail: Exit Interstate 240 onto Douglas Boulevard near Midwest City (about 8 or 9 miles southeast of downtown Oklahoma City). Go north on Douglas Boulevard to the first traffic light and turn right onto 74th Street. Go to the top of the hill and parking lot on the left (north) side of 74th Street. The trails are all around you, to the east and west in the trees.

Look Ma, no hands. I am so sure his mom would be beside herself with pride from that stunt. Mine would be reminding me of all the times I have cracked up doing stuff like that. Somewhere on the trail at Stanley Draper Lake.

If you follow the single-track, exiting the parking area to the east, you will enter the trees and wind back and forth, gradually popping out near Post Road and a big set of power lines. There are soon so many forks and side trails that your only hope for following the accepted route is to find some arrows from a prior race or to pick up a pal from one of the many locals sure to be hanging out and swapping tall tales in the parking area or along the trail. Otherwise just ride around, sticking to the perimeter of the trails and making a large counterclockwise loop. Soon you will see the obstacle course and buildings on the air force base.

You may just sort of wander here as you like. There are trees in the center of the square mile these trails cover and along Douglas Boulevard. When you get near Douglas Boulevard, you will cross through a gully near the road. A branch under the road here will take you to more single-track that winds around the land on the west side of Douglas Boulevard, almost all the way to the runway at Tinker Air Force Base. This section probably has the hardest parts and most technical challenges available, so hardheads take note. Check it out.

On the opposite side of 74th is another small parking area. Leading to the south, toward the highway and the lake, is a double-track that will take you to the motorcycle areas on the north end of the lake. These are considerable, so if you are going to be here for a while, try to find an afternoon to lend some exploring to this area also. I try to stay away from the motorcycles when I can, so I generally leave this area alone. It is sandy and harassed by throttle-jockeys, but some of it is beautiful. And it's open. If you want to focus on this area, you may park on the dirt roads just about anywhere around the north end of the lake and just cruise. Again, check it out.

Sources of additional information:

Al's Bicycle Shop
562 West Main
Norman, OK 73069
(405) 364-8787

Notes on the trail: There are trails, and then there are trails. And then there are more trails, and trails again. Parking by 74th Street gives you the opportunity to explore what this area offers and the ability to return to your car to resupply. This allows you to execute many tactical forays into the bush with a minimal amount of temporal resistance. Check it out, again and again.

RIDE 57 *CLEAR BAY TRAIL*

This trail is a nice six-mile loop of sandy single-track along the shores of Lake Thunderbird. Though it is called the Clear Bay Trail, you actually must start from the South Dam area, because the trail is closed to bicycles at the Clear Bay trailhead. The trail is essentially a pair of loops connected in sort of a figure-eight arrangement. There are a few short side trails that run down to the water, but the trail mostly stays in the trees out of sight of the lake.

This is fairly gentle riding. There are no severe climbs or dangerous technical challenges, but a few spots may be very soft, ankle-deep sand. There are also some tree roots on the mild climbing sections. All in all, this is a trail nearly anyone can enjoy, and a lot of riders do. On a busy weekend you will definitely run across (hopefully not into) some other cyclists and probably more than a few hikers.

Since there are several pieces of single-track, it is wise to go right at each branch or fork you come to. This will keep you on track and take you onto each piece of the entire series of loops. When you get near Clear Bay, you will see signs on the trees announcing that bicycles are only allowed on the roads in this area. Please obey and respect these trail rules and remember your etiquette when encountering other trail users.

General location: Lake Thunderbird is about 9 miles east of Norman on OK 9. This puts you in the center of the state, about 20 miles southeast of Oklahoma City.

Elevation change: The lowest point you ride is near the lake, at about 1,040′ of elevation. The highest point you reach is up to maybe 1,140′.
Season: This trail gets enough traffic to stay open all season; it never grows over. There is no hunting of any kind on this land, so if you hear gunshots it probably means a bank robbery or something. The sandy soil is very durable, and you should be okay riding here shortly after some rainfall—it drains well in most places.
Services: There is a rest room building at the trailhead, and water is available there, too. The only pay phones are by the highway at the headquarters building for the Clear Bay Unit, not at the trailhead in the South Dam Unit, where we start. There is a convenience store with gas and assorted supplies a few miles west of the South Dam Unit. Norman has a couple of good bike shops, less than 10 miles away.
Hazards: Running over a pedestrian or into a tree represent the major dangers on this trail. In the summer, there is a concentration of poison ivy that should be avoided at all costs. Riding on the sections that are closed to bikes would be hazardous—not to you, but to our sport, for sure. Low-hanging branches and tree roots that cross the trail may present some significant opportunities to find the ground; take care and watch for these. There may also be a soft spot or two along the trails, so don't try to carry too much speed through any of the turns where the sand is getting powdery.
Rescue index: This trail carries a good rescue index, because it has a fairly high traffic level. You are never very far from the road—out of sight, but within reach. Surviving will depend on getting to the phones at the entrance to the Clear Bay Unit or flagging down a motorist along the highway or a park road. The nearest ambulance is probably back in Norman, though, at least 6 or 7 miles away.
Land status: This trail lies within Little River State Park.
Maps: The rangers do not have maps. (This is unusual.) The quad for this trail is Little Axe.
Finding the trail: From Interstate 35 and OK 9 in Norman, go east on OK 9 about 10 miles. You will pass the headquarters and entrance for the Clear Bay Unit. Keep going another mile to the turn into the South Dam Unit. Turn left (north) and go a short distance, until you see a parking lot and picnic pavilion on the left. A sign marks the trailhead.

Behind the trail sign you will see a paved hiking trail making a loop down toward the lake, through the trees. Hang a right on the trail and follow it until you are right by the lake. Start looking around and you will see dirt single-track heading off to the right, into the trees. That is the trail. Follow it, and turn right every time you come to a fork in the trail. This will keep you on the perimeter of the double loop and let you maximize your mileage.

Keep going gradually west until you reach the spurs to the park road in Clear Bay. These are posted as off-limits to bikes. You will be winding around

RIDE 57 *CLEAR BAY TRAIL*

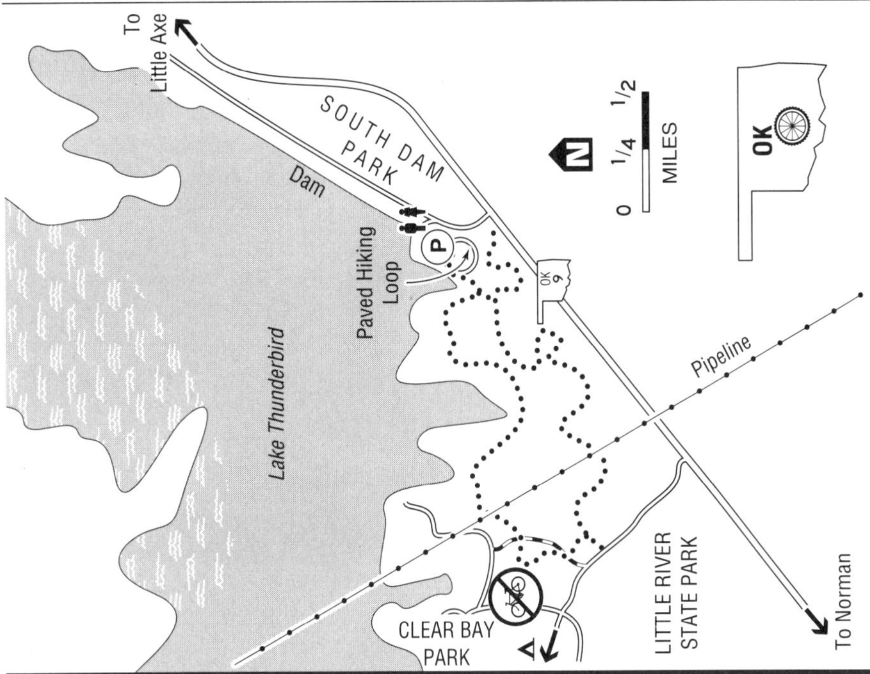

through the trees, and soon you will have looped back around and reached forks that you have already passed. Keep going right at the forks, and you will end up running into the paved park road, just south of the parking area. If you miss the spur that cuts over to the road, you will eventually find yourself back at the paved hiking loop. Turn right on the paved trail, and it will carry you back up the hill to the trailhead. Easy as pie.

Sources of additional information:

Little River State Park
Route 4, Box 277
Norman, OK 73071
(405) 360-3572

Oklahoma Tourism and Recreation Department
Division of State Parks
2401 North Lincoln Boulevard
Oklahoma City, OK 73105
(405) 521-3411

The Clear Bay Trail is another gentle place to take the chronologically disadvantaged members of your group. Whichever way you bias that statement, you are on your own.

Oklahoma Tourism and Recreation Department
Literature and Information
Box 600000
Oklahoma City, OK 73146-6000
(405) 521-2409
(800) 652-6552

Notes on the trail: You can camp over in Clear Bay Park and have all the Oklahoma City rides within about a 45-minute drive, max. The facilities are clean, the park is quiet, and the scenery is relaxing. The trails here are easy and would in my opinion be a good choice for a tandem crew or family-type outing with kids on BMX-type bikes. It is also a trip that would be fairly gentle on a nonhardhead spouse or pal.

RIDE 58 *TWELVE MILES OF HELL*

Okay, so it's not exactly 12 miles, and it's not really hell. They call it that because the local bike shop has a race here every February and it is usually cold as hell.

If you ride the race route, which changes every year, you can ride between 12 and 15 miles. Most will be rocky single-track, but a few parts will be gravel roads. These trails are pretty demanding technically and physically. A couple of spots are downright dangerous, and anytime you find yourself on a steep downhill where you cannot see the bottom, you should be extremely cautious. The section called The Kevinator is a perfect example of this rule. You drop off the back side of a mountain in a frenzied descent and are required to make a turn about halfway down, both to stay on the trail and to avoid riding headfirst into a gully. If your brakes go out, you are headed for a Care Flight helicopter or the morgue. During the race they park a couple of the biggest guys here with orders to tackle anyone headed for the edge.

This mountainous land is part of the local army base, Fort Sill. We used to come here when I was a kid and watch the military demonstrate their artillery and tanks. It was a popular field trip for Oklahoma Boy Scout troops. They would shoot off a few cannon, and maybe a tank or two would blast some targets. Just the sort of stuff juvenile males live for.

The trails we will ride are all a safe distance from the live firing ranges. You may hear some explosions from time to time, or maybe see a tank in the distance. Just ignore them. One thing you should be cautious of is that there may be live buffalo running loose on this land. If you see any, stay as far away from them as possible. They may not have very good eyesight, but they can run over 30 miles per hour and would squash you like a bug if you got underfoot. Give them a wide berth.

As I mentioned in the introduction to Oklahoma, the Buffalo Soldiers built Fort Sill. Well, the Wichita Mountains Bicycle Club and the Flying Pigbutts are some of the guys who built and maintain the mountain bike trails here. With humorous names like The Kevinator, Beck's Quest, Landrum's Landing, The Tally Whacker, and The Do Drop In, the trails at Fort Sill promise many thrills (and have broken several collarbones). Be careful and live to ride another day.

It may seem cheesy that I do not give you directions to the trailhead for this ride, but there is a very good reason for me not to. The local bike club, the Wichita Mountains Bicycle Club (WMBC), has an agreement with the army base that only members of their club will ride on the trails they built. I know a loophole that allows us to get around this technicality. We will make you honorary members of the WMBC and give you verbal instructions to find the start. All you have to do is swing by the local bike shop, headquarters of the WMBC, and schmooze the folks there. Ask for Mike or Allen—they will guide you to the trailhead. We don't want to irritate the army guys, because it is only by their good graces that we enjoy riding in this excellent mountain biking area.

General location: This trail is on Fort Sill Military Reservation, in the southwest corner of the state.

Key to numbered features

1. Start Hill
2. Power Line Hill
3. Slab of Death
4. Over by the Bones
5. Do Drop In
6. Bike Breaker
7. Speed Chute
8. The Kevinator
9. B. Q.'s Baby
10. Beck's Quest
11. Not B. Q.
12. Over by the Dead Trees
13. The Barn Doors
14. Tally Whacker Hill
15. The Yellow Brick Road
16. The Horseshoe
17. No-name Hill
18. Big Chain Ring
19. The Road that's Not There

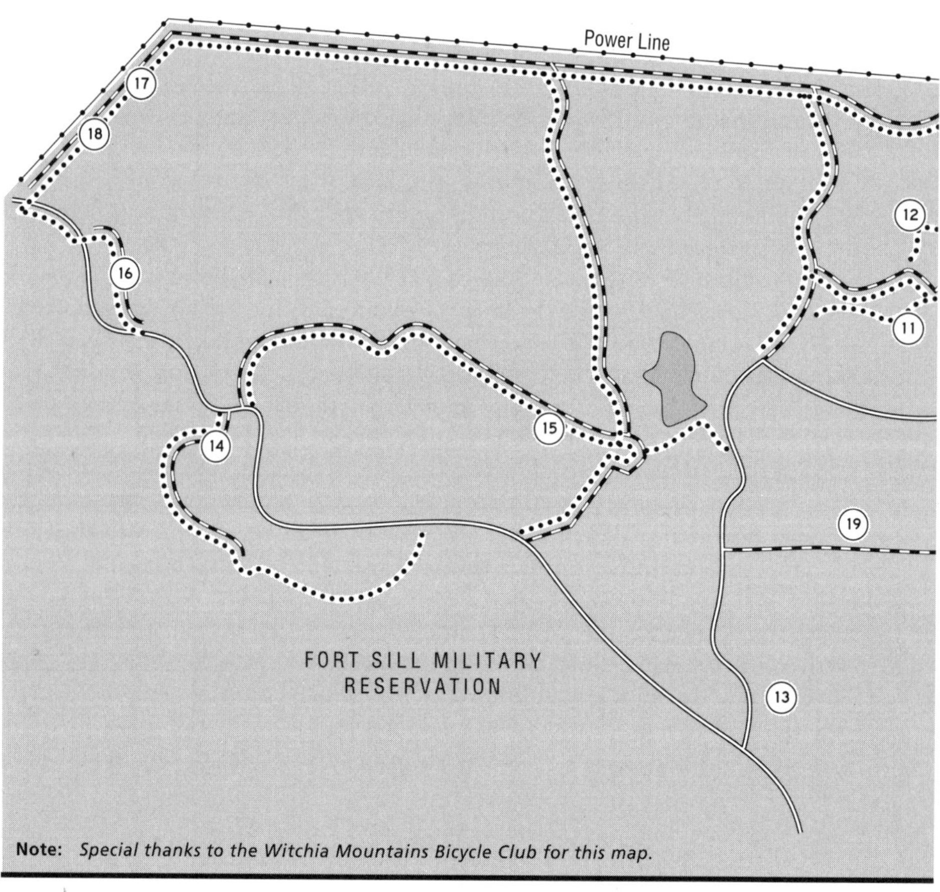

Note: *Special thanks to the Witchia Mountains Bicycle Club for this map.*

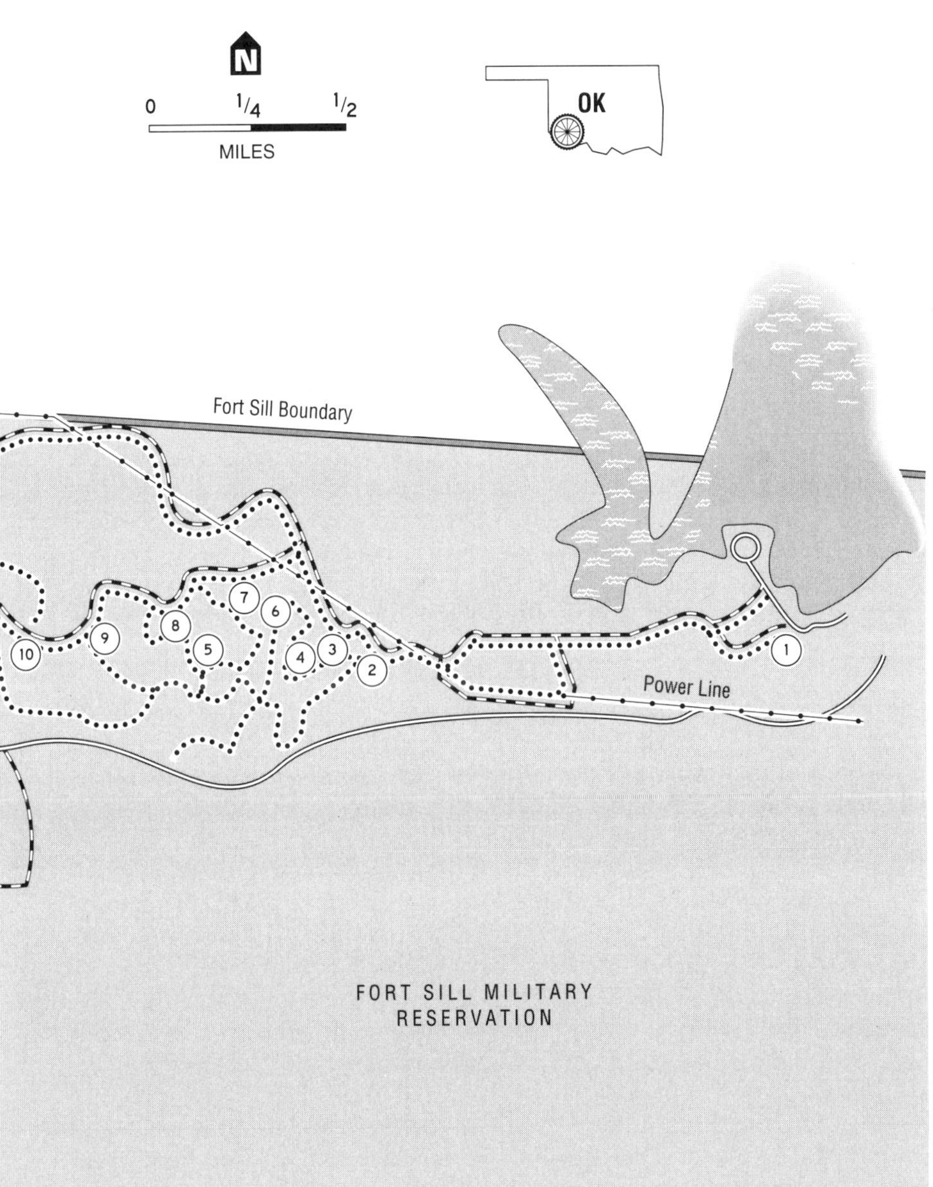

N
0
1/4
1/2
MILES
OK
Fort Sill Boundary
Power Line
FORT SILL MILITARY
RESERVATION
1
2
3
4
5
6
7
8
9
10

Elevation change: The elevation at the trailhead is the lowest point you will pass, at about 1,390′ above sea level. The highest point, the top of Beck's Quest, is around 1,710′.

Season: This trail grows over real bad in summer if there has been a lot of rain the previous spring. This makes many sections difficult or impossible to traverse. Also, hunting *is* allowed on these lands, so during deer season you must ride somewhere else. The best time to ride here is in February. This is when the race is held and therefore when the trail is in the best shape and marked the best.

Services: A picnic pavilion and playground are located near the trailhead. There you will find chemical toilets and water, but little else. The nearest pay phone does not exist. There are convenience stores on the way to the base, but only before you enter the Fort Sill grounds. If you need any supplies, stop and get them before you enter Fort Sill. The nearest bike shop is Mud Sweat & Gears, only a few miles from Fort Sill, in Lawton.

Hazards: Boys and girls, you could die or get mangled very easily while riding here; the trail is very tricky in places. The trails are covered with loose gravel, they are steep and technical, and many of them lead along or by dangerous drop-offs and gullies. Although they are officially only located in the Wichita Mountains Wildlife Refuge, it is not unheard-of to find bison wandering around on the land around the trails. *These things are extremely dangerous if you get too close to them.* Just stay at a distance and all will be well. The fact that deer hunting is allowed around the trails is enough to keep you away during season. If you have any doubt, call the Fish and Wildlife folks and ask when the season is open.

Rescue index: Your only hope of being rescued here if you get hurt is to have a healthy partner to retrieve emergency personnel. If you ride alone and crash, you could be decomposing before someone happens by and finds you. Almost all sections of the trail are remote, far from any access for an ambulance. A helicopter is the only way you could be evacuated in an emergency.

Land status: This land is all part of Fort Sill Military Reservation.

Maps: I want to take a second to thank someone for taking time out of his days to make me a map with all the place-names marked. Mike Thompson (the Mud in Mud Sweat & Gears) knows this trail like I know my name. Thanks, Mike—see you in February. The quad that brings us data for this trail is Mount Scott.

Finding the trail: I am not going to tell you how to find this trail, because as I said earlier, the agreement the Wichita Mountains Bicycle Club has with Fort Sill is that only members of the club are allowed to ride here. There is an easy way to get around this rule. Stop by Mud Sweat & Gears bike shop in Lawton and say "hi." Mike and the fine folks at the shop will tell you how to get there. The army just does not want a bazillion people coming out to ride their land unless they have been indoctrinated with the "code of the hills." Mike and company will tell you anything pertinent to riding on the trails so that the

Flying Pigbutt Racing's Jeff Tally showing us how to get a place along the Twelve Miles of Hell named for you.

army guys are happy. We ride here only because they like us, so we need to keep it that way. Go by the shop—they will give you directions.

To find Mud Sweat & Gears, go to Lawton and go west from Interstate 44 onto Cache Road. After a few miles you will pass a traffic light at 52nd Street, and very soon you will see a shopping center on the south side of Cache Road. Turn left into the shopping center. At the far west end of the complex you will see the bike shop. Go in and say "hello" and get directions to the trailhead.

Sources of additional information:

Wichita Mountains Bicycle Club
(405) 355-1808

Mud Sweat & Gears
5340 Northwest Cache Road
Lawton, OK 73505
(405) 355-1808

Fort Sill Army Base
Public Affairs and Community Relations
(405) 442-3024

Fishing and hunting information
(405) 442-3314

Notes on the trail: This is a most excellent trail, one of the best in the whole book. In the distance to the north of the trailhead you will notice a big mountain, the tallest peak in the area—Mount Scott, which reaches 2,464′. A road that leads up to the top of the mountain is a popular ride for local roadies. The trip to the top is a piece of work, and the ride back down will keep you on the edge of your seat. Hold on tight and make sure your brakes are in good shape.

RIDE 59 *MEDICINE BLUFFS RIDE*

I am going to leave you with one of the most fascinating areas I explored while building this guide. I have not had time to really get to know this area as thoroughly as I want to, and there is much of it I have not ridden yet. So I am not going to describe any particular route through it—I am going to turn you loose and tell you to wander around a little and let your instincts guide you. Spend half an hour driving the paved perimeter before you ride. You will get a feel for what is what and where is where, then you can jump off into it.

There are places of magical beauty here. For centuries this has been a high holy place for the Indians of the region, and many a medicine man has built a prayer fire to the spirits and spent a long lonely night atop one of the bluffs waiting for a sign. In fact, the Indian medicine men are why it is so named. Lots of other serious stuff has gone down here throughout the years. Early dwellers with broken hearts committed suicide by taking that big step from one of the 300-foot-tall cliffs along the creek. There are even legends of the famous war chief Geronimo leading a cavalry troop to their death by tricking them over the edge and into the creek below. Nowadays the Special Forces troops use these cliffs for rappelling practice, but the memory of an earlier time lingers on. I think you will see what I mean after you have been here awhile.

The area in question is roughly three miles long by one mile wide. It is laced with easy gravel roads and serious rocky double-track, and it's ringed with pavement, so you can only get just so lost. Some of the roads will lead you down to Medicine Creek through thick wooded areas, and some will take you to the top of the bluffs to gaze down across the winding creek. Explore, take a chance, try a road just to see where it goes. You can spend an afternoon gradually making your way around the bluffs, then return to your parking spot with tired legs and a calm mind.

There are three things in this world that make me dizzy-headed: certain females, certain automobiles, and certain locations in Texas and Oklahoma. This area is definitely one of the latter. It is somewhere I plan to get much more familiar with. Take your time—pack a few pralines and an extra bottle. Enjoy some of the rich aura that surrounds the Medicine Bluffs.

General location: The Medicine Bluffs area is a few miles north of Lawton in the southwestern part of the state.
Elevation change: Medicine Creek lies around 1,110′ to 1,120′ above sea level, and the top of the highest bluff is at least 1,400′.
Season: As is the case with much of the land on Fort Sill, hunting is allowed during deer season. The roads around the bluffs are "all-weather gravel" and generally will be rideable any time of year. Heavy rainfall will make for pretty messy riding, so I normally stay on the pavement when the conditions are wet.
Services: There is a pay phone at the Fish and Wildlife Department headquarters right across Apache Gate Road from the Medicine Creek Park campground. Water and chemical toilets are also available in the campground. The nearest convenience stores are outside the base and located all around Lawton. The nearest bike shop is Mud Sweat & Gears on Cache Road in Lawton. Go visit them—they are good folks.
Hazards: The main hazard you have to face while riding here is the automobile threat. All of the roads you will cross or follow are open to automobile traffic, so there will be cars around. As I mentioned above, it would not be healthy to ride around here much during deer season, so dig out your road bike. I would venture to say there are a fair many snakes living in this area, so it would be wise to keep your eyes peeled for them if you decide to get off the bike anywhere along the way.

Some places within our riding area here are off-limits. If you see something that looks like a prison, take heed. It is the camp stockade, and some tough guys are kept in there. Stay away from the razorwire and you will be okay. Just figure that if your road ends or you see signs telling you not to approach, you should go another way. It does not take a rocket scientist to figure out that you can get into trouble around here. Use your noodle and live to ride another day.
Rescue index: You have a very good shot at getting saved if you get stranded or hurt here, because there is generally some traffic through these roads. As I've already said many times, having a healthy partner to fetch assistance is always the easiest route to any rescue. A cellular phone might be a handy item to have stuffed into your pocket, on any ride.
Land status: Fort Sill Military Reservation. You can go to prison for carrying drugs or other contraband onto the premises.

This land is all generally open to the public, so the secretive behavior I described in the previous ride is essentially unnecessary. It is open because the military decided we are cool and they do not mind a bit if we ride some around here. Let's not do anything to jeopardize our current warm relationship with "the man." Also bear in mind that the GATE you drove through getting here is LOCKED SHUT after about 11 P.M. or so. When it is time to go home, don't dillydally.
Maps: The only detailed map I have seen is the quad for this area—namely, Fort Sill.

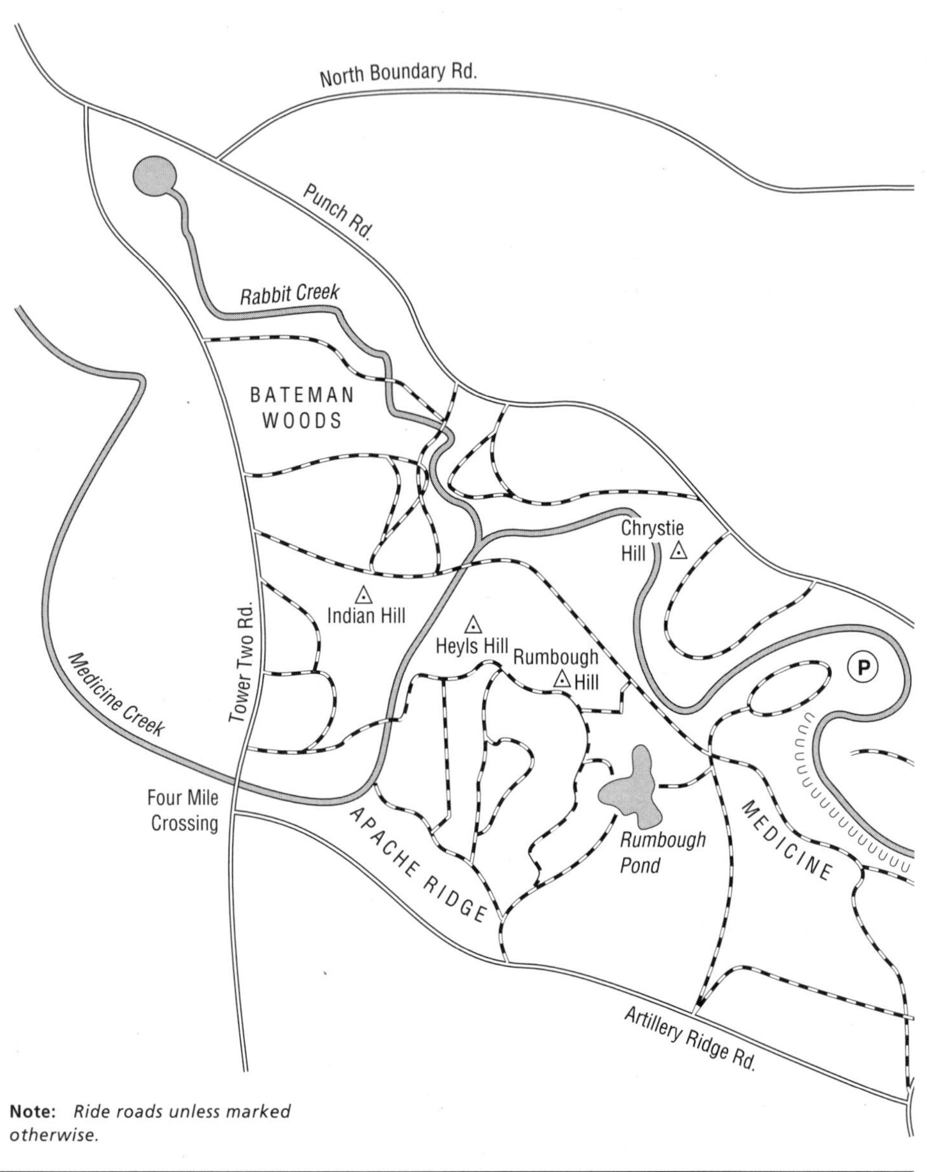

Note: *Ride roads unless marked otherwise.*

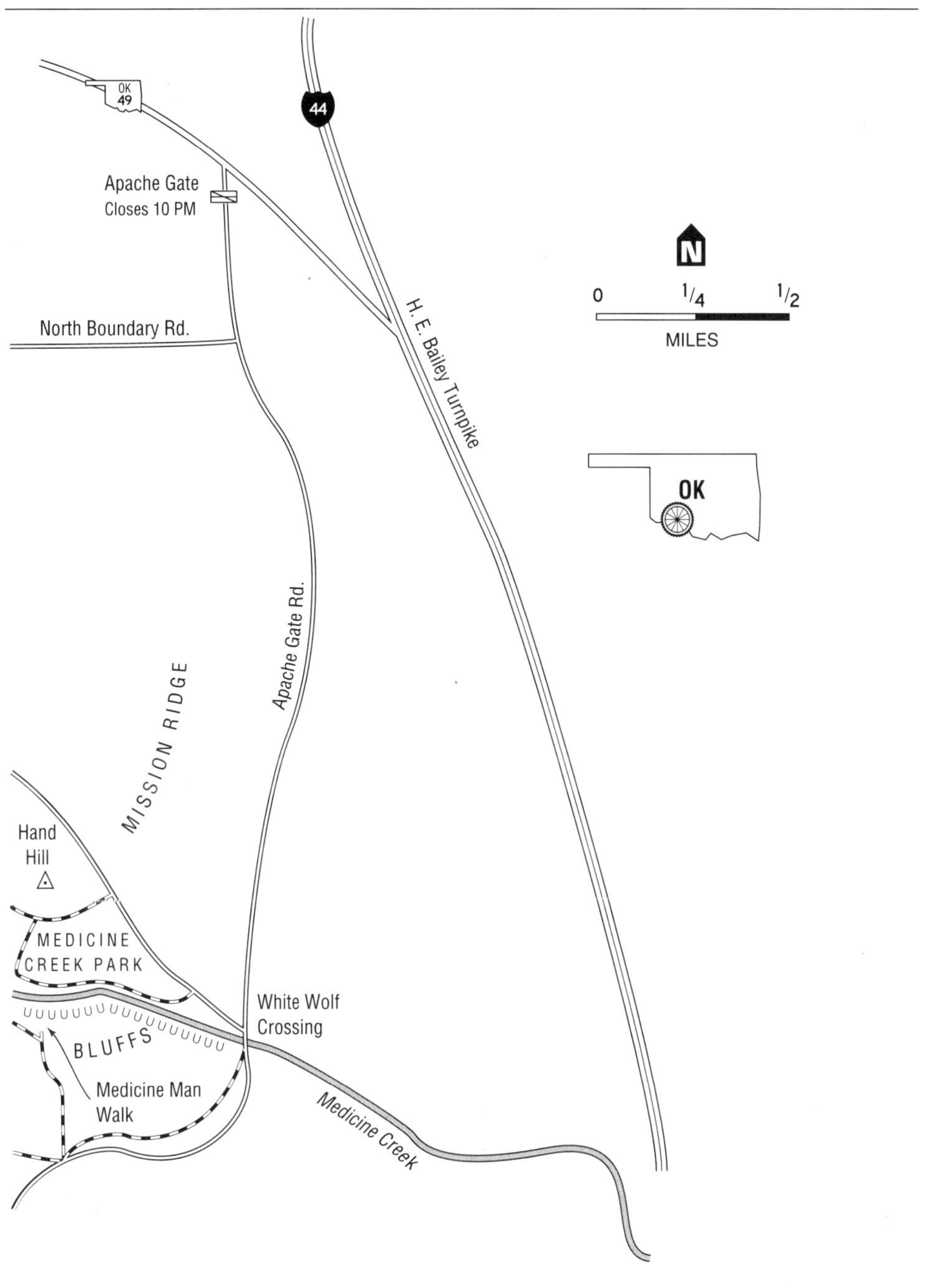

OK 49
44
Apache Gate
Closes 10 PM
North Boundary Rd.
H. E. Bailey Turnpike
0
1/4
1/2
MILES
OK
Apache Gate Rd.
MISSION RIDGE
Hand Hill
MEDICINE CREEK PARK
White Wolf Crossing
BLUFFS
Medicine Man Walk
Medicine Creek

It doesn't get much better than this. From a few miles away you would never guess the Medicine Bluffs hide idyllic spots like this, but there are several in the vicinity.

Finding the trail: I like to park at the picnic area near Medicine Creek Park, close to White Wolf Bridge on Apache Gate Road. Before setting out I strongly recommend a quick half-hour drive around the perimeter to familiarize yourself with the area you are preparing to tackle. It will give you some idea of where you are when you see landmarks later, when you're on the bike. It is an easy area to learn.

From Mud Sweat & Gears on Cache Road in Lawton go east on Cache Road to 52nd Street and go north to Gate #6. At that point you enter Fort Sill. Go north until the road curves to the right (east), then turn left onto the first paved road. This is Tower Two Road. Go north on Tower Two Road, past Tower Two, and turn right onto Artillery Ridge Road at Four Mile Crossing. You will go east until Bateman Road (about 2 miles). This is the first paved road you reach, right by a large complex of base buildings. Go left (north) on Bateman Road. It will wind around a little until it crosses White Wolf Bridge and becomes Apache Gate Road. Turn left onto the next paved road—Punch Road. You are in Medicine Creek Park now. You may park in the picnic area on the right and ride from here.

If you like (or if you are smart), you can make a tour of the perimeter of the area we will ride by going roughly west on the pavement of Punch Road until you reach the first paved road (about 3 miles). This is Tower Two Road again.

Turn left and go south until you reach Four Mile Crossing and Artillery Ridge Road again. Turn left onto Artillery Ridge Road and follow it back to Bateman Road. Turn left again and proceed to Medicine Creek Park.

Park somewhere in the picnic area and choose a route from the map. I would tend toward making a rough loop around the bluffs in a clockwise rotation. Go south on the pavement of Bateman/Apache Gate Road to Artillery Ridge Road and turn right. Follow Artillery Ridge Road to the first dirt road to the right and follow it north toward the bluffs. Explore, gradually working your way to the west and north.

You may ride up to the top of one of the bluffs on the gravel roads visible in the distance, or you may just ease around the western end of the bluffs, cross the creek at one of the many double-tracks you will find back in the trees, and wind up back on the pavement of Punch Road. At this point, take a right (east) turn, and soon you will return to Medicine Creek Park and your vehicle.

Since the whole area is ringed with pavement, you may just stay back in the trees or along Medicine Creek and wander until you are tired. Then it is an easy matter to hop on the pavement and slip back to Medicine Creek Park and a drink or potty break. Have fun, take your time, and bring plenty of film. Maybe some of the army guys will be climbing down the bluff with their rappelling equipment; that is always interesting to watch.

Sources of additional information:

Wichita Mountains Bicycle Club
(405) 355-1808

Mud Sweat & Gears
5340 Northwest Cache Road
Lawton, OK 73505
(405) 355-1808

Fort Sill Army Base
Public Affairs and Community Relations
(405) 442-3024

Fishing and hunting information
(405) 442-3314

Notes on the trail: Pack a praline or two and park your behind up by Medicine Man Walk for a respite from the world. Hang out for a while, rest your legs, and go grind a few more miles. The view is as awesome as this place is timeless.

On your way to the ride you will pass the aforementioned Tower Two, a tall concrete structure that looks like a big machine-gun nest or something. A historical plaque there offers up the history of this thing. Guys used to get in there and spot for the artillery on the far side of the base. Sounds like fun for all ages.

These bluffs are a land formation that geologists tell us forms the eastern end of the Wichita Mountains—sort of my segue to the end of the book. Thank you for following me as we have toured Texas and Oklahoma. I hope it has been enjoyable. Or at the very least interesting and informative. See you on the trails.

Appendix I

A BRIEF GUIDE TO TEXAS STATE PARKS

I will take a few moments of your time here to give the State of Texas and the Texas Parks and Wildlife Department a big pat on the back for the excellent park system they have built for us. As far as I know, we have the best state park system in the country, maybe the world, and I am proud of it. Some of the prettiest locations and nicest facilities you will find anywhere can be enjoyed by anyone with a few dollars for an entrance fee or camping permits.

You will find Texas parks to be clean and safe places to enjoy time with your family. You will find that the staff is knowledgeable, friendly, sincere, and falling over backwards to provide you with "quality of experience." Though some parks may be less developed than others, you will find that most have a complete selection of activities for the whole family. Some cater more to specific crowds, such as equestrian groups, rock climbers, or hikers, and some even focus heavily on mountain bikers. One interesting aside is that my club, DORBA, in cooperation with the Texas Parks and Wildlife Department, helped many other Texas mountain bike clubs catalogue all the state parks with mountain bike trails. As a result, by the time you read this book, you should be able to pick up a free brochure at the headquarters building of any park. It will list all the parks with trails where you can ride unhassled, and it will also give a brief description of each trail and other interesting tidbits. *De nada.*

To maximize your enjoyment, it is necessary to get current on a few other details:

For a fee of $25 you may purchase a Texas Conservation Passport that gets you in any park that charges day use fees. Camping is additional but discounted with the passport. I may be mistaken, but I think just about all Texas state parks charge day use fees nowadays, so for the avid traveling mountain biker the $25 is a worthy investment. Amen.

Most state parks lock the entrance gate every night around 10 P.M. and don't open it again until 8 A.M. the next day. For paid campers, this is only a slight inconvenience, because you get the combination to the lock with your campsite receipt. If you are planning to drive into an area late at night or very early in the morning, you should call the ranger and see if you can make any arrangements to maybe pay with a credit card and get the combination. Give it a shot or wait until business hours to arrive.

Typical office hours are 8 A.M. to 5 P.M., but a few of the most popular parks may staff the headquarters building later in the evening. You may still camp if you arrive and the office is closed, of course, by either doing a prepay at the main entrance or waiting until the following morning, when someone will visit your campsite to check you in. Since collecting money is a fairly high priority around here, you may get visited earlier in the morning than you desire. Though I seldom sleep in when I am camping, occasionally it will happen—usually when I have not prepaid.

Only a very few parks allow hunting, but coincidentally, those are some of the parks with trails open to mountain bikers. From fall through spring it would be advisable to call ahead and check on the status of trails in the park. The same advice holds concerning weather-related trail closures, so if in doubt, dial it out. From time to time there will be other activities and conditions that may make parts of the park off-limits to you. Don't get mad at the ranger if you drive 200 miles and find out the trails are closed to bikes because of the weather or some event taking place that weekend. I hope this guide will give you enough alternatives that you can find somewhere else to ride.

Another fun item is the magazine of the park system, *Texas Parks and Wildlife*. Each month, astounding photographs and in-depth articles about beautiful places you did not know existed can arrive in your mailbox. A one-year subscription is only $10 and is a bargain at that price. Contact 'em at the address below.

Last but certainly not least, we all owe Governor Pat Neff (governor of Texas from 1921 to 1925) a debt for establishing the State Parks Board in 1923. Thank-yous also go out to the National Park Service, Civilian Conservation Corps, Works Progress Administration, and National Youth Administration for developing and constructing the facilities at many of our fine state parks.

For further information, contact the following:

Texas Parks and Wildlife Department
4200 Smith School Road
Austin, TX 78744-3291
(800) 792-1112 for information only

TPWD Reservation Center
P.O. Box 17488
Austin, TX 78760-7488
(512) 389-8900 for reservations only

Appendix II

A BRIEF GUIDE TO CLUBS AND OTHER PERTINENT GROUPS

Maybe you are the club-joining type, and maybe you are not. Being a pretty solitary soul, I thought I was not until I met the members of DORBA. Then I realized I could really enjoy being part of something cool and getting involved. Now I love to brag about my pals and all the constructive stuff WE do and all the fun WE have.

I am going to confess that the typical mountain bike club is a pretty informal lot and may tend to keep a low profile. What happens is, people get tired of being the only ones doing anything, so they drop out from time to time. As a rule of thumb, the typical active core group for any volunteer organization is about 10% of the total membership. A larger club has a larger active member base and gets more done with less wear and tear on the members. A smaller club finds a handful of folks running the show and getting things done in the same amount of time. You do the math.

Since club presidents come and go, it is difficult to give you an accurate telephone number that will always be an easy way to contact the club in your area. Here are some numbers; good luck. If you have trouble getting through, or if you would like to find out about clubs in your area or an area you are going to visit, the best place to start is the local bike shop. They usually know who is doing what and often are the headquarters for a local club or maybe employ a member or two.

A finer, more knowledgeable, more caring, more fun-to-ride-with group of people you will not meet in any other sport. Be sociable and meet some locals when you visit a new area. That is by far the best way to find out about local rides and meet people. Don't be bashful—these are great folks, and fun like there is no tomorrow. Good folks all.

Here is a list of clubs I know about or have heard about or have read about. There are surely more I have not heard of, but this list covers Texas and Oklahoma pretty well. Some are dedicated mountain biking clubs, and some are road clubs with strong off-road involvements. If their locale is not apparent from the name, I have tried to add a blurb giving you the name of their home city. For instance:

The buck stops here. This photograph shows several cogs in the DORBA wheel. This is us taking care of business at a monthly meeting.

Alamo Trail Blazers (San Antonio)
Austin Ridge Riders: Tom Delaney (512) 453-1955
Caprock Bike Club, P.O. Box 475, Quitaque, TX 79255
Central Texas Trailblazers: Robert McEntire (817) 939-6499
Chihuahuan High Desert Riders (Lajitas): Mike or Gay (915) 371-2602
Corpus Christi Off-Road Bicycle Riders Association
Dallas Off-Road Bicycle Association: (214) 579-5540
Denton Area Mountain Bike Association: Bike-O-Rama
Desert Ratz Mountain Bike Club (El Paso): Brad or Rick (915) 585-1085
El Paso Bicycle Club: (915) 584-4455:
Flying Pigbutts Racing: Gary Loafman (405) 355-8993
Giddings Area Bicycle Association: Bicycle Country (409) 542-0964
Houston Area Mountain Bike Riders Association: (713) 856-9732
Kerrville Bicycle Club
Oklahoma Earth Bike Fellowship: Jim Flemming (405) 787-3003 or Joseph Mills (405) 235-3553
Red Dirt Pedalers: Chris DuRoy (405) 372-2525
San Angelo Bicycle Association: Don Ickles (915) 947-2675
South Texas Off-Road Mountain Biking Club: B & J Bicycle Shop (210) 826-0177
Tyler Bicycle Club: (903) 534-8890
Wichita Mountains Bicycle Club: Mud Sweat & Gears (405) 355-1808

And of course we have our sanctioning bodies and political machines. If you are interested in racing or want to get involved with the indoor side of our sport, check with the following:

National Off-Road Bicycle Association (NORBA)
National Headquarters
One Olympic Plaza
Colorado Springs, CO 80909
(800) 72-NORBA

International Mountain Bicycling Association (IMBA)
1634 Walnut Street, #301
Boulder, CO 80302

Texas Bicycle Coalition (TBC)
P.O. Box 1121
Austin, TX 78767
(512) 476-RIDE

Texas Trails Network (TTN)
P.O. Box 2858
Grapevine, TX 76099

Rails-to-Trails Conservancy
National Headquarters
1400 16th Street, NW
Suite #300, Department 292
Washington, DC 20036
(202) 797-5400

Over the years my cycling has brought me into contact with some neat sources for maps. The Texas State Highway Department is a great source of most excellent county road maps of Texas. Might come in handy someday.

State Department of Highways and Public Transportation
Attention: D-10 MS
P.O. Box 5051, West Austin Station
Austin, TX 78763-5051
(512) 465-7397

Special thanks to all the guys over at One Map Place, maps of any time or any place. They will help you stay found.

One Map Place
212 Webb Chapel Village
Dallas, TX 75229
(214) 241-2680

Appendix III

HONORABLE MENTIONS

Here are some trails or areas I was unable to investigate or include in the main body of the book for one reason or another. Just because I wrote a book does not mean I know everything there is to know about every place you can ride. I live to find places I have never been to before; nothing is better than a new trail. I am going to name-drop these and leave the exploring to you. So if you get bored with the 59 rides in my book, have at it.

TEXAS

White Rock Lake Trail: A paved jogging trail around Dallas's White Rock Lake. The far north trailhead is located near LBJ Freeway and Hillcrest, and from there the trail is a 7-mile out-and-back down to the lake, where it connects to a 10-mile loop around the lake, giving you about 24 miles round-trip of easy riding when the trails near Dallas are too muddy to ride.

Cedar Hill State Park's Pond and Talala Loops: These are hiking trails in the park but do not get ridden a lot because we have the DORBA Trail. Some worthy views—just take it easy on the peds.

Isle du Bois Trails: Located in Lake Ray Roberts State Park's Isle du Bois Unit. About 16 miles of very sandy single-track and double-track, so heavily used by the equestrian set as to be totally useless to mountain bikes. It is legal to ride there, but nobody does.

Red River Cycle Ranch: Hard, sandy, dangerous, and fun riding at this motocross motorcycle park. Located in North Texas near the town of Muenster, on the banks of the Red River. If you can stand the smell of castor bean oil and the scream of two-stroke engines, this can be a very invigorating riding experience. For information contact the Red River Cycle Ranch, Bulcher, TX, (817) 995-2903, or Coy Mosley, (817) 995-2889.

Cross Timbers Trail at Lake Mineral Wells State Park: This is a nice, easy, sandy trail, but it is usually chewed into ankle-deep powder by the horsy set and may be less than fun for the typical mountain biker.

Lake Lewisville State Park Trail: This is about three miles or so of easy, flat, wide single-track located north of The Colony on Lake Lewisville, near Dallas.
Piney Creek Equestrian Trails in Davy Crockett National Forest: Another experience in deep sandy single-tracks. There are over 30 miles of trails open, but they are hard riding because of the conditions left over after the horses have been there.
Sam Houston National Forest Off-Road Vehicle Areas: Another sea of ankle-deep powder. Over 60 miles of trails are open, but hard riding is the rule of thumb because of the conditions.
Matagorda Island Trail (or just about anywhere along the Gulf Coast beaches): Usually quite rideable in spite of the soft sandy conditions. Can be fun.
Galveston Seawall: Paved for ten miles, very easy riding, and can be fun unless severely crowded.
Austin Veloway: Austin has a closed-loop bike path called the Veloway where many local road bikers train. The Veloway is a 3.2-mile paved loop, mostly flat, with one fairly sharp hill. Ask at local bike shops for directions.
Choke Canyon State Park Trail: Easy 3-mile single-track out-and-back, lots of game to look at. The rangers act all innocent, but it appears they dump cracked corn in the middle of the paved park roads to get the deer, turkey, and javelina out where you can see them. About an hour south of San Antonio.
Kerrville State Park Trails: Easy to moderate 3-mile single-track loop. Very nice location on the banks of the Guadalupe River.
Kelly Creek Ranch: Private ranch near Kerrville that has tons of single-track. They host a leg of the Texas State Mountain Bike Championships every year.
The River Road, Paint Gap Road, Grapevine Hills Road, Pine Canyon Road, and Juniper Canyon Road: You can ride anywhere in Big Bend National Park that you can drive your car. There are several gravel "improved" or "unimproved" roads in the park that make for nice riding. These locations are all very remote and should be attempted only by experienced riders with a burning desire to explore.
Comanche Creek Trail near Lajitas, and Terlingua Ghost Town near Terlingua: There are some nice places to ride in the vicinity of but not within the boundaries of Big Bend National Park. Check with guide services in the vicinity of Lajitas and Terlingua.
Lajitas, Texas, to San Carlos, Mexico: For really adventurous riders only. You can take the ferry (a rowboat) across the Rio Grande and ride the dirt roads of Mexico. Once you have ridden the 20 miles or so to San Carlos, a trail will lead you up to an old waterfall that is visible from town, supposedly a good place for a picnic (or a bottle of Herra Dura, according to unnamed sources). It would be advisable to check with some of the guide services in the area to get information on the riding in Mexico before you attempt this trip. Just remember, the ferry guy goes home at dark or thereabouts. It might suck having to swim the river with your bike slung across your back. Try not to miss that last ferry run of the day.

Boquillas, Mexico: You may also take the small ferry (rowboat) across from Boquillas Crossing in Big Bend National Park to go ride a little around the small village of Boquillas in Mexico. The riding mostly consists of tooling around on dirt roads, but some trails lead up into some of the canyons. Ask the locals.

OKLAHOMA

Jean-Pierre Chouteau Trail: A beautiful, flat, and easy trail that parallels the Verdigris River for 60 miles, from Catoosa to Fort Gibson, in northeastern Oklahoma. This trail has a lot of possibilities and would be in the book, but it was so overgrown when I tried to ride it that the trail literally disappeared about six miles after the start. I saw the biggest water moccasin ever on this trail.

John Zink Ranch Trails: Another motorcycle ranch, home of the 1994 International Six Day Enduro. Near Tulsa. Said to offer some awesome riding.

The Stillwater Cycle Park: Another motorcycle park. It has a selection of riding opportunities, from a motocross area with jumps to long and short enduro courses. More deep sand, but lots of fun terrain too. Go south of Stillwater, Oklahoma, 4 miles to the dirt road, then go west about 2 miles and look for the sign on the south side of the road.

Platter Flats to Lakeside Trail: A multi-use trail on the Oklahoma side of Lake Texoma. This trail stretches 16 miles, from the Platter Flats area to the Lakeside area. Mostly real pretty single-track, but many stretches are very sandy. This trail is not well marked in many places and is hard to follow. Might be okay during seasons when the horse crowd is not heavily using it.

Lake Murray Motorcycle Area: Near Ardmore, Oklahoma. Miles and miles of trails, but once again, very sandy.

Lake Altus Motorcycle Area: I have only heard about this—I have never been there (yet). Open for bikes.

Author's Afterword

Okay, kids, what have we learned?

There are trails you can't touch when the wet seasons are upon us, and there are some places you DO NOT GO during deer season. There are lots of good people out there working hard to maintain places for us to ride unhassled, people who spend so much time off-bike pestering other people that they do not have time to ride.

There are places you only get to see if you schmooze the right folks. There are places you can break a sweat, and there are places you can take the kids.

This is where I grew up, people, and I want you to enjoy your time on the trails. I want you to have fun, because I do when I ride on these trails. And that really matters to me. Having fun—that's what it is all about. This thing we call a sport.

Maybe we will meet someday; maybe we will share an afternoon. Maybe we will pass and never know it. Ride like that—like you might be passing someone you could like, every time another trail user goes by. That person might be good people.

If you see somebody point a camera at you and tell you to "say titanium," that is probably me. Stop and say "hey."

Once again, thank you to all those hard-working souls who keep the trails open, and thank you to anyone who ever bought a kid his or her first bike. That's what got me started.

Adios, amigos y amigettes. Good luck to all you beginner-class racers, you are the salt of the earth. Eat poop, all you male sport-class veteran racers. *Track! I said, track!*

Chuck Cypert

Afterword

LAND-USE CONTROVERSY

A few years ago I wrote a long piece on this issue for *Sierra* magazine that entailed calling literally dozens of government land managers, game wardens, mountain bikers, and local officials to get a feeling for how riders were being welcomed on the trails. All that I've seen personally since, and heard from my authors, indicates there hasn't been much change. We're still considered the new kid on the block. We have less of a right to the trails than horses and hikers, and we're excluded from many areas, including:

a) wilderness areas
b) national parks (except on roads, and those paths specifically marked "bike path")
c) national monuments (except on roads open to the public)
d) most state parks and monuments (except on roads, and those paths specifically marked "bike path")
e) an increasing number of urban and county parks, especially in California (except on roads, and those paths specifically marked "bike path")

Frankly, I have little difficulty with these exclusions and would, in fact, restrict our presence from some trails I've ridden (one time) due to environmental damage and a chance of blind-siding the many walkers and hikers I met up with along the way. But these are my personal views. The author of this volume and mountain bikers as a group may hold different opinions.

You can do your part in keeping us from being excluded from even more trails by riding responsibly. Many local and national off-road bicycle organizations have been formed with exactly this in mind, and one of the largest—the National Off-Road Bicycle Association (NORBA)—offers the following code of behavior for mountain bikers:

1. I will yield the right of way to other nonmotorized recreationists. I realize that people judge all cyclists by my actions.

2. I will slow down and use caution when approaching or overtaking another cyclist and will make my presence known well in advance.
3. I will maintain control of my speed at all times and will approach turns in anticipation of someone around the bend.
4. I will stay on designated trails to avoid trampling native vegetation and minimize potential erosion to trails by not using muddy trails or short-cutting switchbacks.
5. I will not disturb wildlife or livestock.
6. I will not litter. I will pack out what I pack in, and pack out more than my share whenever possible.
7. I will respect public and private property, including trail use signs and no trespassing signs, and I will leave gates as I have found them.
8. I will always be self-sufficient, and my destination and travel speed will be determined by my ability, my equipment, the terrain, the present and potential weather conditions.
9. I will not travel solo when bikepacking in remote areas. I will leave word of my destination and when I plan to return.
10. I will observe the practice of minimum impact bicycling by "taking only pictures and memories and leaving only waffle prints."
11. I will always wear a helmet whenever I ride.

Now, I have a problem with some of these—number nine, for instance. The most enjoyable mountain biking I've ever done has been solo. And as for leaving word of destination and time of return, I've enjoyed living in such a way as to say, "I'm off to pedal Colorado. See you in the fall." Of course it's senseless to take needless risks, and I plan a ride and pack my gear with this in mind. But for me number nine smacks too much of the "never-out-of-touch" mentality. And getting away from civilization, deep into the wilds, is, for many people, what mountain biking's all about.

All in all, however, NORBA's is a good list, and surely we mountain bikers would be liked more, and excluded less, if we followed the suggestions. But let me offer a "code of ethics" I much prefer, one given to cyclists by Utah's Wasatch-Cache National Forest office.

Study a Forest Map Before You Ride
Currently, bicycles are permitted on roads and developed trails within the Wasatch-Cache National Forest except in designated Wilderness. If your route crosses private land, it is your responsibility to obtain right of way permission from the landowner.

Keep Groups Small
Riding in large groups degrades the outdoor experience for others, can disturb wildlife, and usually leads to greater resource damage.

Avoid Riding on Wet Trails
Bicycle tires leave ruts in wet trails. These ruts concentrate runoff and accelerate erosion. Postponing a ride when the trails are wet will reserve the trails for future use.

Stay on Roads and Trails
Riding cross-country destroys vegetation and damages the soil.

Always Yield to Others
Trails are shared by hikers, horses, and bicycles. Move off the trail to allow horses to pass and stop to allow hikers adequate room to share the trail. Simply yelling "Bicycle!" is not acceptable.

Control Your Speed
Excessive speed endangers yourself and other forest users.

Avoid Wheel Lock-up and Spin-out
Steep terrain is especially vulnerable to trail wear. Locking brakes on steep descents or when stopping needlessly damages trails. If a slope is steep enough to require locking wheels and skidding, dismount and walk your bicycle. Likewise, if an ascent is so steep your rear wheel slips and spins, dismount and walk your bicycle.

Protect Waterbars and Switchbacks
Waterbars, the rock and log drains built to direct water off trails, protect trails from erosion. When you encounter a waterbar, ride directly over the top or dismount and walk your bicycle. Riding around the ends of waterbars destroys them and speeds erosion. Skidding around switchback corners shortens trail life. Slow down for switchback corners and keep your wheels rolling.

If You Abuse It, You Lose It
Mountain bikers are relative newcomers to the forest and must prove themselves responsible trail users. By following the guidelines above, and by participating in trail maintenance service projects, bicyclists can help avoid closures that would prevent them from using trails.

I've never seen a better trail-etiquette list for mountain bikers. So have fun. Be careful. And don't screw things up for the next rider.

Dennis Coello
Series Editor

Author's Glossary

a.k.a.	also known as; if a trail I describe has an alias, I like to tell you
bayou	a small river or large creek
berm	a banked turn; opposite of off-camber; like the inside of a bowl
big ring	the largest sprocket of the front gears on your bike; good for high-speed flat cruising
blue-hole	a deep spot in a creek or river, suitable for swimming in; when you see one, you will know why they are called that
BMX	a kid's bike. Well, lots of mountain bikers started out as kids, and they were doing off-roading before there was mountain biking. BMX is the style of off-road riding done with very durable single-speed bikes like you see the kids riding. They do some amazing tricks with those machines
bridge	any construction allowing you to cross a stream or ditch and not get your tires wet—i.e., a bridge passes over a creek and you are not required to go all the way to the bottom of the ditch to get to the other side
CamelBak™	a personal hydration system invented by a guy from Texas. A very popular and useful addition to any cycling experience. It consists of a poly bladder that can be filled with ice and drink, then fitted into a small insulated backpack arrangement. The flexible straw that feeds you from the bladder has a bite-valve and fits nicely under a helmet strap to be easily accessible for a quick draught
CCOSP	Collin County Open Spaces Commission
dip	a depression in the trail large enough to get your whole bike into with neither wheel outside.

DORBA	the Dallas Off-Road Bicycle Association; North Texas mountain bike club with roughly 500 members; DORBA builds and maintains almost all of the mountain bike trails in the Dallas–Fort Worth Metroplex
DPARD	Dallas Parks and Recreation Department; the agency that operates City of Dallas park facilities
flags	pieces of surveyor's tape tied to trees and objects along a trail to mark the route
FM	Farm to Market Road; Texas is crisscrossed with paved two-lane roads that were built to allow farmers and ranchers to have roads they can use to get, like the name says, from farm to market; generally well maintained, though they may not be heavily trafficked—might even have a shoulder sometimes
gonzo	foolishness; devil-may-care riding; looking for Mister Bustyerass
granny-ring	the smallest front sprocket on your bike; good for that low-speed grind up a long difficult hill; whew, I'm tired
gully	a dry streambed or other type of wash where the water runs during rain; dry otherwise
hard right- or left-hander	an immediate turn of the slightly-more-or-less-than-90-degrees variety
hairpin	a very tight turn of more than 90 degrees of arc, usually more like 180 degrees
high desert	the typical elevation of the desert floor in the parts of the Chihuahuan Desert contained by Texas is 2,000 or so feet; this is far enough above sea level as deserts go that it is normally called "high desert"
hybrid	an on- or off-road bicycle having European 700C wheels that are slightly smaller than American 27-inch wheels; hybrids are like a real heavy duty version of a road bike
IMBA	International Mountain Bicycling Association, the worldwide organization dedicated to promoting responsible mountain bike activities
kiosk	whatever handy little sign structure that shows you (typically) a map of the trails, or whatever relevant information the kiosk builders considered pertinent to riding the trails

marbles	small pebbles or pieces of rock that litter the surface of a trail and make control and bike handling a tricky affair
m-dolphins	chemical enzymes your glands produce to make pain feel good. Known to medical science as endorphins
moguls	short-spaced small dips in the surface of a trail; not to be confused with washboarding; more like a quick series of hard large bumps
mountain bike	a bicycle specifically designed to be ridden off-road, typically having 26-inch wheels
Mister Bustyerass	the ground where you fall, a rock you skin a knee on, a tree that tears your jersey; anything dangerous or abrasive
Mudhole Surfer	a rider without a helmet
NORBA	the National Off-Road Bicycle Association, the sanctioning body for American mountain bike racing
off-camber	any turn on a slope that requires you to lean in toward the slope, putting only the very edge of your tire in contact with the ground; a common feature of switch-backs; like the outside of a bowl
OK	an Oklahoma State Highway; generally wider and usually has a shoulder, as opposed to relatively narrow FMs
OTB	over the bars; as the name implies, this athletic maneuver is a particularly nasty form of dismount; this separation of rider and bike is achieved by one of two methods: the good one and the bad one; the good one involves landing feet-first, while the other often includes a headache; not to be confused with any Olympic events
peds	pedestrians—mountain bikers who did not bring their bikes
Porta-potty	a chemical toilet, like those you see around construction sites
powder	very loose and very fine material making up the surface of a trail; may be several inches deep; not sand, exactly—more like dust
PR	Park Road; the roads in parks, strangely enough; they are usually paved

radius	the rate of directional change related to a turn or bend in the trail; if the turn gets tighter through its course, the radius is decreasing; if the turn starts tight and bends less and less through its course, its radius is increasing
relief	terrain contour or elevation changes; generally, information about relief indicates that the property in question possesses considerable differences in elevation
RR	Ranch Road, related to Farm-to-Market roads only in a different part of Texas
rut	a small ditch across or on the trail; not a purposeful construction; usually caused by water erosion or tire tracks
slalom	S-turns parallel to the direction water rushes down a gully; may be a lot of fun or a frightening experience, depending on how fast the slaloms are (like if the gully runs downhill) and how good your vision is
SNA	State or Scenic Natural Area; sort of like a state park without all the appurtenances of state park infrastructure—i.e., nothing but primitive camping facilities
S-turn	left right left right left right, etc.; looks like an exaggerated letter **S** from the air
sweeper	a gradual turn in the trail, less than 90 degrees, not tight enough to prevent it from being taken at speed
switchback	a series of hairpins zigzagging up the face of a very steep incline in order to make the trail rideable; switchbacks normally involve some off-camber and bermed places where the direction reversals occur
tank	a pond is typically called a tank in the southern Midwest
TPWD	Texas Parks and Wildlife Department; the agency responsible for operating state parks
TTN	Texas Trails Network; a group of concerned trail users dedicated to acquiring and protecting lands that will be used for public trails
twisty-turnies	any series of fast turns that requires pitching the bike around expertly, if you want to shave seconds from a lap time (see **S**-turn)
TX	a Texas State Highway; generally wider than relatively narrow FMs, and usually has a shoulder

USACE	United States Army Corps of Engineers; those kind folks with the United States Army who build bridges and reservoirs and levees
USGS	United States Geological Survey; in this book I use "USGS" to refer to topographical maps produced by the federal government's surveyors
washout	a rut or ditch caused by erosion; way too common in some places
water crossing	any place you cross the actual bed of a stream and your tires can get wet; if it is dry it is not a water crossing, only a dry streambed or gully, but it may revert at any time
WMA	Wildlife Management Area; a parcel of land set aside for hunting and/or fishing, often crisscrossed with trails and unpaved roads; outside of hunting season, many of these facilities are practically abandoned except for the casual camper and may offer miles of mountain bike trails to the hearty enthusiast

Glossary

This short list of terms does not contain all the words used by mountain bike enthusiasts when discussing their sport. But it should serve as an introduction to the lingo you'll hear on the trails.

ATB	all-terrain bike; this, like "fat-tire bike," is another name for a mountain bike
ATV	all-terrain vehicle; this usually refers to the loud, fume-spewing three- or four-wheeled motorized vehicles you will not enjoy meeting on the trail—except, of course, if you crash and have to hitch a ride out on one
bladed	refers to a dirt road that has been smoothed out by the use of a wide blade on earth-moving equipment; "blading" gets rid of the teeth-chattering, much-cursed washboards found on so many dirt roads after heavy vehicle use
blaze	a mark on a tree made by chipping away a piece of the bark, usually done to designate a trail; such trails are sometimes described as "blazed"
blind corner	a curve in a road or trail that conceals bikers, hikers, equestrians, and other traffic
BLM	Bureau of Land Management, an agency of the federal government
buffed	used to describe a very smooth trail
catching air	taking a jump in such a way that both wheels of the bike are off the ground at the same time
clean	while this may describe what you and your bike won't be after following many trials, the term is most often used as a verb to denote the action of pedaling a tough section of trail successfully
combination	This type of route may combine two or more configurations. For example, a point-to-point route may integrate

a scenic loop or out-and-back spur midway through the ride. Likewise, an out-and-back may have a loop at its farthest point. (This configuration looks like a cherry with stem attached; the stem is the out-and-back, the fruit is the terminus loop.) Or a loop route may have multiple out-and-back spurs and/or loops to the side. Mileage for a combination route is for the total distance to complete the ride

dab — touching the ground with a foot or hand

deadfall — a tangled mass of fallen trees or branches

diversion ditch — a usually narrow, shallow ditch dug across or around a trail; funneling the water in this manner keeps it from destroying the trail

double-track — the dual tracks made by a jeep or other vehicle, with grass or weeds or rocks between; mountain bikers can ride in either of the tracks, but you will of course find that whichever one you choose, and no matter how many times you change back and forth, the other track will appear to offer smoother travel

dugway — a steep, unpaved, switchbacked descent

endo — flipping end over end

feathering — using a light touch on the brake lever, hitting it lightly many times rather than very hard or locking the brake

four-wheel-drive — this refers to any vehicle with drive-wheel capability on all four wheels (a jeep, for instance, has four-wheel drive as compared with a two-wheel-drive passenger car), or to a rough road or trail that requires four-wheel-drive capability (or a one-wheel-drive mountain bike!) to negotiate it

game trail — the usually narrow trail made by deer, elk, or other game

gated — everyone knows what a gate is, and how many variations exist upon this theme; well, if a trail is described as "gated" it simply has a gate across it; don't forget that the rule is if you find a gate closed, close it behind you; if you find one open, leave it that way

Giardia — shorthand for Giardia lamblia, and known as the "backpacker's bane" until we mountain bikers expropriated it; this is a waterborne parasite that begins its life cycle when swallowed, and one to four weeks later has its host (you) bloated, vomiting, shivering with chills and living in the bathroom; the disease can be avoided by "treating" (purifying) the water you acquire along the trail (see "Hitting the Trail" in the Introduction)

gnarly — a term thankfully used less and less these days, it refers to tough trails

hammer — to ride very hard

hardpack — a trail in which the dirt surface is packed down hard; such trails make for good and fast riding, and very painful landings; bikers most often use "hard-pack" and "hard-packed" as an adjective, and "hardpacked" as an adjective only (the grammar lesson will help you when diagramming sentences in camp)

hike-a-bike — what you do when the road or trail becomes too steep or rough to remain in the saddle

jeep road, jeep trail — a rough road or trail passable only with four-wheel-drive capability (or a horse or mountain bike)

kamikaze — while this once referred primarily to those Japanese fliers who quaffed a glass of saké, then flew off as human bombs in suicide missions against U.S. naval vessels, it has more recently been applied to the idiot mountain bikers who, far less honorably, scream down hiking trails, endangering the physical and mental safety of the walking, biking, and equestrian traffic they meet; deck guns were necessary to stop the Japanese kamikaze pilots, but a bike pump or walking staff in the spokes is sufficient for the current-day kamikazes who threaten to get us all kicked off the trails

loop — This route configuration is characterized by riding from the designated trailhead to a distant point, then returning to the trailhead via a different route (or simply continuing on the same in a circle route) without doubling back. You always move forward across new terrain, but return to the starting point when finished. Mileage is for the entire loop from the trailhead back to trailhead

multi-purpose — a BLM designation of land that is open to many uses; mountain biking is allowed

ORV — a motorized off-road vehicle

out-and-back — a ride where you will return on the same trail on which you pedaled out; while this might sound far more boring than a loop route, many trails look very different when pedaled in the opposite direction

pack stock — horses, mules, llamas, et cetera, carrying provisions along the trails . . . and unfortunately leaving a trail of their own behind

point-to-point — A vehicle shuttle (or similar assistance) is required for this type of route, which is ridden from the designated trailhead to a distant location, or endpoint, where the route ends. Total mileage is for the one-way trip from trailhead to endpoint

portage — to carry your bike on your person

pummy — volcanic activity in the Pacific Northwest and elsewhere produces soil with a high content of pumice: trails through such soil often become thick with dust, but this is light in consistency and can usually be pedaled; remember, however, to pedal carefully, for this dust obscures whatever might lurk below

quads — bikers use this term to refer both to the extensor muscle in the front of the thigh (which is separated into four parts) and to USGS maps; the expression "Nice quads!" refers always to the former, however, except in those instances when the speaker is an engineer

runoff — rainwater or snowmelt

scree — an accumulation of loose stones or rocky debris lying on a slope or at the base of a hill or cliff

signed — a "signed" trail has signs in place of blazes

single-track — a single, narrow path through grass or brush or over rocky terrain, often created by deer, elk, or backpackers; single-track riding is some of the best fun around

slickrock — the rock-hard, compacted sandstone that is great to ride and even prettier to look at; you'll appreciate it even more if you think of it as a petrified sand dune or seabed, and if the rider before you hasn't left tire marks (from unnecessary skidding) or granola bar wrappers behind

snowmelt	runoff produced by the melting of snow
snowpack	unmelted snow accumulated over weeks or months of winter—or over years in high-mountain terrain
spur	a road or trail that intersects the main trail you're following
squid	one who skids
switchback	a zigzagging road or trail designed to assist in traversing steep terrain: mountain bikers should not skid through switchbacks
talus	the rocky debris at the base of a cliff, or a slope formed by an accumulation of this rocky debris
technical	terrain that is difficult to ride due not to its grade (steepness) but to its obstacles—rocks, logs, ledges, loose soil . . .
topo	short for topographical map, the kind that shows both linear distance and elevation gain and loss; "topo" is pronounced with both vowels long
trashed	a trail that has been destroyed (same term used no matter what has destroyed it . . . cattle, horses, or even mountain bikers riding when the ground was too wet)
two-wheel-drive	this refers to any vehicle with drive-wheel capability on only two wheels (a passenger car, for instance, has two-wheel drive); a two-wheel-drive road is a road or trail easily traveled by an ordinary car
water bar	An earth, rock, or wooden structure that funnels water off trails to reduce erosion
washboarded	a road that is surfaced with many ridges spaced closely together, like the ripples on a washboard; these make for very rough riding, and even worse driving in a car or jeep
whoop-de-doo	closely spaced dips or undulations in a trail; these are often encountered in areas traveled heavily by ORVs
wilderness area	land that is officially set aside by the federal government to remain natural—pure, pristine, and untrammeled by any vehicle, including mountain bikes; though mountain bikes had not been born in 1964 (when the United States Congress passed the Wilderness Act, establishing the

National Wilderness Preservation system), they are considered a "form of mechanical transport" and are thereby excluded; in short, stay out

wind chill a reference to the wind's cooling effect upon exposed flesh; for example, if the temperature is 10 degrees Fahrenheit and the wind is blowing at 20 miles per hour, the wind-chill (that is, the actual temperature to which your skin reacts) is minus 32 degrees; if you are riding in wet conditions things are even worse, for the wind-chill would then be minus 74 degrees!

windfall anything (trees, limbs, brush, fellow bikers) blown down by the wind

Bibliography

A hearty thanks to the following contributors and sources:

Beckos y Ricardo. *A Knobby-Headed Guide to Mountain Biking in Austin and Central Texas.*

Fehrenbach, T.R. *Lone Star: A History of Texas and the Texans.* New York: Macmillan, 1968.

Gong, Linda, and Gregg Bromka. *The Mountain Biker's Guide to Colorado.* Birmingham, Ala.: Menasha Ridge Press/Falcon Press, 1994.

Leckie, William H. *The Buffalo Soldiers.* Norman: University of Oklahoma Press, 1967.

Madison, Virginia Duncan, and Hallie Crawford Stillwell. *How Come It's Called That? Place Names in the Big Bend Country.* Albuquerque: University of New Mexico Press, 1958.

Miller, Ray. *Texas Parks: A History and Guide.* Houston: Cordovan Press, 1984.

National Park Service, Division of Publications. *Big Bend: Official National Park Handbook.* Washington, D.C.: GPO, 1983.

Neidhardt, Ralph, and Bill Pellerin. *Mountain Biking the Houston Area.* Houston: Texas Bicycle Map Company,

Big Bend Natural History Association/National Park Service. *Road Guide to Backcountry Dirt Roads in Big Bend National Park.* Norman: Paragon Press,

Surkiewicz, Joe. *The Mountain Biker's Guide to Central Appalachia.* Birmingham, Ala.: Menasha Ridge Press/Falcon Press, 1993.

ABOUT THE AUTHOR

When Chuck Cypert's fingers aren't stuck to a keyboard somewhere (he is on the payroll of a Dallas-based manufacturer of computerized response equipment and enjoys being a computer nerd), the author may be found in the garage maintaining his stables of bikes or possibly out riding one of them.

An avid cyclist since his dad gave him his first tricycle, Chuck has been involved with the Dallas Off-Road Bicycle Association (DORBA) since 1990 and is presently their Director of Activities. He possesses the rare and useless talent of being able to eat Tex-Mex food or barbecue with one hand and type hopelessly bad Spanish phrases with the other, all the while espousing the virtues of the driving styles of various Formula One pilots.

I call it mild annoyance. Photo by Cheryl Sams.

Kennis, his female roommate of ten years, and he share a variety of pets. The main ones are a squeaky black cat named Isis and a painfully noisy cockatiel named Tango—the turtles ran away. Chuck's plans for the future don't include any new pets for the household.

DENNIS COELLO'S AMERICA BY MOUNTAIN BIKE SERIES

Happy Trails

Hop on your mountain bike and let our guidebooks take you on America's classic trails and rides. These "where-to" books are published jointly by Falcon Press and Menasha Ridge Press and written by local biking experts. Twenty regional books will blanket the country when the series is complete.

Choose from an assortment of rides—easy rambles to all-day treks. Guides contain helpful trail and route descriptions, mountain bike shop listings, and interesting facts on area history. Each trail is described in terms of difficulty, scenery, condition, length, and elevation change. The guides also explain trail hazards, nearby services and ranger stations, how much water to bring, and what kind of gear to pack.

So before you hit the trail, grab one of our guidebooks to help make your outdoor adventures safe and memorable.

Call or write
Falcon Press or Menasha Ridge Press

Falcon Press
P.O. Box 1718, Helena, MT 59624
1-800-582-2665

Menasha Ridge Press

Menasha Ridge Press
3169 Cahaba Heights Road, Birmingham, AL 35243
1-800-247-9437